5,000 AWESOME FACTS

(About Everything!)

3

NATIONAL GEOGRAPHIC
WASHINGTON, D.C.

CONtENTS

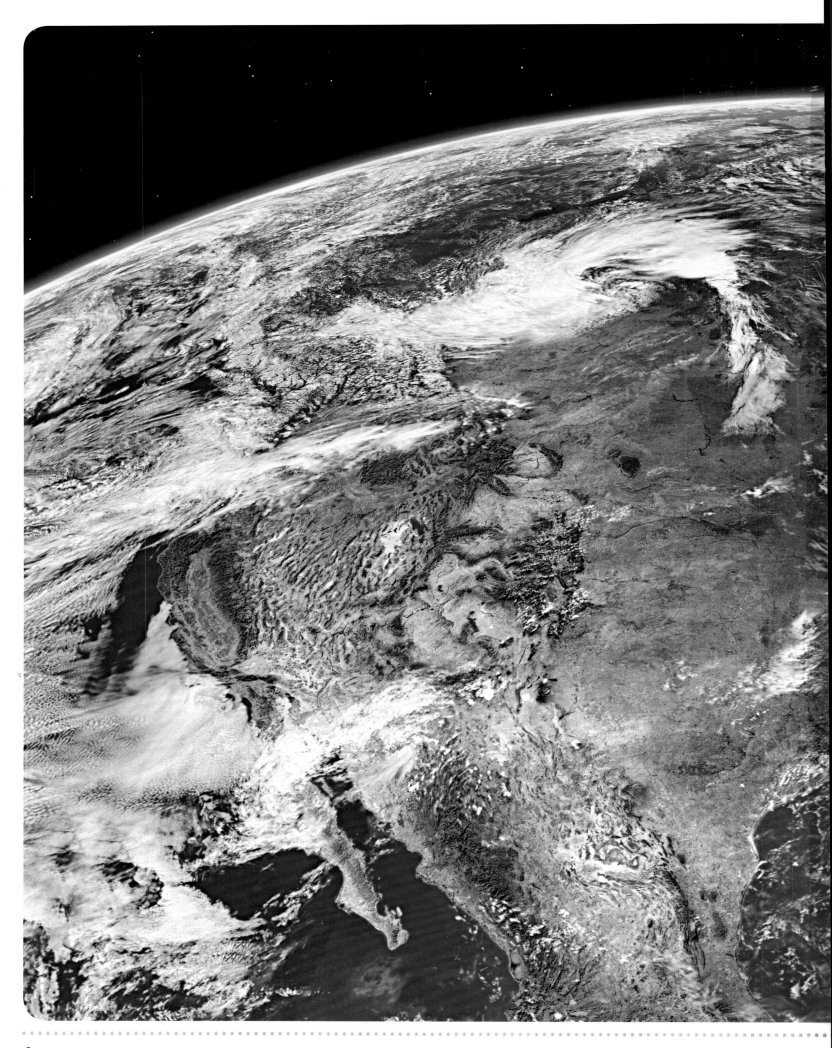

FACT

1

OUR PLANET,
Earth,
is about
4.55 billion
years old.

(Follow the facts at the bottom and count the facts!)

15 FERRIS WHEEL FACTS

❶ The **WORLD'S FIRST** Ferris wheel—designed by engineer George Ferris for the Chicago World's Fair in 1893—cost 50 cents to ride and could hold **MORE THAN 2,000 RIDERS** at once.

❷ Original Ferris wheels were turned by powerful **STEAM ENGINES**. Most modern wheels run on **ELECTRICITY**.

❸ You can ride a **HUMAN-POWERED** Ferris wheel in India, with park employees using their **BODY WEIGHT** to help turn the wheel.

❹ The **NEW YORK WHEEL** will tower more than **60 STORIES** over **NEW YORK CITY**, making it one of the **WORLD'S TALLEST** Ferris wheels.

❺ A roller coaster whips through the middle of the **BIG O** wheel in Tokyo, Japan—one of the only Ferris wheels to operate without a **CENTER AXLE** or **SPOKES**.

❻ The **PACIFIC WHEEL** in Santa Monica, California, U.S.A., is the only entirely **SOLAR-POWERED** Ferris wheel on the **PLANET**.

❼ The **CAPTAIN WHEEL** outside of Washington, D.C., U.S.A., is decorated with 1.6 million **LED** lights that **CHANGE COLOR** to the beat of **MUSIC**.

❽ Turkmenistan is home to the **LARGEST ENCLOSED** Ferris wheel in the world, a 156-foot (47.5-m)-tall ride built inside a **GLASS** and **MARBLE** structure.

TO MAKE YOUR HEAD SPIN

9 Despite being damaged during WORLD WAR II, the 120-year-old Wiener Riesenrad in VIENNA, AUSTRIA, still spins with 15 of its original 30 cars.

10 The TRANSPORTABLE Roue de Paris wheel—that has popped up in PARIS, ENGLAND, BANGKOK, and AMSTERDAM—can be DISMANTLED in 60 HOURS and built in 72 HOURS.

11 Each year, more than **3.7 MILLION PEOPLE** take a spin on the **LONDON EYE,** Europe's largest Ferris wheel built to mark the **NEW MILLENNIUM** in 2000.

12 It takes **30 MINUTES** to make a **FULL ROTATION** on the **SINGAPORE FLYER,** a massive wheel that's nearly as tall as the **WASHINGTON MONUMENT.**

13 An artist created a PEDAL-POWERED Ferris wheel, powered by a TRIO OF RIDERS simultaneously pedaling to propel and rotate the ride.

14 The TIANJIN EYE looms large over a SIX-LANE BRIDGE in northern China, with cars and pedestrians **PASSING BELOW** the **394-FOOT (120-M)** wheel.

15 With a **TIME DISPLAY** at the center of a giant Ferris wheel, the **COSMO CLOCK 21** in Yokohama, Japan, can claim to be the world's **LARGEST CLOCK.**

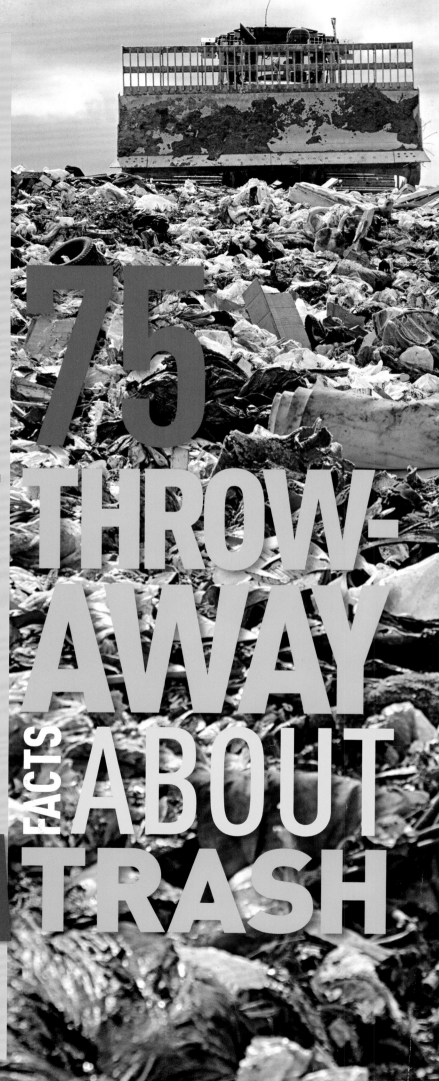

75 THROW-AWAY FACTS ABOUT TRASH

1 In 2012, Americans produced 251 million tons (227.7 million MT) of household and business waste. It would take 26.7 million garbage trucks to haul this amount of trash!

2 More than 100 cities and counties in the United States have passed legislation that bans the use of plastic bags in stores.

3 It takes 500 years for a Styrofoam cup to decompose.

4 A man in Cancún, Mexico, used 150,000 plastic bottles to create the base for his own personal floating island.

5 People in the U.S. buy 29 billion bottles of water each year. That's more plastic water bottles than any other country in the world!

6 The first garbage truck was invented by George Roby Dempster in 1935.

7 IN ONE YEAR, AMERICANS DISPOSED OF MORE THAN 150 MILLION CELL PHONES —THAT'S ONE PERSON THROWING AWAY FIVE CELL PHONES EACH SECOND.

8 San Francisco, California, U.S.A., has the highest recycling rate of any city in that country.

9 Studies show that the more repetitive your diet (eating the same things day after day), the less food you throw away.

10 It's estimated that 22 to 55 million tons (20 to 50 million MT) of used electronics are thrown away worldwide each year.

11 By studying what was discarded in ancient landfills, archaeologists learn about the daily life of people in ancient civilizations.

12 A college student designed the recycling symbol in 1970 for a contest about raising awareness for the environment. He won $2,500 for creating a logo that is now recognized worldwide.

13 Recycling one million laptops saves the energy equivalent of the electricity used by 3,657 homes in the United States in one year.

14 Americans throw away enough trash to fill more than 73,000 garbage trucks every day.

15 *Plastiki*, a catamaran made from 12,500 recycled plastic water bottles, sailed 8,000 miles (12,875 km) from San Francisco, California, to Sydney, Australia, in a little more than four months in 2010.

16 About one out of every six big trucks in the United States is a garbage truck.

17 One of the first journalists to interview J. K. Rowling threw away the copy of *Harry Potter and the Philosopher's Stone* that was given to him during the interview. A first edition of this book would now be worth about $40,000.

18 The United Nations estimates that about one-third of all the food produced every year worldwide never gets eaten.

19 The Belaz 75710 is the biggest dump truck in the world. It can haul a load of up to 504 tons (457.2 MT).

20 Plastic debris at sea is carried away by ocean currents into large, circulating whirlpools called gyres. There are five major gyres in the world's oceans.

21 An anthropology professor in Tucson, Arizona, U.S.A., started the Garbage Project. He and his students studied the trash local residents threw away to learn more about society.

22 Landfills are made with plastic liners on the bottom to prevent any contamination from getting into the nearby groundwater.

23 On your next car trip you might just be riding on top of used tires. Tires are recycled to make asphalt for highways.

24 A 500-YEAR-OLD WOODEN BED, USED BY ENGLISH KING HENRY VII, WAS FOUND DUMPED IN A PARKING LOT IN CHESTER, ENGLAND.

25 In 1997, the Great Pacific Garbage Patch—a floating island composed of tiny pieces of plastic and other marine debris—was discovered by a boat captain who was racing in a yacht competition.

26 Floating plastic in the ocean harms marine life. Sea turtles often eat plastic bags, and albatrosses mistake small pieces of plastic as fish eggs and feed them to their young.

27 Eat your veggies! Why? Fruits and vegetables are the most wasted kind of food worldwide.

28 The founder of Adopt-a-Highway got the idea for this roadside litter pickup program when he was driving in his car and saw trash flying out of the back of a pickup truck in front of him.

29 Recycled plastic bottles are used to make the material that goes in backpacks or sleeping bags.

30 John W. Hammes invented the garbage disposal in 1927. He was looking for ways to make it easier for his wife to clean up the kitchen.

31 Each year, on average, an American family of four people throws away an amount of trash that weighs the same as a large sports utility vehicle (SUV).

32 Frito-Lay started packing SunChips in a bag that was 100 percent compostable. The eco-friendly bag came with a drawback—it made a noise about as loud as a jackhammer when handled.

33 Recycling one ton (0.91 MT) of aluminum cans saves the equivalent of 26 barrels of oil.

34 WHILE MOST HALLOWEEN CANDY IS EATEN, A LARGE AMOUNT OF VALENTINE'S DAY CANDY IS THROWN OUT.

35 Solid waste can be combusted—burned—and turned into energy.

36 Composting is nature's way of recycling. When organic waste is put into soil, microorganisms break it down to simpler, reusable parts.

37 Residents of New York City throw away more than three million tons (2.72 million MT) of trash each year. That amount of trash would weigh more than 13,000 Statues of Liberty.

38 According to the United Nations, 1.46 billion tons (1.32 billion MT) of trash are generated worldwide each year. Only a fraction is recycled.

39 Only one percent of Sweden's trash ends up in landfills. The rest is either recycled or incinerated and converted into energy, mostly for heating but also for lighting.

40 Garbage collectors have a dangerous job. In the United States, it is ten times deadlier than most other jobs.

41 The MIT Trash Track project followed where trash went after it was thrown away by using electronic location tags. Some items traveled across the country before finally being disposed of!

42 Trash buried in a landfill can take an incredibly long time to decompose because the trash is not exposed to air or water, which helps it break down. Landfills like this are called "dry tombs."

43 Since 1990, the Recology Solid Waste and Transfer Station in San Francisco, California, has sponsored an artist in residence. The artist can use any discarded materials from the site to make art out of the trash.

44 IN CANADA A GARBAGE DISPOSAL IS CALLED A GARBURATOR.

45 Every year, people in developed countries waste about the same amount of food that is produced in all of sub-Saharan Africa.

46 Strong magnets are used at recycling centers and at landfills to sort out some metal objects.

47 Oops! Not realizing a plastic bag of trash was part of an artwork display at the Tate Britain—an art museum in London, England—an employee accidentally threw it away.

48 Some landfills capture methane gas emitted from the decaying garbage and convert it into power.

49 In the 19th century, pigs would roam the streets of big cities like Washington, D.C., to eat food scraps residents threw in the streets.

50 To cut down on waste and washing up, and to encourage people to be eco-conscious, some restaurants have started charging diners for any food left on their plates.

51 A woman in New York City once discovered a stolen painting worth $1 million dollars in the trash.

52 Americans are composting almost five times as much yard waste today compared to what was composted in 1990.

53 A COMPANY IN CALIFORNIA, U.S.A., HAS CREATED GLU6, "THE GLUE THAT SAVES PLANET EARTH." THE GLUE TURNS RECYCLED STYROFOAM PRODUCTS, LIKE TAKEOUT FOOD CONTAINERS AND CUPS, INTO GLUE FOR CRAFTS.

54 When there was a shortage of food during World War II, the U.S. government started encouraging people to clean their plates, with the motto "Don't Waste It!"

55 Containers and packaging make up the largest portion of municipal waste.

56 Lots of people turn old things into new ones. One designer recycled an old suitcase into a double-decker cat bed.

57 More than 95 percent of all food waste could have been composted.

58 Laid out end-to-end, the amount of plastic bags Americans use each year would circle the Equator 1,330 times.

59 In Sweden, recycling centers are located less than a quarter of a mile (300 m) from any residential area.

60 The group Keep America Beautiful sponsors a Recycle-Bowl competition for schools in the United States. The winning school wins the national title of America's Top Recycling School.

61 When a manager at Harvard University saw all the furniture that was left behind when students moved out of the dorms, he organized Harvard's Habitat for Humanity Annual Stuff Sale.

62 Mount Trashmore in Virginia Beach, Virginia, U.S.A., was one of the first landfills to be made into a city park after the landfill was filled up and closed.

63 Since 2011, an artist has sold more than 1,400 clear cubes full of trash picked from the streets of New York City.

64 Every ton of mixed paper that is recycled can save the energy equivalent of 165 gallons (625 L) of gasoline.

65 Glass is 100 percent recyclable and can be used over and over again.

66 The Mbeubeuss dump in Senegal, Africa, stretches over 432 acres (175 ha). That would cover more than 4,000 basketball courts.

67 A hotel in the Netherlands is called the Hotel Trash Deluxe. But don't worry, you won't be sleeping with trash. Many of the hotel's decorations are crafted from recycled materials.

68 The United States makes up less than 5 percent of the world's population but creates 30 percent of the world's garbage.

69 An artist created a seven-foot (2-m)-tall statue of Optimus Prime of the Transformers out of old car parts.

70 In Pakistan, Oscar the Grouch's name is Akhtar and he lives in an oil barrel instead of a trash can. In Turkey, he lives in a basket and goes by the name of Kirpik.

71 A bioreactor landfill adds a controlled amount of air and water to the waste to speed up decomposition.

72 An employee of a trash removal company found $16,500 worth of ancient Maya artifacts in a cardboard barrel in an apartment he was cleaning out.

73 A documentary movie about people who pick through trash in a Rio de Janeiro, Brazil, landfill was nominated for an Oscar in 2011.

74 USED SCRAP PAPER AND METAL ARE TWO OF THE LARGEST U.S. EXPORTS BY VOLUME.

75 A ski slope is being constructed on top of a high-efficiency, waste-to-energy plant in Copenhagen, Denmark.

1 With a land area of 570,374 square miles (1,477,262 sq km), Alaska is LARGER than the U.S. states of Texas, California, and Montana combined.

2 Eleven different languages are spoken among Alaska's NATIVE PEOPLE, who make up about 16 percent of the state's population.

3 The United States purchased Alaska from Russia in 1867 for $7.2 million—that's less than TWO CENTS AN ACRE!

4 Just 51 miles (82 km) from Russia, Alaska is CLOSER TO ASIA than it is to the mainland United States.

5 Alaska's capital city, JUNEAU, was originally called Harrisburg after the first miner to strike GOLD there.

6 There are NO ROADS leading in or out of Juneau—it's only accessible by BOAT, FERRY, OR PLANE.

7 About 1 in every 87 residents of Alaska is a licensed AIRPLANE PILOT.

8 A 9.2-magnitude earthquake struck Alaska on March 27, 1964—the BIGGEST EARTHQUAKE in North America to date.

9 Alaska's THOMPSON PASS once received more than 81 feet (24.7 m) of snow in a single year. Added up, that would be taller than an EIGHT-STORY BUILDING!

10 In Fairbanks, Alaska, it's illegal for a MOOSE to walk on a sidewalk. It was also illegal to have an ELEPHANT anywhere in the state until 1995.

11 There are close to 150,000 BEARS living in Alaska—that's about one for every five people in the state.

12 You can see the aurora borealis—or NORTHERN LIGHTS—an average of 243 days a year in Fairbanks.

13 About 5 percent of Alaska—some 29,000 square miles (75,110 sq km)—is covered by GLACIERS.

35 AWESOME FACTS ABOUT ALASKA

14 Alaska has 39 MOUNTAIN RANGES that include 17 of the 20 highest peaks in the United States.

15 There are more than 12,000 RIVERS in the state. The longest? The YUKON, which ranks third in length among all U.S. rivers.

16 In 1998, a miner found a GOLD NUGGET about as big as a softball in northern Alaska.

17 Alaska contains 1,800 named ISLANDS, including the 100-mile (161-km)-long Kodiak Island, which is nearly three times the size of Rhode Island.

18 An 11-YEAR-OLD BOY once scaled the peak of 20,320-foot (6,194-m)-high DENALI (Mt. McKinley)—the youngest ever climber to do so.

19 There are more than 3 million FRESHWATER LAKES in Alaska; 94 of them larger than ten square miles (25.9 sq km).

20 Alaska is the only state name that you can type on one row of a KEYBOARD.

21 Alaska has 70 potentially ACTIVE VOLCANOES—that's about 80 percent of all the active volcanoes in the United States.

22 Alaska is the only state to have COASTLINES on three different bodies of water: the Arctic Ocean, the Pacific Ocean, and the Bering Sea.

23 Every spring you can spot PODS OF BELUGAS from the banks of the Naknek River in south-western Alaska, where the white WHALES come to feed on rainbow trout.

24 A fisherman once caught a 97-pound (44-kg) KING SALMON in the Kenai River in south central Alaska.

25 The town of CHICKEN, Alaska, has a population of about 17, with no phone service and no electricity.

26 UNALASKA, NORTH POLE, MARY'S IGLOO, and DEADHORSE are all names of towns in Alaska.

27 With a depth of nearly 9,000 feet (2,743 m), the GREAT GORGE in Alaska's Ruth Glacier is deeper than the Grand Canyon.

28 A seventh-grader from Seward designed the STAR PATTERN on Alaska's state flag in 1926.

29 DOG MUSHING is the official sport of Alaska—and the practice of using dogs to pull SLEDS has been used in the state for thousands of years.

30 During the summer, Anchorage gets about 20 hours of DAYLIGHT and the sun doesn't set until around midnight.

31 Thanks to Alaska's famous BORE TIDE, surfers can ride ten-foot (3-m)-tall waves in the ocean just outside of Anchorage.

32 *Akutaq*—also known as ESKIMO ICE CREAM—is made of whipped berries, seal oil, and freshly fallen snow.

33 Because there aren't many GROUNDHOGS in Alaska, the state observes MARMOT DAY every February 2 instead.

34 Alaska's DENALI NATIONAL PARK is about half the size of Switzerland.

35 There are more CARIBOU than people in Alaska.

aurora borealis in Alaska

1. The strongest part of a hurricane is a wall of storms that swirl around the hurricane's center or "eye." 2. Storms used to be named randomly but today names are pulled from a rotating list written by an international group called the World Meteorological Organization. 3. **The United States first began naming storms in 1953 and only used female names. It wasn't until the end of the 1970s that male names were included.** 4. The idea that storms should be named after women stems from the 1941 novel *Storm*. In the book, the storm's name is Maria. 5. "Arlene" has been used more than any other name for Atlantic storms. 6. **Storm surge is when a hurricane or tropical storm causes the water level to rise far above normal.** 7. Storm surges that occur during high tide can cause the water to rise more than 20 feet (6 m). 8. Most of the damage caused by Hurricane Katrina in 2005 was due to storm surge flooding when the water level rose almost as tall as a three-story building! 9. **Tornadoes come from extreme thunderstorms and have winds reaching up to 300 miles an hour (483 km/h).** 10. The damage caused by a tornado can stretch over an area up to 1 mile (1.6 km) wide and 50 miles (80.5 km) long. 11. Tornadoes can be impossible to see until swirling dust, dirt, or other debris caught in the funnel cloud make them visible. 12. **Research shows that tornadoes are most common between the hours of 3 p.m. and 9 p.m.** 13. It is rare, but tornadoes can strike twice—in Guy, Arkansas, U.S.A., three tornadoes struck the same church within 24 hours. 14. The most damage and injury caused by tornadoes comes from flying objects and debris. 15. **Tornadoes that form over water are called waterspouts and are most common in the Florida Keys, U.S.A.** 16. Some people believe that shooting something large, like a cannonball, into a waterspout will make it disappear, but there is no scientific proof to back it up. 17. *Sharknado* was a 2013 movie about a waterspout in Los Angeles, California, U.S.A., that lifted sharks (computer-generated images) out of the Pacific Ocean and carried them to land, wreaking havoc. 18. **Snowspouts—waterspouts in winter conditions—are rare but do occur in places like Antarctica, Scandinavia, and Canada.** 19. Astraphobia is an abnormal fear of thunder and lightning and comes from the Greek word for lightning: *astrape*. 20. 1994 Hurricane/Typhoon John lasted 31 days, making it the longest tropical cyclone to date. 21. **Thunderstorms occur more often in the United States than anywhere else.** 22. It's estimated there are up to 40,000 thunderstorms every day around the world—that's 14.6 million per year. 23. Tornadoes can last anywhere from a few seconds to more than an hour, but most are under ten minutes. 24. **Hail is basically frozen rain. These balls of ice form when winds in thunderstorms carry raindrops high up where they freeze (and often grow in size) before falling.** 25. In 2001, a hailstorm in Kansas, U.S.A., caused more damage than any other hailstorm in the United States—the damage estimated at about $2 billion. 26. The heaviest hailstone ever recorded fell in Kansas in 1970 and weighed 1.67 pounds (0.76 kg). 27. **The Empire State Building in New York City, New York, U.S.A., is hit by lightning about 100 times a year.** 28. A nor'easter is a storm from the northeast in the Mid-Atlantic and New England states of the United States. A nor'easter in 1888 killed about 400 people. 29. The Marvel character "Storm" has the power to control the weather, creating things like lightning, snow, rain, and hurricanes. 30. **In the *Star Wars* films, the soldiers that fight for the Emperor and the Imperial cause are called Storm Troopers.** 31. A haboob is a superstrong dust and sand storm that creates walls as high as 3,300 feet (1 km). *Habb* is an Arabic word for "wind." 32. Haboobs happen in hot and dry areas like the Sahara and in Arizona and Texas, U.S.A. 33. *Catatumbo* lightning in Venezuela is an "eternal storm" that lights up the sky about 160 nights per year and has done so for thousands of years. 34. The word "tornado" comes from the Spanish word *tronada*, which means "thunderstorm." 35. Tornadoes are funnel-shaped rotating columns of air that stretch from powerful thunderstorms above down to the ground. 36. **Sometimes the wind stops completely and the air feels strangely still—with no movement or sound—right before a tornado strikes.** 37. In April of 1974 the United States was hit with the worst tornado outbreak it has ever seen: 148 tornadoes struck 13 states in 16 hours. 38. Oklahoma City, Oklahoma, U.S.A., has been struck by more tornadoes than any other city in the United States. 39. **A green sky or sounds similar to a roaring train are two signs that there may be a tornado coming.** 40. Hurricane hunters fly into hurricanes, as low as they can, to study them—typically at altitudes from 1,000 feet (305 m) to 10,000 feet (3 km). 41. Hurricane hunters drop a measuring instrument that looks like a paper towel tube on a parachute, called a dropsonde, into the hurricane's eye to take measurements of the storm. 42. **Even though many more storms form over the ocean, about five hurricanes hit the coast of the United States every three years.** 43. Hurricanes move at about 10 to 20 miles an hour (16 to 32 km/h) but can be as fast as 40 miles an hour (64 km/h). 44. Typhoons, hurricanes, and cyclones are different names for the same thing: "Typhoons" are west of the International Date Line, "hurricanes" are east of that point, and "cyclones" are in the Indian Ocean. 45. **Hurricanes only form over warm waters of 80°F (26.7°C).** 46. In 1968 a storm with a sweet name hit Texas: Tropical Storm Candy. 47. Only three extreme hurricanes have hit the United States since the beginning of the 20th century: "Labor Day," in Florida, 1935; "Camille," in Mississippi, 1969; and "Andrew," in Florida, 1992. 48. **Elephants seemed to sense the 2004 Indian Ocean tsunami and came to the rescue of foreign tourists—allowing them to ride on their backs to the safety of the nearby jungle.** 49. The word "hurricane" developed from two gods: Hurakan, a one-legged Maya god who was believed to send floods and storms, and Hurican, the Carib god of evil. 50. In an ice storm, freezing rain falls and causes a layer of ice to glaze over every surface it touches. The thickest ice ever collected was eight inches (20 cm) deep! 51. **After a storm, someone in North Carolina, U.S.A., backed out of a parking spot and left an ice sculpture of the front of their Jeep attached to the curb.** 52. In a bad ice storm, even thin layers of ice

100 FIERCE FACTS ABOUT STORMS

that form over power lines and other structures can cause major damage because they weigh so much. 53. The "First North American Blizzard of 2010," as it is called, had many nicknames, including Snowmageddon, Snowpocalypse, and SnOMG. 54. **A blizzard is a snowstorm with winds of more than 35 miles an hour (56 km/h). Visibility in a blizzard is so bad it's impossible to see beyond one-quarter mile (400 m) for three hours or more. 55.** In 1985 Dairy Queen came out with the Blizzard—soft-serve ice cream blended with toppings. It was very popular, selling more than 175 million cupfuls that year. 56. Every winter it's estimated that about one septillion snowflakes fall—and no two are alike. 57. **The first ever European account of a hurricane was written by Christopher Columbus when he encountered a tropical cyclone in 1494. 58.** *Derecho* is the Spanish word for "straight ahead" and the word used to describe strong, violent windstorms that leave tornado-like destruction but, unlike a tornado, travel in a straight line. 59. In May of 1998, a *derecho* created winds clocking in at 128 miles an hour (206 km/h) in Wisconsin, U.S.A. 60. **Red sprites are rare reddish lightning bolts above thunderstorms that look like fireworks or giant jellyfish. 61.** Names for different types of lightning include anvil crawler, bolt from the blue, bead lightning, and ribbon lightning. 62. A thunderstorm is considered "severe" if it creates any one of the following: winds of 58 miles an hour (93 km/h) or more, hail at least the size of a penny, or tornadoes. 63. **Tropical Cyclone Olivia struck Australia in 1996 and holds the record for fastest gusts of wind, at 253 miles an hour (407 km/h). 64.** In 1979, Super Typhoon Tip hit Japan. It was the largest tropical cyclone to date, stretching across 1,350 miles (2,173 km). That's the distance from New York City to Dallas, Texas! 65. Animals such as frogs and fish have "rained" from the sky. The animals are carried into the sky by strong winds and then they fall down, making it look like rain. 66. **Ball lightning is a circle of light a few feet wide that happens, only rarely, seconds after a lightning strike. Scientists don't know what causes it. 67.** The longest lasting tropical cyclone lasted 31 days in August and September of 1994. It crossed the date line (twice) so it is called both Hurricane and Typhoon John. 68. Kampala, Uganda, has more thunderstorms than anywhere else in the world: about 240 each year. 69. **All thunderstorms create lightning, sometimes as far as 10 miles (16 km) away from the storm's rains. 70.** "Thundersnow" occurs when it is thundering and snowing at the same time. 71. The air around bolts of lightning cause thunder. Energy from the lightning heats the air to 18,000°F (9,982°C) and it quickly expands, causing the noise. 72. **Hundreds of people are injured from lightning each year in the United States, but the chance of being struck is only 1 in 600,000. 73.** It's safe to touch a person who has been struck by lightning since the human body does not retain electricity. 74. In 2010 in Pakistan an elderly lady's cow saved her life during a flash flood by carrying her, swimming through the rough waters for hours until they reached land. 75. **The shape of a raindrop depends on its size—small raindrops look like spheres while larger ones stretch out and look more like hamburger buns. 76.** Floods are the most damaging natural disaster in the United States and can be caused by hurricanes, winter storms, and nor'easters. 77. Humans don't generally notice the small (P) shock waves that come before the big destructive (S) waves in an earthquake—but animals can. 78. **In 1949 one foot (0.3 m) of snow dropped across the city and beaches in Los Angeles, California. 79.** There are coin-operated machines called Tornado Simulators that allow a person to step inside and experience 100-mile-an-hour (161-km/h) winds. 80. Snowflakes can be as large as six inches (15 cm) wide! 81. **"Snow White in a Snowstorm" is a work of art of 2006 consisting of just a layer of white polystyrene and acrylic on a rectangular wooden board. 82.** NASA uses satellites in space to measure rain. The Tropical Rainfall Measuring Mission measured around seven inches (18 cm) of rainfall on land during Hurricane Sandy in 2012. 83. The Pineapple Express is a type of rainstorm that originates in the tropics of Hawaii and goes up into the Pacific Northwest. It typically causes flooding and mudslides. 84. **For a tropical cyclone to be classified as a hurricane, cyclone, or typhoon, its winds much reach 74 miles an hour (119 km/h) or higher. 85.** Each year, 21 names in alphabetical order are used to name Atlantic tropical storms. Why not 26? Because it is hard to find names that start with *Q, U, X, Y,* or *Z.* 86. If more than 21 storms occur in the Atlantic Ocean, they begin to take their names from the Greek alphabet. 87. **Ringo Starr, drummer with the Beatles pop group, first played for a group called Rory Storm and the Hurricanes. 88.** The Great Red Spot on Jupiter is a hurricane-like storm that's lasted for more than 300 years with winds topping out at 250 miles an hour (402 km/h). 89. Neptune has storms with winds whipping around at 1,600 miles an hour (2,575 km/h). 90. **A solar storm is an explosion in the sun's atmosphere. Often, when the particles streaming from the explosion hit Earth, it creates lights called auroras that are usually seen from places closest to the North and South Poles. 91.** The Halloween Solar Storms of 2003 created colorful auroras that danced across the sky and were seen as far south as Florida and Texas, U.S.A. 92. In 1992, Steven Spielberg was on the island of Kauai, Hawaii, U.S.A., shooting *Jurassic Park* during the most powerful hurricane to hit Hawaii. It was called Hurricane Iniki. 93. **Filmmakers used a stocking and chicken wire to create the tornado in the film *The Wizard of Oz*. It rotated with a motor and was pushed along a track. 94.** In March 2014, a fire tornado, also called a fire whirl or fire devil, was captured on film ripping through Denver, Colorado, U.S.A. 95. Airplanes are often struck by lightning in flight—and planes can even trigger a strike. But people flying inside are not affected by it because the lightning flows around the outside of the plane. 96. **"Storm spotters" look at the different shapes of clouds to see if a storm is coming. 97.** People have compared the deafening sound of a tornado to a jet engine or a freight train. 98. Tornadoes are so powerful they can dig a hole in the ground up to three feet (1 m) deep. 99. **Nebraska, Colorado, and Wyoming typically have more hailstorms than anywhere else in the U.S. 100.** Sharks tend to swim to deeper waters before a storm. Scientists have tagged some

1 DOLPHINS and PORPOISES are actually TOOTHED WHALES.

2 A BABY BLUE WHALE weighs about as much as an ADULT HIPPOPOTAMUS.

3 BALEEN WHALES use fringe-like bristles instead of teeth TO TRAP thousands of TINY pieces of FOOD.

4 Although blue whales are the HEAVIEST animals ever to live on Earth, they are up to 50 feet (15 m) SHORTER than the biggest dinosaur.

5 SPERM WHALES are some of the DEEPEST-DIVING whales, reaching depths of 6,700 feet (2 km).

6 The LUNGS of sperm whales COLLAPSE WHEN THEY DIVE to help them handle the PRESSURE at great depths.

7 The vaquita porpoise is the SMALLEST MEMBER of the whale and dolphin family; it would take about 3,000 of them to EQUAL THE WEIGHT of a blue whale.

8 BOTTLENOSE DOLPHINS are often trained to perform TRICKS such as jumping through hoops.

9 The male NARWHAL HAS ONLY TWO TEETH, one of which grows into a SPIRAL TUSK that measures up to 8.8 feet (2.7 m) long.

10 A narwhal's tusk grows right through its UPPER LIP.

11 A FIN WHALE pees enough to FILL THREE BATHTUBS each day.

12 The HEAD of a sperm whale is nearly ONE-THIRD of its TOTAL BODY LENGTH.

13 Blue whales EAT 2.2 TONS (2 MT) of KRILL each day.

14 Humpback whales USE RINGS OF BUBBLES called BUBBLE NETS to trap fish at the water's surface.

15 Hundreds of years ago, Europeans sold NARWHAL TUSKS as UNICORN HORNS.

16 Southern right whales SAIL through the water by holding their tails in the air and LETTING THE WIND MOVE THEM.

17 Sperm whales SLEEP IN GROUPS, FLOATING VERTICALLY in the water.

18 Blue whale POOP contains nutrients that FERTILIZE PLANKTON, which in turn FEED FISH.

50 WHOPPING FACTS ABOUT WHALES

19
When whales **DIVE AND RESURFACE,** they help **MIX OCEAN WATERS** from top to bottom, bringing **NUTRIENTS UP FROM THE DEEP.**

20
Gray whales **SUCK FOOD** from the sandy ocean floor.

21
When gray whales search for food **HIDDEN IN THE SAND,** they **PLOW TROUGHS** in the ocean floor.

22
Whale carcasses that fall to the ocean floor take carbon with them; some scientists think this sinking carbon could **HELP FIGHT GLOBAL WARMING.**

23
The **BIG KNOBS** on a humpback whale's face are actually **HAIR FOLLICLES.**

24
Blue whales are the **LOUDEST ANIMALS ON EARTH;** their calls are as loud as a **ROCKET LAUNCH.**

25
When hunting, **KILLER WHALES**—also known as orcas—create **WAVES TO WASH SEALS** off of ICE FLOES.

26
AMAZON RIVER DOLPHINS start out dark **GRAY** but turn **PINK** and even **WHITE** as they **AGE.**

27
Whales **POKE THEIR HEADS** out of the water to get a better **FEEL FOR THEIR SURROUNDINGS,** a behavior called **SPYHOPPING.**

28
The **BOWHEAD WHALE,** which lives in the Arctic Ocean, has a layer of **BLUBBER THAT IS TWO FEET (61 CM) THICK.**

29
The **FIN WHALE** can **SWIM** at speeds up to 23 miles an hour (37 km/h)—about the same speed as the **FASTEST HUMAN RUNNER.**

30
Whales communicate using **WHISTLES** and **PULSES** that sound like **SQUAWKS** and **SCREAMS** to the human ear.

31
DIFFERENT PODS of whales have their own **DIALECTS,** or variety of sounds.

32
Whales and dolphins—and even seals and penguins—sometimes swim by **PORPOISING, THAT IS, LEAPING IN AND OUT** of the water.

33
Orcas sometimes **EAT OTHER WHALES.**

34
The **COLOR PATTERN** and **SHAPE** of a humpback whale's fins are **AS UNIQUE AS HUMAN FINGERPRINTS.**

35
A whale's **EARWAX** is laid down in layers, **LIKE TREE RINGS,** so it can be **USED TO TELL HOW OLD** the animal is.

36
The **EARWAX PLUG** removed from a whale can be **TEN INCHES (25.4 CM) LONG.**

37
Musicians in Winnipeg, Canada, created **MUSIC** that **THEY PLAYED** underwater to **WILD BELUGA WHALES.** The whales **SANG ALONG.**

38
BOWHEAD WHALES can live for **MORE THAN 200 YEARS**—their cold, Arctic habitat helps **SLOW THE AGING PROCESS.**

39
A whale **HUNTED IN ALASKA, U.S.A.,** in 2007 contained weapon fragments that **DATED BACK TO 1879.**

40
Female **HUMPBACK** whales **MEET UP** year after year, just like **OLD FRIENDS.**

41
A WHITE WHALE MIMICKED the sounds of **HUMAN SPEECH** so well, one of his handlers got out of the water because **THE WHALE TOLD HIM TO DO SO.**

42
A blue whale can completely **OPEN AND CLOSE** its 19.7-foot (6-m) jaws in **LESS THAN TEN SECONDS.**

43
Unlike fish, which swish their tails from **SIDE TO SIDE,** whales move their tail fins, called flukes, **UP AND DOWN AS THEY SWIM.**

44
"OLD TOM," an orca that lived in the waters off Australia, and its pod **HELPED HERD** baleen whales so whalers could **HUNT THEM MORE EASILY.**

45
Although whales live in the ocean, a **MOTHER HUMPBACK** and her daughter **SWAM 75 MILES (121 KM) UPRIVER** in California, U.S.A.

46
Male **HUMPBACK WHALES** sing songs; they change these songs every two to three **MONTHS** to match those sung by other humpback whales.

47
In 2013 a pod of **SPERM WHALES ADOPTED** a **DOLPHIN** with a **CURVED SPINE,** allowing it to become part of their pod.

48
HIPPOS are the **CLOSEST LIVING RELATIVES** of whales.

49
The **HEART** of a blue whale is the size of a **VOLKSWAGEN BEETLE.**

50
Captive **DOLPHINS** in Port-Saint-Père, France, **SING** humpback **WHALE SONGS** at night.

1 ARCHAEOLOGISTS FOUND A **2,000-YEAR-OLD** STONE TOILET THAT COULD BE **FLUSHED** WITH **PIPE WATER** IN A CHINESE TOMB.

2 Instead of using **TOILET PAPER**, ancient Romans would **WIPE** themselves with a **SHARED SPONGE** on a stick.

3 Public toilets were common in **ANCIENT ROME**. Some could **SEAT 80 PEOPLE** at one time.

4 Up until the 18th century, people in major cities like **LONDON** and **NEW YORK** relieved themselves in **CHAMBER POTS**—then dumped the **WASTE** into the **STREET.**

5 King Louis XIV's toilet was designed to look like a **WOODEN THRONE.** Legend has it that the famous **FRENCH** leader would **RELIEVE** himself while conducting **COURT** sessions.

6 A **TOILET** is also known as a **LOO, JOHN, LAV, LATRINE, PRIVY, HOPPER,** and the **HEAD.**

25 FACTS ABOUT TOILETS TO FLUSH

7 THE FIRST-EVER PUBLIC BATHROOMS, INTRODUCED IN LONDON IN 1851, COST **ONE PENNY** PER VISIT.

8 FLUSHING THE TOILET CAN USE MORE THAN 200 GALLONS (757 L) OF WATER EVERY DAY. THAT'S ENOUGH TO FILL NEARLY THREE BATHTUBS.

9 There are nearly **2,000 PORTABLE** toilets lined up at the **START** of the **NEW YORK CITY** Marathon.

10 In 1957 a **TOILET** appeared on **TELEVISION** for the **FIRST TIME** during an episode of the hit show *Leave It to Beaver.*

11 YOU VISIT THE BATHROOM ABOUT **2,500 TIMES A YEAR.** THAT EQUALS A TOTAL OF ABOUT **THREE YEARS ON THE TOILET** DURING THE AVERAGE LIFETIME.

12
The World Toilet Association—that works to bring **SANITATION** to **DEVELOPING COUNTRIES**—has deemed November 19 as **WORLD TOILET DAY.**

13
A **BOA CONSTRICTOR**—measuring about **5.5 FEET LONG (1.7 M)**—was recently **REMOVED** from a **TOILET** in an **OFFICE BUILDING** in San Diego, California, U.S.A.

14
A SCIENCE MUSEUM IN **JAPAN** ONCE FEATURED A BATHROOM-THEMED EXHIBIT WHERE VISITORS **SLID** INTO A **GIANT TOILET** TO LEARN MORE ABOUT WHAT HAPPENS TO THINGS YOU **FLUSH.**

15
SCULPTOR Clark Sorensen in San Francisco, California, U.S.A., has created **COLORFUL URINALS** in the shape of **FLOWERS.**

16
The **NUMI** is a $5,000 toilet with a **HEATED SEAT**, a foot warmer, lights, and a **STEREO SYSTEM.**

17
Three people ran the 2014 **LONDON MARATHON** dressed as toilets. The **FASTEST** completed the race in 2 hours, 57 minutes.

18
The International Space Station **TOILET SYSTEM** converts **URINE** into **DRINKING WATER.**

AWAY

19
A SMARTPHONE APP called AIRPNP helps you find the closest **BATHROOM** in a city then **RENT** its use. Fees range from $1 to $100.

20
In Indiana, U.S.A., a man once **BROKE 46 WOODEN** toilet seats over his **HEAD** in **ONE MINUTE.**

21
AT THE **OUTHOUSE RACE** IN SAGINAW, MICHIGAN, U.S.A., EACH TEAM BUILDS A **COVERED** TOILET, MOUNTS IT ON **SKIS**, THEN RACES ON A **SNOWY** TRACK—WHILE ONE TEAM MEMBER **SITS** INSIDE.

22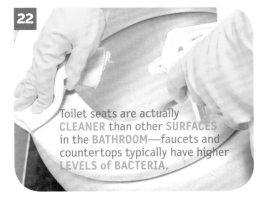
Toilet seats are actually **CLEANER** than other **SURFACES** in the **BATHROOM**—faucets and countertops typically have higher **LEVELS** of BACTERIA.

23
A **TRADING CARD** featuring **BATMAN** sitting on the **TOILET** once went on sale for $3,500.

24
A **BELGIUM** company put together a TOILET PAPER roll CHAIN out of 92,080 ROLLS, measuring nearly SIX MILES (9.7 KM) long.

25
ECO-FRIENDLY ELECTRIC toilets use **HEAT** to burn human **WASTE** into **ASH**, which you then **THROW** into the **GARBAGE.**

15 CRUNCHY FACTS ABOUT

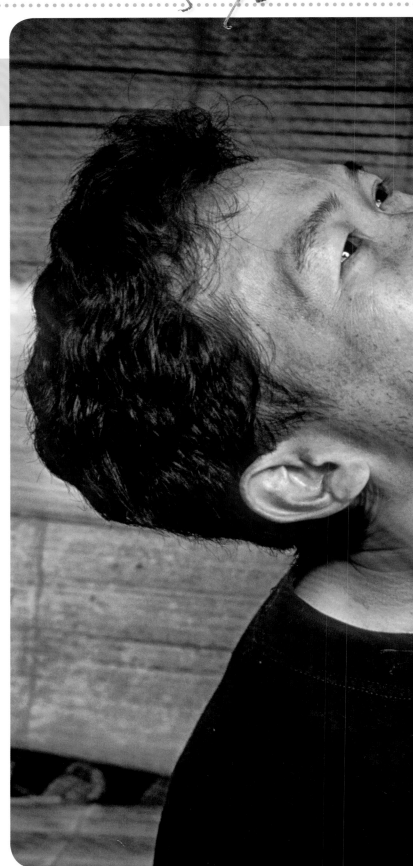

❶ The Food and Agriculture Organization of the United Nations estimates that **TWO BILLION** people worldwide depend daily on **INSECTS** for food.

❷ **NATIVE AMERICANS** roasted **BEETLES** over coals and ate them like **POPCORN.**

❸ Supporters of bug-eating—and the practice of using insects as food—are known as **ENTOMOPHAGISTS.**

❹ To make bugs tastier, they're often fed **ORGANIC GRAINS** and **VEGGIES** by **INSECT FARMERS.**

❺ **FLIES** that feast and develop on different types of **CHEESE** tend to take on the flavor of their host.

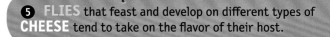

❻ More than **1,900 INSECT SPECIES** are eaten by people around the world.

❼ "CHIRPS"—tortilla chips made with beans, rice, and finely ground **CRICKET FLOUR**—come in flavors like barbecue, sea salt, and aged cheddar.

❽ The edible bug business is said to generate more than **20 MILLION DOLLARS** a year worldwide.

EATING INSECTS

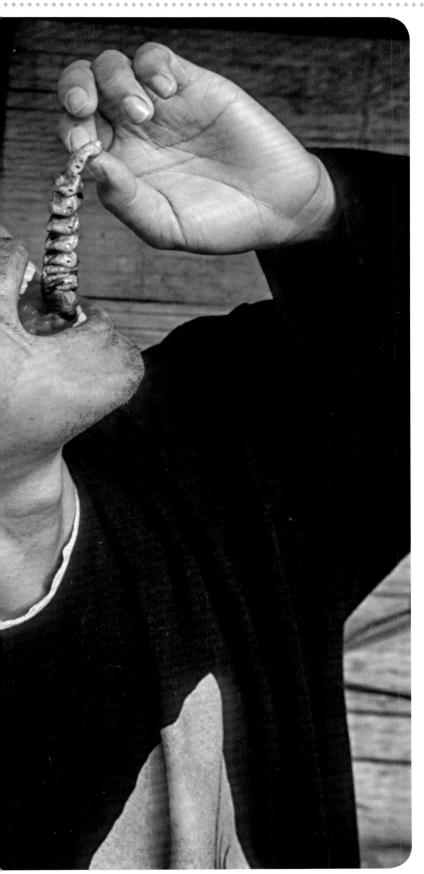

9 At bug-themed "**PESTAURANTS**," you can order GRASSHOPPER BURGERS, roasted crickets, Mexican spice mealworms, and **ANT LOLLIPOPS.**

10 In certain parts of Mexico, **STINKBUGS** are ground up, mixed with chilies, and served in TACOS.

11 Ounce for ounce, both GRASSHOPPERS AND CATERPILLARS pack more protein than a hamburger.

12 People in Ghana gather WINGED TERMITES and roast them or add them into BREAD.

13 In Southeast Asia, the larvae (caterpillars) of RED PALM WEEVILS are often eaten DEEP FRIED or live after marinating in SOY SAUCE.

14 A French company sells CANNED cheese-and-bacon-flavored WATER BUGS and WASABI MEALWORMS.

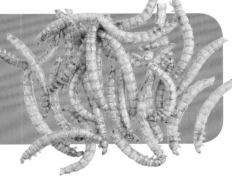

15 A company in Stockholm, Sweden, has come up with a concept called INSECTCITY— a city that would be entirely DEPENDENT on INSECT PROTEIN.

1 Gravity pulls things together—it never pushes them apart.

2 The force of gravity not only keeps our feet on the ground, it also keeps the moon orbiting Earth and Earth orbiting the sun.

3 Ancient Greeks noticed the natural motion of planets and stars but were unaware of gravity.

4 Sir Isaac Newton was the first person to describe the nature of gravity, more than 300 years ago.

5 The force of gravity is exerted by all things—the more mass an object has, the stronger its gravitational pull.

6 The International Space Station is kept in orbit because of Earth's gravitational pull.

7 An object dropped inside the space station doesn't look like it's falling because the object and the space station are falling together at the same rate.

8 What most people call zero gravity—when that object falls but doesn't appear to do so—is actually called microgravity.

9 OBJECTS ORBITING EARTH ARE IN FREE-FALL: THEY CONTINUALLY FALL, BUT NOT TOWARD THE GROUND.

10 An object in free-fall is weightless.

11 NASA has special airplanes that can achieve microgravity without leaving Earth's atmosphere. As the planes zoom toward Earth, the people inside experience weightlessness.

12 One of NASA's microgravity planes is called the "Vomit Comet."

13 The plane NASA used before the Vomit Comet was used to film scenes of weightless astronauts for *Apollo 13*, a movie based on a real mission to the moon that almost ended in disaster.

14 In order for a space shuttle to reach orbit, it has to travel to an altitude of 80 miles (129 km) above Earth and reach a speed of 17,500 miles an hour (28,164 km/h).

15 To reach such high speeds, a space shuttle needs half a million gallons (1.9 million L) of liquid hydrogen and liquid oxygen.

16 THE STRENGTH OF GRAVITATIONAL PULL DEPENDS PARTLY ON DISTANCE. WHEN SOMETHING IS TWICE AS FAR AWAY, GRAVITY PULLS ON IT ONLY A QUARTER AS MUCH. AN AIRPLANE FLYING AT 15,000 FEET (4,600 M) EXPERIENCES FOUR TIMES MORE GRAVITATIONAL PULL THAN A PLANE AT 30,000 FEET (9,100 M).

17 The sun's gravitational pull on Mercury is greater than on any other planet because Mercury is the closest planet to the sun.

18 Gravity pulls harder as objects get closer to Earth, so objects travel faster (and hit the surface harder) when they are dropped from greater heights.

19 Earth's gravity pulls us toward the ground at an accelerating rate of 32.2 feet per second squared (9.8 m/sec^2)—in other words, for every second we fall toward the ground, we move 32.2 feet per second faster than we did the second before (assuming no air resistance).

20 A brick and a feather will hit the ground at the same time if they are dropped from the same height in a chamber without air.

21 NASA spacecraft navigate using flybys past planets and moons. They use the gravitational pull of the planet or moon to slingshot around it, which increases the spacecraft's speed and changes its direction of travel.

22 When the spacecraft Cassini does a flyby around Saturn's moon, Titan, it speeds up by 2,625 feet per second (800 m/sec).

23 Cassini changes speed because it steals a tiny bit of orbital speed from Titan as it goes by.

24 The Voyager spacecraft used flybys past Jupiter, Saturn, Uranus, and Neptune to reach the outer edges of our solar system.

25 NASA has 500-foot (152-m)-tall towers that allow objects to be tested in free-fall. When air is removed, it takes five seconds for the object to reach the bottom of the tower from the top.

26 Roller coasters and other amusement park rides put riders into free-fall, but only for a few seconds.

27 When water boils in microgravity, it forms one big wobbly bubble, rather than thousands of tiny ones. Bubbles rise when gravity pulls cooler water down; without gravity, the bubbles can't go anywhere, so they join together.

28 Every object that has mass—even the tiniest speck—has its own gravity and attracts other objects.

29 Black holes are created when stars at least 25 times the mass of our sun run out of fuel and collapse under their own gravitational pull.

30 The strongest gravitational pull in the universe comes from a black hole. It is so strong, not even light can escape.

31 When a dying star collapses into a black hole, all of the matter from that star is condensed into a single point, called a singularity.

32 A snowball-size black hole would have the mass of ten Earths in a singularity smaller than a snowflake.

33 The gravity from a black hole is so great that it bends light traveling past it.

34 One way astronomers find black holes is by looking for places where a galaxy shows up multiple times in the same picture. This happens because the black hole bends the galaxy's light.

35 IF YOU WERE TO BE PULLED INTO A BLACK HOLE, YOUR BODY WOULD BE STRETCHED LIKE A PIECE OF SPAGHETTI. SCIENTISTS CALL THIS THE NOODLE EFFECT.

36 Saturn has "shepherd moons." The gravitational pull of these moons is what keeps the particles and rock fragments of Saturn's rings orbiting in distinct paths.

37 Tides—changes in water level along shorelines—are caused by the gravitational pull of the moon.

38 When the moon pulls on Earth's oceans, it causes water to bulge outward—this causes low tide.

39 When the sun, moon, and Earth are aligned, the sun's gravitational pull adds to the moon's pull to create extra-high tides and super-low tides.

40 The force of gravity near Earth's surface is called normal gravity and is given the value 1 g.

41 A Formula 1 race car driver experiences 3.5 g-forces while rounding corners and as much as 5 g-forces when braking. Many drivers hold their breath during these maneuvers to keep from passing out.

42 GRAVITY HELPS KEEP OUR BONES STRONG: ASTRONAUTS LOSE 1.5 PERCENT OF THEIR BONE MASS EACH MONTH THEY ARE IN SPACE.

43 Most people pass out when they experience 4 or 5 g's, because g-forces move blood into the arms and legs, starving the brain of oxygen.

44 If a 100-pound (45.4-kg) person stood on the surface of the sun, they would weigh 2,707.2 pounds (1,228 kg).

45 Because of microgravity, astronauts can lose bone density and muscle mass. They exercise six days a week to prevent this from happening.

46 It takes three to four years to recover the bone mass lost during a six-month stay aboard the International Space Station.

47 Because Earth is not a perfect sphere, its gravitational pull varies from one place to another.

48 Hudson Bay, Canada, is an area of low gravity because glaciers up to 2 miles (3.2 km) thick indented Earth's surface during the last ice age.

49 You shrink by about half an inch (1.3 cm) each day, from the time you get up until the time you go to bed; this is caused by gravity pulling down on your body all day.

75

FORCEFUL FACTS ABOUT GRAVITY

an apple on a tree—before it falls
under the force of gravity

50 After just two to three days in space, the amount of blood in an astronaut's body decreases by up to 22 percent.

51 Mountain ranges increase Earth's gravitational tug because there is more mass in those areas.

52 Astronauts who spend six months on the space station return to Earth up to three inches (7.6 cm) taller than they were when they left.

53 For the first few weeks in space, astronauts' faces get puffy and their legs slim down because there is no gravity to pull blood down toward their feet.

54 Astronauts who have returned to Earth after spending months in space let go of things, forgetting that gravity will cause them to fall.

55 When a flame burns on Earth, gravity pulls cold, dense air down while warm air rises; this causes the flame to taper to a point at the top.

56 FLAMES IN SPACE ARE SHAPED LIKE DOMES BECAUSE THERE IS NO GRAVITY TO PULL THE COLD AIR DOWN.

57 A person who weighs 100 pounds (45.4 kg) on Earth would weigh 130 million pounds (59 million kg) on the surface of a white dwarf star.

58 When someone cries in space, their tears stick to their eye and face in a big, jiggly ball.

59 Albert Einstein determined that gravity warps space and time, much like a bowling ball on a trampoline would cause it to bend and bow.

60 The stronger the gravitational pull of an object, the more it warps the space–time "trampoline."

61 Researchers at the University of Oxford, in Oxford, U.K., say that gravity is the reason time always moves forward and not backward.

62 According to scientists, there may be two universes—ours, which runs forward in time, and another one that runs backward.

63 Astronauts can't taste their food for the first few days in space because their sense of smell weakens, affecting taste.

64 NASA scientists built a chamber that used a superstrong magnet to lift mice off the ground—defying gravity.

65 The GravityLight is a lamp that uses the tug of gravity on a weighted pulley to power a light for 25 minutes with no batteries or electricity.

66 Although we can judge whether an object will fall if we are standing upright, we are not good at predicting the effects of gravity when lying down.

67 Fighter pilots wear antigravity suits that squeeze the legs and abdomen during high-g maneuvers. This keeps blood moving to their heads, even at 8 or 9 g's.

68 A typical sneeze generates 2.9 g-forces.

69 If you jump from a height of three feet (0.9 m) and land with stiff legs, you will experience about 100 g's upon landing.

70 Fighter pilots who regularly experience 2 to 6 g's build stronger, denser bones.

71 Astronauts used a loop of wire to blow bubbles aboard the International Space Station. When they stuck the loop in plain water, the water clung to the wire, bending like rubber, but not breaking.

72 THE GRAVITATIONAL TUG OF EARTH CHANGES MINUTE BY MINUTE.

73 Salt and pepper used by astronauts aren't tiny particles— they're in a liquid, to keep them from floating away when shaken onto food in microgravity.

74 A clock sitting just one foot (30.5 cm) off the ground ticks slightly faster than one sitting on Earth's surface.

75 A 100-pound (45.4-kg) person standing on the surface of a neutron star (a star that exploded before collapsing into a ball just 12.5 miles— 20.1 km—across) would weigh 14 trillion pounds (6.4 trillion kg).

35 FACTS ABOUT CHEESE

1 There are more than 2,000 **VARIETIES** of **CHEESE** made around the world.

2 In one year, a single **DAIRY COW** can produce enough milk to make cheese for 1,800 **PIZZAS**.

3 **CHEESEMAKING** is believed to date back to some time around 7,500 B.C., soon after **SHEEP** and **GOATS** were first domesticated.

4 Some ancient Roman houses had a **SPECIAL ROOM** just for **MAKING CHEESE**, called a careale.

5 It only takes a **FEW HOURS** to make cheese, but the **AGING** process—that boosts **FLAVOR**—lasts for **MONTHS** or **YEARS**.

6 Scientists have discovered **CHEESE-COOKING POTS** in **FRANCE** that date back to 5,000 B.C.

7 Remnants of **3,800-YEAR-OLD CHEESE** were recently discovered in the graves of **CHINESE MUMMIES**.

8 Queen Victoria of England received a **GIANT BLOCK** of cheddar cheese as a **WEDDING GIFT** in 1869. It was made from the milk of more than **700 COWS!**

9 The holes in Swiss cheese, called **EYES**, are caused by carbon dioxide **GAS BUBBLES** produced during fermentation.

10 **MICE** don't actually like the **TASTE of CHEESE**, a study showed.

11 The U.S. produces nearly **11 BILLION POUNDS** (about 5 million MT) of cheese per year—enough to provide 1.5 pounds (0.7 kg) for every **PERSON** on the **PLANET**.

12 President Andrew Jackson once left a 1,400-pound (635-kg) block of cheddar cheese to age in the **WHITE HOUSE** lobby for two years before serving it to **GUESTS** at a party.

13 Some types of cheese are so **SMELLY** that they've been **BANNED** from being carried or eaten on **PUBLIC BUSES** and **SUBWAYS** in France.

14 The scent of **EXTRA STINKY** Vieux Boulogne, a soft cheese from France, has been described as "six-week-old **EARWAX**."

15 Someone who **SELLS** cheese is known as a **CHEESEMONGER**.

16 A scientist has created cheese out of **BACTERIA** collected from people's stinky **FEET**, belly buttons, and **TEARS**.

17 A team of chefs once **WHIPPED UP** a 2,469-pound (1,120-kg) serving of **MACARONI AND CHEESE** using 286 pounds (130 kg) of cheese and 56 pounds (25 kg) of butter.

THAT DON'T STINK

18 Cheddar gets its name from the **VILLAGE OF CHEDDAR** in Somerset, U.K., where the **ORANGE** cheese was first made.

19 Cheese company Kraft cranks out about **7.2 BILLION SLICES** of American cheese per year.

20 *Lactococcus lactis*, the bacterium used to make cheddar, Colby, and Monterey Jack cheese, is the **STATE MICROBE** of Wisconsin, the largest producer of cheese in the U.S.

21 More people **STEAL CHEESE** from stores than any other **SHOPLIFTED** item.

22 A professional cheese **SCULPTOR** known as the Cheese Lady once created a 120-pound (54-kg) human-size **MICKEY MOUSE** out of a giant block of cheddar.

23 **MOOSE** cheese is considered among the world's most **EXPENSIVE** cheese—selling for around $500 per **POUND** ($1,100 per kg).

24 **BUFFALO** mozzarella is made from the milk of 1,500-pound (680-kg) water buffalo—that is said to have more **CALCIUM, PROTEIN,** and **IRON** than cow's milk.

25 Every other year, cheesemakers from more than 24 **COUNTRIES** compete at the **WORLD CHAMPIONSHIP** Cheese Contest. (The U.S. was the **BIG CHEESE** in 2014.)

26 Collectively, people in **GREECE** eat **MORE** cheese than in any other country on the planet, **CHOMPING** on average nearly 72 pounds (33 kg) each per year.

27 The largest block of **CHEDDAR** ever produced was made in 1989 by a cheesemaker in Oregon, U.S.A. It weighed **56,850 POUNDS (25,787 KG).**

28 On average, it takes 1.2 **GALLONS** (4.5 L) of **MILK** and 600 gallons (2,271 L) of **WATER** to make one pound of cheese.

29 Contrary to popular belief, eating cheese **BEFORE BED** has not been proven to give you **NIGHTMARES** or weird **DREAMS.**

30 There is an **ORANGE** Crayola **CRAYON** called "macaroni and cheese."

31 For an **APRIL FOOL'S DAY** joke, **NASA** once released a statement "proving" that the **MOON** was made of **GREEN CHEESE.**

32 Leftover cheese **BRINE**—salty water used to make cheese—can be used to treat **ICY ROADS.**

33 Some **DAIRIES** hire "cheese graders"—people who **SMELL** and **TASTE** cheese for a **LIVING.**

34 After a cheese shop owner found a **FORGOTTEN** 40-year-old block of cheese in his **REFRIGERATOR,** he sold it for $160 per pound.

35 The dish called **HEAD CHEESE** contains no cheese: It's actually a jellied **SAUSAGE** made of **BOILED** pig's parts.

1. One cup of undisturbed soil contains more than 200 billion living things. 2. In order to equal the height of the world's tallest tree, found in Redwood National and State Parks in California, U.S.A., 63 six-foot (1.8-m)-tall men would have to stand on top of one another. 3. Found in Great Basin National Park, Nevada, U.S.A., the oldest tree on record started growing just 600 years after the ancient Egyptians settled near the Nile River. 4. The world's biggest underground chamber is the Miao Room cavern in China—it could hold water from 4,312 Olympic-size swimming pools. 5. Northern lights shimmer across the sky when charged particles from the sun cause Earth's atmosphere to glow. 6. We smell rain because raindrops trap tiny bubbles that rocket through the droplet and explode on the surface, releasing scented fizz. 7. A beaver dam in Wood Buffalo National Park, Canada, is 2,800 feet (853 m) across—big enough to be seen from space. 8. The highest point on the Maldives, a group of 1,200 islands in the Indian Ocean, is just four feet (1.2 m) above sea level—the height of an average 7-year-old. 9. The world's largest living thing is thought to be a humongous fungus in Malheur National Forest in Oregon, U.S.A., that covers 2,385 acres (965 ha) of land. 10. Gran Cenote, a water-filled sinkhole in Mexico, is the entrance to the 130-mile (209.2-km)-long underwater Sistema Sac Actun cave system. 11. The longest insect migration in the world takes place across the Indian Ocean: Dragonflies fly more than 4,350 miles (7,001 km) from India to Africa. 12. Tsingy de Bemaraha National Park in Madagascar is home to a forest of limestone "needles." *Tsingy* is a local word meaning "where one cannot walk barefoot." 13. Five-story-tall Blood Falls in Antarctica oozes red water from an ancient lake trapped under Taylor Glacier. The lake is salty and full of iron, which turns the water red. 14. At the Bay of Fundy in Canada, high tide can swell as high as 53.5 feet (16.3 m) against the seaside cliffs—the height of a three-story building. 15. The Alleys of Stone in Las Majadas, Spain, form a natural maze in which visitors can get lost if they don't follow the marked paths. 16. If you replaced the wood in the world's largest tree with water, it would take more than 1.5 Olympic-size swimming pools to fill the tree. 17. Large rocks "sail" across a dry lake bed in Death Valley, California, U.S.A., leaving grooved trails in their wake. 18. Glaciers store about 75 percent of the world's fresh water. 19. More than six million cubic feet (168,000 cu m) of water flows over Niagara Falls every minute. 20. Bamboo can grow 1.2 inches (3 cm) an hour. 21. The Amazon rain forest is 2.1 million square miles (5.5 million sq km)—that's more than three times the size of Alaska. 22. When wet, the Salar de Uyuni salt flats in Bolivia perfectly mirror the sky, creating a landscape that seems to go on forever. 23. Old Faithful in Yellowstone National Park in Wyoming, U.S.A., erupts because the park sits on the caldera of a massive volcano. 24. Large

wandering glider dragonfly

100 BREATH-TAKING
FACTS ABOUT NATURE'S WONDERS

sphere-shaped stones cover the floor of the Valley of the Moon in Argentina. 25. A diving peregrine falcon travels more than three times as fast as a cheetah in full sprint. 26. Off the coast of Belize, the Blue Hole sinkhole is sufficiently wide and deep to stack four Boeing 747 airplanes inside. 27. The water surrounding deep-sea vents can reach 750°F (400°C). 28. The Three Eyes, or Los Tres Ojos, in the Dominican Republic are subterranean lakes filled by an underground river. 29. Major Oak, a tree in Sherwood Forest, Nottingham, England, is 1,000 years old. Its largely hollow trunk gave rise to rumors that Robin Hood used it as a hideout. 30. The deepest point on Earth, the bottom of the Mariana Trench in the South Pacific, lies 35,838 feet (10,923 m) below sea level—that's deeper than Mount Everest is tall. 31. Over the course of 5,000 years, iron released from mining activity has caused Spain's Rio Tinto river to run red. 32. **Mount Everest is the tallest mountain in the world, reaching 29,029 feet (8,848 m) above sea level.** 33. **The Gulf Stream current flows across the northern Atlantic Ocean at four miles an hour (6.4 km/h).** 34. Arches National Park in Utah, U.S.A., is home to more natural stone arches than any other place in the world. 35. **Dust and air bubbles trapped in Greenland and Antarctic ice sheets contain hundreds of thousands of years of information about Earth's climate.** 36. A stalactite in Doolin Cave, Ireland, is 23 feet (7 m) long, weighs 10 tons (9 MT), and is about 400,000 years old. 37. The Sargasso Sea, located in the Atlantic Ocean, is the only sea surrounded entirely by water. 38. **Ocean currents create the boundaries for the Sargasso Sea.** 39. The Alps mountain range crosses 11 European countries. 40. Lake Sørvágsvatn in the Faroe Islands of Northern Europe sits at the top of a bluff that's 98 feet (30 m) above the Atlantic Ocean. 41. **The Atlantic Ocean, Mediterranean Sea, and Red Sea all border the Sahara.** 42. Although glaciers usually move slowly, Kutiah Glacier in Pakistan put the pedal to the metal in 1953, moving more than the length of a football field each day for three months. 43. Visitors can reach the three natural stone bridges in Chongqing, China, by glass elevator or by climbing 1,000 steep steps. 44. **Antelope Canyon, with its red, ribbon-like walls, is owned and maintained by the Navajo Nation in Arizona, U.S.A.** 45. Black smoker deep-sea vents can form chimneys as tall as an 18-story building at the bottom of the ocean. 46. Naturally shaped stones that resemble pine trees dot the landscape in the Stone Forest of China. 47. **Dragon's blood trees on Yemen's island of Socotra look like flying saucers.** 48. **The 150 million Mexican free-tailed bats that roost inside Bracken Cave in Texas, U.S.A., snap up 140 tons (127 MT) of insects each night.** 49. The Great Lakes of North America hold 84 percent of the surface freshwater (water found in streams, rivers, and lakes) in North America. 50. **Swirls of blue marble overhang General Carrera Lake on the Chile-Argentina border. The Marble Caves were carved by 6,000 years of water wearing away the rock.** 51. **Wild emu wander among jagged spikes of sculpted sand, called the Pinnacles, in Nambung National Park, Australia.** 52. Millions of monarch butterflies spend the winter clustered in trees at just 12 areas in the mountains of Mexico. 53. **Fully intact skeletons of horses, camels, and rhinos can be seen in the Ashfall Fossil Beds State Historical Park in Nebraska, U.S.A.** 54. **The mist rising from Victoria Falls on the Zambezi River in Zimbabwe can be seen more than 12 miles (19 km) away.** 55. The sulfur yellow crater of Dallol volcano in Ethiopia sits 157 feet (48 m) below sea level. 56. **Arctic terns migrate from the Arctic to the Antarctic and back each year—a round-trip of 44,000 miles (71,000 km).** 57. **More than 300 100-million-year-old dinosaur tracks trail across the rocks of Dinosaur Ridge in Morrison, Colorado, U.S.A.** 58. The Silver Dragon tidal wave reaches up to 30 feet (9 m) high when it races up the Qiantang River in Jiaxing, China, as the tide rushes in. 59. **The dry valleys of Antarctica are so dry that the bodies of animals that die there are preserved and turn into mummies.** 60. The black sand beaches of Muriwai in New Zealand stretch for 37 miles (60 km) and are home to 1,200 pairs of seabirds called gannets during nesting season. 61. Barrel waves (that curl over along the top) can be up to 0.6 mile (1 km) long at Skeleton Bay, Namibia. 62. **More than 3,300 hot spring pools in the Huanglong National Scenic Area in China are bright blue, green, yellow, and white, from calcium bicarbonate in the water.** 63. Brave kayakers can paddle through caves carved on the underside of glaciers in Resurrection Bay near Seward, Alaska, U.S.A. 64. The grass-covered Chocolate Hills in the Philippines aren't edible, but they do contain marine fossils that are millions of years old. 65. **Leatherback sea turtles swim up to 3,700 miles (6,000 km) to lay their eggs.** 66. **The coldest place on Earth is in eastern Antarctica—temperatures can drop to minus 133.6°F (−92°C).** 67. The tundra is one of the harshest environments on Earth. Tundras can be found in the Arctic, Antarctic, and on mountain tops—anywhere it's cold, windy, and dry. 68. **Two lakes continue to exist in the Sahara, fed by water from underground.** 69. To reach the misty rain forest on Cape Melville, Australia, you must scale nine miles (15 km) of house-size boulders. 70. The Rocky Mountains run 3,000 miles (4,800 km) from northern Canada to New Mexico, U.S.A. 71. **Lake Powell in Utah, U.S.A., has more shoreline than the West Coast of the United States.** 72. Inside Greenland's ice sheet lies a lake the size of West Virginia, U.S.A. 73. A volcano in Iceland gushed lava for several months, at times spewing enough lava to cover a football field every 5.5 minutes. 74. **Several lakes in western Australia have bubble-gum pink water.** 75. **Ice crystals in glaciers can grow to be the size of baseballs.** 76. Clashing warm and cold ocean waters create fog every day on Grand Banks, Newfoundland, making it the foggiest place on Earth. 77. **Blue flames erupt from a volcano on the island of Java, Indonesia.** 78. **Storms produce 1.2 million lightning strikes per year where the Catatumbo River flows into Lake Maracaibo in Venezuela.** 79. The Greek island of Santorini has red, white, and black sand beaches. 80. **Mount Erebus in Antarctica has been erupting continuously since at least 1841.** 81. **Coral reefs house as much as 25 percent of ocean life.** 82. Meghalaya, India, gets 467 inches (11.9 m) of rain each year—more than half of which falls during the June and July monsoon. 83. **People in Meghalaya, India, train the roots of rubber trees to form natural bridges.** 84. There are more forests in Russia than in any other country. 85. Fire helps to maintain grasslands by killing off trees—grasses survive because they grow from the bottom up. 86. **A whopping 93.5 feet (28.5 m) of snow fell on Mount Rainier in Washington, U.S.A., in the winter of 1971–1972.** 87. **Rivers fan out into deltas as they reach the ocean, creating wetlands that purify the water.** 88. Ice shelves extending off Antarctica calve icebergs longer than the island of Oahu, Hawaii, U.S.A. 89. **The oldest crystals on Earth formed 4.276 billion years ago.** 90. **The biggest volcano in the world—the size of the British Isles—lies hidden under the Pacific Ocean east of Japan.** 91. If you compare the inside of an apple to our planet, our atmosphere is thinner than the apple's skin. 92. **The strongest storms on Earth occur east of the Andes mountains in Argentina.** 93. **The Atlantic Ocean gets wider by one inch (2.5 cm) each year.** 94. The Colorado River runs dry before it reaches the Gulf of California because people in seven U.S. states and Mexico use the water. 95. **Along the East African Rift Valley, the east coast is slowly splitting off from the rest of the continent. An ocean will eventually form between the two.** 96. Elaborate ice crystals decorate the inside of glacier caves in the Arctic. 97. The hills of Zhangye Danxia in China are striped with red, blue, and yellow stone. 98. **Natural Bridge, a 215-foot (65.5-m)-long limestone bridge in Virginia, U.S.A., is the largest natural land bridge in North America.** 99. Visitors exploring the forest near La Colle-sur-Loup in southern France may happen upon sculptures made using forest materials by artist Spencer Byles. 100. The plant-covered beaches of Panjin, China, turn bright red in the fall.

1
Japan is made up of 4 MAIN ISLANDS and almost 4,000 SMALLER ISLANDS.

2
In Japan, people use money called YEN.

3
More than 127 MILLION PEOPLE live in Japan. Of that, about 12.7 million people LIVE IN THE CAPITAL, Tokyo, alone!

4
The DRAGON'S TRIANGLE, a region of the Pacific Ocean near Japan, was believed to be a MYSTERIOUS PLACE WHERE SHIPS WENT MISSING.

5
Japanese BULLET TRAINS, called *Shinkansen*, carry passengers at SPEEDS OF 168 MILES AN HOUR (270 KM/H).

6
Sometimes these trains are SO FULL, train workers PUSH PEOPLE through the doors to PACK THEM IN.

7
The main RELIGIONS in Japan are SHINTO, BUDDHISM, and CONFUCIANISM.

8
People who celebrate the SHINTO religion believe that forests, mountains, waterfalls, and other NATURAL FEATURES HAVE SOUL-LIKE SPIRITS.

9
Japanese people BOW when they GREET ONE ANOTHER.

10
Japan has nearly 1,500 EARTHQUAKES EACH YEAR, with minor tremors EVERY DAY.

11
In the past, most BUILDINGS were made from WOOD, partly because it HOLDS UP well during EARTHQUAKES.

12
The LARGEST EARTHQUAKE ever recorded in Japan MOVED THE ENTIRE ISLAND OF HONSHU EIGHT FEET (2.4 M).

13
The TSUNAMI caused by the earthquake TRAVELED ACROSS THE PACIFIC OCEAN. It was still SIX FEET (1.8 M) HIGH when it reached California.

14
The tsunami created a GIANT WHIRLPOOL in one of the harbors.

15
The word TSUNAMI is Japanese for "HARBOR WAVE."

16
In Japan, people are allowed to take naps at work—as long as they STAY UPRIGHT.

17
Japan is home to 109 VOLCANOES.

18
The Japanese word for Japan is *NIPPON*, which means "ORIGIN OF THE SUN."

19
On average, Japanese women LIVE LONGER than people from other nations.

20
Japan is the ONLY COUNTRY with an EMPEROR AND EMPRESS.

21
MOUNT FUJI, the HIGHEST VOLCANO AND MOUNTAIN in Japan, is actually THREE VOLCANOES STACKED ON TOP OF ONE ANOTHER.

22
Climbers have to PAY TO USE THE TOILETS on Mount Fuji.

23
JAPANESE CHERRY BLOSSOMS, called *sakura*, CHANGE COLOR, fading from dark pink to white.

24
The Japanese SCHOOL YEAR STARTS IN APRIL, at about the time when cherry blossoms bloom.

25
Hōryū-ji, a 1,400-year-old TEMPLE, remained standing through 46 MAJOR (magnitude 7.0 or greater) EARTHQUAKES.

26
The world's SHORTEST ESCALATOR can be found in Kawasaki—it is just 2.7 FEET (82.3 CM) from the BOTTOM TO THE TOP.

27
The AINU are a NATIVE PEOPLE of Japan; of the 24,000 Ainu living today, only ten still SPEAK the native language.

28
The Japanese language is WRITTEN USING CHARACTERS called kanji.

29
There are more than 60,000 KANJI, but fewer than 2,000 are TYPICALLY USED in books and newspapers.

30
The Japanese style of comic book known as MANGA is so popular, MANGA CAFÉS have libraries of nothing but manga.

31
MANGA characters have huge eyes and no nose, and are often shown IN MOTION.

32
Although NINJA were SPIES AND ASSASSINS thought to fight against samurai warriors, MANY SAMURAI WERE ALSO NINJA.

33
The NINJA MUSEUM of Iga-ryu features a building with TRAPS AND FAKE HALLWAYS.

50 INCREDIBLE FACTS ABOUT JAPAN

34 A NINJA MOVES SILENTLY— sometimes by walking with their feet in their palms and the BACKS OF THEIR HANDS to the ground.

35 The Mr. Kanso restaurant in Osaka ONLY SERVES CANNED FOOD.

36 SUMO involves two large, LOINCLOTH-WEARING wrestlers who each try to force the opponent out of a ring.

37 The sport of KENDO, or Japanese fencing, originated from a type of sport SAMURAI used for training.

38 RICE is such an important part of Japanese food that *gohan*, their word for COOKED RICE, also means "MEAL."

39 Leaving CHOPSTICKS STICKING UP out of a bowl of rice is considered OFFENSIVE unless it is done AT A FUNERAL.

40 KARAOKE, which means "EMPTY ORCHESTRA" in Japanese, originated in Japan in the early 1970s.

41 Japanese hold FORGET-THE-YEAR PARTIES, called *bonenkai*, throughout December to help PUT THE PROBLEMS of the past year BEHIND THEM.

42 Japanese drink 80 percent of the COFFEE grown in the BLUE MOUNTAINS OF JAMAICA.

43 In people's homes, TOILET SLIPPERS are worn in the bathroom to avoid TRACKING GERMS to other parts of the house.

44 BLOWFISH, which contains a TOXIN that's deadlier than cyanide, is considered a specialty dish in Japan, even though it KILLS FIVE PEOPLE EACH YEAR.

45 The FIRST NOVEL, *The Tale of Genji*, was written by a JAPANESE WOMAN more than 1,000 YEARS AGO.

46 Until the mid-1800s, BLACKENED TEETH were considered BEAUTIFUL in Japan.

47 Fishmongers at the TSUKIJI MARKET in Tokyo sell MORE THAN 2,000 TONS (1,814 MT) of fish and seafood EACH DAY.

48 About 73 percent of Japan is COVERED WITH MOUNTAINS.

49 CAPSULE HOTELS have cubicles that are just large enough for ONE PERSON TO LIE DOWN IN.

50 Japanese people consider CROOKED TEETH so attractive, some even PAY to have their teeth "snaggled."

Shinkansen bullet train

1 The first KNOWN food truck—a COVERED WAGON with WINDOWS—hit the streets of Providence, Rhode Island, U.S.A., in 1872, selling SANDWICHES and PIES to local workers.

2 Chuck wagons—that served COWBOYS in the WILD WEST—were specially designed for COOKING, with separate areas for food prep and cleaning.

3 The popular fast-food chain Carl's Jr. began as a FOOD CART specializing in HOT DOGS.

4 The earliest versions of food trucks were known as ROACH COACHES because of their questionable SANITARY standards.

5 THE MOBILE FOOD MOVEMENT HAS TAKEN OFF IN AUSTRALIA, WITH ABOUT 50 FOOD TRUCKS ROVING AROUND MELBOURNE ALONE.

6 FOR ALMOST 100 YEARS, TUBBY ISAAC'S FOOD STALL IN LONDON, ENGLAND, SOLD JELLIED EELS—CAUGHT IN THE THAMES RIVER—TO EAT.

25 FOOD

7 FOOD TRUCKS make close to **$800 Million** a YEAR in the United States alone.

8 A TOTAL OF **121 VEHICLES** GATHERED TOGETHER FOR A 2014 EVENT IN FLORIDA—THE **LARGEST EVER** PARADE OF FOOD TRUCKS.

9 MONDAY IS TYPICALLY THE BUSIEST DAY FOR FOOD TRUCKS.

10

After Hurricane Sandy in 2012, food trucks in the NEW YORK CITY area served more than 100,000 MEALS, including 11,000 FREE LUNCHES in just one day.

11 THE GREAT FOOD TRUCK RACE IS A U.S. TV SHOW IN WHICH FOOD TRUCKS COMPETE FOR SALES. THE WINNER GETS $100,000.

12 TokyoDog, a food truck based in Seattle, Washington, U.S.A., sells a FOOT-LONG HOT DOG with ingredients that include TRUFFLES, CAVIAR, and FOIE GRAS.

13
One truck based in Atlanta, Georgia, U.S.A., uses its profits to support a local HOMELESS SHELTER—making enough money to feed three people with the profits from selling just ONE MEAL.

14
IN A SPAN OF SIX MONTHS DURING 2011, 250 FOOD TRUCKS OPENED UP IN AUSTIN, TEXAS, U.S.A.

GYRO EXPRESS

15
STREET FOOD is eaten by nearly **2.5 BILLION** people every day.

18
One NEW YORK CITY food truck sells a $666 burger made of KOBE BEEF wrapped in GOLD LEAF with LOBSTER.

16
Most mobile food carts are attached to MOTORCYCLES in Bangkok, THAILAND.

17
FOOD BIKES are another way to serve portable meals, selling everything from COFFEE to TACOS.

19
Because of CITY RESTRICTIONS, some food trucks around the United States have to move every **30 MINUTES** to a DIFFERENT LOCATION.

TRUCK FACTS TO SNACK ON

20
You can order REINDEER SAUSAGE from the Beez Neez food truck in Portland, Oregon, U.S.A.

23
AN ECO-FRIENDLY FOOD TRUCK IN MINNEAPOLIS, MINNESOTA, U.S.A., RUNS ON USED VEGETABLE OIL FROM ITS OWN DEEP FRYER.

21
A SUPERCOMPUTER picked the menu for a food truck at a MUSIC FESTIVAL —coming up with meals such as SWISS-THAI ASPARAGUS QUICHE.

22
In PORTLAND, OREGON, groups of food trucks known as PODS gather together in one location, acting as an OUTDOOR food court.

25
A NEW YORK CITY food cart sold "PUP CAKES," fish and chip–flavored BISCUITS and other treats just for DOGS.

24
The FLAMING WHEELS food truck serving noodles and beef nachos in Kuala Lumpur, Malaysia, features an exterior with RED and ORANGE flames painted on each side.

❶ At the Cowal Highland Gathering in Scotland, **KILT-WEARING** participants compete to see who can **TOSS 28-POUND (12.7-KG) BOULDERS** the farthest.

❷ In the sport of **SPEEDRIDING**, skiers strap on a **PARACHUTE** so they can soar over rock walls, crevasses, and snow drifts as they **SHOOT DOWN** a mountain.

❸ During **RELAY HORSE-RACING**, jockeys **JUMP FROM ONE HORSE TO ANOTHER** while galloping at high speeds.

❹ Each year, the World **STAND UP PADDLEBOARD** Championship welcomes paddlers to race around an **11-MILE (18-KM) OCEAN COURSE**—all while remaining **UPRIGHT** on their **BOARD.**

❺ **HOUSE RUNNING** involves walking quickly down the sides of buildings **FACE DOWN** while secured by ropes and harnesses. It is popular in **GERMANY** and **NEW ZEALAND.**

❻ The wild sport of **ICE CROSS** blends **DOWNHILL SKIING** and **MOTOCROSS RACING**—with athletes coursing down a steep, twisty course, reaching speeds of up to **45 MILES AN HOUR (72 KM/H).**

❼ Tommy Caldwell was one of a pair of **ROCK CLIMBERS** who recently reached the top of El Capitan's Dawn Wall in Yosemite National Park. He **SCALED 3,000 VERTICAL FEET (914 M)**—without any climbing equipment except ropes.

❽ **WATER CATAPULT** fans are **FLUNG 50 FEET (15 M)** into the sky from a **GIANT FLOATING AIRBED** before **CRASHING** into the **WATER** below.

GO TO THE EXTREME

9 An **EXTREME MOUNTAINEER** once ran 1,250 miles (2,012 km) along the Great Himalaya Trail in 49 days—the world record for the **FASTEST TIME** across Nepal, the highest elevated country in the world.

10 Fearless **FREEDROPPERS** leap from extreme heights onto huge trampolines, performing **TWISTS**, **TURNS**, and **FLIPS** as they drop.

11 The sport of **PARKOUR**— or freerunning—involves **CLIMBING**, flipping, **ROLLING**, and **LEAPING** over **URBAN TERRAIN**, like **LIGHT POSTS**, buildings, and rooftops.

12 **DAREDEVIL** photographers known as **ROOFTOPPERS** scale to the top of some of the **WORLD'S TALLEST** buildings for **SPORT** (and for amazing pictures).

13 Deep Water Soloing (DWS) involves MOUNTAIN CLIMBERS scaling **SEA CLIFFS** and LAKESIDE LEDGES—and using the **WATER** as their **SAFETY NET**.

14 A GERMAN man recently **ROLLED** down the 18,606-foot (5,671-m) Mount Davamand in IRAN—on a **UNICYCLE**.

15 Competitive **STREET LUGERS**—who race down **STEEP HILLS** while lying face-up on a modified **SKATEBOARD**— can reach SPEEDS of up to 97 miles an hour (156 km/h).

1 "Raptor" is another word for bird of prey.

2 The American kestrel is the smallest falcon in North America—it weighs the same as 34 pennies!

3 BALD EAGLES SOMETIMES STEAL FISH RIGHT OUT OF ANOTHER BIRD'S TALONS!

4 Benjamin Franklin once said he wished the bald eagle wasn't chosen to be a national emblem of the United States because it had "bad moral character."

5 A bald eagle nest in Vermilion, Ohio, U.S.A., weighed more than two tons (1.8 MT).

6 Black vultures don't have a voice box, so they communicate by hissing and grunting.

7 California condors can survive up to two weeks without eating!

8 When vultures get hot, they often urinate on their legs! The evaporating liquid lowers their body temperature.

9 In the 1980s, the California condor population fell to just 22 birds. Thanks to protection and breeding programs, the species has rebounded. Today, there are 230 California condors in the wild.

10 Cooper's hawks grab their prey with their talons and kill it by squeezing it.

11 When large herds of bison roamed the United States in the 19th century, ferruginous hawks made their nests partly out of bison bones and wool.

12 The golden eagle sometimes fights off coyotes and bears that try to eat its prey.

13 Golden eagles, rough-legged hawks, and ferruginous hawks have feathers all the way to their toes.

14 Ospreys rack up as many as 160,000 flight miles (257,500 km) during their 20-year lifetime.

15 The peregrine falcon lives on every continent but Antarctica.

16 Harris's hawks often hunt in groups; each bird in the group takes a turn in chasing down the prey.

17 In the 1700s, Russian empress Catherine the Great used merlins, a type of small falcon, to hunt skylarks for sport.

18 Be careful if you're walking near a northern goshawk's nest—the birds are known to attack people who get too close.

19 The golden eagle is the national animal of many countries, including Albania, Austria, Germany, Mexico, and Kazakhstan.

20 Ospreys have barbed padding on their feet that helps keep the fish they catch from wriggling away.

21 An osprey's success rate for catching a fish when it dives in the water is as high as 70 percent.

22 Turkey vultures have a strong sense of smell that allows them to detect dead animals.

23 "Peregrine" means wanderer. Peregrine falcons migrate along the same route as far as 15,500 miles (25,000 km) every winter.

24 Peregrine falcons are hunted by great horned owls and eagles.

25 Peregrine falcons aren't finicky eaters—they have been known to eat 450 different bird species.

26 PRAIRIE FALCONS TAKE BATHS IN THE DUST.

27 Great horned owls are also known as cat owls.

28 During courtship, male and female red-tailed hawks sometimes grab each other while in flight, clasp talons, and fall. Before they hit the ground, they let go and swoop up.

29 Groups of migrating hawks are called kettles.

30 Generations of ospreys keep building on to the same nest. Eventually the nest can be big enough to hold a person!

31 An adult snowy owl eats some 1,600 lemmings (a gerbil-like rodent) every year.

32 Unlike most owls, which are nocturnal, snowy owls hunt during the day and night.

33 Burrowing owls are so named because they live in underground burrows that were dug by prairie dogs or squirrels.

34 Burrowing owls line their nests with dung to attract insects, which the owls then, in turn, eat.

35 WHEN ALARMED, YOUNG BURROWING OWLS MAKE A HISSING CALL THAT SOUNDS LIKE A RATTLESNAKE.

36 Old-fashioned Western movies often used the raspy screams of red-tailed hawks as sound effects when eagles or hawks were filmed.

37 Great horned owls don't have horns. They have tufts of feathers that look like ears. (Their ears are actually further down on the sides of their head.)

38 A great horned owl can grab prey more than twice its weight.

39 When captured, elf owls play dead until they are released.

40 American kestrels hide their extra kills in bushes and grass clumps and come back for it on days when they're hungry.

41 Raptors all have a similarly designed beak—curved at the top with sharp edges for ripping meat.

42 A harpy eagle's rear talons are the same length as a grizzly bear's claws.

43 Most birds have stiff feathers that cause them to make a whooshing sound when they fly. However, owls have soft feathers, so they fly in silence.

44 Turkey vultures don't have a voice box so they don't communicate by sound like other birds.

45 Owl pellets contain the bones and hair of prey that they are unable to digest. So, you can find out what an owl has eaten by examining its pellet.

46 In Greek and Roman mythology, the goddess of wisdom was represented by an owl.

47 A café in Tokyo called Fukoro no Mise ("Shop of Owls") has live owls on display.

48 Researchers found that barn owls can detect prey even in total darkness.

49 Blue jays often swoop around and make noisy calls at raptors during the day to make them move out of their territory.

50 Owls don't have teeth—they use their sharp beaks to rip their food or swallow it whole.

51 American kestrels sometimes perch on foul poles during evening sports games to hunt moths and other insects attracted to the stadium's bright lights.

52 The word "vulture" comes from the Latin word *vellere*, which means to pluck or tear.

53 Sharp-shinned hawks eat the heads of their prey before giving the rest to their young.

54 Gyrfalcons—the world's largest falcons—sometimes take a bath in freezing cold water.

55 NORTHERN HAWKS CAN SPOT A VOLE—A TYPE OF SMALL RODENT — HALF A MILE (0.8 KM) AWAY.

56 Rough-legged hawks sometimes build their nests with caribou bones.

57 Great horned owls have been called the "tigers of the sky" because of their excellent hunting skills.

58 Raptors have three eyelids that not only keep their eyes moist, but protect their eyes in flight and when feeding excited young.

osprey hunting for fish in a Florida lagoon

75 FACTS ABOUT BIRDS OF PREY TO FEAST ON

59 In most raptor species, females build the nest, while males gather the building materials.

60 It can take up to ten years of molting before a bald eagle develops its white head and tail feathers.

61 California condors often lay their eggs directly on the dirt floor of a cliff edge or cave.

62 Kites that you fly on a string are named after the kite, a type of raptor that seems to hang in the wind.

63 OSPREYS DIVE FOR FISH AND SOMETIMES COMPLETELY SUBMERGE THEMSELVES IN THE WATER.

64 Owls' eyes are fixed in their socket, so the birds have to turn their head to look sideways.

65 Merlins mimic non-threatening pigeons in flight so they can sneak up on prey.

66 The elf owl roosts in a saguaro cactus during the day.

67 People in Mongolia use golden eagles in sport to catch prey, like rabbits.

68 Some golden eagles eat tortoises.

69 When ospreys carry fish in their talons, the fish's head faces forward. This position helps the bird reduce drag (a slowing force) while flying.

70 Because of their "ghost-like" appearance, some cultures think barn owls are omens of death.

71 Owls can turn their heads 270 degrees from side to side.

72 Harpy eagles, which live in Central and South America, eat sloths, porcupines, and monkeys.

73 Great horned owls are one of a few animals that prey on skunks.

74 Peregrine falcons can be found living in cities preying on pigeons and starlings.

75 The California condor's wingspan is ten feet (3 m)—that's almost the length of four skateboards.

the Russian rocket
Vostok seen from below

1 The word "rocket" comes from the old Italian word *rocce*, which meant LONG, THIN TUBE.

2 The MORE POWERFUL THE EXPLOSION inside a rocket—and the faster the exhaust races out the end—the FASTER THE ROCKET WILL TRAVEL.

3 Jet engines get the OXYGEN they need to operate from the air, but rockets travel to space, where there is no air, so they must CARRY THEIR OWN supply of oxygen.

4 Liquid fuel must be KEPT SEPARATE from the oxygen supply until the rocket is READY TO IGNITE.

5 Three people—one Russian, one German, and one American—are credited with INVENTING THE FIRST SPACE ROCKETS. They were WORKING INDEPENDENTLY of one another.

6 Germany's V-2 rocket, developed during World War II, was powered by FUEL MADE FROM POTATOES.

7 A TOP-SECRET operation to relocate German rocket scientists to the U.S. following World War II was CODE-NAMED OPERATION PAPERCLIP.

8 SPUTNIK, THE FIRST SATELLITE made by humans, was the size of a BEACH BALL and weighed 184 pounds (83 kg).

9 Space-bound rockets BURN IN STAGES, each one IGNITING, BURNING, and FALLING OFF before the next section ignites.

10 When the United States first tried to LAUNCH A SATELLITE into space, the rocket lifted just four feet (1.2 m) before FALLING TO THE GROUND AND EXPLODING.

11 The FIRST PERSON TO ORBIT EARTH, Russian cosmonaut Yuri Gagarin, rode the rocket Vostok to an altitude of 187 miles (300.9 km) and WHIZZED AROUND THE PLANET in 108 minutes.

12 A single SOLID-FUEL ROCKET BOOSTER weighs about 1.3 million pounds (590,000 kg) when it is launched.

13 EXPLODING BOLTS were used to SEPARATE solid rocket boosters from the space shuttle.

14 When astronaut SHANNON WALKER went to the International Space Station, she took the watch Amelia Earhart wore when she flew across the Atlantic.

15 Want your body to spend ETERNITY IN SPACE? A company will ROCKET YOUR ASHES into deep space for just $12,500.

16 John P. Stapp rode a rocket sled that reached a SPEED of 632 MILES AN HOUR (1,017 KM/H), earning him the title of "fastest man on Earth."

17 The LIQUID OXYGEN used in most rockets must be kept at MINUS 297.4°F (−183°C) so it doesn't turn into a gas. That's almost twice as cold as the coldest day in Antarctica.

18 When NASA launched the Juno spacecraft to study Jupiter, it had three Lego mini-figures on board: Galileo Galilei, the Roman god Jupiter and his wife, Juno.

19 The very FIRST ROCKETS were used for FIREWORKS IN CHINA about 900 years ago.

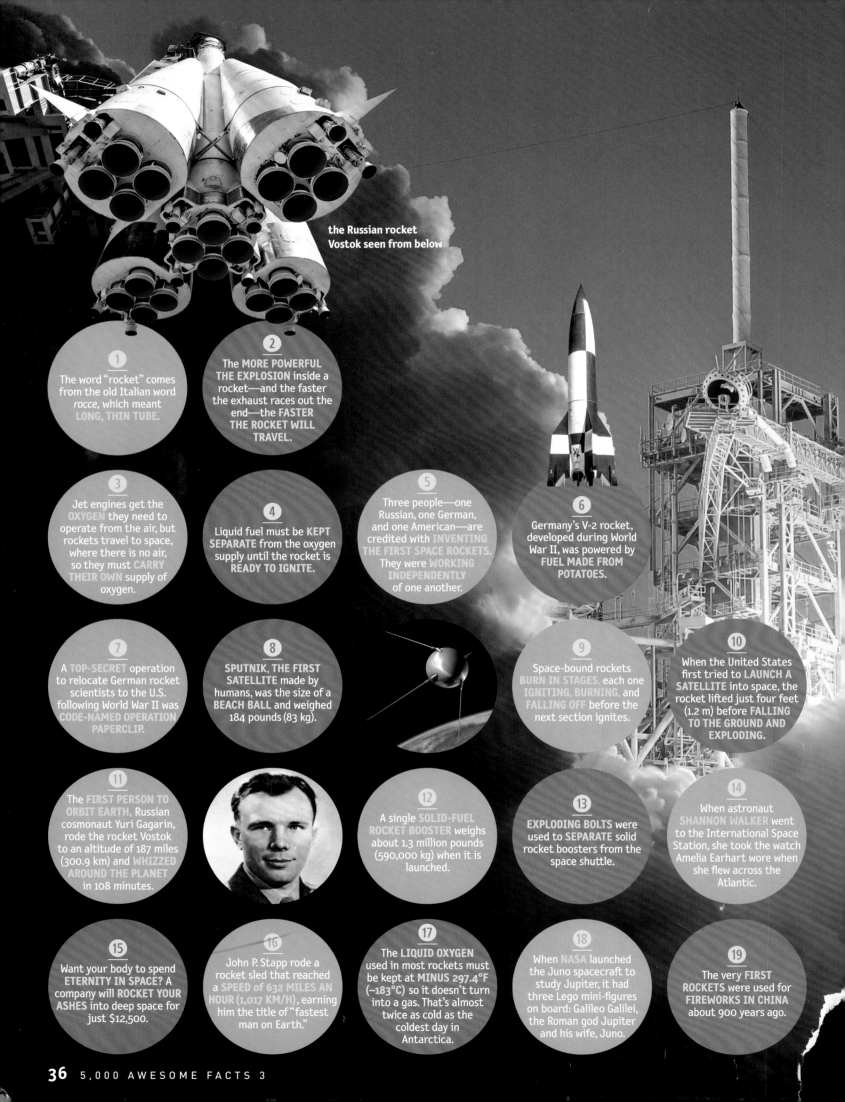

35 EXPLOSIVE FACTS ABOUT ROCKETS

the space shuttle lifting off from its launchpad

20 SCIENTISTS HAVE ROCKETED INTO SPACE: insects, fish, turtles, cats, dogs, rabbits, algae, fungi, monkeys, apes, mice, mold, jellyfish, newts, quail eggs, and spiders.

21 The shuttle's reusable solid rocket boosters were the WORLD'S LARGEST ROCKETS. Each measured half the length of a football field.

22 Airborne rockets sometimes BOUNCE LIKE A POGO STICK because fuel moves around unevenly.

23 Space shuttle rocket boosters were FISHED OUT OF THE OCEAN, CLEANED, and REUSED after each launch.

24 The X-15 rocket is the FASTEST PLANE ON RECORD, traveling more than seven times the SPEED OF SOUND.

25 The creator of the original *Star Trek* told designers that the starship ENTERPRISE shouldn't have any rockets.

26 The words "ROCKETS' RED GLARE" in the Star Spangled Banner refer to rockets FIRED BY BRITISH WARSHIPS on Fort McHenry in Maryland, U.S.A., during the War of 1812.

27 Just two minutes into its flight, the space shuttle flew FASTER THAN A BULLET.

28 The X-15 rocket plane is also the HIGHEST-FLYING PLANE ever, with a maximum altitude of 67.1 miles (108 km)—NINE TIMES HIGHER than a typical commercial plane flies!

29 The amount of THRUST (forward motion) from most rockets is EQUAL TO THE POWER GENERATED BY 13 HOOVER DAMS.

30 The Atlas V travels SO FAST, you could fly from Denver, Colorado, to New York City, N.Y., U.S.A., in just 2 MINUTES and 16 SECONDS.

31 Scientists are making rockets using MAGNETS AND PLASMA (very hot gas) that may run on HYDROGEN—an element so abundant, rockets could REFUEL IN DEEP SPACE.

32 MODEL ROCKETS run on "rocket candy," a mixture that is HIGH IN SUGAR.

33 "Rocket" is another name for ARUGULA—a lettuce-like plant often used in salads.

34 The candy store ROCKET FIZZ makes its own soda in flavors that include bacon, buffalo wing, and ranch dressing.

35 A wealthy man STARTED BUILDING ROCKETS because he wants his company to carry people TO AND FROM THE MOON—and Mars.

1. *Rafflesia arnoldii* is a huge flower that grows in the rain forests of Indonesia and smells like rotting meat when it blooms. 2. Edible flowers, like nasturtium, calendula, and violets, have been used in cooking for hundreds of years. 3. Giant water lily pads are six feet (1.8 m) across and are strong enough to hold the weight of a human. 4. There are about 400,000 species of flowering plants in the world. 5. A 125-million-year-old fossil found in China is the earliest evidence of a flowering plant found to date. 6. The leaves of the "sensitive plant," *Mimosa pudica*, fold up when touched. 7. A flower called "bird of paradise" looks like orange birds in flight. 8. Roses cost Americans twice as much around Valentine's Day as they do the rest of the year. 9. Tulips continue to grow after they are cut—up to a whole inch (2.5 cm)! 10. The Japanese believe chrysanthemums bring happiness and joy. The annual chrysanthemum festival is called the Festival of Happiness. 11. Money plants have pink or purple flowers and their seedpods look like silver dollars when they dry. 12. Thomas Jefferson grew money plants in his gardens and wrote about them in his journals. 13. Saffron is a spice that comes from a type of crocus flower: 75,000 flowers are needed for one pound (454 g) of saffron. 14. Flowers of the *Dracula simia* orchid look like dancing monkeys. 15. Singers LeAnn Rimes, Judy Garland, Barbra Streisand, and Dolly Parton all have roses named after them. 16. Orchids can grow just about everywhere—except for deserts. The only continent they cannot grow on is Antarctica (that is one giant frozen desert). 17. Pumpkin and squash flowers can be stuffed with cheese and fried. Yum! 18. Hummingbirds drink nectar from up to 1,000 flowers every day. 19. "Anthophobic" is a term used to describe someone who has a fear of flowers. 20. Pollen is transferred between flowers—the process of pollination—by wind or by animals that include insects, birds, and bats. 21. Jasmine and Lily were two of the most popular baby names from 2000 to 2010. 22. In addition to dancing monkeys, other orchid flowers resemble moths, naked men, monkey faces, dancing girls, laughing bumblebees, parrots, and flying ducks. 23. Many flowers had meanings attached to them during the 1800s. Daisies meant innocence, camellias meant graciousness, rhododendron meant beware, and red tulips were considered a declaration of love. 24. "Flowers" is the name given to a lumpy mass of the yellow, pollen-like powder of the chemical element sulfur. 25. Foxglove, also called "fairy fingers," "fairy gloves," and "fairy bells," is highly poisonous. 26. From its roots up to its yellow flower head, the dandelion plant is edible—in fact, it's good for you. 27. Dandelion roots can be used to make a substitute for coffee. 28. The word "dandelion" comes from the French term *dent-de-lion,* which means "lion's tooth." 29. Dinner plate dahlias have huge, colorful blooms that can be up to ten inches (25 cm) in diameter. 30. An estimated 18 million flowers are used on the floats each year in the Rose Parade in Pasadena, California, U.S.A. 31. Scarlet pineapple sage has red flowers and smells like ripe pineapple. 32. Brightly colored marigolds are used to celebrate Dia de los Muertos, or Day of the Dead, in Mexico. 33. The scent of lavender is known to have a calming effect, reduce stress, and even relieve digestive gas. 34. During the middle of the 17th century, tulips were so expensive in Holland that the bulbs were used as money. It was known as tulip mania. 35. The largest flower garden in the world is in the United Arab Emirates: the Dubai Miracle Garden, home to more than 45 million flowers. 36. Every other August since 1971, the people of Brussels, Belgium, build a carpet made of flowers, covering 19,000 square feet (1,800 sq m) on the Grand Place, the city's central square. 37. Daffodil bulbs range in price from about $1 to $100! 38. For decoration, almost 2,000 miles (3,219 km) of oleander is planted along freeways in southern California. Oleander is chosen because it is hardy and drought resistant. 39. Every single part of the oleander plant is extremely poisonous. 40. Dicentra, also known as the "bleeding heart," has yellow, pink, red, or white heart-shaped flowers that dangle from its stem. 41. Some florists sell "tie-dyed" roses with swirls of rainbow colors splashed throughout each bloom. They get the effect by slicing the stems in three sections and placing each one in a different color dye. 42. Sticking the stem of a white carnation in blue food coloring overnight will turn the flower blue.

43. The flowers on the purple passionflower are said to look like something from outer space. 44. The seeds from sunflowers can be used to make "sun butter," a tasty alternative to peanut butter. 45. There are many different types of sunflowers with interesting names, for example "sunzilla," "lemon queen," and "chocolate cherry." 46. The sunflower is the state flower of Kansas,

100 BLOOMING FACTS ABOUT FLOWERS

field of sunflowers

U.S.A. In some parts it grows so wild it is considered a nuisance. 47. Sunflower stems, leaves, and flowers are used to make food for cows. 48. One sunflower plant grown in Michigan, U.S.A., in 2004 had 837 flower heads. 49. Native Americans grew sunflowers and used them for food, dye, medicine, and building materials. 50. Fragrant flowers such as roses and lavender can be chopped up and used to make a flowery sugar for baking or teas. 51. Snapdragons look like they have mouths. If you squeeze them on either side the blossom will open and close its "mouth" like a puppet. 52. *Mirabilis jalapa* is also called "the four o'clock flower" because its blooms open in the late afternoon and close in the morning. 53. *Physalis alkekengi* is called the "Chinese lantern flower" because its flowers look like little paper lanterns. 54. Children have used hollyhock flowers to make miniature dolls for hundreds of years. 55. Roses are called the "queen of the flowers" and have been around since 1700 B.C. 56. Several episodes of *The Muppet Show* feature singing puppet flowers, including a rose with fangs. 57. The jade vine grows wild in the Philippines and is pollinated by bats that are attracted to the flower's nectar. 58. The ghost orchid is an endangered plant that grows in the swamps of Florida, Cuba, and the Bahamas. Its name comes from its rare flower—when it blooms, it appears to float, like a ghost. 59. Snowdrop, Christmas rose, and camellia will flower in the snow. 60. Camellias are large shrubs covered with flowers and can live as long as 200 years. 61. The rose is the official flower of the United States. New York, Oklahoma, Georgia, Idaho, and North Dakota also have chosen it as their state flower. 62. The leaves of the carnivorous butterwort look like they've been slathered in butter because they're covered with a sticky substance that catches bugs. 63. The flowers of the butterwort look like little purple or pink orchids. 64. Desert tortoises eat flowers such us lupine, forget-me-nots, blazing star, and coreopsis. 65. "Forcing" a flower bulb means growing it indoors and "forcing" it to bloom when it wouldn't normally do so—like in winter. 66. Some cactus flowers open and last only a day while others stay open for weeks. 67. Native to Africa, kniphofia is also known as "torch lily" and "red hot poker" because of its tall spikes of red, orange, and yellow flowers. 68. Some flowers, like Lady Banks climbing rose, bloom only once a year. 69. Dracula orchids attract flies with their mushroom-like "mouths" that look and smell like mushrooms the flies like to eat. 70. Some candy companies make flower-flavored candy like violet, rose, and orange blossom. 71. Before the flowers of the *Psychotria elata* completely open, they look like bright red lips. 72. The blooms of the rare *Impatiens bequaertii* look like dancing ballerinas. 73. Before an orchid from Colombia called *Anguloa uniflora* completely opens, it looks like a swaddled baby. 74. The 40-foot (12-m)-tall Queen of the Andes plant blooms once every 80 to 100 years and then dies. 75. Some people believe that playing music to their flowers helps them grow. There is no scientific evidence for this. 76. Prince Charles of England once said he talks to his flowers and they respond. 77. In *Alice in Wonderland*, a garden of flowers sing to Alice and then call her a weed and chase her out of the garden. 78. The bat flower is native to China and has long hanging whiskers and dark petals that spread out like a bat's wings. 79. Desert agave grows in the southwestern deserts of the United States and takes up to 20 years to bloom. Native Americans used it for food, building material, and shoes. 80. The desert plant, ocotillo, can look dead but once it rains it springs to life and soon grows red tubular flowers that hummingbirds love. 81. Mule deer and bighorn sheep eat the flowers of the brittle bush, a desert relative of the sunflower. 82. The center of the coneflower feels like a bunch of pins when you touch it. 83. Sea holly, also called "rattlesnake master," was used by Native Americans to cure rattlesnake bites. 84. Each flower of the milkweed plant, a favorite of monarch butterflies, releases hundreds of seeds. 85. Nosegay, tussie-mussie, and posy are old-fashioned small bouquets of flowers given as gifts, often tied with lace or ribbon. 86. Some people claim pouring soda pop into the vase helps cut flowers last longer. 87. Dictamnus is also called "burning bush" or "gas plant" because it is highly flammable during the summer months when it is covered with a sticky lemon-scented goo. 88. *Angelica archangelica* was used throughout history as people believed it could cure just about everything—including the plague. It was even believed to ward off evil spirits. 89. The word "daisy" comes from "day's eye" because daisy flowers open in the morning, showing their bright yellow "eye," and close at night. 90. The game of plucking petals off a daisy while saying, "he/she loves me, he/she loves me not" is thought to have originated in France. 91. NASA astronauts have experimented with growing sunflowers and sunflower seeds in space. 92. Dandelions' parachute-like seeds can travel in the wind as far as five miles (8 km). 93. Legend holds that if you make a wish and blow the seeds off a dandelion in one breath it will come true. 94. A giant flower made out of more than 100,000 Lego pieces was featured at a 2015 festival in Australia. It took more than 400 hours to build. 95. A lei is a Hawaiian necklace, usually made of fresh flowers. The most common flowers used are orchids and plumeria. Traditionally, it is rude to refuse a lei or remove it in front of the person who gifted it. 96. Freesia, honeysuckle, and lilacs all have sweet smells that have been compared to candy. 97. The *Bulbophyllum phalaenopsis*, a hairy pink orchid from New Guinea, smells like rotting rodents when it opens. 98. The orchid *Aristolochia salvadorensis* looks like Darth Vader from *Star Wars*. 99. The scent of jasmine is used in more than 80 percent of women's perfumes. 100. Joseph's coat climbing rose is always multicolored, with each rose opening in multiple shades of orange, pink, and gold.

50 DUSTY FACTS ABOUT ANCIENT RUINS

1 The Great Wall of China is the **MOST VISITED** ancient ruin, with about ten million visitors per year.

2 The 1,000-year-old Montezuma Castle is a 5-story 20-room castle **BUILT** into a **CLIFF** in Arizona, U.S.A.

3 Diocletian's Palace in Croatia, built between A.D. 295 and 305, is made of the same white sandstone that the **WHITE HOUSE** is made of.

4 The ancient homes in Derinkuyu, Turkey, a city from the seventh century, were built with **UNDERGROUND ROOMS** and tunnels 280 feet (85 m) deep.

5 The **UNDERWATER RUINS** of Samabaj in Guatemala sat on what was once an island. Researchers believe a volcano destroyed the city in A.D. 250.

6 In Kourion, Cyprus, a 3,500-seat **ANCIENT THEATER** sits on top of a cliff over the Mediterranean Sea and is still used for performances today.

7 The aqueduct over the Gardon River in southern France was built from A.D. 40 to 60 **WITHOUT MORTAR**— the glue that typically holds stones together.

8 The **LION GATE** in the ancient city of Mycenae, Greece, dates back to the 13th century B.C. when it served as a grand doorway to the palace.

9 Visitors can take a **CABLE CAR** up a cliff more than 1,300 feet (400 m) in Israel in the Judean Desert to the ruins of the palace of Herod the Great.

10 **RUINS** from the set of the 1977 movie *STAR WARS* stand in the open deserts in Tunisia.

11 The remains of the ancient city Pompeii, Italy, were not found until 1,700 **YEARS AFTER** the eruption that destroyed it.

12 The ancient city Pavlopetri, dating back to 2800 B.C., lies underwater in southern Greece and is considered the **OLDEST UNDERWATER CITY.**

13 The Inca built Machu Picchu, a city made of stone high in the Andes mountains, without using **WHEELS** or **IRON TOOLS.**

14 It's common for hikers to get **ALTITUDE SICKNESS** climbing up 13,800 feet (4,206 m) above sea level to see the ruins of Machu Picchu, an ancient city in Peru.

15 Ruins of **CLEOPATRA'S PALACE** were found under the Mediterranean Sea off Alexandria, Egypt, in the 1990s. Coins, sphinxes, and temples were unearthed.

16 The African country Zimbabwe got its name from the massive Shona ruins there. The Shona word *dzimbahwe* means **"BIG HOUSES OF STONE."**

17 Recreational scuba divers can **EXPLORE** the ruins of an **ANCIENT SUNKEN CITY** in Yonaguni, Japan.

18 In 2007, a circle of stones similar to **STONEHENGE** was found underwater in **LAKE MICHIGAN**, U.S.A.

19 It's been estimated that it would have taken **600 MEN** to move just one of the biggest **STONES** used to **BUILD STONEHENGE.**

20 No one knows how the ancient people of Tiahuanaco managed to cut and move the **ENORMOUS STONES** that fit together like a puzzle in Bolivia.

ruins at Machu Picchu, Peru

21

The ruins of the largest Roman temple in the world stand in eastern Lebanon: The **TEMPLE OF JUPITER** has 65-foot (20-m)-high columns.

22

Visitors can swim in an ancient **SACRED POOL** in Pamukkale, Turkey. The ruins of the Roman "spa city," called Hierapolis, date back to the second century B.C.

23

The world's first known temple was built at Göbekli Tepe in **TURKEY**, in about **10,000** B.C.

24

THOUSANDS of **ANCIENT TOMBS** from the fourth century B.C. are in Italy's Lazio region. Many have painted frescoes, a style of wall painting, inside.

25

The ruins of the Sacred Garden of Lumbini in Nepal mark the exact spot where it's believed **BUDDHA** was **BORN** in 623 B.C.

26

Dolmens are **ANCIENT TOMBS** made from balancing giant stone slabs. In addition to human remains, artifacts have been found inside some dolmens.

27

KOREA has more dolmens than any other country in the world.

28

The ancient temples at Mnajdra in Malta were built so the people could tell **WHAT TIME OF YEAR** it was by the way the sunlight shined between the stones.

29

No one knows why the bustling ancient city of **CAHOKIA** came to an end by A.D. 1400. Today, its ruins continue to be uncovered in Illinois, U.S.A.

30

China's first emperor, **QIN SHI HUANGDI**, had a giant underground city built where he would be buried. The tomb is close to the modern city of **XI'AN**.

31

In the 1700s, it was popular for rich families in **ENGLAND** to build rooms in their **HOMES** similar to those in **ANCIENT ROME**.

32

A tomb **FULL OF JADE**, a precious stone, was uncovered in the Maya ruins at Palenque in Mexico.

33

One of the casts of those killed from a **VOLCANO** in Pompeii, Italy, in A.D. 79 is a **DOG**.

34

9,500-year-old **TEETH** and **BONES** were found among the ruins of an ancient city underwater in the Gulf of Cambay, India.

35

The Arènes de Nîmes in Nimes, France, is a Roman **AMPHITHEATER** built during the first century and used for gladiator fights. Today it hosts concerts.

36

Peruvian **HAIRLESS DOGS** live among ruins along the coast of Peru in Lima that date back to A.D. 500.

37

Lego sells sets with pieces and instructions to build ruins such as **AMAZON ANCIENT RUINS** and **PHARAOH'S FORBIDDEN RUINS**.

38

The filmmakers of the 2008 *Indiana Jones and the Kingdom of the Crystal Skull* were accused of using the stolen real **CRYSTAL SKULL** as the basis of the film.

39

Cloaca Maxima is the ancient **ROMAN SEWER** that was built back in the sixth century B.C.

40

In ancient ruins in Japan, researchers found a **WILD BOAR BONE** that they believe was used in the late third century for fortune telling.

41

ROBOTS with **CAMERAS** are often used to safely explore underground ancient ruins.

42

Hundreds of **MYSTERIOUS YELLOW SPHERES** were found underneath the ancient Temple of the Feathered Serpent outside Mexico City, Mexico.

43

Ruins from the **ONLY KNOWN** Viking settlement in North America are at L'Anse aux Meadows, Canada.

44

The Pantheon in Rome, Italy, was **BUILT TWICE**. The original, built in A.D. 27, was destroyed by a fire in A.D. 80 and was rebuilt in about A.D. 125.

45

The ruins of a medieval crypt in Rome, Italy, are decorated with the **BONES** of **MORE THAN 4,000 MONKS**.

46

In 2014, construction workers found a 200-year-old ship underneath the former site of the **WORLD TRADE CENTER** in New York City, U.S.A.

47

Ruins from an ancient Maya city found in the jungles of Mexico include a doorway entrance shaped like a **MONSTER'S MOUTH**.

48

A Canadian woman flew to Italy to return a piece of an **ANCIENT THEATER** she had stolen from **POMPEII** 50 years after she took it.

49

More than 11,000 years ago the Ancestral Pueblo people of New Mexico, U.S.A., built their homes by making bricks out of **VOLCANIC ROCK**.

50

IGUANAS hang around the ruins of Uxmal, an ancient Maya town in Yucatán, Mexico.

1 The PROMINENT CLAWS on a sloth's foot are also known as TOES. There are TWO-TOED and THREE-TOED sloths—and a total of SIX KNOWN SPECIES.

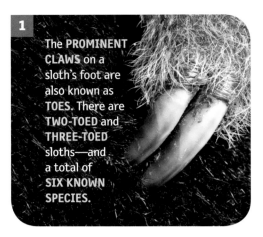

2 Sloth babies STAY with their MOTHERS for more than SIX MONTHS before they HEAD OFF on their own.

3 Most sloths are found high in the TREETOPS of the RAIN FORESTS in CENTRAL and SOUTH AMERICA.

4 Sloths move about 120 FEET (37 m) per day— at a TOP SPEED of about TWO INCHES (5 cm) per second.

5 Danitsja, a sloth living at a RESCUE CENTER in SURINAME, learned to be POTTY TRAINED. (She's since been RELEASED back into the WILD.)

6 The word "sloth" comes from the Middle English term *slouthe*, meaning slow. The animal's common name wasn't used until *500* years later.

25 SLUGGISH FACTS ABOUT SLOTHS

7 It can take up to ONE MONTH for sloths to COMPLETELY DIGEST a meal.

8 A sloth's stomach can make up to ONE-THIRD of its body weight—more than DOUBLE that of other animals its size.

9 Most sloths POOP just ONCE A WEEK.

10 A scientist once found 980 BEETLES living in the FUR of a single SLOTH.

11 SLOTHS CLEAN THEIR FUR WITH THEIR FRONT PAWS— NOT WITH THEIR MOUTH.

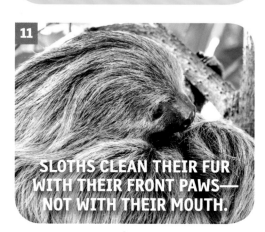

12 Sloths are extremely VULNERABLE on the ground: More than HALF of all sloth DEATHS in the WILD occur during their weekly BATHROOM EXPEDITIONS.

13 A CERTAIN SPECIES OF MOTHS LIVES EXCLUSIVELY ON SLOTHS, SPENDING THEIR ENTIRE ADULT LIVES IN THE ANIMAL'S FUR.

14 MOST SLOTHS IN THE WILD ARE **TINTED GREEN** BECAUSE OF THE **ALGAE** GROWING ON THEIR COAT. THIS HUE HELPS THEM **BLEND** INTO THEIR **HABITAT**.

15 International Sloth Day is CELEBRATED annually around the world on OCTOBER 20.

16 Sloths have VERY WEAK hind legs. On the ground, they use their SHARP CLAWS and STRONG front legs to DRAG themselves forward.

17 Sloths are **GOOD SWIMMERS**, and have been **SPOTTED** paddling along in **RIVERS** and **STREAMS**.

18 HUGE **SWIMMING** SLOTHS—NAMED *THALASSOCNUS*—LIVED ALONG THE **BEACHES** OF **PERU** EIGHT TO FOUR MILLION YEARS AGO.

19 THREE-TOED SLOTHS CAN **TURN THEIR HEADS** ALMOST **ALL THE WAY AROUND**, THANKS TO AN EXTRA **NECK VERTEBRA**.

20 *MEGATHERIUM*, A **GIANT PREHISTORIC SLOTH**, WEIGHED AS MUCH AS AN **ELEPHANT** AND WAS AS TALL AS A **GIRAFFE**.

21 Baby sloths SQUEAK. Adult sloths are much less verbal, typically only HISSING if they're THREATENED.

22

Each day, sloths in **CAPTIVITY** sleep for up to **19 HOURS** and up to about **9 HOURS** in the **WILD**.

23 THERE'S A GIANT STATUE OF A SLOTH IN MIAMI, FLORIDA, U.S.A., THAT IS NEARLY AS TALL AS A TWO-STORY BUILDING.

24

Sloths have such a STRONG GRIP that they've been known to continue hanging UPSIDE DOWN from a tree even after they die.

25 A PASSERBY ONCE MISTOOK A DEAD SLOTH FLOATING IN A PANAMA CREEK FOR AN **ALIEN**. PHOTOS OF THE ANIMAL WENT **VIRAL**, EARNING IT THE NICKNAME "PANAMA E.T."

1 Fuels are burned to **PROVIDE ENERGY** for heat and light, and to power machines. **BIOFUELS** come from **ANIMALS, PLANTS, FUNGI,** and **BACTERIA.**

2 THE BIOFUEL METHANE from cow digestion is **DOWNRIGHT EXPLOSIVE:** Cows filled a German barn with methane—a greenhouse gas—and **BLEW THE ROOF RIGHT OFF!**

3 Cows in Argentina wear **BACKPACKS THAT CAPTURE THE METHANE THEY PRODUCE.** That methane may eventually be used to power remote farms.

4 *E. COLI* BACTERIA may make you sick, but they can also be engineered to produce biofuel that can **POWER A TRUCK'S ENGINE.**

5 *E. coli* reproduce **EVERY 30 MINUTES.** In a day, one bacterium can become **281 TRILLION BACTERIA.**

6 INSECTS ARE BIOFUELS for plants such as the sundew. Sticky leaves **TRAP THE INSECTS,** which are digested to provide the plant with energy.

7 The biofuel methane may have **CAUSED THE WORST EXTINCTION** on Earth, 20 million years **BEFORE DINOSAURS** began to roam.

8 Scientists think gassy **PLANT-EATING DINOSAURS** like *Apatosaurus* produced enough methane to keep the planet **WARM AND TOASTY.**

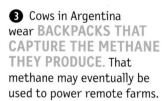

refueling and changing tires on a car during a NASCAR race

ABOUT **BIOFUEL**

9 If **BIOFUEL MADE FROM ALGAE** were used to **POWER AIRPLANES,** we would need to grow enough algae to cover the **ENTIRE COUNTRY OF IRELAND.**

10 **THE FUEL ETHANOL** can be made from sugar beet, sugarcane, wheat, grass, corn, sorghum, barley, and the **LEFTOVER PARTS OF MOST PLANTS**— anything that can't be eaten by people or other animals.

11 **ELEPHANT DUNG** powers the Munich Zoo in Germany. Gas from decomposing dung **PROVIDES HEAT AND ELECTRICITY** for the animal buildings.

12 Biofuels for vehicles **AREN'T NEW:** Early truck engines ran on **PEANUT OIL.**

13 **COFFEE** may soon be **POWERING TRUCKS** in addition to fueling people.

14 The **EXHAUST** from cars and trucks powered by **RECYCLED RESTAURANT GREASE** smells like french fries.

15 National Association for Stock Car Auto Racing (NASCAR) **RACE CARS** run on fuels that are **15 PERCENT ETHANOL,** also known as drinking alcohol.

75 ENERGY FACTS THAT WILL CHARGE YOU UP

1 Energy is the ability to do work. There are many different forms of energy, including electrical, chemical, thermal (heat), radiant (light), mechanical, and nuclear.

2 Energy cannot be created or destroyed. It just changes from one form to another.

3 In August 2003, a computer malfunction caused the largest widespread power grid failure in the history of the United States—some 50 million people lost power.

4 ANCIENT ROMANS USED UNDERGROUND HEATING SYSTEMS TO WARM THEIR PUBLIC BATHHOUSES.

5 Researchers in the United Kingdom have created a device that can turn urine into electricity.

6 The British energy drink Lucozade was first invented by a chemist in 1927 to help sick people recover from illnesses like a cold.

7 It takes a depth of ten feet (3 m) of prehistoric plant material to produce one foot (30 cm) of coal.

8 A person watching 60 minutes of YouTube videos and using other Google services every day requires about the same energy in one month as driving a car for one mile (1.6 km).

9 The Seattle School District in Washington, U.S.A., saved $20,000 by turning out the lights in all their vending machines.

10 Jelly Belly Sport Beans are jelly beans that provide energy to the body during exercise.

11 The word "energy" comes from the Greek word *energeia*, which means activity.

12 Students, faculty, and friends from the EARTH University in Costa Rica set a world record by pedaling on bicycles connected to a generator to keep 1,600 Christmas lights lit for 24 hours.

13 Ivanpah, the world's largest solar power plant, uses 300,000 software-controlled mirrors to track the sun. It's located in the Mojave Desert, California, U.S.A.

14 You can be stylish and be green! Tommy Hilfiger designed a solar-powered jacket that can be used to keep your cell phone charged.

15 THE TALLEST TOWERS FOR WIND TURBINES CAN BE TALLER THAN THE STATUE OF LIBERTY.

16 The Three Gorges Dam on the Yangtze River in China is the largest hydroelectric power plant in the world.

17 A new type of energy bar will give you something to chirp about. One of the main ingredients is crickets!

18 The Pedal-A-Watt device allows you to pedal a stationary bike and store your energy in a power pack. Ride for an hour and you can power your laptop for ten hours.

19 Kinetic energy is the energy an object contains when it's in motion. A basketball has kinetic energy only when you pass or shoot it.

20 In 2014, a family-size solar-powered car traveled from Los Angeles to San Francisco, California, U.S.A., powered just by the sun.

21 The Toyota car company's first hybrid electric car was named "Volta," in tribute to Alessandro Volta, the scientist who invented the electric battery.

22 On average, wind needs to be traveling at least 14 miles an hour (23 km/h) before its energy can be converted into electricity.

23 THE EIFFEL TOWER HAS TWO WIND TURBINES INSIDE. THEY POWER THE GIFT SHOP, MUSEUM, AND RESTAURANTS ON THE FIRST FLOOR.

24 All of the energy used on the island of Samsø, Denmark, comes from wind power.

25 The solar-powered plane *Solar Impulse 2* set a world record in 2015 for the longest nonstop flight when it flew for 117 hours from Japan to Hawaii.

26 The state of Texas produces more power from wind energy than any other state in the United States.

27 Energy "vampires" are electronic devices, such as cell phone chargers, that use electricity all day and night, even when they are plugged in but not in use.

28 The United States produces more energy from the natural heat of the ground (geothermal energy) than any other country in the world.

29 Some cities in Scandinavia pump warm geothermal water underneath roads and walkways to help melt snow.

30 Some cars can run on vegetable oil instead of gasoline.

31 In the first six months of 2015, Costa Rica used only "green" energy sources (no fossil fuels) for all its electricity needs.

32 A 36-foot (11-m)-tall wind turbine that looks like a tree was "planted" in Paris, France.

33 A BATTERY MADE FROM A BOILED POTATO CAN PRODUCE TEN TIMES MORE ENERGY THAN A BATTERY FROM A RAW POTATO.

34 Sound is a form of energy. It's created when an object vibrates and produces sound waves.

35 About 68 percent of the universe is made up of a mysterious force scientists call dark energy.

36 A Btu isn't text lingo—it stands for "British thermal unit," which is a precise way to measure the heat content of fuels.

37 A bolt of lightning contains enough energy that, if harnessed, could toast 100,000 slices of bread.

38 Iceland has so many volcanoes and hot springs, it uses geothermal energy to power nine out of ten homes.

39 New gaming consoles use almost as much energy in standby mode as they do when they are turned on.

40 The most energy-efficient appliance in a kitchen is the microwave.

41 Windmills were used to pump water in Persia as early as 900 B.C.

42 Scientist Michael Faraday, who discovered the electric generator, never went to college. He taught himself by reading science books.

43 The total amount of energy in the universe always remains the same.

44 Thomas Edison, who developed electric light, had six children. He nicknamed one of them "Dot" and another "Dash" in reference to Morse code messages sent by telegraph.

45 Using the "sleep" feature on your desktop computer can save about $30 in energy costs every year.

46 Fish ladders help migrating fish swim over hydroelectric dams. A fish ladder is a series of rising pools that fish leap into to scale the dam.

47 The Crayola company uses renewable energy from a 20-acre (8-ha) solar farm. It provides enough power to make 1 billion crayons and 500 million markers in a year.

48 It would take 25 large power plants to provide the electricity needed to keep all the refrigerators in the United States running for a whole year.

49 If every house in the United States replaced just one lightbulb with a new energy-efficient bulb, the amount of energy saved could light three million homes for a year.

50 The Grand Coulee Dam on the Columbia River in Washington state, built in 1949, is the largest hydropower plant in the United States.

51 Newly designed solar backpacks receive enough power from the sun to keep cell phones, MP3 players, and other small appliances charged.

52 Tiny microbes found in pandas' poop may help scientists discover a way to convert waste materials from plants into eco-friendly biofuel for the cars of the future.

53 FEELING ZONKED? SNACKS HIGH IN PROTEIN AND COMPLEX CARBOHYDRATES PROVIDE A LONG-LASTING ENERGY BOOST—THINK CHEESE AND CRACKERS OR A PB&J.

54 The Sihwa Lake Tidal Power Station in South Korea is currently the largest wave-energy facility in the world. The station turns wave power into electricity.

55 Caffeine is the most common ingredient in energy drinks.

56 The Swedish ship *Tûranor PlanetSolar* completed a journey around the world in 584 days powered completely by the sun.

57 Piezoelectricity is electrical energy produced by mechanical pressure, as with walking feet.

58 Mexico's Sustainable Light program distributed 22.9 million energy-efficient lightbulbs, for free, to people living in Mexico.

59 At the central train station in Stockholm, Sweden, the ventilation system captures the body heat from commuters and then converts it into energy to heat a nearby office building.

60 TOP THAT! A MAN BALANCED FOUR ENERGY DRINK CANS ON HIS THUMB FOR MORE THAN TEN MINUTES.

61 In Tokyo, Japan, special floors have been installed at some busy subway stations to convert the energy from heavy foot traffic into electricity that is used to power lights, signs, and turnstiles.

62 Potential energy is the energy an object has because of its position. A stretched rubber band stores elastic potential energy. Let go of the rubber band and this energy is released.

63 Lemons can power lightbulbs— by using a copper and a steel wire, lemon juice (an acid) converts chemical energy to electrical energy.

64 Why give your dog a bone when it can have a canine energy bar instead? Veterinarians recommend giving canine energy bars to only very active dogs.

65 Researchers in Barcelona, Spain, have invented a device that can convert light into energy in just 50 quadrillionths of a second.

66 Scientists are working on developing technology similar to the energy force fields in the *Star Wars* movies that could create a buffer around objects protecting them from the shock waves of nearby explosions.

67 Solar ovens provide a solution in developing countries where food is typically cooked over a wood fire. They save forests and provide clean energy.

68 The Geysers, located north of San Francisco, California, U.S.A., is the largest geothermal power plant in the world. It produces enough energy to power 725,000 homes.

69 Playing a vigorous game of racquetball takes about two times as much energy as canoeing.

70 When Hurricane Sandy made landfall in 2012, it contained twice as much energy as the atomic bomb dropped on Hiroshima, Japan.

71 AS OF 2014, 90 PERCENT OF ALL ENERGY IN THE UNITED STATES WAS CREATED FROM NONRENEW-ABLE ENERGY SOURCES SUCH AS PETROLEUM, NATURAL GAS, AND COAL.

72 The United States has 86 plants in 25 states that burn trash and convert it to electricity. The smaller European country of Germany has 80.

73 The United States uses about 18 percent of all the energy produced globally. That's higher than any other country.

74 Researchers have created a cloth with miniscule materials that can take the energy used when pressing on it and use it to power an LED light.

75 Buildings covered in "green" roofs—with plants and gardens— help insulate the building and lower the cost to both heat and cool the building.

solar panel array in Shanghai, China

35 FACTS ABOUT

1 Male emperor penguins keep their eggs warm by balancing them on their **FEET** and covering them with a layer of skin called a **BROOD POUCH**.

2 **BALD EAGLES** usually have from one to three **EGGS**.

3 Female turtles use their rear legs as **SCOOPS** to dig out a **NEST** for their eggs.

4 **OSTRICH HENS** all lay their eggs in the nest of the most dominant female in the **HERD**.

5 If **FIREFLY** eggs are disturbed before they hatch, the larvae inside will **GLOW** with short pulses of light.

6 From 1885 until 1916, the **HOUSE OF FABERGÉ** created elaborately **JEWELED ORNAMENTAL** eggs for Russia's imperial family. The eggs are worth millions of dollars today.

7 Female **LEATHERBACK TURTLES** migrate to the same **BEACH** where they were hatched to lay about 80 eggs in a sandy nest.

8 April 16 is **NATIONAL EGGS BENEDICT DAY**, a day to celebrate the breakfast dish that consists of an English muffin with a poached egg and Canadian bacon.

9 Cadbury creme eggs with the **CREAMY YOLK CENTER** sold in the United Kingdom are six grams (0.2 ounces) heavier than those sold in the United States.

10 The extinct **ELEPHANT BIRD**, a flightless bird that inhabited **MADAGASCAR** until the 17th century, laid 12-inch (30.5-cm)-long eggs.

11 Every year some 35,000 people attend the **WHITE HOUSE EASTER EGG ROLL**, a tradition since 1878.

12 About 400 species of **SHARKS** lay eggs; the rest give birth to **LIVE YOUNG**.

13 Natural objects can be used to dye **EASTER EGGS**: blueberries for **BLUE**, the spice turmeric for **YELLOW**, and the spice paprika for **ORANGE**.

14 There are no eggs in an **EGG CREAM**. The classic diner drink is made from milk, **SELTZER WATER**, and chocolate syrup.

15 The "**EGGMAN**" is the main villain in the video game series **SONIC THE HEDGEHOG**.

16 The **INCUBATION TEMPERATURE** of an alligator's egg determines if it becomes **MALE** or **FEMALE**. Higher temperatures produce **MALE** alligators.

17 Portuguese chefs mixed 145,000 **CHICKEN EGGS** with hundreds of pounds of oil and butter to make an **OMELET** weighing 14,225 pounds, 1.5 ounces (6.466 MT).

18 **A MCDONALD'S FRANCHISE OWNER** invented a device that could be placed on the **GRILL** to form perfectly **ROUND** eggs for the **EGG MCMUFFIN** sandwich.

19 Turtle **HATCHLINGS** use a sharp tooth, called a **CARUNCLE**, to break open their shells.

20 A stone bridge in **LIMA, PERU**, is reportedly held **TOGETHER** by egg whites—an ingredient in the mortar between the stones.

21 The **DUCK-BILLED PLATYPUS** and the **ECHIDNA** are the only mammal species that lay eggs.

22 Baby chickens can **BREATHE** through their **SHELLS**.

EGGS THAT WON'T CRACK

23 A queen **BEE** can lay up to 1,000,000 eggs during her **LIFETIME**—that's as many as **2,000 PER DAY**.

24 Rocks that have been smoothed by rivers are often **MISTAKEN FOR FOSSILIZED DINOSAUR EGGS**. Dino egg shapes include **TORPEDO-SHAPED** and **PERFECT SPHERES**.

25 Mackerel fish **RELEASE EGGS** into the water to be fertilized, and the largest **MACKEREL** can carry 1,000,000 eggs.

26 Some fish **EGGS**—like those of sea catfish—hatch while they are being carried in their **DAD'S** mouth.

27 About 1 in 1,000 chicken eggs has a **DOUBLE YOLK**.

28 Some chickens lay eggs with **GREEN** or **BLUE SHELLS**.

29 The **WHITE** part of an egg is called **ALBUMEN**; the egg **YOLK** is known as **VITELLUS**.

30 During the Renaissance, artists such as **LEONARDO DA VINCI** painted with tempera paints. These paints can be made by **COMBINING AN EGG** with **WATER** and color pigments.

31 **OOLOGY** is the **STUDY** of **BIRD** eggs.

32 Researchers observed a **DEEP-SEA OCTOPUS** guarding her clutch of eggs for **53 MONTHS**. This is the longest **EGG-BROODING PERIOD** of any animal.

33 The eggs of many species of **SHARKS AND SKATES** are enclosed in a tough, protective case **CALLED A "MERMAID'S PURSE."**

34 **CAVIAR** is another name for fish eggs. The most expensive caviar comes from **CRITICALLY ENDANGERED STURGEON**.

35 Butterflies will lay their **EGGS ON LEAVES**. Be careful not to disturb them as the eggs of some species can die if they are cut from their **ORIGINAL LEAVES**.

nest and eggs of a blackbird

50 VAMPIRE FACTS TO SINK YOUR TEETH INTO

Bran Castle, Romania

1
By its **ENGLISH** definition, a **VAMPIRE** is an "**UNDEAD**" **HUMAN** that relies on sucking blood from the living to survive.

2
According to legend, vampires can't see themselves in **MIRRORS** because they **LACK SOULS.**

3
The idea of vampires started **LONG AGO.** A grave in Poland from the 1600s is partly **STAKED TO THE GROUND,** supposedly so the body won't rise from the dead.

4
Many people living today in a small Serbian village **CARRY GARLIC** in their **POCKETS** to protect them from the ghost of Sava Savanović, "Serbia's first vampire."

5
Grobniks are Bulgarian vampires that eat **DEAD ANIMALS,** and *algul* are Arabic vampires that eat **RICE.**

6
In addition to garlic, people have used **PEPPERCORNS,** grains of **RICE,** and **POPPY** and **SESAME SEEDS** to protect themselves from vampires.

7
VAMPIROLOGY is the study of vampires, and one who studies them is called a **VAMPIROLOGIST.**

8
SANGUIVORIPHOBIA, or "fear of blood-eaters," is the term used to describe an irrational fear of vampires.

9
One of the first **VAMPIRE MOVIES** ever made was *NOSFERATU* in 1922. It was an adaptation of Bram Stoker's 1897 novel, *DRACULA.*

10
One of the oldest known blood-guzzling vampires is an Assyrian and Babylonian monster called **EKIMMU,** from 4000 B.C.

11
Dolmens—giant stones put over ancient tombs —may have been placed over dead **SUSPECTED VAMPIRES** to prevent them from entering back into the world.

12
Instead of eating seeds like most finches, the **VAMPIRE FINCH** pecks at seabirds and feeds on their **BLOOD.**

13
Although there is no evidence of their actual existence, vampirologists have found more than 600 **DIFFERENT SPECIES** of vampires in folklore.

14
Fans of the vampire series **TWILIGHT** flock to its real-world setting— the town of **FORKS** in Washington State, U.S.A.

15
Bram Stoker was inspired by 15th-century Romanian nobleman **VLAD THE IMPALER** when he created the character of **DRACULA.**

16
In China, a *GYONSHEE* is a **VAMPIRE.** The name also refers to the legendary **HOPPING CORPSE** of China that acts like a zombie.

17
Prince Charles of the United Kingdom is a **DESCENDANT** of Vlad the Impaler.

18
There are **TOURS** in Romania that explore Bran Castle —where Vlad was imprisoned—the subject of vampires, and the legend of **DRACULA.**

19
Balkan folklore says that **MELONS** and **PUMPKINS** left out for ten days or more turn into **TOOTHLESS VAMPIRES.**

20
Vampire moths, of the genus *CALYPTRA,* occasionally drink human blood through **PIERCINGS** of the skin.

21

The vampire name Nosferatu comes from the Greek word *nosophorus*, which means "PLAGUE CARRIER."

27

For about $1,500 you can buy a velvet-lined COFFIN BED.

33

More than THREE MILLION AMERICAN ADULTS dressed up as vampires for Halloween in 2012.

39

According to a recent census, 4 percent of Americans believe vampires are REAL.

45

Some BABY PACIFIERS are made with vampire teeth painted on to give the appearance of a VAMPIRE BABY.

22

VAMPIRE-SLAYING KITS from the 1800s have been found that include things like stakes, holy water, salt, and garlic.

28

In 2005, a group of people started the New Orleans Vampire Association for people who ARE VAMPIRES.

34

In the cartoon *Monster High*, DRACULAURA is a vegetarian vampire and the adopted daughter of Count Dracula. She's 1,600 years old.

40

A *kappa* is a sumo-wrestling Japanese vampire that lives in the water. When an animal comes by for a drink, the kappa drags it in and BITES its REAR.

46

According to Eastern European lore, a VAMPIRE SLAYER called a "dhampir" has a VAMPIRE FATHER and a HUMAN MOTHER.

23

Archaeologists have found many graves containing 500-year-old skeletons with STAKES through their CHESTS. Perhaps the stakes were used to kill vampires.

29

Vampire MITES are infecting honeybees in the United Kingdom with a virus that DEFORMS the bees' wings.

35

Vampire cereal monster mascot COUNT CHOCULA'S tagline is "I want to eat your cereal!"

41

One Florida man who believes he is a vampire ran for PRESIDENT of the UNITED STATES in 2012.

47

After biting a member of Italy's soccer team during the 2014 WORLD CUP, player Luis Suárez fell victim to many VAMPIRE JOKES.

24

VAMPIRIC WITCHES are common in Spain. One of them, BRUJA, looks like a normal, beautiful woman by day, but by night she HUNTS FOR CHILDREN.

30

Many contact lens companies make VAMPIRE CONTACT LENSES that come in colors like red, orange, and gold.

36

An animal that FEEDS ON BLOOD is called "HEMATOPHAGOUS."

42

A ROLLER COASTER called the VAMPIRE has a Gothic theme and blasts organ music in an amusement park in London, England.

48

Some companies sell CHERRY LIQUID CANDY packaged in something that looks like a BLOOD BAG.

25

Instead of antlers, the male Siberian musk deer grows LONG, VAMPIRE-LIKE FANGS, inspiring the nickname, "vampire deer."

31

Some people have their TEETH SHAVED into PERMANENT FANGS.

37

Scientists developed a drug made out of VAMPIRE BAT SPIT to help stroke victims.

43

There are VAMPIRE TOURS through the French Quarter in New Orleans, Louisiana, U.S.A., where visitors can see where so-called vampires roamed in the 1800s.

49

In 2010, a woman in COLORADO, U.S.A., backed her car into a CANAL because, she said, she was trying to get away from a vampire.

26

Sesame Street's COUNT is a VAMPIRE. The muppet was inspired by Dracula and has a "counting habit," which was considered a vampire trait in Europe.

32

A disease called PELLAGRA is linked to the ORIGINATION of vampire folklore. Symptoms include sensitivity to sunlight, pale skin, and red lips.

38

In 2011 some people accused actor Nicolas Cage of BEING A VAMPIRE because a photo of a similar-looking man from the 1800s had surfaced.

44

Central America is home to VAMPIRE ORCHIDS that have BLOODRED flowers, often with contorted "faces" and long, pointy sepals.

50

The AXEMAN African vampiric witch supposedly turns into a bat at night and finds someone sleeping with an uncovered BIG TOE, which she cuts and drinks from.

TURN ON
100
FACTS ABOUT
TV

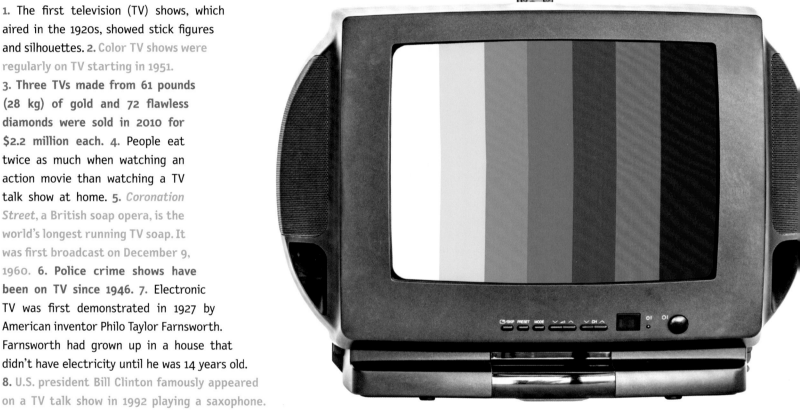

a 1990s TV set

1. The first television (TV) shows, which aired in the 1920s, showed stick figures and silhouettes. 2. Color TV shows were regularly on TV starting in 1951.

3. Three TVs made from 61 pounds (28 kg) of gold and 72 flawless diamonds were sold in 2010 for $2.2 million each. 4. People eat twice as much when watching an action movie than watching a TV talk show at home. 5. *Coronation Street*, a British soap opera, is the world's longest running TV soap. It was first broadcast on December 9, 1960. 6. Police crime shows have been on TV since 1946. 7. Electronic TV was first demonstrated in 1927 by American inventor Philo Taylor Farnsworth. Farnsworth had grown up in a house that didn't have electricity until he was 14 years old.

8. U.S. president Bill Clinton famously appeared on a TV talk show in 1992 playing a saxophone.

9. As people watch Internet-streamed shows on tablets and phones, they are watching less traditional television. 10. The typical American household spends from 2.5 to 5 hours a day watching TV. 11. At the 1939 New York World's Fair, Franklin D. Roosevelt became the first president to appear on TV. It was only broadcast to a handful of TVs. 12. Americans watch more TV than any other country. (Italians are the second highest viewers.) 13. Americans get their news from the TV more than any other source. 14. The outbreak of World War II caused the sales and production of TV sets to drop. 15. From 1945 to 1948, sales of TVs rose 500 percent. 16. By 1960, 85 percent of U.S. households had a TV set. 17. By 1994, 99 percent of American households had at least one TV. 18. The first practical wireless remote control used to operate a TV was invented in 1957. 19. In the series *T.U.F.F. Puppy*, the initials are for Turbo Undercover Fighting Force. 20. Actress Sofía Vergara earns $325,000 per episode for her role on the TV show *Modern Family*. 21. Up until 1967, most TV shows were filmed in black and white. 22. Before the first transatlantic satellite signal was received in 1962, it would take days to learn of news in distant lands. 23. In 1970, TV manufacturers started to use fiber optic cables—rods of glass and plastic—instead of copper. The cables transmitted information 65,000 times faster. 24. U.S. president Dwight Eisenhower's 1952 campaign was the first to introduce political TV ads. 25. In 1963, 45 percent of all households with TVs turned their set on after it was announced that U.S. President John F. Kennedy had been assassinated. 26. The first U.S. congressional hearing on TV violence was held in 1952. 27. *The Tonight Show* is the longest running talk show. It debuted in 1954. 28. In 1956, the host of *The Ed Sullivan Show* at first thought Elvis Presley's

dancing wasn't appropriate for his family show, but he changed his mind after Elvis soared in popularity with teenagers. **29.** An estimated 600 million TV viewers watched the moon landing on July 20, 1969. **30. When the Beatles first performed on TV in the U.S. in 1964, 40 percent of all Americans tuned in to watch. 31.** The actor who voiced Shaggy in the *Scooby-Doo, Where Are You!* cartoon series was a vegetarian and asked the producers that Shaggy be one, too. **32.** Scooby-Doo's real name is Scoobert. **33. When *The Jetsons* aired in 1962, it showed a device that allowed characters to video chat. 34.** Although the TV show *Little House on the Prairie* was meant to take place on a prairie in the Midwest, it was filmed almost entirely in Southern California. **35.** Mick, the dog-actor who plays Stan on *Dog With a Blog*, was rescued by his animal-trainer owners. **36. With more than 114 million people tuning in, the 2015 Super Bowl was the most-watched TV show ever in the U.S. 37.** *SpongeBob SquarePants* was originally going to be called *SpongeBoy Ahoy!* **38.** U.S. president Barack Obama once said SpongeBob was his favorite TV character. **39. First Lady Michelle Obama made a cameo appearance on *iCarly* to raise awareness about supporting U.S. military families. 40.** Originally, Marge Simpson from the cartoon series *The Simpsons* was going to have bunny ears under her blue beehive hair. **41.** Before he founded the shoe company Toms, Blake Mycoskie competed on the reality TV show *The Amazing Race*. **42. R2-D2 once appeared on *Sesame Street* and fell in love with a fire hydrant. 43.** *Sesame Street*'s Mr. Snuffleupagus's full name is Aloysius Snuffleupagus. **44.** Big Bird is 8 feet, 2 inches (2.5 m) tall. **45. The creators of *The Brady Bunch* considered calling it *The Brady Brood*. 46.** In 2012, about 1,000 people gathered in New York City's Time Square at 1 a.m. to watch the Mars rover landing on a giant TV. **47.** Twice as many main characters die in children's animated films than in adult films, a study found. **48. The actor who played Spock in the original *Star Trek* TV series once owned a pet store. 49.** "Watching the box" is a British expression for watching TV. **50. When the British TV show *Sherlock Holmes* aired in China, the names for Sherlock and Dr. Watson were changed to Curly Fu and Peanut. 51.** More than 63 million music tracks from the TV show *Glee* were sold during its first 100 episodes. **52.** Four-year-olds who were given a test after watching *SpongeBob* for nine minutes scored significantly worse than ones who watched an educational show or colored pictures instead. **53. In 2011, *American Idol* had 577 product placements (products that are intentionally placed on the TV show for advertising purposes). 54.** A TV news broadcaster in Ecuador anchored the news for 47 years—longer than any other news anchor. **55.** The longest on-screen TV kiss—that occurred on a morning news show in Oklahoma, U.S.A.—lasted 3 minutes and 47 seconds. **56. The world's largest TV set, Zeus, has a 370-inch (940-cm) screen and costs $1.7 million. 57.** A Swedish man once set the record for quickly punching ten TV sets: He smashed all ten in less than eight seconds while wearing boxing gloves. (Don't try this at home!) **58.** Mr. Rogers's mother hand-knitted all the sweaters he wore on *Mister Rogers' Neighborhood*. **59. TVs were first used onboard an airplane in 1932. 60.** The longest-running TV variety show—*Waratte Iitomo! ("It's Okay to Laugh!")*— aired in Japan for more than 31 years. **61.** *Candid Camera*, which first aired in 1948, was the first TV show to regularly feature non-acting members of the public. **62.** *Dragnet* was the first movie based on a TV show. **63.** Superman has appeared in four live-action TV series. **64.** *Sazae-san*, a cartoon series from Japan, has been on the air since 1969. **65. A TV commercial for the perfume Chanel N°5 cost $33 million to produce. 66.** Soap operas have been on TV since 1946. **67.** Soap operas got their name because serial dramas on radio were often sponsored by soap companies. **68. Nielsen is a company that studies what people watch and then releases ratings of the most popular TV shows. 69.** When a movie advertisement appears on TV, more than 50 percent of viewers pay attention to the ad. **70.** A 1946 boxing match that aired on TV was the first time a company (in this case Gillette, which makes razors) sponsored a show. **71. More than 219 million Americans tuned in to watch the 2012 Summer Olympic Games in London. 72.** NBC stations broadcasted the 2012 summer Olympic Games, airing 5,535 hours of coverage. **73.** From 1982 to 2013, a British man named David St John made more than 30 appearances as a contestant on TV quiz shows. **74. Miranda Cosgrove, who starred on *iCarly*, made up to $180,000 per episode, the highest paid child actress per TV episode. 75.** *The Flintstones* was originally going to be called *The Flagstones*. **76.** A chef in Mexico who hosted a cooking show for 46 years set a world record for longest career as a TV chef. **77. When it premiered in 1963, Julia Child's *The French Chef* became the first cooking show to air on U.S. public TV. 78.** The 2015 finale of *The Great British Bake Off* TV series was viewed by more than 13.4 million people—a U.K. viewing record. **79.** *Dora the Explorer*'s Map and Swiper characters are voiced by the same actor. **80. The Superman suit worn in the 1955 TV series *Adventures of Superman* sold for $129,800. 81.** *Doctor Who*, which first aired in 1963, was originally created to be a family educational program, where two of the original characters were science and history teachers. **82.** On the animated show *Arthur*, the main character, Arthur, is an aardvark and he wears bunny slippers. His best friend, Buster, is a rabbit, and he wears aardvark slippers. **83. *The Magic Roundabout*, shown on British TV in the 1960s and 1970s, was originally a French children's motion animation program. Among the characters were Brian, a snail, and Dougal, a shaggy dog. 84.** The first science-fiction show ever broadcast on TV appeared from Czechoslovakia in 1938. **85. In 2005, a live TV show about the Japanese number puzzle sudoku aired in the United Kingdom. 86.** Shortly after Mr. Potato Head was first advertised on TV in 1952, more than $4 million worth of Mr. Potato Head toys were sold. At the time, the toy consisted of plastic body parts for a real potato. **87.** The first TV game show, which aired in 1938, was called *Spelling Bee*. Contestants on the show were asked to spell various words. **88. In 2009, 114 people watched a FIFA World Cup match on TV underwater. 89.** The original name for *Wheel of Fortune* was *Shopper's Bazaar*. **90.** The signatures on the green brick wall at the Asphalt Café on the TV show *Victorious* belong to the cast and crew. **91. The real name of the host of *Jeopardy!* isn't Alex Trebek—it's George Trebek. (Alex is his middle name.) 92.** Fergie, of the band the Black Eyed Peas, was the voice of Sally in several *Peanuts* TV specials. **93.** *A Charlie Brown Christmas* first aired on TV in 1965. **94. *The Wizard of Oz* first aired on TV 17 years after it played in movie theaters. 95.** Longtime talk show host Oprah Winfrey once gave away a car to every single person in her studio audience. **96.** *The Tonight Show* host Jimmy Fallon has a Ben & Jerry's flavor of ice cream named after him called The Tonight Dough Starring Jimmy Fallon. **97. The first TV remote control was called Lazy Bones. 98.** Early remote controls were connected to the TV with a long cord. **99.** *Sesame Street*'s Count von Count has a pet octopus named Octavia. **100. Cookie Monster's real name is Sid.**

1
Vikings SAILED LONG DISTANCES from their homes in Scandinavia from A.D. 800 to 1066.

2
Vikings are known for their RAIDS AND PLUNDER, but they also traded with people from other countries.

3
The name "Viking" means "A PIRATE RAID" in the Old Norse language.

4
In about A.D. 1000, about 500 years BEFORE CHRISTOPHER COLUMBUS came to the American continent, Vikings visited what is now Canada.

5
Vikings BELIEVED IN THOR, the god of thunder, and LOKI, a mischief-maker who could shape-shift into different kinds of animals.

6
Vikings were expert boat BUILDERS and SAILORS.

7
KEELS—spines along the bottom of Viking boats—made the boats EASY TO STEER.

8
Because Viking boats were designed to FLOAT HIGH IN THE WATER, they could easily land on shore.

9
The Vikings' "long houses" where families lived had ROOFS COVERED IN GRASS to help keep in the heat.

10
In the winter, Vikings ate DRIED FISH that they prepared during the warmer months.

11
Viking longships were also called DRAGONSHIPS.

12
Fenrir Greyback, a WEREWOLF IN THE HARRY POTTER SERIES, was named after a giant wolf from ancient Viking mythology.

the prow of a replica Viking longboat

13
"Berserkers" was the name of Viking warriors who WORE BEAR AND WOLF SKINS and howled in battle like wild animals.

14
Vikings CAME FROM what is today SCANDINAVIA—Denmark, Norway, and Sweden.

15
Vikings left Scandinavia and TRAVELED TO OTHER COUNTRIES, including Britain and Ireland.

16
Some Vikings STOLE FROM OTHER LANDS, but others became farmers, craftsmen, and traders.

17
Eastern ROMAN EMPERORS HIRED Vikings as guards.

18
Vikings who traveled in the East learned about THE GAME OF CHESS and brought the game back to their native land.

50 FACTS ABOUT VIKINGS TO SETTLE

19

Viking women wore BROOCHES made of GOLD.

20

To START a FIRE, Vikings struck IRON against a FLINT to make a spark.

21

Vikings landed in southern Britain in A.D. 787, BATTLED with Britons, and then left. But it was the start of a long STRUGGLE between the two groups.

22

Vikings launched their ships into the water by PUSHING them over LOG ROLLERS.

23

The English CALLED THE VIKINGS "DANES," even though they came from what is today Denmark, Sweden, and Norway.

24

Norwegian Vikings, also called NORSE, sailed to northern Scotland and settled on the ORKNEY and SHETLAND ISLANDS.

25

Vikings raided WALES and settled on the ISLE OF MAN, located between the islands of Great Britain and Ireland.

26

Vikings practiced PAGANISM, where they believed in more than one god and sacrificed animals to please the gods. They often robbed Christian churches.

27

For 500 YEARS, starting in about A.D. 900, Vikings RULED northern Scotland.

28

Contrary to popular belief, VIKING HELMETS did not have horns.

29

To protect themselves in battle, Vikings sometimes wore CHAIN MAIL jackets, where metal rings were laced together to avoid the penetration of a spear.

30

France's Normandy got its name from the fact that it was founded by Danish Vikings—it was "LAND OF THE NORTH-MEN."

31

Viking men often wore a KIRTLE, a long shirt that hung to their knees.

32

Vikings TRADED in Constantinople (now Istanbul, Turkey), with people from AFRICA, ARABIA, AND ASIA.

33

At feasts, Vikings held competitions in WRESTLING, FENCING, and ARCHERY.

34

Vikings built up their STRENGTH by throwing HEAVY ROCKS.

35

Vikings wore ICE SKATES made from ANIMALS' BONES tied to their feet to navigate frozen landscapes.

36

Vikings usually ate BREAKFAST and DINNER, but didn't eat LUNCH.

37

Vikings used HORSES that were the size of today's PONIES.

38

Viking SHIPS had one big sail made from WOOL.

39

At the FRONT END of a Viking ship there was usually a CARVED WOODEN HEAD.

40

Viking BABIES were given THOR HAMMERS as CHARMS.

41

A LONGSHIP had room for from 40 to 60 oarsmen.

42

Vikings TRADED when they needed SUPPLIES, but they also paid for things with GOLD and SILVER COINS, whose value was based on WEIGHT.

43

Vikings had SLAVES, who were often people captured in a VIKING RAID.

44

Viking children played with carved WOODEN DOLLS.

45

Vikings made WHISTLES from the BONES OF BIRDS.

46

When there wasn't wind to SAIL THE SHIP, Vikings ROWED the BOAT.

47

Viking ships COULD SAIL AS FAST AS ten miles an hour (16 km/h)—about as fast as you ride a bike. Sea crossing could take months.

48

The STEERING OAR on a Viking ship was on the right-hand side of the ship. The Norse word for steering board is *stjórnborði*—now known as "starboard."

49

Two Viking ships that were used for FUNERALS were found BURIED in Norway. They are now in a MUSEUM in Oslo.

50

To navigate while at sea, Vikings looked for LANDMARKS on the coast; they also relied on the position of the SUN and STARS.

1 BIOLUMINESCENT ORGANISMS ARE PLANTS, ANIMALS, OR FUNGI THAT **GLOW IN THE DARK.** THE GLOW IS CAUSED BY A **CHEMICAL REACTION** THAT RELEASES ENERGY.

2 VELVET BELLY LANTERNSHARKS WARD OFF DANGER WITH A BIOLUMINESCENT SPINE THAT'S SORT OF LIKE A LIGHT SABER.

3
MICROSCOPIC PLANTS AND ANIMALS THAT **DWELL IN THE OCEAN** PRODUCE BIOLUMINESCENCE WHEN THEIR ENVIRONMENT IS **DISTURBED** BY WAVES AND MOVING BOATS.

4 THE HUMAN BODY GLOWS, BUT THE LIGHT IT GIVES OFF IS TOO WEAK TO BE SEEN BY OUR EYES.

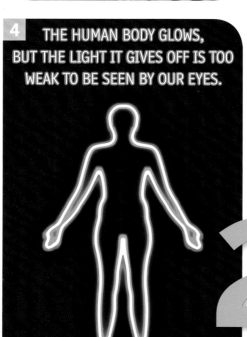

5 **EIGHTY PERCENT** *of the world's glowing organisms* **LIVE IN THE OCEAN.**

6 COMB JELLIES (RELATIVES OF JELLYFISH) **HAVE** MORE BIOLUMINESCENT SPECIES **THAN** ANY OTHER **GROUP OF ANIMALS.**

25 GLOWING FACTS ABOUT

7
PHYTOPLANKTON— TINY PLANT-LIKE ORGANISMS IN THE SEA—PRODUCE A **BLUE GLOW.**

8 Since **VAMPIRE SQUID DON'T HAVE INK**, they squirt out a sticky, **BIOLUMINESCENT MUCUS** to confuse predators. This allows them to make a **QUICK GETAWAY.**

9
The ability to bioluminesce has evolved **MORE THAN 40 TIMES** in bacteria, fungi, sponges, jellyfish, beetles, shrimp, sharks, and more.

10 SCIENTISTS IN SEOUL, SOUTH KOREA, HAVE CREATED CATS AND DOGS THAT **GLOW** RED.

11
Although most marine animals glow blue or green, some flash **PURPLE, RED, PINK, ORANGE, or YELLOW.**

12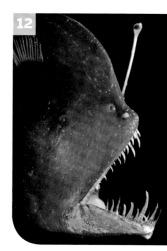
The deep-sea anglerfish **DANGLES AN ILLUMINATED, FLESHY LURE** in front of its mouth to attract prey— then it **GOBBLES THEM WHOLE.**

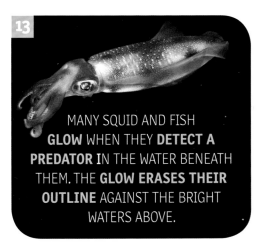

13 MANY SQUID AND FISH **GLOW** WHEN THEY **DETECT A PREDATOR** IN THE WATER BENEATH THEM. THE **GLOW ERASES THEIR OUTLINE** AGAINST THE BRIGHT WATERS ABOVE.

14 FIGHTER-JET PILOTS USE **BIOLUMINESCENT** TRAILS CHURNED UP BY AIRCRAFT CARRIERS IN THE OCEANS BELOW TO FIND THEIR WAY "HOME" AT NIGHT.

15 Scientists at Syracuse University in Syracuse, New York, U.S.A., used the **GLOW FROM FIREFLIES** to create **LIGHTS THAT DON'T NEED ELECTRICITY.**

16 FEMALES OF A CARNIVOROUS FIREFLY SPECIES **MIMIC THE FLASHES** OF ANOTHER SPECIES IN ORDER TO **CATCH DINNER.**

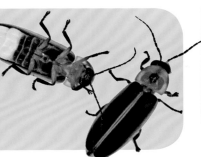

17 **GLOWWORMS** THAT CLING TO THE CEILING OF CAVES IN NEW ZEALAND USE THEIR GLOWING BODIES TO **ATTRACT MOSQUITO-LIKE INSECTS**—AND THEN SNARE THEM WITH STICKY "FISHING LINES" THEY MAKE FROM SILK AND GOBS OF MUCUS.

BIOLUMINESCENCE

18 SOME **POTATO PLANTS** HAVE BEEN GENETICALLY MODIFIED TO GIVE A BIOLUMINESCENT **GLOW** WHEN THEY **NEED TO BE WATERED.**

19 Each day, bioluminescent critters SWIM FROM THE OCEAN SURFACE TO THE DEPTHS and back again as part of the BIGGEST MIGRATION in the world.

20 Scientists **DON'T KNOW WHY** mushrooms glow: Some may **ATTRACT INSECTS** that help spread spores, but others may glow **JUST TO RELEASE HEAT.**

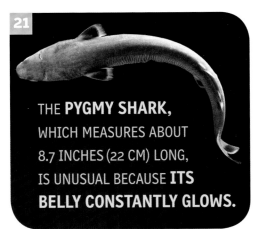

21 THE **PYGMY SHARK,** WHICH MEASURES ABOUT 8.7 INCHES (22 CM) LONG, IS UNUSUAL BECAUSE **ITS BELLY CONSTANTLY GLOWS.**

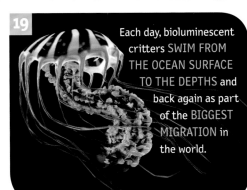

22 SCIENTISTS DISCOVERED SEVEN SPECIES OF MARINE WORMS THAT HAVE **GLOWING "BOMBS,"** OR BULB-LIKE STRUCTURES THAT **BURST WITH A SUDDEN FLASH OF LIGHT.**

23 Scientists have identified 71 different species of **GLOWING MUSHROOMS.**

24 EACH SPECIES OF FIREFLY FLASHES A UNIQUE PATTERN IN ORDER TO ATTRACT MATES OF THE SAME SPECIES.

25 In order to FILM A REAL GIANT SQUID, scientists used a fake squid that FLASHED LIGHT to attract it.

❶ *MINECRAFT*—one of the most popular video games in history—is known as a **"SANDBOX"** game since there is **NO END** and the **USER DECIDES** what to build and construct.

❷ **MINECRAFT STEVE**—the blockhead lead character in the game—is neither **MALE** nor **FEMALE,** according to the game's creator. The character is meant to represent a **HUMAN BEING** with no specific gender.

❸ Some **14,000 PEOPLE** purchase *Minecraft* EVERY DAY—and there are more than **1,000** LOGINS per hour.

❹ There are more than **50 MILLION** *Minecraft* users WORLDWIDE: That's a number larger than the entire POPULATION of **SPAIN.**

❺ *Minecraft*'s creator **MARKUS "NOTCH" PERSSON** wrote an **ADVENTURE GAME** for his father's COMPUTER when he was **EIGHT YEARS OLD.**

❻ An **EARLY VERSION** of *Minecraft* was known as *CAVE GAME,* which PERSSON created in his **SPARE TIME** while working on ANOTHER JOB.

❼ In real life, a *Minecraft* **BRICK** would be about the size of a **DISHWASHER.**

❽ One *MINECRAFT* player has **"WALKED"** 919 miles (1,480 km) on a **THREE-YEAR JOURNEY** in the game. That's like walking from **NEW YORK** to FLORIDA, U.S.A.

MINECRAFT

Minecraft Steve

9 Through its **BLOCK BY BLOCK** program, the UNITED NATIONS has used *Minecraft* to DIGITALLY REIMAGINE run-down areas around the world, like parks and neighborhoods.

10 It took just **50 MINUTES** for an Australian man to build a *Minecraft* tunnel with 10,502 BLOCKS—setting the mark for the **LONGEST TUNNEL** ever recorded in the game.

11 More than 3,000 schools in over **40 COUNTRIES** are using *MinecraftEdu*, an educational version of the game that teaches about subjects like **GEOGRAPHY** and **ART.**

12 An AUSTRIAN GAMER once spent 24 HOURS, 10 MINUTES playing *MINECRAFT* without **STOPPING**—the LONGEST anyone's ever played the game.

13 *Minecraft* has won the GOLDEN JOYSTICK award for the best **DOWNLOADABLE** game.

14 **YOUTUBE** videos of *Minecraft* users navigating the game are among the **MOST VIEWED** clips worldwide, some snagging up to **30 MILLION** hits per **WEEK.**

15 *Minecraft* players have **RE-CREATED** famous landmarks like the **HOGWARTS SCHOOL** from the *Harry Potter* movies, and **DISNEYLAND,** complete with **WORKING RIDES.**

75 GRAND FACTS ABOUT TINY THINGS

1 The smallest remote-controlled helicopter is about the size of two U.S. quarters side-by-side.

2 PhinDeli Town Buford, the official name of a town in Wyoming, U.S.A., is considered the world's least populated town. It has one resident.

3 Pygmy elephants living in Borneo are tiny by elephant standards. Standing about eight feet tall (2.4 m), they are the smallest elephants, but they boast extra long ears and tails.

4 A man once made a tiny sculpture of the Empire State Building out of a single toothpick!

5 The smallest car that is legally allowed to drive on U.S. roadways is two feet (0.6 m) high, four feet (1.2 m) long. It seats one.

6 THE SHORTEST FULL-GROWN DOG STANDS 3.8 INCHES (9.7 cm) TALL—AS TALL AS A COFFEE MUG!

7 Not only is Vatican City the smallest country in the world, it has the lowest population of any country: Only about 800 people live there.

8 A Planck is the smallest unit of time—it's the amount of time it takes light to travel, in a vacuum, across the smallest distance, called a Planck length.

9 A microbe found in hydrothermal vents on the seafloor off of Iceland is considered the world's smallest organism. Its cells are 400 nanometers across. (A nanometer is one billionth of a meter.)

10 The smallest bones in the human body are those of the inner ear: the incus, malleus, and stapes.

11 Romania has the smallest paper money of any country—the 10-bani note is about one-tenth the size of a U.S. dollar.

12 The bumblebee bat is only about one inch (2.5 cm) long—the size of a large bumblebee!

13 *National Geographic Kids* set a record for the world's smallest magazine cover. It is so small that 2,000 magazine covers could fit on a single grain of salt!

14 A Chinese puzzle-making company once made a 1,000-piece jigsaw puzzle that was smaller than a piece of notebook paper.

15 THE BILL AND TAIL OF THE BEE HUMMINGBIRD— THE WORLD'S SMALLEST BIRD—MAKE UP HALF ITS BODY LENGTH, WHICH IS ABOUT TWO INCHES (5 CM).

16 Not all dinosaurs were huge: *Microraptor zhaoianus* is considered the smallest non-avian bird found. It was just 2.5 feet (0.8 m) long.

17 A MOVIE THEATER IN GERMANY HAS JUST NINE SEATS!

18 The Hoffman's dwarf centipede has 41 pairs of legs but is less than half an inch (1.3 cm) long.

19 Most hummingbird nests are about the size of a walnut shell.

20 A 570-SQUARE-FOOT (53-SQ-M) HOTEL IN GERMANY CAN ACCOMMODATE ONLY TWO GUESTS AT A TIME.

21 A Russian man made a fully functional Rubik's Cube that was about half the size of a nickel!

22 British scientists created the world's smallest snowman, which was only ten micrometers (ten millionths of a meter) across. They etched on eyes, a nose, and a mouth with an ion beam.

23 The smallest stars—neutron stars—have three times the mass of our sun but have a diameter of only 6 to 19 miles (10 to 31 km).

24 The Atacama Desert in Chile is considered the world's smallest desert with an area of 40,600 square miles (105,200 sq km). It's also considered the driest place on Earth.

25 U.K. scientists created a Christmas card so small that 8,276 of the cards could fit on one postage stamp.

26 THE WORLD'S SMALLEST FROG IS THE SIZE OF A HORSEFLY.

27 The common octopus is the size of a flea when it is born.

28 A German man once made a map of the Western Hemisphere from atoms. Its width is one-fiftieth the thickness of a human hair.

29 Finger Twister is just like the real game of Twister but miniature. You play with your fingers on a board, not your hands and feet.

30 The Irukandji jellyfish is small but deadly. It's just one inch (2.5 cm) across, but its sting is poisonous.

31 The pygmy mouse lemur is among the smallest primates in the world— its head and body are less than 2.5 inches long (6 cm), but its tail is twice that length.

32 When born, grizzly bear cubs only weigh as much as four sticks of butter!

33 A dust mite is a mere 0.008 inches (0.2 mm) long, but the average bed has up to 1.5 million dust mites living on it.

34 The royal antelope—the world's smallest antelope—lives in the rain forest of West Africa and stands the same height as a jug of milk.

35 Scientists created what's called "the world's smallest movie"—a 93-second animation entirely made out of individual atoms moving around that depict a boy playing.

36 Pygmy three-toed sloths, found in Panama, are about 40 percent smaller than their mainland relatives.

37 Pygmy goats are about 15 inches (38 cm) shorter than regular goats and are sometimes kept as pets.

38 A TV commercial advertising a Canadian music and video TV channel lasted all of 1/60th of a second.

39 The elf owl, which stands just five inches (13 cm) tall, will play dead if it's captured.

40 The smallest blood vessels in the human body are capillaries, which connect veins and arteries. They are a fiftieth as thin as a baby's hair.

41 Ebenezer Place, a street in Wick, Caithness, Scotland, is the world's shortest street at just 6.75 feet (2.06 m) long.

42 The word "eunoia" is the shortest word in the English language that contains the five major vowels. It means "beautiful thinking."

43 Fennec foxes are the world's smallest foxes but have giant bat-like ears that keep them cool in the desert heat.

44 King Louis XIX of France had a very short reign as French monarch in 1830. He was king for a total of 20 minutes.

45 A NEW ZEALAND MAN USED A 3-D PRINTER TO MAKE A WORKABLE HAND DRILL THE SIZE OF HIS THUMBNAIL.

46 German scientists have created an engine that is less than a micrometer (1 millionth of a meter) in length that can run on a single atom.

47 The pink fairy armadillo—the smallest armadillo—is the size of a soda can.

48 The blue whale is the largest animal to have ever lived on Earth, but its main food source, krill, is just 2.4 inches (6 cm) long. It eats up to four tons (3.6 MT) of krill per day!

49 Krill may be the length of two paperclips, but it is estimated that the total weight of all the Antarctic krill in the oceans is more than the weight of all the humans on Earth.

50 The shortest acceptance speech made by an actor winning the Oscar at the Academy Awards was just six words spoken by Joe Pesci: "Well, it's my privilege. Thank you."

51 THE WORLD'S SMALLEST VOLCANO—FOUND IN COLOMBIA—IS ABOUT AN INCH (2.5 CM) TALL!

52 Researchers are designing easy-to-carry drones small enough to fit in a firefighter's pocket to help get into small places to aid in search and rescue.

53 The smallest salamander living in the U.S. is about the size of a quarter and doesn't have any lungs!

54 Canadian scientists made a book so small that it can only be read with an electron microscope. It tells the story of "Teeny Ted" winning a turnip contest.

55 The smallest organ in the human body is the pineal gland, located near the center of the brain. It produces a hormone that affects how you sleep and wake up.

56 Little blue penguins, also called fairy penguins, are the smallest penguin species. Standing a little over one foot high (30 cm), they get their name from their indigo blue feathers.

57 An artist and scientist collaborated to sculpt the smallest human figure—made of polymer, which are molecules strung together to form chains—that is as tall as a sheet of paper is thick!

58 A designated park in Portland, Oregon, U.S.A., is about the size of a large truck tire and sits in the middle of a busy street. It contains a tree and some small plants.

59 The Admiral Dot Miniature Gallery in Oakland, California, U.S.A., displays tiny art that must be observed with a magnifying glass.

60 Monaco is the world's third smallest country but has the most millionaires in relation to the number of people living there.

61 A Brazilian man chips away at pencils to make tiny sculptures, like of Elvis wearing sunglasses, out of the graphite that stand on the pencils' tips.

62 A British artist who makes microscopic models out of individual grains of sand has to hold his breath while he works. One exhale could destroy everything!

63 The world's smallest snake is half as long as a pencil and as skinny as a spaghetti noodle.

64 An artist spent 2,000 hours making a perfectly scaled-down model of Manhattan, New York, U.S.A., out of balsa wood that, when finished, wasn't much bigger than a doormat.

65 The world's smallest bone china tea set, made to celebrate the Queen of England's 60-year reign, is so small that the cup and saucer can balance on a person's fingertip.

66 Instead of "It's a Small World," Walt Disney planned on calling the famous park ride "Children of the World."

67 IN TERMS OF VOLUME, YOU COULD FIT 24,462 MERCURY PLANETS—THE SMALLEST PLANET IN OUR SOLAR SYSTEM —INSIDE JUPITER, OUR LARGEST.

68 At birth, a koala bear is about the size of a bee.

69 The shortest movie ever nominated for an Academy Award was called *Fresh Guacamole* and lasted 100 seconds.

70 What's considered the world's shortest airline flight—between islands in northern Scotland—lasts only 47 seconds!

71 Minifigures—also known as Lego people—measure exactly four bricks high (without a hat).

72 A woman in Azerbaijan has a collection of 2,913 miniature books— all under 2.75 inches (7 cm) high.

73 A kishu, a tiny variety of mandarin orange, is smaller than a golf ball.

74 *Tinkerbella nana*, also known as Tinkerbell fairyfly, is just 0.00984 inches (0.25 mm) long, one of Earth's smallest insects.

75 "Teacup" dogs are extra small dogs of traditional breeds—like poodles, Chihuahuas, and terriers.

35 FACTS ABOUT MAGNETISM

1 Magnetism is a FORCE that repels or attracts OBJECTS that are usually made of metal.

2 Every magnet has two poles—a NORTH and SOUTH pole.

3 Earth has its own magnetic field, which protects our PLANET from damaging COSMIC RAYS that stream through space.

4 The area around a magnet can ACT like a force field. Its STRENGTH varies depending on how close the object is to the field.

5 Lodestone is a rock with magnetic properties. It was used as a compass to show ANCIENT TRAVELERS the way.

6 Nickel, cobalt, and IRON are the most COMMON magnetic metals.

7 You can FIND magnets in computers, TVs, fans, and washing machines.

8 The word "magnetism" comes from a region in ASIA MINOR called MAGNESIA where a type of magnetic iron ore is found.

9 William Gilbert, a doctor to QUEEN ELIZABETH I of Britain, is considered the FATHER of the science of magnetism for his EXPERIMENTS with magnets.

10 Homing PIGEONS have magnetite in their BEAKS. It helps them NAVIGATE because they can sense Earth's magnetic field.

11 JUPITER has the strongest magnetic FIELD of all the planets. Its METALLIC hydrogen core gives it a magnetic field 19,000 times stronger than Earth's.

12 Since magnets always have two DIFFERENT poles, they are called DIPOLAR.

13 Some early PHILOSOPHERS thought that lodestone, which moved on its own due to its magnetic properties, POSSESSED A SOUL.

14 Small flecks of IRON DUST are mixed into PAINT to make magnetic paint.

15 Some ROLLER COASTERS use magnetic BRAKES.

16 The CHINESE used the first compasses in SHIP NAVIGATION during the Song dynasty (960–1279). The technology was adopted by MIDDLE EASTERN and EUROPEAN sailors.

17 Earth has a SOLID inner core of iron that is about the size of the MOON. It has an OUTER core made of LIQUID iron. The total size of the core is about the size of MARS.

THAT STICK

18 To play **VINYL RECORDS** with little distortion, the McIntosh MT5 turntable uses **MAGNETS** so that the platter that plays the records floats on a cushion of air.

19 Magnetic fields are measured in **TESLA UNITS.** These units were named after the Serbian-American inventor Nikola Tesla, who invented an alternating current motor.

20 Electric currents can produce magnetic fields when **ELECTRICITY** is passed through a **COIL OF WIRE.** When the electric power is off there is no magnetic field.

21 A 29-inch (74-cm)-tall **MAGNETIC SCULPTURE** of the **GOLDEN GLOBE AWARD** was created in a Los Angeles, California, U.S.A., hotel in 2011.

22 Your brain has a very **WEAK** magnetic field. Scientists can measure it using a magnetoencephalogram, or **MEG,** which maps brain activity.

23 In 1928 a German engineer named Fritz Pfleumer patented magnetic tape, which could be use to **RECORD SOUND.**

24 Magnetic fields can't be **SEEN OR TOUCHED.**

25 Junkyards use superstrong magnets to lift **OLD CARS** and other **SCRAP METAL** off the ground.

26 The **MILKY WAY** has its own magnetic field, but don't worry, it won't sweep you away. The **GALAXY'S** magnetic field is about one-hundredth of a refrigerator magnet's.

27 A magnetic resonance imaging (MRI) scanner contains a strong magnet. It uses a **MAGNETIC FIELD AND RADIO WAVES** to see inside your body.

28 Scientists at the University of California, Berkeley, created a 3-foot (0.9-m)-long magnet that is 300,000 times as strong as **EARTH'S MAGNETIC FIELD.**

29 **MAGLEV TRAINS** use the power of electromagnetism to **ELEVATE** the train above the tracks, which cuts down on friction and allows the train to travel faster.

30 Marvel Comics' Magneto can **INCREASE HIS STRENGTH** through electromagnetism and shape magnetic fields to move metals.

31 **HEATING** a magnet can destroy its magnetic properties but **COOLING** it won't.

32 Designers have created magnetic **"ZUBITS,"** which attach to your shoelaces so you never have to lace them again. They snap into place, taking the place of the bow.

33 Computer **HARD DRIVES** use magnets to store all of your pictures, movies, documents, and files.

34 **VOLVO ENGINEERING** has created a road with magnets that could be used to control **SELF-DRIVING** cars traveling at speeds of 90 miles an hour (145 km/h).

35 **"MAGNETIC ATTRACTION"** is the pulling power that brings things together, including people with similar tastes, thoughts, and beliefs.

1. Soccer balls were once made out of inflated pigs' bladders wrapped in leather. 2. More than 2,000 years ago, soldiers in China played an early version of soccer. 3. The ancient Maya played a soccer-like game with rubber balls called *pok-ta-pok.* 4. In medieval England, players kicked around a leather-covered glass bottle filled with cork shavings—helping it float if it fell in the river. 5. In eighth-century England, hundreds of people would gather to play "mob football"—a no-rules game similar to soccer that could last all day. 6. To combat the violence brought on by mob football, the British monarchy passed laws that would imprison anyone caught playing. 7. The name "soccer" came from Brits calling the sport "association football"—"soc" coming from "association." 8. Soccer is known as "football" or "footie" in most countries. 9. The first set of official soccer rules were created at Cambridge University in the U.K. in 1848. 10. A handwritten soccer rules book, penned in 1857, sold at auction for $1.42 million. 11. Whistles were introduced in the game in 1878. Before that, referees used handkerchiefs or sticks or shouted to make calls. 12. London's oldest professional football club, Fulham F.C., formed in 1879. 13. King Henry VIII—who reigned over England from 1509 to 1547—had "football boots," or soccer shoes, made by his personal shoemaker. 14. Rugby originated from soccer—the main differences being that you could carry the ball and use your hands. 15. Soccer goalkeepers are allowed to touch the ball with their hands or arms—all other players must use their feet or head only. 16. The FIFA World Cup, the soccer championships held every four years, is the biggest sporting event on the planet. 17. The first World Cup, in 1930, welcomed 13 countries. Today, 32 countries meet up every four years. 18. The United States won the first ever women's World Cup held in 1991. 19. A total of 3,429,873 fans attended the 64 matches held during the 2014 World Cup. That's about half the population of host city Rio de Janeiro. 20. 173,850 people attended the 1950 World Cup final in Brazil—the highest attendance of any soccer match ever. 21. Germany has appeared in a record-setting eight World Cup Finals. They've won four. 22. Goalkeepers wear different color uniforms than their teammates to stand out against opposing players on the field. 23. Two teams once went head-to-head for more than 40 hours during a marathon indoor soccer game in Cochrane, Canada. 24. Table soccer—also known as foosball—was first played in Europe during the 1920s. 25. The world's longest foosball table extends the length of two soccer fields, and can accommodate over 330 players. 26. More than 3,000 soccer balls were used during the 2014 World Cup. 27. Most soccer players run a total of about seven miles (11.3 km) per match. 28. A soccer ball weighs a little more than a full

GOOOOAL!
100 SOCCER FACTS THAT SCORE

A player makes an overhead kick.

can of soda. **29.** **The mascot for the 2014 World Cup was an armadillo named Fuleco.** **30.** Russia and Qatar will host the next two men's World Cups, in 2018 and 2022, respectively. **31.** Scoring three goals in one match is known as a hat trick. **32.** László Kiss, a pro player from El Salvador, scored a hat trick in just seven minutes during a 1982 match. **33.** The Australian men's national team goes by the nickname the "Socceroos." **34.** After the Cameroon men's team beat Spain to win the gold medal at the 2000 Olympics, the country's president declared a national holiday to celebrate. **35.** In soccer, a tackle means to take a ball from another player with your feet. **36.** Soccer is sometimes referred to as "the beautiful game." **37.** Argentinian soccer star Lionel Messi is said to be worth more than $261 million, making him the most valuable athlete in the world. **38.** In 2012, Messi scored 91 goals in one season, a record for the most scores in a calendar year. **39.** In most countries, a soccer player's uniform is called a kit and cleats are called hooves. **40.** The Inuit—indigenous people in the Arctic—once played a game where they'd boot a heavy ball stuffed with grass, caribou hair, and moss across the tundra. **41.** Soccer balls have remained basically the same size and shape for the past 120 years. **42.** An Iranian man once juggled a soccer ball with his feet for 30 hours nonstop—setting a new world record. **43.** Soccer and water polo were the first team sports added to the Olympics in 1900. **44.** Women's soccer joined the Olympic lineup in 1996. **45.** U.S. national team head coach Jürgen Klinsmann is also a helicopter pilot. **46.** In 2013, a Bosnian player named Asmir Begovic scored a goal from 301 feet, 6 inches (91.1 m) away—the longest goal scored in soccer. **47.** A record-setting crowd of 2,149 once simultaneously dribbled soccer balls for ten minutes in four cities across the U.S. **48.** Just two men have won the FIFA World Cup as both player and coach: Brazilian Mário Zagallo and German Franz Beckenbauer. **49.** A Belgian professional soccer team signed a 20-month-old boy to their roster in 2013. **50.** The oldest athlete to play in a men's World Cup was 43 years old. The youngest? 17. **51.** American superstar Mia Hamm began her international career at the age of 15—making her the youngest woman to play for the U.S. at the time. **52.** A building at the Nike headquarters in Beaverton, Oregon, U.S.A., is named after Mia Hamm. **53.** The United States' player Abby Wambach has more than 160 career international goals—the most international goals ever scored by a male or female player. **54.** Many Brazilian soccer stars—like Pelé and Ronaldo—are so famous, they go by only one name. **55.** Pelé scored 1,281 goals in his 20-year-long career, the most ever of any soccer player. **56.** The penalty card system in soccer was inspired by a traffic light: Yellow means caution or a warning; red means stop, or an ejection. **57.** You may get a yellow card if a referee thinks you're faking an injury. **58.** In 1966, a dog named Pickles found a stolen World Cup trophy in London—and received a cash reward for sniffing it out. **59.** Brazil is the only country to qualify for the World Cup all 16 times it has been held. They've won 5 times. **60.** Brazil has never won a World Cup on their home turf. **61.** The United States' team is the only team to reach the semifinals in every Women's World Cup. **62.** The 2014 World Cup was the first to use goal-line technology, including computers to help referees make calls. **63.** When a goal is scored in a World Cup game, a special watch worn by the referees displays the word "goal." **64.** Some pro players are able to shoot at speeds of more than 74 miles an hour (120 km/h)— faster than a speeding car. **65.** In 1937, the BBC aired portions of a soccer match between two English soccer teams—the first game ever to be televised. **66.** More than one billion people watched the 2014 World Cup Final between Germany and Argentina. **67.** Soccer became a popular sport for British women during World War I. **68.** The Japan women's national soccer team is known as Nadeshiko, which means "beautiful flower" in Japanese. **69.** Bicycle kicks, headers, banana kicks, booters, and scissor kicks are all soccer skills. **70.** Using 40,781 balloons, artists created a four-story-tall sculpture of soccer players heading a ball into a goal. **71.** The Australian national soccer team once beat American Samoa 31–0, the largest margin of victory in an international match. **72.** A ten-year-old girl once "juggled" a soccer ball for 5,000 toe touches without letting the ball hit the ground. **73.** The original World Cup trophy was made of papier-mâché until it was destroyed by heavy rains in 1951. **74.** The FIFA's Women's World Cup trophy, made of pure silver covered with 23-carat gold, is worth about $30,000. **75.** U.S. pro player Michael Bradley played for his father, coach Bob Bradley, during the 2010 FIFA World Cup. **76.** American soccer star Clint Dempsey once recorded a rap album. **77.** North Korea's Rungrado May Day Stadium, which can seat 150,000 people, is considered the biggest soccer arena in the world. **78.** The entire Congo national soccer team was reportedly killed by lightning during a game in 1998 . **79.** Italian player Giuseppe Meazza's shorts fell off when he was taking a penalty shot in a semifinal match in the 1938 World Cup. **80.** A scientist has created a soccer ball grown from pig bladder cells in his lab. **81.** Nearly half of the world's soccer balls are made in one city in Pakistan. **82.** In 2013, the U.S. men's soccer team defeated Costa Rica during a match held in a driving snow storm. **83.** From 2002 to 2011, Portuguese soccer coach José Mourinho's teams won every match they played at home—a total of 150 wins. **84.** The U.S. women's team has more World Cup points than any other country's in the world. **85.** Some 30 percent of American households have at least one member who plays soccer. **86.** The number of youth soccer players in the United States has doubled, to 4.04 million players, since 1990. **87.** With about 24.5 million kids playing nationwide, soccer is the second most popular youth sport in the U.S., behind basketball. **88.** India recently launched the Indian Super League, a brand-new professional soccer organization. **89.** Recep Tayyip Erdogan, the president of Turkey, once played professional soccer. **90.** In hot conditions, soccer players may lose enough sweat to almost fill up a gallon jug. **91.** Stoke City Football Club in the U.K. has a light blue hippopotamus for a mascot. **92.** Bosnia and Herzegovina, which played its first World Cup in 2014, went by the nickname "Humanitarian Stars." **93.** A "cap" in soccer refers to how many international matches a player has partaken in. **94.** American soccer player Kristine Lilly collected a record-setting 352 caps throughout her career. **95.** Kristine Lilly is also the only woman to play in five Women's World Cups. **96.** In 2005, female Mexican soccer star Maribel Domínguez signed a contract with a men's professional team but was not allowed to play. **97.** When a ball is not moving during a match, it's known as a "dead ball." **98.** There are no zeroes in soccer. When the score is 3–0, you say, "three nil." **99.** A bank in Doha, Qatar, created a soccer ball taller than two giraffes stacked on top of each another. **100.** A British man once bounced a soccer ball off of his mouth for a consecutive 158 times in 2012.

1

The first cereal was invented in the 1800s and was called **GRANULA**.

2

According to cereal mascot Cap'n Crunch's uniform, he is **NOT** a captain. He is a **COMMANDER**.

3

Dr. Alexander Anderson discovered puffed rice when he experimented with **EXPLODING SEEDS**—Quaker Oats later sold it as "the food shot from guns."

4

A cereal from the 1980s called **FRUITY YUMMY MUMMY** had the tagline "Fruity Yummy Mummy makes your tummy go yummy! Heh, heh, heh!"

5

Huitlacoche, corn covered in **GRAY FUNGUS**, is a nutritious gourmet breakfast item in Mexico.

6

A typical breakfast for a **NASA ASTRONAUT** on the space shuttle includes coffee, granola, a breakfast roll, and a pear.

7

Many zoos offer programs where visitors can enter before the zoo opens and eat breakfast **WITH THE ANIMALS**.

8

A cereal from the 1970s was called **FREAKIES**.

9

You can **DRIVE THROUGH** a **GIANT DOUGHNUT** at a shop in California, U.S.A., called the Donut Hole.

10

SUGARCRISP was the first cereal to have a cartoon commercial. It featured three mascot bears named **DANDY, HANDY**, and **CANDY**.

11

Nicknames for coffee include **JOE, JAVA, ROCKET FUEL**, and **MUD**.

12

Breakfast literally means to "**BREAK** the **FAST**" since it is the first meal after sleeping.

13

The first Lucky Charms mascot **WALDO THE WIZARD** had the catchphrase "**IBBLEDEBIBBLE DELICIOUS**."

14

Mascot **BIG MIXX** of Big Mixx cereal was part rooster, part pig, part moose, and part wolf.

15

When doughnuts first appeared in New Amsterdam they were called *olykoeks*, which means "**OILY CAKES**" in Dutch.

16

In Hong Kong, one popular breakfast is porridge with a **WHOLE CRAB** in it.

17

Studies show that students who eat breakfast do **BETTER IN SCHOOL** than those who skip a morning meal.

18

It takes about **FOUR** oranges to make one glass of **FRESHLY SQUEEZED** orange juice.

50 BREAKFAST
FACTS TO START
YOUR DAY WITH

19
A Denny's in New York City sells a "GRAND SLAM" for $300. It comes with EGGS, SAUSAGE, BACON, PANCAKES, and champagne.

20
The QUEEN OF ENGLAND typically has a simple breakfast: cereal, dried fruit, and macadamia nuts.

21
The public can make reservations to have breakfast at the WHITE HOUSE. It happens one weekend out of every month.

22
Taco Bell sells a WAFFLE TACO: scrambled eggs, cheese, and bacon or sausage wrapped inside a waffle.

23
Dunkin' Donuts sells a GLAZED DONUT breakfast sandwich with bacon and egg sandwiched between two halves of a doughnut.

24
McDonald's Big Breakfast with hotcakes and a large biscuit packs as many calories and grams of fat as HALF A PEPPERONI PIZZA.

25
SCRAPPLE, a breakfast food made from pork scraps, cornmeal, and spices molded together in a loaf, dates back to 16TH-CENTURY GERMANY.

26
Some called it a NATIONAL TRAGEDY when a flood caused a shortage of Eggo frozen waffles in 2009. Kellogg's had to ration the item to stores across the U.S.

27
The waffle's history can be traced back to the STONE AGE when cakes of cereal were cooked on hot stones.

28
In Spain, fried sticks of dough called CHURROS are a popular breakfast item. They are typically eaten with (and dunked into) a warm, thick chocolate drink.

29
Michael Phelps's TYPICAL BREAKFAST was often 3 fried egg sandwiches with cheese, lettuce, tomato, fried onions, and mayonnaise, an omelet, grits, toast, and pancakes.

30
Retired basketball player Shaquille O'Neal likes an egg white omelet and FRESH ORANGE JUICE for breakfast. He has never tried coffee.

31
A bright GREEN SMOOTHIE can be made with Granny Smith apples, avocado, and spinach or kale.

32
The world's LARGEST STACK OF PANCAKES was made out of 242 pancakes and measured 2 feet 11 inches (89 cm) high.

33
Breakfast is SERIOUS in Van, a city in eastern Turkey. People line up at popular breakfast-only restaurants for a spread of breads, olives, eggs, cheese, honey, and tea.

34
In 2013 a French pastry chef named Dominique Ansel invented a pastry called the CRONUT. Like the word, the pastry is a combination of a croissant and doughnut.

35
A CREEPY CLOWN named KRINKLES was a mascot for a cereal from the 1960s called Sugar Krinkles.

36
In Scotland, KIPPERS— smoked herring—are often eaten for breakfast, along with porridge.

37
Americans spend more than $7 BILLION on cereal each year.

38
Many people like eating cold pizza for breakfast, but some Domino's Pizza outlets produce hot BREAKFAST PIZZA with ham, egg, and cheese topping.

39
February 9 is NATIONAL BAGEL DAY in the United States.

40
It takes 12 MINUTES for the average American to eat breakfast.

41
Throughout Latin America, many children have COFFEE and milk with their breakfast.

42
U.S. president Calvin Coolidge ate breakfast in bed while having PETROLEUM JELLY rubbed into his head.

43
A cereal called GRINS & SMILES & GIGGLES & LAUGHS said it came out of a computer monster named Cecil when his funny bone was tickled.

44
388 people in China had BREAKFAST IN BED together for charity in 2014.

45
French toast is NOT actually FRENCH. It originated across medieval Europe at the same time, and there are records of the dish in France, Spain, and Germany.

46
It is AGAINST THE LAW to eat a breakfast sandwich while driving in Nova Scotia, Canada.

47
A typical breakfast for an elephant at the zoo is 6.5 pounds (3 kg) of BRAN mixed with water.

48
A traditional Japanese breakfast is miso soup, rice, and side dishes that include FISH, EGG, SEAWEED, and PICKLED VEGETABLES.

49
Before the 1970s, BAGELS were transported on ropes or string around New York City.

50
In 1971 the dye in pink Franken Berry cereal caused children to have PINK POOP.

1 In 1810, Robert Stewart, a **FUR TRADER** living at Fort Astoria in western Oregon, became the **FIRST PERSON** to use what is now the Oregon Trail.

2

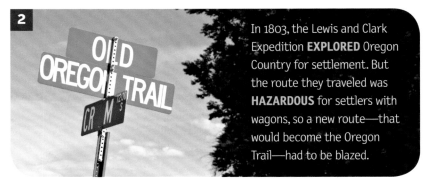

3 It took Robert Stewart **TEN MONTHS** to travel the 2,000 MILES (3,219 km) from Fort Astoria to **ST. LOUIS, MISSOURI.**

In 1803, the Lewis and Clark Expedition **EXPLORED** Oregon Country for settlement. But the route they traveled was **HAZARDOUS** for settlers with wagons, so a new route—that would become the Oregon Trail—had to be blazed.

4 In 1836, a **FAMILY MADE THE OREGON TRAIL TREK** by wagon. The wagons were **ABANDONED** 200 miles (322 km) **BEFORE THE END** because of rough trail.

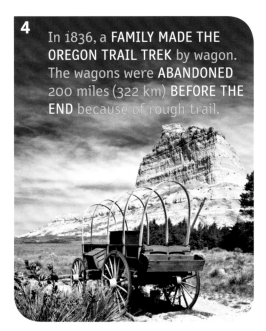

5 IN 1843, A **WAGON TRAIN**, MEANING A CARAVAN OF WAGONS, OF 1,000 PEOPLE TRAVELED FROM MISSOURI TO OREGON. THEIR JOURNEY BECAME KNOWN AS THE GREAT MIGRATION.

6 The Oregon Trail, which extended from Independence, Missouri, to Oregon City, near present-day Portland, was **ONE OF TWO MAIN ROUTES** to the **AMERICAN WEST**. (The second was the southerly Santa Fe Trail, used mostly for trade with northern Mexico.)

7 Since 1818, Britain and the United States had **JOINT OCCUPATION** of Oregon country, but settlers on the Oregon Trail created **PRESSURE** for it to become American, which it did under a 1846 treaty.

USA 29
Oregon Trail
1843-1993

8

BY **1846**, THOUSANDS OF PEOPLE HAD MADE THE LONG, DANGEROUS JOURNEY ACROSS THE OREGON TRAIL TO GAIN CHEAP LAND AND A BETTER LIFE.

25

9 The **BEST TIME** of year to leave Missouri for the treacherous four-month trek west was **APRIL OR MAY**—right after the **SPRING SNOW**. This allowed pioneers to reach their destination before an **EARLY FALL** snow.

10 MANY FAMILIES HEADED WEST **OVERLOADED** THEIR WAGONS AND HAD TO **DUMP SUPPLIES**—LIKE TOOLS, GUNS, FOOD, AND EVEN PRIZED **PIANOS**—BY THE SIDE OF THE TRAIL.

11 The Oregon Trail crossed through **TERRITORIES** occupied by **NATIVE AMERICANS,** who were usually **TOLERANT** of the **WAGON TRAINS.**

12 The Oregon Trail started in **INDEPENDENCE, Missouri,** because many travelers had arrived in nearby St. Louis by **STEAMSHIPS** from the eastern United States.

13 Just like today's truck stops, FORTS AND SETTLEMENTS WERE SET UP ALONG THE OREGON TRAIL TO OFFER SUPPLIES TO TRAVELERS.

14 Travelers helped out other settlers by leaving **MARKERS** along the trail and **WARNINGS** like "contaminated water." Messages were written on paper, painted on trees and rocks, and even carved in skulls!

15 Among the biggest _____ along the Oregon Trail were long stretches—sometimes 50 miles (80 km)—without SOURCES OF WATER.

16 About 10 percent of pioneers attempting the trip died—often from illness or injury.

17 Pioneers on the trail **COVERED AN AVERAGE 15 TO 20 MILES (24 TO 32 KM) PER DAY**—a snail's pace compared to today, where you can travel three times that far in a car in one hour on a highway.

18 A COMMON DELAY along the trail was **FLOODING**, when streams and rivers became too deep and wide to cross. Travelers had no choice but to wait.

19 People who **DIDN'T HAVE WAGONS** sometimes traveled with a **HANDCART**, which had two big wheels, a platform for carrying things, and handles for people to pull it.

ENDURING FACTS ABOUT THE OREGON TRAIL

20 TRAVELERS **HUNTED BUFFALO** AND **SMALL ANIMALS,** AND ALSO **PICKED WILD BERRIES.**

21 In the early years of the Oregon Trail, pioneers **HIRED A TRAPPER** to help guide them. Later, the trail was sufficiently **WORN** and **WELL MARKED** that a guide wasn't needed.

22 More than 2,000 miles (3,219 km) of **TRAILS AND GROOVES** left by pioneers can **STILL BE SEEN** along the Oregon National Historic Trail today.

23 **MILK COWS** were brought along to walk the trail and provided **FRESH MILK.** Milk in the wagon was churned to butter by the **CONSTANT BUMPS** in the wagon!

24  Pioneers used oxen to pull their wagons instead of horses because they needed less food, could pull heavier loads, and were not desired by thieves or Plains Indians.

25 *The Oregon Trail* video game that was popular **25 years ago** can now be played online. Players face the same trials as **pioneers.**

1 **TIDE POOLS** are like windows to the ocean's floor. They are made during **LOW TIDE** when shallow pools of water form in rocky shores—life usually found at the bottom of the ocean can be seen.

2 **ADULT SUNFLOWER SEA STARS** use their 15,000 **TUBE FEET**—like tiny suction cups—to get around and catch **PREY.**

3 **MARINE SNAILS** like the **WAVY TURBAN** and **PERIWINKLE** species have **GILLS** instead of lungs.

4 Tide pool creatures have special features to cope with the tough environment. Crabs can **GROW** a new **CLAW** and mussels, limpets, and barnacles can **STICK TO ROCK.**

5 **SEA ANEMONES** in Southern California, U.S.A., reproduce by **CLONING** themselves. To do this, each one can split in half and become **TWO ANEMONES.**

6 **SANDCASTLE WORMS** create a glue-like cement to build "sand castles" in a honeycomb pattern.

7 The **GIANT KEYHOLE LIMPET** poops through a hole in the center of its **VOLCANO-LIKE** body.

8 The colorful Spanish shawl **SEA SLUG** eats animals with **STINGING CELLS** and then uses **THOSE STINGERS** for its own protection.

TIDE POOL CREATURES

9 The **GLUE** created by **ACORN BARNACLES** is strong enough to keep them attached to rocks, ships, and other hard surfaces. Scientists have been studying this substance to improve **DENTAL GLUE.**

10 Most anemones are **IMMOBILE** but, when necessary, the **APPLE ANEMONE** can **MOVE** around by stretching, swaying, and moving its tentacles.

11 Up to **20 WORMS** live in spaces along a **BAT STAR'S** arm. The worms snack on leftovers from the bat star's meals.

12 **SOME MUSSELS** can live for up to **50 YEARS.**

13 Tunicates, or **SEA SQUIRTS,** look like long, **RUBBERY TUBES.** Water squirts out of the top of one tube as they eat algae and bacteria through the other.

14 A **MAGNET** can pick up a **GUMBOOT CHITON**—the largest of the 650 species of these oval, shelled, simple animals—because of the mineral magnetite in its **TEETH.**

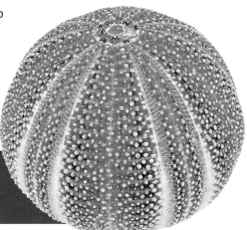

15 When a **SEA URCHIN** dies all of its **SPINES FALL OFF.**

1 Elephants are pachyderms—a word with Greek origins meaning "thick skinned."

2 Rhinos, tapirs, horses, hippos, and pigs are also classified as pachyderms.

3 An elephant's skin can be thicker than five smartphones stacked on top of one another.

4 AFRICAN ELEPHANTS ARE BIGGER THAN INDIAN ELEPHANTS AND HAVE BIGGER EARS AND TUSKS.

5 Elephants don't sweat. Instead, they keep cool—and keep their skin protected from the sun—by coating themselves with dirt and mud.

6 Female elephants are called cows and males are known as bulls, and a baby is called a calf.

7 Male African elephants continue to grow throughout their lives.

8 An African elephant can knock down a tree in seconds and will then chomp on its leaves and fruit.

9 Because of their thick skin and size, healthy adult elephants have no natural predators.

10 In South Africa, elephants are being trained to use their trunks to sniff out bombs and land mines.

11 Elephants are known to mourn the loss of a fellow herd member.

12 Elephants have been observed displaying fear when they find the remains or bones of other elephants—a behavior unique in the animal kingdom.

13 Elephants can produce sounds louder than the noises you'd hear at a construction site.

14 During ancient times in India, armored elephants were used in wars to carry soldiers and break through enemy lines.

15 To protect their young from the sun and bugs, adult elephants will toss sand on them and stand over the little ones as they sleep.

16 Despite the vast size difference, elephants are closely related to the rock hyrax, a small furry mammal found in Sub-Saharan Africa.

17 An adult elephant must drink close to 60 gallons (227 liters) of water every day to survive. That's enough to fill up an entire bathtub!

18 AFRICAN AND ASIAN ELEPHANTS ARE CAPABLE OF MIMICKING HUMAN VOICES LIKE PARROTS, AND HAVE ALSO BEEN KNOWN TO IMITATE THE SOUND OF TRUCK ENGINES.

19 Koshik, an Asian elephant living in captivity, can mimic the Korean words for "hello," "good," "no," "sit down," and "lie down."

20 Elephants digest just about 40 percent of the food they eat—the rest of it, including seeds and grass, is expelled from their body as waste.

21 Acacia trees sometimes sprout from elephant's dung since the seeds are still intact after the leaves pass through the animal's digestive system.

22 Elephants have incredible memories. Individual elephants can identify old friends even after being apart for years.

23 Some elephants can be trained to paint by clutching a brush in their trunk. A painting created by a group of eight elephant artists sold for $39,000 at auction in 2005.

24 The height of an Asian or African elephant at the shoulder is roughly equal to twice the circumference of their front foot.

25 Elephants don't run. Researchers consider their fast movements a "trot" because they always keep at least two feet on the ground, unlike other vertebrates who lift all four feet at once while running.

26 Despite not being able to run, elephants have been clocked trotting at a speedy 25 miles an hour (40 km/h)—almost as quick as the world's fastest man.

27 Elephants, great apes, humans, magpies, and dolphins are the only animals that are able to recognize themselves in a mirror.

28 In one study, African elephants displayed the ability to recognize human voices and distinguish between gender, age, and accents.

29 Elephants have been observed using sticks to scratch themselves in hard-to-reach places.

30 Elephants don't like bees. They purposefully avoid snacking on trees that host hives. Even a recording of the buzzing insects will chase them away.

31 A team of scientists from Russia and Korea are working on creating an elephant–woolly mammoth hybrid by inserting the extinct species' deoxyribonucleic acid (DNA) into African elephant cells.

32 One Asian elephant living in a zoo in Taiwan died at the age of 86—far exceeding the animal's average life expectancy of 60.

33 THROUGHOUT THE DAY, ELEPHANTS TAKE QUICK CAT NAPS ON THEIR FEET. AT NIGHT, THEY LIE DOWN AND SNOOZE SOUNDLY FOR A FEW HOURS.

34 At the annual Elephant Round-Up in Surin Province, Thailand, hundreds of elephants are gathered together to parade around town—then feast on fruits, vegetables, and sugarcane.

35 A California, U.S.A., man has a collection of more than 10,000 different elephant-themed items, including artwork, stuffed animals, and jewelry.

36 Baby elephants are born blind and rely on their mothers, plus their keen sense of hearing and trunks, to navigate their way around.

37 Not long after giving birth, a mother elephant will select "babysitters" from the herd to look after her calf while she recovers and regains her strength.

38 A curious elephant once snatched a tourist's video camera in Zimbabwe, kicking it around and even putting it in his mouth—all while the camera captured the funny footage.

39 Some elephants living in captivity wear specially made boots to help protect their feet.

40 A male elephant can slurp down over 53 gallons (200 L) of water in less than five minutes.

41 When soundly sleeping, some elephants will snore loudly.

42 YOUNG ELEPHANTS SOMETIMES THROW TEMPER TANTRUMS WHEN THEY'RE UPSET, MUCH LIKE HUMAN TODDLERS DO.

43 A young African elephant's tusks—which are much smaller than an adult's—are called tushes.

44 In certain parts of Africa, olive baboons follow elephants around so they can drink from the water wells dug up by the larger animals.

45 Asian elephants keep their ears in constant motion to fan away the heat and cool themselves.

46 Elephants are excellent swimmers.

47 Asian elephants stay with their mothers for several years and don't reach full size until they're about 17 years old.

48 Elephant herds follow ancient seasonal migration routes, and are always led by the eldest animal in the group.

49 Asian elephants are almost completely hairless, while African elephants have tufts of hair near their mouths and on their tails.

50 Although it's highly illegal to poach elephants for their ivory tusks, more than 12,000 elephants are killed by poachers each year.

51 In one study, elephants learned how to use step stools to reach food hidden in trees.

52 A 31-year-old cow named Curve gave birth to an extremely rare set of twins at a game reserve in South Africa.

53 Doctors in Thailand have fit two elephants that lost their legs in land mine accidents with prosthetic limbs—making them the world's first "bionic" pachyderms.

54 TWO-THIRDS OF AN ELEPHANT'S BODY WEIGHT RESTS ON ITS FRONT LIMBS—THAT'S ABOUT 3,000 POUNDS (1,360 KG)!

55 An elephant's long eyelashes aren't just there to look pretty: They keep sand, dirt, and debris from getting in its eyes.

56 From 1868 to 1917, the national flag of Siam—present-day Thailand—featured an elephant on a red background.

57 DURING WORLD WAR I IN ENGLAND, CIRCUS ELEPHANTS WERE USED TO HAUL SCRAP METAL AND PLOW FIELDS.

58 Aside from a herd, a group of elephants is also sometimes called a parade or a memory.

59 Studies show that elephants are able to sniff out thunderstorms some 150 miles (241 km) away.

60 African elephants have more than five times the number of genes dedicated to the sense of smell than humans.

61 After 145 years of featuring elephants in its famous circus, Ringling Bros. and Barnum & Bailey will retire its entire herd by 2018.

62 An elephant's eyeball is about the size of a Ping-Pong ball.

63 A SOUTH AFRICAN FAMILY ONCE FOUND A LOST BABY ELEPHANT IN THEIR YARD, THEN TRACKED DOWN HER HERD AND RETURNED HER TO THE WILD.

64 Elephants sometimes gather in groups of up to 1,000 individuals around watering holes.

65 In certain Asian countries, rare "white" elephants—actually albinos that are pinkish in color with light eyelashes—were once kept by kings as a symbol of power, wealth, and good luck.

66 The largest elephant on record was an adult male African elephant that weighed close to 24,000 pounds (10,886 kg) and was 13 feet (4 m) tall at the shoulder.

67 *Deinotherium*—a giant prehistoric pachyderm—was taller than a giraffe and weighed nearly twice as much as today's African elephants.

68 Female elephants can have babies until they are about 50 years old, and typically have a new calf every three or four years.

69 The thousands of muscles in an elephant's trunk allows it to be flexible and delicate enough to pick up an object as small as a grain of rice off the ground.

70 AN ELEPHANT'S TRUNK IS POWERFUL ENOUGH TO LIFT AN OBJECT WEIGHING MORE THAN AN ADULT LION.

71 Contrary to popular belief, elephants are not afraid of mice.

72 Some grooms at Indian weddings ride in on elephants for good luck—with people paying more than $8,000 to rent the animals for a few hours.

73 You can buy paper made out of elephant dung.

74 A pair of elephants living in captivity were spotted dancing and swaying in time to classical music.

75 Elephant Appreciation Day is celebrated in the United States annually on September 22.

75 BIG FACTS ABOUT ELEPHANTS

A group of elephants bathe in a river in Sri Lanka.

35 COOL FACTS ABOUT

1 The North Pole is the NORTHERN END of Earth's axis and lies in the ARCTIC OCEAN.

2 American explorer ROBERT E. PEARY claimed to reach the North Pole by DOGSLED in 1909, but others disputed that he actually made it.

polar bear in the Arctic

3 When your COMPASS POINTS NORTH, it's pointing not to the North Pole but to Earth's magnetic pole, where Earth's magnetic field points downward.

4 When Robert E. Peary supposedly reached the North Pole, he said he TOOK POSSESSION of the region for the United States, but he had no authority to do that.

5 POLAR BEARS occasionally wander to the North Pole from farther south in the Arctic looking for food.

6 You can spend the night in a HOTEL MADE OF ICE in Jukkasjärvi, Sweden— a city near the North Pole.

7 There ISN'T ANY LAND in the North Pole—it's just floating ice.

8 The North Pole is WARMER than the South Pole— by about 14°F (7°C) in summer and 36°F (20°C) in winter, on average.

9 EVEN DURING THE SUMMER the North Pole is FREEZING! Temperatures average 32°F (0°C).

10 The North Pole experiences only ONE SUNRISE and ONE SUNSET every year because there the sun is always above the horizon in SUMMER and below the horizon in WINTER.

11 You can buy a "Northpole Communicator" to receive daily updates from SANTA AND THE ELVES for the month of December.

12 Since the North Pole sits on DRIFTING ICE, North Pole researchers work on DRIFTING RESEARCH STATIONS set up to move with the moving ice pack, or sea ice.

13 Researchers monitor the ICE PACK, temperature, currents, WEATHER, and MARINE LIFE.

14 Street names in North Pole, Alaska, include SANTA CLAUS LANE, ST. NICHOLAS DRIVE, and HOLIDAY ROAD.

15 ARCTIC COD, found at the North Pole, are one of the most important prey species for whales, seals and polar bears.

16 The Arctic tern—that has the LONGEST MIGRATION ROUTE in the world, traveling 44,000 miles (71,000 km)—spends its spring and summer at the North Pole.

17 The North Pole experiences up to 24 hours of SUNLIGHT in summer and 24 hours of DARKNESS in winter.

18 In the 19th century, A TEAM OF SWEDISH EXPLORERS tried to fly over the North Pole in a HYDROGEN BALLOON but failed.

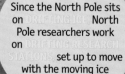

THE NORTH POLE

19 The **FIRST VERIFIED EXPEDITION** to the North Pole was conducted by Norwegian explorer Roald Amundsen in 1926. **HE FLEW** in an airplane over the pole.

20 Powerful ships called **ICEBREAKERS** are used to navigate around the North Pole today.

21 **THE INUIT** live in **REGIONS** close to the North Pole, including Greenland, Russia, and Canada, but not at the North Pole proper.

22 The North Pole **DOES NOT BELONG** to a specific country.

23 In spite of its name, North Pole, Alaska, **IS NOT NEAR** the North Pole. It's about 1,700 miles (2,735 km) away.

24 HOH OHO is the **CANADIAN ZIP CODE** for the North Pole.

25 Narwhals—inspiration for mythical **UNICORNS**—live in Arctic waters near the North Pole. A **NARWHAL'S TUSK** grows up to ten feet (3 m) in length.

26 The North Pole is in **ALL THE TIME ZONES.**

27 The wobbling axis means the North Pole **MOVES** about 30 feet (9 m) every seven years.

28 From the North Pole, all directions are **SOUTH!**

29 Icebreakers cut through the ice at the North Pole to **TRANSPORT GOODS.** This route is much quicker than traveling all the way to Central America through the Panama Canal.

30 The **U.S. NUCLEAR SUBMARINE** *Nautilus*—that could remain submerged for several weeks—reached the North Pole in 1958.

31 Because Earth's **AXIS WOBBLES,** it causes the exact location of the North Pole to wobble with it.

32 **RUSSIA** placed a **TITANIUM FLAG** on the ocean floor beneath the North Pole in 2007.

33 **POLARIS,** the North Star, sits almost motionless above the North Pole.

34 The **ICE** at the North Pole is six to ten feet (2 to 3 m) **THICK.**

35 The **OCEAN BELOW THE NORTH POLE** is more than 13,000 feet (3,960 m) deep.

SOUTH POLE 9000
TOKYO 6043
EQUATOR 10002
BEIJING 5564
WASHINGTON 5683
NEW-YORK 6501
TORONTO 5164

1. The first map to call the new world "America" was created in 1507 by German mapmaker Martin Waldseemüller. The Library of Congress bought it in 2003 for $10 million. 2. Robert Louis Stevenson's *Treasure Island* is thought to be based on Norman Island in the British Virgin Islands. 3. The U.S. Declaration of Independence does not have an invisible map on the back of it as shown in the 2004 movie *National Treasure*. 4. Jaro Hess's 1930 "The Land of Make Believe" map includes more than 50 fairy-tale characters and places. 5. Early mapmakers would put fake cities on their maps to catch forgeries of their work. 6. A map that shows legal property lines is called a cadastral map. 7. London cab drivers study city maps to pass the "knowledge test" of 25,000 streets and 20,000 landmarks in London, United Kingdom. It's considered the hardest geography test in the world. 8. The first known map of the United States with the American flag on it dating back to 1784 was sold at an auction for $1.8 million dollars. 9. In 2006, a rare-map dealer admitted to stealing 97 antique maps from libraries in the United States and England. 10. People thought they could see the lost city of Atlantis on Google Earth, but it was actually a computing error. 11. The 1964 New York World's Fair featured a road map of New York State embedded in the pavilion floor with dimensions of 130 x 166 feet (39.6 x 50.6 m). 12. The first world ocean floor map was published in 1977 by the U.S. Office of Naval Research. 13. Because Earth is round, mapmakers use mathematical equations called projections to represent it correctly on a flat map. 14. Before satellite images were available, surveyors would take photographs from airplanes to create maps. 15. Ancient Polynesians made charts of the ocean currents with bamboo sticks and seashells. Ocean currents were represented by curved wood, and seashells were used for islands. 16. The "Tabula Peutingeriana" was a map created by ancient Romans around A.D. 250. It shows all the major roads of the Roman Empire. 17. In 1855 the physician John Snow determined the source of a cholera outbreak in London, United Kingdom, by plotting all the cases on a map of the city. The source was a water pump near Cambridge Street and Broad Street. 18. Edmond Halley not only predicted the comet that would be named after him, he also was the first person to create a weather map of the world's trade winds, which are the pattern of surface winds that blow from the east in the tropics. 19. The ancient Greek astronomer Ptolemy had a great influence on mapmaking. His book *Geography* was translated into Arabic in the 800s and into Latin in the 1300s. 20. In the late 1500s, mapmaker Gerardus Mercator was the first to call a collection of maps an atlas. 21. A hydrographer is a person who studies and maps the ocean floor. 22. To map the ocean's depths, scientists use echo-sounding equipment on a boat to measure how long it takes

100 MAP FACTS

sound waves to travel to the seafloor and back. 23. A giant bunny in the Italian Alps was spotted on Google Earth. 24. One of George Washington's first jobs was as a public land surveyor, people who take measurements to determine boundaries. 25. The U.S. Geological Survey (USGS) published more than 55,000 topographic maps in the 20th century. 26. The first nautical charts were called portolan charts and date back to the European Middle Ages. 27. When maps were first printed in the 1600s, any color other than black was painted on by hand. 28. One map made by the California Department of Conservation estimates that there were 13,500 gold mines in California during the Gold Rush of 1849. 29. Surveyors use a telescope-like instrument called a theodolite to measure the horizontal and vertical angles of the land. 30. Google Maps first started including street view images—where you can see actual images of the street scene—in 2007. 31. A schedule of where the Google Maps street cars are driving is posted on Google's website. 32. The method called LIDAR (Light Detection and Ranging) uses light from lasers to measure distances. 33. In 2000, archaeologists discovered a map of three constellations—including one that has been recognized as the Pleiades—painted on the walls of a cave in Lascaux, France, that are about 20,000 years old. 34. The global positioning system (GPS) that a car or cell phone uses is made up of 24 satellites flying 12,645 miles (20,350 km) above Earth. It uses the satellites to determine your exact location. 35. The geographic center of the United States is located in South Dakota, about 17 miles (27 km) west of Castle Rock in Butte County. 36. A map of China carved into stone dates back to the mid-1100s. 37. A bathymetric map shows what land looks like under the water. 38. A geodesist surveys the distance and direction between points on, under, or above Earth's surface. 39. The geodetic center for North America is Meades Ranch Triangulation Station in Osborne County, Kansas, U.S.A. It is the origin point for all governmental mapping. 40. Two places located exactly on the opposite sides of a globe are called antipodes. The antipode of Portugal is New Zealand. 41. A globe is considered to be the most accurate map of Earth because it is a sphere like the planet. 42. The largest rotating globe is 41.5 feet (12.65 m) in diameter and tilts at 23.5 degrees (which is the same tilt as Earth's). It is located at a mapping company in Yarmouth, Maine, U.S.A. 43. Some ancient petroglyphs etched on rocks may show the geography of the nearby area. 44. Contour maps are illustrated with lines joining points of equal height above sea level. They highlight mountains and valleys. 45. The Coast Survey, established in 1807, is the oldest scientific agency of the U.S. government. It was established to survey and chart the country's coasts. 46. A map created in 1500 by Juan de la Cosa, the mapmaker who sailed with Christopher Columbus, was found in a Paris bookstore in 1832 and was later sold to the Queen of Spain. 47. In 1841 John C. Fremont was commissioned by the U.S. Congress to survey and create maps of the Oregon Trail. It took him four years to complete. 48. The Inuit carved small wooden maps, shaped like the coastlines, to be held in one's hand to navigate along coastal waters. 49. During World War II, maps with escape routes were smuggled in Monopoly games and delivered to prisoners of war in Germany. 50. A research study done in Northern Ireland showed that fishermen could create a map as accurate as a scientific one using only their mental images of fishing grounds. 51. Some Native American stories can be used to map sacred places of the tribe. 52. For almost 100 years, California was depicted as an island on maps. 53. David Rumsey, one of the largest private map collectors in the United States, has made more than 30,000 maps from his collection available to the public to view online. 54. An isotherm is a line drawn on a map that connects places with the same temperature. 55. An isobar is a line drawn on a map that connects locations with the same atmospheric pressure. 56. A team of astronomers with the Sloan Digital Sky Survey (SDSS) have created a 3-D map of the universe that includes more than three million astronomical objects. 57. During World War I, the British Ordnance Survey created almost 33 million military maps for the armed forces. 58. The National Library of Scotland has made more than 130 trench maps of World War I battlegrounds available online. 59. A cognitive map is a mental image of a person's physical location or space. 60. The satellites in the global positioning system (GPS) circle the planet twice each day. 61. The master control station of the global positioning system (GPS) is at Schriever Air Force Base in Colorado Springs, Colorado, U.S.A. 62. The U.S. Geological Survey (USGS) monitors a real-time earthquake map. Thousands occur every day, but we can't feel most of them. 63. A map from Hereford Cathedral in the United Kingdom created in about 1300 shows a world surrounded on the edges by monsters. At the time, things that were unknown were considered dangerous. 64. In 2013, Mikheil Kvrivishvili, a graphic designer from Moscow, Russia, won a competition to re-design the map showing Boston's metro system. 65. In the online game *GeoGuessr,* you must guess the location of a random Google Maps street view. 66. The current London Underground tube map was created in 1933 by Harry Beck, an electrician who worked for the subway system. 67. It took J. K. Rowling only a few minutes to sketch a map of Hogwarts because she knew Harry Potter's world so well. 68. Alaska has very few roads, with only 12 route numbers for the whole state. 69. The "Loneliest Road in America" is the section of U.S. Route 50 that goes through Nevada, U.S.A. You won't find many people along it. 70. Scientists at IBM created a complete 3-D map of the world that is only 22 by 11 micrometers—small enough that 1,000 of the maps could fit on a grain of salt. 71. Google used a camel to map the Liwa desert in Abu Dhabi, United Arab Emirates. 72. A planisphere is a chart of the stars (usually small and portable) that can be rotated to show you the position of the stars for any given date. 73. The first free map of London's Underground subway system

TO PIN-POINT

was given out more than 100 years ago, in 1908. 74. You can stand in four states—Utah, Arizona, Colorado, and New Mexico—at Four Corners, the only place where this is possible in the United States. 75. The International Date Line, an imaginary line in the Pacific Ocean, marks the place where the date changes by one day. It's not straight but zigzags so that countries are not divided in two. 76. The southernmost point in the United States is located in Ballast Key, Florida. 77. From early October to early March, Cadillac Mountain in Maine is the first place to see the sunrise in the continental U.S. 78. In 2011, NASA's Lunar Reconnaissance Orbiter created the highest resolution map of the lunar surface ever. 79. Maps of the human brain made by using magnetic resonance imaging (MRI) help neuroscientists better understand the function and structure of the human brain. 80. National Geographic's 1988 map of Mount Everest included information taken from the space shuttle *Columbia.* 81. Google Maps can turn any map showing grids of streets into a *Pac-Man* game you can play. 82. Longitude lines show east and west positions on a globe. These vertical lines converge at the North and South Poles. Latitude lines show north and south positions and are parallel to the equator. 83. Both China and Japan claim eight uninhabited islands in the East China Sea as their territory, known in Japan as the Senkaku Islands. 84. Until the early 1930s, place-names were hand lettered on most maps produced by the National Geographic Society. 85. The creator of the TV show *The Simpsons* says he named the town they live in after Springfield, Oregon, U.S.A. 86. Maps painted on silk from the second century B.C. were found in Hunan Province, China, in the early 1970s. 87. Maps showing countries of the world became outdated in July 2011 when South Sudan became an independent nation. 88. The company that produces London's A–Z maps uses the motto "On We Go." 89. The southernmost point of South America is a tiny island in the Diego Ramírez archipelago. 90. In the U.S., electoral district boundaries are sometimes re-drawn as populations change. 91. Mapmakers can use radar-based systems to help them draw maps. 92. Earth is divided into 24 time zones, each corresponding to the distance the planet rotates in one hour. 93. Britain's Royal Observatory at Greenwich is home to the prime meridian, or 0° longitude. 94. German mapmaker Sebastian Münster created the first map showing Africa as a continent in the mid-1500s. 95. The deepest place on Earth, called Challenger Deep, is near the Philippines in the western Pacific Ocean. 96. General Dwight D. Eisenhower (who would become U.S. president) carried National Geographic maps with him during World War II. 97. A giant, eroded rock structure in Mauritania, Africa, is so large it can be seen from space. It stretches about 25 miles (40 km) across. 98. Scientists are using an imaging technique to uncover faded words on a map that Christopher Columbus probably used to plan his 1492 voyage across the Atlantic. 99. Vision scientists at Massachusetts Institute of Technology have created a computer model that can show just how well someone understands a subway map in just one glance. 100. In 1934, a watchmaker in Toronto, Canada, found an old, weathered treasure map hidden in a watch he was cleaning.

1

GRAVITY on JUPITER is 2.5 times that of gravity on Earth. You would need much more strength in your MUSCLES to lift objects.

2

The end of a CHAMELEON'S tongue is a BALL of muscle that forms a SUCTION cup to snag prey and bring it to its MOUTH.

3

Your muscles move your BONES and TENDONS.

4

A GRIZZLY BEAR has a muscular hump on its back behind its shoulders for DIGGING and TURNING OVER ROCKS.

5

Muscles are MADE up of layers of SLENDER cells called fibers.

6

The human TONGUE can slurp, bend, twist, and in some people even CURL, and for most people it NEVER tires out.

7

Slightly more GIRLS THAN BOYS can roll their tongue into a tube shape. Try it!

8

In Marvel Comics, if a character can lift MORE THAN 800 POUNDS (363 KG) over his or her head, they have SUPERHUMAN strength.

9

The specific number of muscles in the HUMAN BODY differs depending on what system is used to CLASSIFY them.

10

When the muscles in the CALF become TIGHT and very PAINFUL, some people call these cramps a CHARLEY HORSE. They are caused by muscle SPASMS.

11

Whales and SEALS can store extra OXYGEN in their muscles, which lets them STAY UNDERWATER without having to breathe for about ONE HOUR.

12

Each end of a muscle ATTACHES to a DIFFERENT bone, which is HOW our bodies move.

13

Superstrong JAW muscles in the black PIRANHA give it a bite force some 30 TIMES its body weight. Chomp!

14

The cartoon character POPEYE gets his bulging bicep muscles from eating SPINACH. The leafy green is a good source of iron, which is good for your health.

15

Scientists have found that lifting weights for just a SHORT amount of time can give your MEMORY a boost.

16

One cause of muscle CRAMPS is a lack of potassium, a nutrient that muscles need to contract. YOGURT AND BROCCOLI are good sources of potassium.

17

A HERNIA happens when PART OF AN ORGAN (or tissue) bulges through a weak area in a muscle.

18

Chimpanzees are about TWICE as STRONG as humans.

19

BALLET DANCERS use small muscles in their feet to help them when they pose *EN POINTE* on their tiptoes.

20

The GLUTEUS MAXIMUS (GLOOT-ee-us MAK-suh-mus) is a fancy name for the muscle in your REAR END.

21

GOOSE BUMPS happen when small muscles at the end of your HAIR follicles contract, PUSHING up the hairs.

22

Lip muscles contract to pucker up—helpful when playing the TRUMPET or giving someone a A KISS.

23

The idea of exercising until it hurts—no PAIN, no GAIN—has a little truth in it, but you should be careful not to overdo it and cause muscle INJURY.

24

Some insects warm up the muscles they use to FLY by VIBRATING their wings.

25

Before Arnold Schwarzenegger was an ACTOR and GOVERNOR of California he was a world-famous BODYBUILDER.

26

Drinking CHOCOLATE MILK after an intense workout can help replenish TIRED muscles. It's rich in protein and CARBOHYDRATES.

27

Muscles are POWERED by the FOODS you eat.

28

Muscle tissue makes up about 50 PERCENT of an ANTELOPE'S body.

29

Changes in the GENES in some HUMANS, CATTLE, SHEEP, and DOGS can cause them to have 2 to 3 times the muscle mass of other people and animals.

30

Earthworms have two sets of muscles. Contracting the first set makes them LONG and THIN, and contracting the other set makes them SHORT and FAT.

31

A FOSSIL found in Newfoundland, Canada, shows evidence of muscle tissue on an ANIMAL that lived 560 MILLION years ago.

32

White meat in the breast of CHICKENS is rich in muscle fibers that power short bursts of FLIGHT. Dark meat comes from RED fibers used for longer-lasting activities.

33

When you SLEEP your brain usually PREVENTS impulses that MOVE your muscles.

34

When you exercise **STRENUOUSLY**, your muscles deplete the muscle's energy reserves, which leads to **STIFFNESS** and **ACHING** muscles.

35

Electrical **SIGNALS** in nerves initiate muscle **CONTRACTION** and movement.

36

The stapedius muscle in the **EAR** is the **SMALLEST** in the body. It's only 0.05 inches (0.13 cm) long.

37

Octopuses can use muscles to change the **TEXTURE** of their **SKIN** and create **BUMPS** or **SPIKY HORNS**, which helps camouflage them.

38

Your body has three different kinds of muscles: **CARDIAC**, **SMOOTH** (nonstriated), and **SKELETAL** (striated). **MOST** of your muscles are **SKELETAL**.

39

Smooth muscles (like those found in **BLOOD VESSELS**) are not under **CONSCIOUS** control; your **AUTOMATIC** nervous system regulates them.

40

Astronauts on the **INTERNATIONAL SPACE STATION** spend 2.5 hours exercising every day to keep their muscles strong.

41

A recent study found that **ANTIOXIDANTS** in **BLACK TEA** helped muscles recover after intense exercise.

42

Muscles in the eye are **SUPER BUSY**. They may move more than 100,000 times a day.

43

Strenuous exercise, as in a **MARATHON RACE**, produces a buildup of **LACTIC ACID**— an antibacterial liquid—in muscles.

44

Clams use just one muscle—the abductor muscle—to **OPEN AND CLOSE** their shells.

45

Since fish **FLOAT IN WATER** they don't need constant muscle activity to support their bones.

46

House **CATS** have more than 30 muscles in their ears, which allow them to move each ear **INDEPENDENTLY** of the other.

47

Eight separate muscles **MAKE UP** the human **TONGUE**. Of those, four muscles **ANCHOR** the tongue to the neck and head.

48

Pro **ATHLETES** such as **FOOTBALL** players use **ICE** baths to help their muscles recover faster after a hard workout or game. Cold treatment affects **BLOOD FLOW**.

49

Shivering on a **COLD** day is a way that your body **USES** your muscles to create **HEAT** and warm up **YOUR BODY**.

50

One **CATERPILLAR** has about 4,000 muscles.

50 EXTRA-STRENGTH FACTS ABOUT MUSCLES

international marathon in Paris, France

1 The word **"LASER" stands for** "light amplification by stimulated emission of radiation."

2
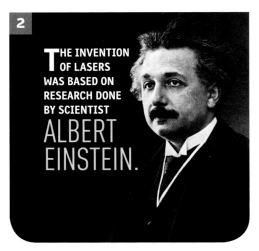
THE INVENTION OF LASERS WAS BASED ON RESEARCH DONE BY SCIENTIST **ALBERT EINSTEIN.**

3 Held in 2012—the 50th anniversary of the invention of lasers— **LASERFEST** was a worldwide series of events showing the use of lasers in modern technology.

4 The name **"BLU-RAY"** came from the **BLUE-VIOLET LASER** used to read the information on a disc.

25 ON-POINT FACTS ABOUT LASERS

5 **PHASERS** ARE LASERS THAT USE SOUND INSTEAD OF LIGHT.

6
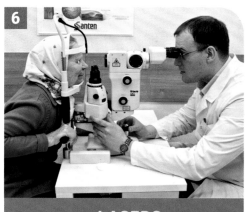
BECAUSE **LASERS** ARE SO POWERFUL AND PRECISE, THEY CAN BE USED FOR SURGERY IN PLACE OF **SCALPELS.** LASERS ARE USED FOR EYE SURGERY, AND EVEN TATTOO REMOVAL.

7 LASERS CAN BE USED FOR **HAIR REMOVAL.** THE LASERS ZAP THE HAIR WITH POWERFUL LIGHT AND SOON STOP THE HAIR FROM GROWING.

8
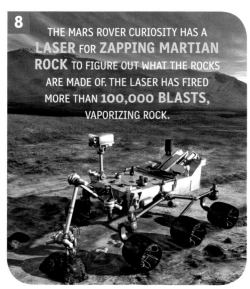
THE MARS ROVER CURIOSITY HAS A **LASER** FOR **ZAPPING MARTIAN ROCK** TO FIGURE OUT WHAT THE ROCKS ARE MADE OF. THE LASER HAS FIRED MORE THAN **100,000 BLASTS,** VAPORIZING ROCK.

9
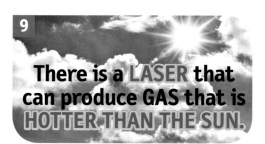
There is a **LASER** that can produce **GAS** that is **HOTTER THAN THE SUN.**

10 THE WORLD'S FIRST LASER WAS CALLED THE **Ruby Laser** BECAUSE THE LIGHT CAME FROM A RUBY GEMSTONE CRYSTAL, MAKING IT BRIGHT RED IN COLOR.

11
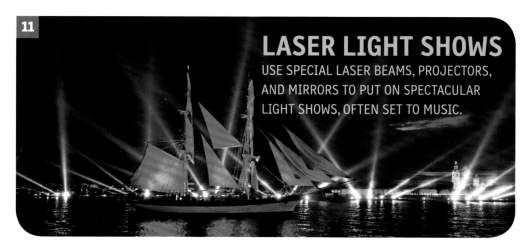
LASER LIGHT SHOWS USE SPECIAL LASER BEAMS, PROJECTORS, AND MIRRORS TO PUT ON SPECTACULAR LIGHT SHOWS, OFTEN SET TO MUSIC.

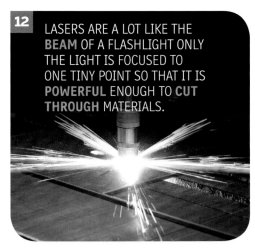

12 LASERS ARE A LOT LIKE THE **BEAM** OF A FLASHLIGHT ONLY THE LIGHT IS FOCUSED TO ONE TINY POINT SO THAT IT IS **POWERFUL** ENOUGH TO **CUT THROUGH** MATERIALS.

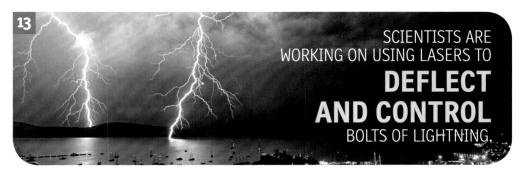

13 SCIENTISTS ARE WORKING ON USING LASERS TO **DEFLECT AND CONTROL** BOLTS OF LIGHTNING.

16 POLICE OFFICERS USE LASERS TO CLOCK THE **SPEED OF CARS** BY MEASURING THE TIME IT TAKES THE LIGHT TO HIT A **REFLECTIVE SURFACE** ON THE CAR AND BOUNCE BACK.

14 THE WORLD'S **FASTEST CAMERA** USES LASERS TO SNAP AN IMAGE EVERY **NANOSECOND**. That's one image every billionth of a second.

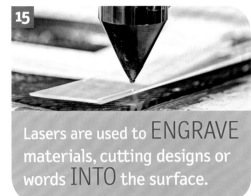

15 Lasers are used to ENGRAVE materials, cutting designs or words INTO the surface.

17 The laser that was used in the film *STAR TREK INTO DARKNESS* from 2013 was 50 times more powerful than previous lasers.

18 California, U.S.A., is home to the WORLD'S LARGEST LASER: an array of 192 LASER BEAMS, 10 STORIES HIGH, and as wide as 3 FOOTBALL FIELDS.

19 Some laser beams are **INVISIBLE** in the air but can be seen in smoke.

20 **OPTICAL TWEEZERS** use laser beams to pick up and handle **MICROSCOPIC OBJECTS**, such as **ATOMS**.

21 In 2015, ten cities in the United States tested **DRIVERLESS CARS** that use radar, cameras, and **LASERS** as sensors to get around without hitting any obstacles.

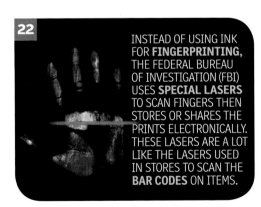

22 INSTEAD OF USING INK FOR **FINGERPRINTING**, THE FEDERAL BUREAU OF INVESTIGATION (FBI) USES **SPECIAL LASERS** TO SCAN FINGERS THEN STORES OR SHARES THE PRINTS ELECTRONICALLY. THESE LASERS ARE A LOT LIKE THE LASERS USED IN STORES TO SCAN THE **BAR CODES** ON ITEMS.

23 IN AN EFFORT TO STOP THE SPREAD OF MALARIA, A SCIENTIST INVENTED A **MOSQUITO-KILLING LASER GUN** CALLED THE **DEATH STAR** THAT TRACKS AND KILLS **MOSQUITOES**.

24 **POINTING A LASER BEAM AT AN AIRPLANE OR HELICOPTER IS ILLEGAL.** THE BEAM CAN REACH ALL THE WAY TO THE AIRCRAFT AND MAKE IT HARD FOR THE PILOT TO SEE.

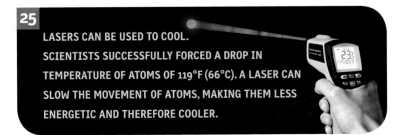

25 LASERS CAN BE USED TO COOL. SCIENTISTS SUCCESSFULLY FORCED A DROP IN TEMPERATURE OF ATOMS OF 119°F (66°C). A LASER CAN SLOW THE MOVEMENT OF ATOMS, MAKING THEM LESS ENERGETIC AND THEREFORE COOLER.

1 The Ugly Animal Preservation Society named the **BLOB FISH,** a bottom-dwelling fish that lives at depths of 2,950 feet (900 m), its GLOBAL MASCOT.

2 The **DUMBO OCTOPUS** gets its name from its prominent fins—even though its total body length is only eight inches (20 cm). Living on the ocean floor, its eight arms are webbed.

3 The AYE-AYE, a primate found only in Madagascar, not only has over-sized ears and big eyes, it has an **EXTRA-LONG MIDDLE FINGER** that it uses to scoop out insect larvae from trees.

4 Hagfish, which **FEED ON THE CORPSES OF DEAD ANIMALS** on the seafloor, produce slime to defend themselves against predators. If an animal bites a hagfish, it may choke on the slime.

5 Male **VISAYAN WARTY PIGS,** which live in the Philippines, have a long snout and wart-like growths on their faces.

6 The annual **WORLD'S UGLIEST DOG CONTEST,** held in Northern California, celebrates unattractive dogs. There are two categories: ugliest mutt and ugliest pedigree.

7 Male proboscis monkeys, which are found only on the island of Borneo, have **OVERSIZE NOSES.** Scientists think their nose may help make **CALLS LOUDER** to attract females.

FACTS ABOUT UGLY ANIMALS

**four-month-old puppy (left)
with his mother (right)**

8 **CHINESE CRESTED HAIRLESS DOGS** only have hair on the top of their heads, their tail, and their feet.

9 India's **PURPLE PIG-NOSED FROG** is stout with short limbs and a pointed snout that looks like a pig's.

10 The mata mata turtle that lives in the Amazon of South America has a **FLAT HEAD**, long neck, and **SPIKEY** outer shell.

11 **HAIRLESS** with pink **WRINKLED SKIN**, the naked mole rat has **WALRUS-LIKE TEETH** that it uses to dig through dirt in its underground burrows.

12 The giant Titicaca water frog, found only in South America's Lake Titicaca, has big **BAGGY FOLDS OF SKIN** that helps it absorb oxygen.

13 The **WRINKLE-FACED BAT** indeed has a wrinkly face covered in skin flaps, which it pulls over its face when it hangs upside-down to sleep.

14 Wrinkly **SPHYNX CATS** look hairless, but most are actually covered in peach-like fuzz.

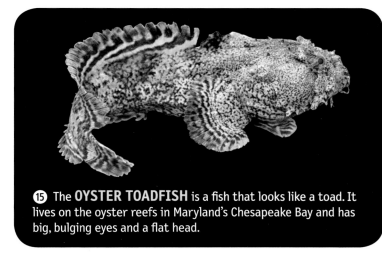

15 The **OYSTER TOADFISH** is a fish that looks like a toad. It lives on the oyster reefs in Maryland's Chesapeake Bay and has big, bulging eyes and a flat head.

1 R.M.S. *Titanic* cost $7.5 million to build in 1912 ($177 million in today's money) and sank on its maiden voyage.

2 IN 2014, A PENNSYLVANIA, U.S.A., MAN ACCIDENTALLY THREW AWAY A $1.25 MILLION-WINNING LOTTERY TICKET.

3 A $125-million satellite burned up in Mars's atmosphere in 1999 because one engineering team used metric measurements and another used standard U.S. measurements and data didn't transfer properly.

4 A $2-billion U.S. Air Force B-2 stealth bomber had an engine fire in 2010. Pilots on board weren't harmed, but it took four years to get the aircraft up and running again.

5 Italy's Tower of Pisa was already leaning ten years after construction began in 1173—and it's still leaning today.

6 Columbus landed on the Caribbean islands in 1492, but that wasn't his intended plan. He thought he had sailed to China and India.

7 Lt. Col. George Custer made a major mistake at the Battle of Little Big Horn in 1876. He expected a small number of Native Americans to fight his troops but thousands came to defend their way of life.

8 The makers of M&Ms passed on being featured in the film *E.T. The Extra-Terrestrial*. Reese's Pieces were used instead and sales soared.

9 A London record company passed on signing the Beatles to their label in 1962, just before the pop group rocketed to stardom.

10 In the 2006 Olympics, American snowboarder Lindsey Jacobellis thought she had a sure victory, so she did an unnecessary trick in the air, which caused her to fall and lose the gold.

11 Ivory brand soap—that floats in water—was invented by accident in 1878. Extra air got into the batch, causing the soap to float.

12 Western Union, which specialized in telegraphs, turned down a patent for Alexander Graham Bell's telephone in 1876 because they didn't think it would be a success.

13 A cleaning worker at an Italian art gallery recently threw away a piece of modern art valued at $15,000. She mistook it for trash.

14 When a batch of too-thick-tissue paper was accidentally shipped to Scott Paper Company in 1907 to turn into toilet paper, the company made it into "sani towels," or paper towels.

15 The Trojans accepted the Greeks' gift of a huge wooden horse. They brought the horse into Troy, and later the Greek warriors who were hiding in the horse sacked the ancient city.

16 IN THE 2002 OLYMPICS, A MALE CHINESE SPEED SKATER FELL AND TOOK OUT EVERYONE IN THE RACE EXCEPT THE SKATER WHO WAS LAST, WHO SKATED ON TO WIN GOLD.

17 London's Millennium Dome, built as a tourist attraction to celebrate the third millennium, didn't attract enough people and was sold and converted to a stadium.

18 The Apollo 13 moon mission in 1970 was quickly doomed when an oxygen tank in the service module exploded. The crew had to orbit the moon, but couldn't make a landing. All three astronauts survived.

19 In 1937, the airship *Hindenburg* left Germany for New Jersey, but it burst into flames, likely because a spark ignited the highly flammable hydrogen gas inside that gave it lift.

20 In 1856, when a college student was trying to make an anti-malaria drug from tree bark, he created a purple sludge instead. He invented—unintentionally—the first synthetic dye, which he called "mauve."

21 The personal helicopter, invented in the 1950s, let a person stand on a platform and steer by shifting their weight, but the blades sometimes wobbled and kicked up rocks and dirt.

22 In 1985, Coca-Cola announced it was changing its formula for Coke and renamed it "New Coke." Consumers protested and within three months the company reverted to its old formula.

23 The *Spruce Goose*, a flying boat meant to carry 700 soldiers to battle, took millions of dollars to develop in the 1940s but it flew only one mile (1.6 km) during tests.

24 In the United States, Washington's Tacoma Narrows Bridge, completed in 1940, was a suspension bridge, but the region's strong winds weren't considered and the bridge collapsed.

25 In 1912, a man dove from the Eiffel Tower hoping his newly designed winged suit would let him glide to safety. It didn't.

26 In 1928, when a scientist accidentally left a petri dish lid off a sample, mold grew, killing the bacteria around it. The mistake was a medical breakthrough: penicillin, a type of antibiotic, was discovered.

27 A chemist who was trying to make a type of rubber that wouldn't be broken down by jet fuel accidentally spilled the concoction on her shoe. She realized that the spilled spot stayed clean while the rest got dirty—and stain-resistant Scotchgard was born.

28 In the 1960 Olympics, a runner from Suriname took a nap before his 800-meter race and overslept, missing the event!

29 WHEN A PHARMACIST FAILED TO MAKE A REMEDY FOR HEADACHES, HE TURNED THE RECIPE INTO COCA-COLA!

30 The Hubble Space Telescope, an in-space observatory that takes pictures of the cosmos, at first sent blurry pictures back to Earth due to a tiny flaw on the main mirror.

31 "Again," "heard," "knew," "school," and "interesting" are among the most commonly misspelled words by third- through eighth-graders.

32 X-rays were invented by accident when in 1895 a German scientist was experimenting with glass ray tubes. He noticed that rays could pass through skin. He took the first x-ray of his wife's hand!

33 The first match was invented in 1827 by accident when a chemist was mixing a bunch of chemicals with a stick. When he scraped the chemicals against the pan, the tip of the stick instantly caught fire.

34 U.S. movie director Steven Spielberg was turned down twice for film school when he was young.

35 When a chemist who was doing experiments didn't wash his hands before eating dinner, he tasted something unexpectedly sweet on his food. He had discovered saccharin, an artificial sweetener.

36 In the first Olympic women's BMX final in 2008, world champion Shanaze Reade tried to overtake the leader on the last bend, crashed spectacularly, and could not finish the race.

37 A rare "Superman" comic worth $175,000 was found inside the walls of a Minnesota, U.S.A., house where it had been used as insulation.

38 Four boys exploring woods in southwestern France in 1940 began to poke around at a hole at a fallen tree and they soon discovered the Lascaux caves underneath, filled with prehistoric wall paintings.

39 Cheese puffs were invented by accident. A machine made for animal feed was accidentally loaded with corn kernels and what came out were hard ribbons. Flavor was added and cheese puffs were born.

40 The 1986 Chernobyl nuclear power plant disaster was caused by an equipment failure during a test.

41 When London's Millennium Bridge first opened, the sway of the bridge made people get dizzy and fall down! An $8 million repair had to be made.

42 SAFETY GLASS WAS ACCIDENTALLY INVENTED IN 1903 WHEN A SCIENTIST DROPPED A GLASS FLASK COATED IN PLASTIC AND IT DIDN'T BREAK INTO PIECES.

43 Two early passenger jets in the 1950s that were made with square windows created structural cracks during flight and caused the planes to break apart.

44 In 1976, Apple co-founder Ron Wayne sold his 10 percent stake in the company for $800, which would have been worth billions today.

45 Russian emperor Tsar Alexander II sold the Alaskan territory to the United States for just $7.2 million—equivalent to about $120 million now.

46 In 1964, Minnesota Vikings defense football player Jim Marshall snagged a fumble and ran 66 yards into the end zone, but it was the wrong team's!

47 In 1914, the ship *Endurance* set off for Antarctica, but would become stuck in ice. For two years the crew had to survive in the harsh polar terrain, but miraculously no one died.

48 IN 1950, THE EAST GERMAN GOVERNMENT ACCUSED AMERICA OF DROPPING COLORADO POTATO BEETLES FROM PLANES TO DESTROY THEIR CROPS. IT WAS NOT TRUE.

49 In the 1948 U.S. presidential election, the first edition of the *Chicago Daily Tribune* wrongly announced Thomas Dewey, not Harry S. Truman, as the new president.

50 In 1992, U.S. President George H.W. Bush became sick at a dinner with the Japanese prime minister and accidentally threw up on him!

51 Holland's Institute of Brilliant Failures thinks there is something to be learned from failures and pays tribute to people who try something different, even if it doesn't work out.

52 Poor design of the John Hancock Tower in Boston, Massachusetts, unveiled in 1976, caused windows to fall out and crash to the pavement below. Some 10,000 windows had to be replaced.

53 Topps baseball card company reversed a photo on the 1957 Hank Aaron card showing him as a left-handed batter.

54 In 2010, 1.5 million coins were printed in Chile that accidentally spelled the country's name as Chiie.

55 In 1993, baseball player Jose Canseco, playing for the Texas Rangers, missed a fly ball, which bounced off his head and over the back wall to give the Cleveland Indians a home run.

56 In the 1982 Stanford versus UC Berkeley football game, the Stanford band thought they had won and marched on the field, but the ball was still in play. Berkeley kept lateral passing and eventually made the touchdown and won the game.

57 When he first started rapping, record companies passed on signing Jay Z to their label, so he sold CDs out of his car.

58 The Chicago Cubs were close to heading to the World Series for the first time in 58 years when a fan deflected a foul ball that the outfielder was ready to catch. The Cubs lost and the fan had to make a getaway from an angry crowd.

59 France's Napoleon Bonaparte tried to invade Russia with a massive army in 1812. Most of the army left because they had not been paid.

60 An art collector planning to sell a Picasso for $139 million accidentally bumped it with his elbow, putting a hole in it!

61 GOOGLE WAS MEANT TO BE NAMED GOOGOL, BUT WHEN CHECKING TO SEE IF THE NAME HAD ALREADY BEEN TAKEN, GOOGLE WAS ACCIDENTALLY TYPED IN.

62 When an engineer accidently left a pen on a hot iron, the ink went shooting out, giving him the idea for the ink-jet printer.

63 There is no real evidence that Isaac Newton was accidentally hit in the head by an apple and this helped him devise the laws of gravity.

64 In the 1936 Olympics, a boxer thought he had lost his fight, so he went out and had a big meal. There was an error in scoring, but when he had to re-weigh in, he was too heavy, and therefore disqualified!

65 A NEW AIRPORT BEING BUILT IN BERLIN, GERMANY, HAS BEEN FOUND TO HAVE MORE THAN 150,000 DEFECTS.

66 J. K. Rowling's manuscript for *Harry Potter and the Sorcerer's Stone* was rejected by numerous publishers before one made her an offer.

67 An American Olympic bobsledder was stuck in a bathroom due to a faulty door at the 2014 Sochi Olympics in Russia. He had to break his way out.

68 A London skyscraper was blamed for reflecting light off of its windows, which melted parts of a car on the street below!

69 William Harrison, the ninth U.S. president, is said to have died after only 30 days in office because he caught a cold after standing outside during his inauguration in the cold without a coat.

70 In an illustration for the *Saturday Evening Post*, U.S. painter Norman Rockwell painted a man with an extra leg!

71 In 1990, a late-night security guard at a Boston museum let in two thieves who said they were police officers. The thieves got away with $500 million in art.

72 In 1897, three men tried to travel to the North Pole by hot air balloon, but the balloon crashed.

73 In 1992, U.S. Vice President Dan Quayle held a spelling bee for sixth graders and he wrongly told a boy he misspelled the word "potato." The president spelled it p-o-t-a-t-o-e!

74 FRANCE RECENTLY SPENT $68 MILLION MAKING TRAINS THAT WERE TOO WIDE FOR THE PLATFORMS.

75 In 1908, a tea dealer handed out loose tea samples in silk pouches. Customers were confused what to do, so they dunked them directly in the water, and tea bags were accidentally invented.

Leaning Tower of Pisa

75 FACTS ABOUT THE BIGGEST OOPS! OF ALL TIME

1 There are 76 percent MORE TWINS BORN in the United States today than 35 years ago.

2 The SCIENTIFIC STUDY of twins is called gemellology.

3 Twins are more likely to be born to a mom who is over the AGE OF 30.

4 Minneapolis and St. Paul, Minnesota, U.S.A., are nicknamed the "TWIN CITIES" because they are two big cities separated only by the Mississippi River.

5 FRATERNAL TWINS are no more genetically similar than brothers and sisters of different ages.

6 Twin sisters living in the U.K. were born in 1911 (the year before the *Titanic* sank!) and still live NEXT DOOR to each other.

7 One in 30 BABIES born in the United States is a TWIN.

8 About 1 IN EVERY 250 pregnant moms is carrying a set of identical twins.

9 Twins are twice as likely to be LEFT-HANDED than single babies are.

10 Some people think twins have a MENTAL CONNECTION—reading each other's thoughts or even feeling each other's pain—but this hasn't been scientifically proved.

11 Even identical twins don't have the same FINGERPRINTS.

12 Once a woman has a set of fraternal twins she is up to FOUR TIMES more likely to have ANOTHER SET.

13 A woman who is a fraternal twin is TWICE AS LIKELY to have twins herself than someone who isn't a twin.

14 NIGERIA has more multiple births (twins, triplets, and more) than ANY OTHER COUNTRY.

15 About 50 PERCENT of PANDAS are born twins.

35 FACTS ABOUT TWINS THAT WILL MAKE YOU DO A DOUBLE TAKE

16 Women who are VEGAN (don't eat animal products) are five times LESS LIKELY to have twins than women who aren't vegan.

17 Some CONJOINED twins (meaning parts of their bodies are connected) can FEEL AND TASTE what the other one touches and eats.

18 A study found that twins start PAYING ATTENTION TO EACH OTHER inside the womb at about 14 weeks.

19 Forty percent of twins INVENT their own LANGUAGE before they even start talking in their native language.

20 Mothers of twins LIVE LONGER, a study found.

21 U.S. astronauts Scott and Mark Kelly are the only set of twins ever to both TRAVEL INTO SPACE.

22 The LANGUAGE made up by twins often DISAPPEARS in childhood after they have learned real vocabulary.

23 You can tell identical twins apart by their BELLY BUTTONS.

24 Sometimes, identical twins MIRROR EACH OTHER: One may have a birthmark on their right arm and the other on their left.

25 TWINS RESTAURANT in New York City is staffed entirely by identical twins who always work the same shift!

26 Mary-Kate and Ashley Olsen, the twins who played MICHELLE on the TV show *FULL HOUSE*, were not identical. Ashley is one inch (2.5 cm) shorter than Mary-Kate.

27 Brook and Robin Lopez are the first twins to PLAY FOR THE NATIONAL BASKETBALL ASSOCIATION (NBA)—Brook plays for the Brooklyn Nets and Robin for the Portland Trail Blazers.

28 Identical twins are always either BOTH BOYS or BOTH GIRLS.

29 OPPOSITE SEX twins make up about one-third of twin births.

30 It is hard to tell sometimes if twins are identical or not! Up to 20 percent of twins THINK they are fraternal when they are ACTUALLY IDENTICAL.

31 There are at least 125 MILLION multiples—meaning twins, triplets, and more!—worldwide.

32 CONJOINED TWINS occur in as few as 1 IN EVERY 200,000 births.

33 William Shakespeare was the FATHER of twins.

34 Jenna and Barbara Bush, daughters of George W. Bush, are the FIRST TWIN CHILDREN of a U.S. president.

35 The actors who played twins Fred and George Weasley in the *HARRY POTTER* FILMS were not natural redheads. They were brunettes.

panda twins

1. A hare can speed along at 35 miles an hour (56 km/h); a tortoise at 1 mile an hour (1.6 km/h). 2. Receptors in your skin send signals to your brain at 1 mile an hour (1.6 km/h)—it's among the slowest speeds found in your body. 3. **Cave paintings from Lascaux, France, from some 20,000 years ago show cattle, deer, and horses running.** 4. Figure skaters use their arms to control how fast they spin. When they pull their arms close to their bodies, they spin faster. 5. A jumbo jet flies at about half the speed of the rotating Earth. 6. **Hummingbirds can beat their wings as fast as 200 times a second.** 7. An elevator in Taiwan's Taipei 101 building (the 4th tallest in the world, with 101 floors) takes just 39 seconds to get from the ground floor to the observation deck on the 89th floor. 8. The deadly black mamba snake, which lives in Africa, can travel as fast as 12 miles an hour (19 km/h) over flat ground. 9. **Winds within the jet stream, air currents that affect weather across the globe, can reach 184 miles an hour (nearly 300 km/h).** 10. Knots are the speed it takes to travel one nautical mile (1.85 km) and are usually used to measure the speed of aircraft and boats. 11. Peregrine falcons can dive through the air at 200 miles an hour (320 km/h) when dropping down to catch prey. 12. **Foods high in simple carbohydrates, like honey, fruits, and milk, provide the quickest energy burst to your body.** 13. The fastest cameras only take 0.1 second from when you press the shutter to when the camera takes the picture. 14. An Internet research firm found that South Korea has the fastest Internet speeds in the world; Japan comes in second.

100 FAST FACTS ABOUT *SPEED*

15. **Even though they can weigh up to four tons (3.6 MT), hippos can run faster than people.** 16. It takes only about five years for a Virginia pine tree sapling to grow into a tree that can be sold as a Christmas tree. 17. The speed of sound varies depending on what material it travels through. 18. **The moon rotates once every 27.32 days; the Earth once every 24 hours.** 19. A cheetah named Sarah who lives at the Cincinnati Zoo ran the 100-meter (109-yard) dash four seconds faster than Usain Bolt, the fastest man in the world. She ran it in 5.95 seconds. 20. The fastest runners in the world take about 180 steps every minute to get their best performance. 21. **The Mach number is the ratio of the speed of an object to the speed of sound, so Mach 1 means you are traveling at the speed of sound.** 22. It took 26 years for a man to solve the Rubik's Cube he bought in 1983. 23. On average, women's hearts beat 78 times a minute, compared to 70 times a minute for men's hearts. 24. **The first All-American Soap Box Derby was held in Dayton, Ohio, U.S.A., on August 19, 1934. Kids raced cars they built down a hill.** 25. Traveling at the speed of light, or 186,000 miles a second (300,000 km/s), might sound like fun, but you'd actually be exposed to so much radiation that you would quickly die. 26. Dolphins use their strong tails to speed through water at speeds of 33 feet a second (10 m/s). 27. **Putting bananas in a paper bag will ripen them faster because the ethylene gas they produce that speeds the process becomes trapped with the fruit.** 28. It takes about 40 days to reach the summit of Mount Everest after departing the camp at the mountain's base. If climbers don't take time to adjust to the altitude, they can get very sick and even die. 29. Earth moves around the sun at a speed of around 70,000 miles an hour (113,000 km/h). 30. **The Jamaican sprinter Usain Bolt, known as the fastest person on Earth, likes to eat Chicken McNuggets during his training.** 31. Researchers found that it takes your brain less than 0.1 second to pick up details in a picture of a landscape. 32. Asia is home to 7 out of 10 of the fastest growing "mega" cities. The fastest? The megacity of Tokyo, Japan.

More than 37 million people live there compared to 1900 when only about 2 million people called the city home. **33. If you were driving at highway speeds through the solar system, it would take you about 4,500 years to reach Neptune. 34.** Want to fall asleep fast? Researchers say that it's best to fall asleep in a room that is about 60 to 68°F (16 to 20°C). **35.** Avalanches are so dangerous because they travel so fast. The snow can reach speeds of 150 miles an hour (241 km/h). **36. Albert Einstein's theory of special relativity holds that as an object speeds up, its mass also increases. 37.** The fastest race cars in the world can blaze at speeds of 270 miles an hour (435 km/h). **38.** A professor at North Carolina State University, U.S.A., had his students figure out how fast Santa's sleigh would need to go to give out all his presents on Christmas. Their answer? A whopping 5,083,000 miles an hour (8,180,295 km/h). **39. Scientists found that one type of tiny bug called a mite moves really fast. If it were the size of a human it would move at the equivalent of 1,300 miles an hour (2,000 km/h). 40.** A perfectly circular racetrack—the Nardò Ring in Italy—gives car manufacturers a place to test drive for speed. The 7.77-mile (12.5-km) track has steep banks so drivers don't need to steer much. **41.** Scientists in China have built a train that can reach speeds of 1,800 miles an hour (2,897 km/h) if there is no resistance from the wind. **42. National Football League (NFL) players wear sensors the size of quarters under their shoulder pads that track their speed and distance traveled on the field. 43.** In 1954, a British medical student named Roger Bannister became the first person to run one mile (1.6 km) in under four minutes in competition. **44.** In a particle accelerator, high-energy atomic particles traveling at nearly the speed of light are made to collide. **45. Sailfish are the fastest fish in the ocean—they leap out of the water at 68 miles an hour (109 km/h). 46.** Fleas release energy through their toes that allow them to jump into the air at speeds of 4.25 miles an hour (6.84 km/h). **47.** A cheesemaker in Wisconsin, U.S.A., sells cheddar cheese that has been aged for 15 years. The maker kept the cheese in an airtight container and at 38°F (3.3°C). **48. Perhaps in an effort of wishful thinking, some racehorses have been named Lickity Split, Fireball, Speed Demon, and Run Run Run. 49.** The springbok, a kind of antelope found in Africa, can run as fast as cars travel on a highway. **50.** Ostriches use half as much energy as humans do to run at their top speed. **51. The Concorde, a supersonic airplane that stopped flying in 2003, cruised at 1,350 miles an hour (2,170 km/h) and could travel between London and New York in under 3.5 hours. 52.** Staghorn corals, which are among the fastest growing corals in the world, can grow four to eight inches (10 to 20 cm) a year. **53.** Olympic swimmers recorded superfast times wearing a swimsuit designed with help from NASA. It made swimmers so fast that it's now been banned. **54. Nerve impulses travel about 268 miles an hour (431 km/h) down your spinal cord to your body. 55.** It took 304 days for Viking 1, the first American spacecraft to land on Mars, to reach the red planet. **56.** The movie The Hobbit was filmed at 48 frames a second, twice the frame rate of most movies, which made it look more like real life. **57. It would take three years of nonstop pedaling to bike to the moon. 58.** As people get older, the hormones important for building muscle mass decrease, which is why it's harder to build muscle as an adult. **59.** Centipedes utilize all of their legs and move a whopping 16.5 inches (42 cm) each second. **60. A woodpecker moves its head at 15 miles an hour (24 km/h) while pecking a tree. 61.** During a penalty shoot-out in soccer, it takes the ball less than half a second to reach the soccer net. **62.** More than 1,000 runners from 24 countries have completed the New York City Marathon (26.2 miles; 42.2 km) at least 15 times. **63. Before National Association for Stock Car Auto Racing (NASCAR) competitions took place in stadiums, races would be held along streets and beaches. 64.** A New York City bus travels a route across Manhattan at an average speed of 3.2 miles an hour (5 km/h). **65.** Green turtles swim at about one mile an hour (1.6 km/h) during their annual migration of hundreds of miles from their feeding ground to beaches where they lay their eggs. **66. Wildfires can travel at speeds of about 12.5 miles an hour (20 km/h). 67.** The International Space Station travels about 5 miles (8 km) every second. **68.** The comic book racer Speed Racer is also known as Mach GoGoGo. **69. If you could drive to Proxima Centauri, the nearest star past our sun, at highway speeds, it would take 40 million years to reach it. 70.** Olympic runners hear an electronic beep instead of a starting gun. Olympic officials changed the sound when they realized athletes farthest from the gun were getting late starts because of how the sound reached their ears. **71.** It took balloon artist John Cassidy only one hour to make an incredible 747 balloon sculptures. **72. Blood flow is slowest in the capillaries to allow for oxygen and nutrient exchange with cells. 73.** The Titanic hit an iceberg at 11:40 at night, but it took it 157 minutes until the ship broke in half. **74.** Since snowflakes are all different, they all fall to Earth at different speeds. **75. Lava from volcanoes flows at about 5 miles an hour (8 km/h), but lava flowing down in channels can reach speeds of 34 miles an hour (55 km/h). 76.** To make a perfect free throw in basketball, you need to maintain a constant speed. **77.** Fingernails grow about three to four times faster than toenails. **78. You blink about 12 times a minute on average. 79.** The speed of wind affects the height of waves in the ocean—if the speed of the wind is slow, no large waves will form. **80.** Sound travels faster through water than air. **81. Staff at the Mount Washington Observatory in New Hampshire, U.S.A., recorded a record-breaking wind gust of 231 miles an hour (372 km/h) on April 12, 1934. 82.** The fastest pitchers in baseball can throw balls at more than 100 miles an hour (161 km/h). **83.** Scientists studying the Jakobshavn Glacier in Greenland found that it is now moving at a speed four times faster than in the 1990s. **84. The world's first speeding ticket was issued in Dayton, Ohio, in 1904. The speed? 12 miles an hour (19 km/h)! 85.** Black bears can run as fast as 25 miles an hour (40 km/h). **86.** Most grasses grow about 2 to 6 inches (5 to 15 cm) a month. **87. A study found that the average third grader reads 150 words a minute, but that by college the average student reads 450 words a minute. 88.** Snails can travel faster on glass than on gravel. **89.** Designers at Arizona State University are working on a jetpack that will give soldiers a boost so they can run as fast as Olympic runners. **90. Snakes can slither by turning their bodies into pleats or squinching up and making parts of their bodies heavier than others. 91.** Elephants and horses run about the same speed (at their fastest gait): 25 miles an hour (40 km/h). **92.** In 2007, it took Patrick Bertoletti just five minutes to eat 47 cream-filled doughnuts. **93. In the sport of cycling around a track, the cyclist in the inside lane must lead for the first lap. 94.** Since wind speed changes over time, instruments that measure it usually average a few readings over a short amount of time to arrive at a final figure. **95.** Salt water boils faster than fresh water. **96. Each game of speed chess only takes about 10 minutes. 97.** Since NASCAR stock cars have a large engine, they can reach speeds of 200 miles an hour (322 km/h). **98.** It takes about 20 minutes after you have started eating for your brain to signal that you are full. **99. Tell that to a Belgian man who ate a 12-inch pizza in just 2 minutes and 19.91 seconds! 100.** Tennis player Sabine Lisicki served a tennis ball during a match at 131 miles an hour (210.8 km/h)—the fastest ever recorded for a female player.

1 Someone who suffers from GEPHYROPHOBIA is afraid of crossing bridges.

2 In 2004, archaeologists looking to extend the subway in New York City, U.S.A., found UNDERGROUND COW TUNNELS used at the turn of the 20th century.

3 The Turkish Marmaray tunnel that runs under the Bosporus Strait is the first rail tunnel to CONNECT TWO CONTINENTS, Asia and Europe.

4 SKYBRIDGE, near Sochi, Russia, is 1,140 feet (347.5 m) long, making it the LONGEST PEDESTRIAN BRIDGE in the world.

5 People used to create bridges by WEAVING VINES together.

6 DRAWBRIDGES in medieval castles were raised from the inside to KEEP INTRUDERS OUT.

7 The Frankford Avenue Bridge in Philadelphia, U.S.A, is the OLDEST BRIDGE IN AMERICA still in use. It was built in 1697.

8 During World War II, British engineer Donald Bailey invented a PORTABLE BRIDGE that could be assembled quickly and hold the weight of tanks.

9 The QUEBEC BRIDGE over the St. Lawrence River in Canada collapsed TWICE during its construction in the early 20th century.

10 The cables that support the GEORGE WASHINGTON BRIDGE in New York City, U.S.A., contain 26,424 twisted wires.

11 The main SUSPENSION CABLES of the Golden Gate Bridge in San Francisco, California, U.S.A., are THREE FEET (0.9 M) IN DIAMETER.

12 Secret tunnels under the ancient Mexican city of TEOTIHUACAN lead to three rooms containing thousands of ancient objects.

13 Before a new LONDON BRIDGE was built, the old one was dismantled and shipped to LAKE HAVASU CITY, Arizona, U.S.A., where it was re-erected in 1972.

14 The 15.2-mile (24.5-km) Laerdal Tunnel in Norway is the WORLD's LONGEST ROAD TUNNEL. It cuts through mountains.

15 If you are scared of heights, don't cross the ROYAL GORGE BRIDGE near Cañon City, Colorado, U.S.A. The Arkansas River is 956 FEET (291 M) BELOW!

16 Ancient Romans built the PONT DU GARD BRIDGE in Avignon, France, more than 2,000 years ago. It's as tall as a 15-story building!

17 Workers have been painting all 120 acres (486,000 sq m) of the SYDNEY HARBOR BRIDGE in Australia ever since it opened in 1932.

18 Engineers now design "SMART" BRIDGES that use modern technology to detect any structural damage.

19 Most bridge failures occur because of EXTREME NATURAL EVENTS such as earthquakes and floods, or from using low-grade building materials.

20 Completed more than 1,400 years ago, the Zhaozhou or Anji Bridge in China is the OLDEST STONE SINGLE ARCH BRIDGE in the world.

21 Gustave Eiffel DESIGNED BRIDGES as well as the Eiffel Tower in Paris, France.

22 When a bus was caught on the TOWER BRIDGE IN LONDON, ENGLAND, as the drawbridge raised up, the driver accelerated and jumped the gap.

23 Inspired by the fairy tale *The Three Billy Goats Gruff*, a CONCRETE TROLL SCULPTURE resides under a highway overpass in Seattle, Washington, U.S.A.

24 In December 2015, FLOODING following heavy rain destroyed a 300-year-old STONE BRIDGE in Tadcaster, England.

25 In less than four months after opening in July 1940, the TACOMA NARROWS BRIDGE in Washington State, U.S.A., COLLAPSED.

26 The TALLEST STRUCTURE in France is the Millau Viaduct bridge in Millau. The roadway is 1,125 feet (343 m) above ground.

27 To create a modern tunnel, engineers use a TUNNEL BORING MACHINE to "chew" through the rock at a rate of 250 feet (76 m) per day.

28 Disney World in Orlando, Florida, U.S.A., is built upon miles and miles of underground tunnels called UTILIDORS, with offices and facilities for the park WORKERS.

29 Medieval armies would launch SNEAK ATTACKS on enemy castles by digging tunnels underneath the MOATS to gain access.

30 The world's first IRON BRIDGE was constructed in 1779 in Shropshire, England, at the start of the INDUSTRIAL REVOLUTION.

31
More than 33.4 miles (53.8 km) long, the Seikan Tunnel in Japan is the LONGEST RAILROAD TUNNEL in the world.

34
Cars won't use the largest tunnel in the United States when completed in 2018—IT WILL CARRY WATER to the residents of New York City.

39
Before the Brooklyn Bridge in New York City was built, the CHIEF ENGINEER died. His son completed it instead.

43
Toronto, Canada, has the largest UNDERGROUND SHOPPING CENTER in the world with 19 miles (31 km) of tunnels linking shopping sites.

48
Venice, Italy, is built on small islands accessed by canals. It's often called the CITY OF BRIDGES because there are more than 400 bridges over the CANALS.

35
Completed in 1998, the AKASHI KAIKYO BRIDGE in Japan can handle up to 180 miles-an-hour (290-km/h) winds and withstand earthquakes.

40
With construction beginning in 1860, the London Underground, also known as the Tube, was the FIRST SUBWAY system in the world.

44
In March 1944, during World War II, 76 prisoners ESCAPED from a Nazi prison camp THROUGH TUNNELS they had dug out underneath the camp.

49
Tunnels aren't always underground. In Kyoto, Japan, there is a 1,000-foot (305-m)-long path underneath a canopy of BAMBOO TREES.

50 BRIDGE AND TUNNEL
FACTS THAT SPAN TIME

36
Some of Rome's tunnels were made using an ancient technique where rocks were HEATED WITH FIRE and then splashed with cold water to break them up.

45
Want a rush? Try bungee jumping 709 feet (216 m) off the Bloukrans Bridge, South Africa. Bungee jumpers experience SEVEN SECONDS OF FREE FALL.

32
Visitors to the CAPILANO SUSPENSION BRIDGE in Vancouver, Canada, walk among the forest trees, 230 feet (70 m) above the river below.

41
Another underground "tube" in London was the MAIL RAIL. This transported the London's mail using DRIVERLESS TRAINS.

37
Small trains called GEOMETRY TRAINS travel along subway lines, taking measurements to see if any of the rails are out of alignment.

46
The Channel Tunnel connects London with France by passing beneath the English Channel. At its deepest, the tunnel sits 250 feet (76 m) below sea level.

33
The roof and sides of COVERED BRIDGES were originally built to cover and protect the bridge's wooden elements from the weather.

42
Part of the Nanpu Bridge in Shanghai, China, is in a SPIRAL SHAPE.

50
Created in the EIGHTH CENTURY B.C., Hezekiah's Tunnel, located underneath the city of JERUSALEM, is one of the world's oldest known tunnels.

38
Spanning 290 feet (88.4 m), LANDSCAPE ARCH in Arches National Park, Utah, U.S.A., has the greatest span of any natural arch in the United States.

47
Visitors to a national park in California can DRIVE through the "Tunnel Log" carved out of a SEQUOIA TREE.

1

IN THE STONE AGE, LIFE EXPECTANCY WAS ONLY

20

YEARS.

2

DURING THE WITCH-HUNT CRAZE IN THE MID-17TH CENTURY, MATTHEW HOPKINS WAS NAMED THE **"WITCH FINDER GENERAL."** HE TRAVELED THROUGH ENGLAND IDENTIFYING WITCHES. MORE THAN 200 PEOPLE WERE KILLED AS A RESULT OF HIS ACCUSATIONS.

3

King Charles VI of France suffered a **STRANGE ILLNESS** in 1392 that caused his hair and **NAILS TO FALL OUT.** It also made him loony.

4

IN ANCIENT ROME, CITIZENS SCRUBBED DAILY IN ELABORATE BATHHOUSES. AFTER THE FALL OF THE ROMAN EMPIRE, BATHING WAS BEYOND THE MEANS OF MOST PEOPLE—AND WAS EVEN CONSIDERED UNHEALTHY!

5

When the **VIKINGS** attacked Paris, France, in 885, the French defended themselves by **POURING BOILING OIL** on the invaders.

6

AMERICAN COLONISTS THOUGHT YOU COULD CURE FEVER AND CHILLS BY EATING AN APPLE PIE THAT HAD A SPIDER WEB BAKED IN IT.

7

One out of every six Londoners died of the **BUBONIC PLAGUE** in 1665. Searchers of the dead went **DOOR-TO-DOOR** to collect corpses.

25 FACTS ABOUT HORRIBLE

8

THE CURE FOR A HEADACHE IN ANCIENT PERU WAS SKULL DRILLING. MANY PEOPLE SURVIVED THE EARLY FORM OF BRAIN SURGERY. SOME EVEN WORE THEIR SKULL CHIPS AROUND THEIR NECKS TO DRIVE AWAY EVIL SPIRITS.

9

ATTILA THE HUN, who sought to conquer much of the Roman Empire in the fifth century, was a calculating and ruthless leader. He even **KILLED HIS OWN BROTHER,** Bleda, in order to secure his rule.

10

Dentists in ancient Egypt recommended putting a **MOUSE** that had just been killed in your mouth as a **REMEDY FOR BAD BREATH.**

11 In 1944 a fire started under the big top of a **RINGLING BROS. AND BARNUM & BAILEY CIRCUS** in Hartford, Connecticut, U.S.A. Almost 200 people were killed in the fire and many burned.

12 In ancient Rome, people were infamous for feasting until they could FEAST NO MORE—and then VOMITING on the floor to make room for seconds, thirds, or fourths.

13 The 13th-century **MONGOL RULER GENGHIS KHAN** caused a stink each time he unleashed his army on kingdoms that were troublesome. **EACH** Mongol soldier traveled with about **TEN HORSES**, and all those horses left **A LOT OF DUNG**.

14 IN 1969, BUZZ ALDRIN BECAME THE FIRST MAN TO PEE ON THE MOON.

15 Poor immigrants coming to America in the early 1900s traveled by ship in CROWDED AND FILTHY CONDITIONS. They weren't able to BREATHE FRESH AIR during the voyage.

16 In ancient Egypt, people with eye irritations were given a **SPECIAL OINTMENT** to apply: **HONEY MIXED WITH HUMAN BRAIN** and maybe a little animal poop folded in.

17 People who lived in castles relieved themselves in the garderobe: **A HOLE CUT INTO A STONE BENCH** over a shaft that emptied into the moat. They wiped with **HAY**.

18 IVAN IV, A 16TH-CENTURY RUSSIAN RULER AND THE FIRST TSAR, WAS KNOWN AS IVAN GROZNY (OR "THE TERRIBLE") FOR THE REIGN OF TERROR HE INITIATED AGAINST THE NOBILITY.

HISTORIES

19 PEOPLE WHO ATTENDED THE FUNERAL OF THE 11TH-CENTURY ENGLISH KING **WILLIAM THE CONQUEROR** WERE IN FOR A SHOCK. HIS STOMACH EXPLODED DURING THE CEREMONY.

20 Life wasn't easy in the 1400s, but it was ESPECIALLY BAD if you lived in what is now the country of Romania. VLAD THE IMPALER, a prince who ruled the region and that many say was the inspiration for DRACULA, had a knack for impaling his victims.

21 The Aztec, a civilization that flourished in Mexico in the 1400s and early 1500s, **SACRIFICED HUMANS** as a way to HONOR THEIR GODS.

22 While the Vikings are known as **BLOODTHIRSTY CONQUERORS,** new evidence suggests their terrible exploits may have been exaggerated by writers of the time.

23 THE ANCIENT XIXIMES OF NORTHERN MEXICO BELIEVED DEVOURING THEIR ENEMIES WOULD GUARANTEE A BOUNTIFUL HARVEST.

24 ANCIENT GREEKS IN ATHENS GOT TOGETHER EVERY YEAR TO VOTE IF ANYONE AMONG THEM WAS BECOMING A TYRANT. THE PERSON WITH THE MOST VOTES WAS BANISHED FROM THE CITY FOR TEN YEARS.

25 In the early 1800s, "BODY SNATCHERS" would dig up corpses and SELL them to medical schools so that students could learn about the HUMAN BODY.

1 The first MONSTER TRUCK, named Bigfoot, came to be because its owner kept breaking parts—each time he replaced one, HE MADE THE TRUCK A LITTLE BIGGER.

2 Each gallon (3.8 L) of fuel a monster truck burns is only enough to travel HALF THE LENGTH OF A FOOTBALL FIELD.

3 The world's LONGEST LIMOUSINE has a swimming pool and a king-size WATER BED inside.

4 3,233 TONKA TRUCK TOYS could fit inside A MINING TRUCK—the mega-vehicle they are designed to look like.

5 Built in the United States in the 1990s, *ROBOSAURUS* is a 30-ton (27.2 MT) giant robot that **TRANSFORMS** from a **SEMI-TRUCK TRAILER** into a fire-breathing, **CAR-EATING** *T. REX* in just two minutes. The driver sits inside the head of the robot.

6 The **LARGEST SHIP EVER BUILT** contains more steel than 3,400 Golden Gate Bridges.

7 A billionaire from the United Arab Emirates built a **21-FOOT (6.4-M)-TALL JEEP** that he uses to tow a GLOBE-SHAPED MOTOR HOME.

8 The largest solar-powered airplane, *SOLAR IMPULSE 2,* has a wingspan greater than that of a Boeing 747 jumbo jet. Yet made of **CARBON FIBER**, it weighs less than a car.

MEGA-VEHICLES

9 The LeTourneau **OVERLAND TRAIN** built in Texas in the 1950s didn't run on tracks. At its full length of 12 cars, the vehicle stretched 572 feet (174 m) and had 54 motors—one for **EACH PAIR OF WHEELS**, which could be steered, allowing the train to **TURN SHARP CORNERS.**

10 Monster trucks can be **HUGE**—some have **TEN-FOOT (3-M)-TALL TIRES!**

11 The biggest **MINING MACHINE** in the world can remove 264,555 tons (240,000 MT) of coal EACH DAY—the weight of more than **1,300 BLUE WHALES!**

12 A U.A.E. billionaire who built a giant Jeep (fact 7) also built a drivable **DODGE POWER WAGON PICKUP** that's so big it contains BEDROOMS, A BATHROOM, AND A CURVED STAIRCASE.

13 The world's largest cargo airplane, the Antonov An-225, IS SO MASSIVE AND POWERFUL that NASA used it to carry an 86-ton (78-MT) **SPACE SHUTTLE** across the United States. Even a jumbo jet can **FIT INSIDE.**

14 The Mil Mi-26 helicopter is the biggest ever built, standing nearly **THREE STORIES TALL.** It is powerful enough to **PLUCK AN AIRPLANE OFF THE GROUND.**

15 The Stratolaunch airplane will be the biggest ever built, with a **WINGSPAN LONGER THAN A FOOTBALL FIELD.** It will carry rockets into the atmosphere before LAUNCHING THEM.

1 THE TARANTELLA DANCE IS NAMED AFTER THE FRENZIED DANCE-LIKE MOVEMENT PEOPLE DID WHEN THEY HAD BEEN BITTEN BY A TARANTULA.

2 November 29 is Square Dance Day in the United States.

3 In the year 1600, Shakespearean actor Will Kemp danced an Irish jig from London to Norwich—about 120 miles (193 km).

4 When Americans began dancing the foxtrot in the early 1900s, church officials disapproved. That disapproval made it one of the most popular dances of all time.

5 Ballet dancers on pointe have a foam-padded toe box that wraps around the toes to support the foot.

6 Ballet dancers train for a year to become strong enough to dance on pointe.

7 A dung beetle will climb on top of a ball of dung and dance in a circle to get its bearings.

8 In Nepal, people love to dance so much—and make others join them—that they have a word that means "to make dance": *nachaune*.

9 Whirling dervishes—people who spin around and around—do so as part of the Sufi tradition of Islam. When a dervish whirls, he imitates the spin of natural objects from atoms to planets.

10 Honeybees dance to tell other bees where to find food. The dance communicates how far to fly and in what direction.

11 The hokey pokey is called the hokey cokey in England.

12 When women perform the maypole dance they move in a circle around a tall, decorated pole. The dance originally came from England, Sweden, and Germany.

13 Most maypole dances are done on May 1, but in Sweden it's a midsummer celebration.

14 Applejack, heel split, and rocking chair are the names of moves in line dancing.

15 IN 1942, 50 ELEPHANTS AND 50 BALLERINAS PERFORMED A CHOREO-GRAPHED DANCE.

16 People aren't the only ones to line dance. Horses can be trained to do it, too, by lining up with people and matching their steps.

17 In the dragon dance, Chinese dancers hold a dragon made of paper or cloth on sticks, making it move and sway.

18 The "Dance of the Swans" in Tchaikovsky's *Swan Lake* is one of the hardest dances in ballet to perform.

19 When the Chinese dragon dance first began 2,000 years ago, it was performed to worship ancestors and pray for rain.

20 An Internet video of the Harlem shake dance was viewed 7.4 million times in just one week.

21 Ballet originated in 15th-century Italy. At the time, everyone participated, not just the ballet dancers.

22 International ballroom dancing is very formal, but the American style allows for dips and spins.

23 The cha-cha originated with voodoo celebrations in Haiti.

24 Michelle Obama, the First Lady of the United States, had a dance-off with Ellen DeGeneres to celebrate the fifth anniversary of Obama's Let's Move campaign.

25 In the Middle East, carvings and paintings up to 9,000 years old provide the oldest evidence of people dancing.

26 Tap dance came from a combination of Scottish, Irish, and English clog dancing and African tribal dances.

27 Dancers avoid getting dizzy when they spin by "spotting"—looking at a fixed spot on the wall for as long as possible before whipping the head around to stare at the spot again.

28 In China, people perform a lion dance to bring good fortune. It takes two people to wear the lion costume for the dance.

29 AFRIKA BAMBAATAA, A REFORMED CRIMINAL, PROMOTED BREAK DANCING AS A POSITIVE ALTERNATIVE TO STREET FIGHTING.

30 King of the Kidz is the only world championship break dance competition for young people.

31 The name "cha-cha" comes from a plant that produces seedpods used as rattles.

32 Bebop, or bop, is a fast-paced version of the jitterbug that people danced to blazing-fast jazz music in the 1940s.

33 The Viennese waltz is the oldest ballroom dance still performed today.

34 Tap dancer Savion Glover wore a motion capture suit to help animators create authentic dance moves for *Happy Feet*'s Mumble, a penguin who loves to dance.

35 Cuttlefish (relatives of squid) do a fluttery dance while flashing colorful patterns over their bodies in order to attract mates and confuse prey.

36 Male manakins (small tropical birds) team up to do a leapfrog dance in order to impress females.

37 Many square dance terms, including "do-si-do," "promenade," and "allemande," come from French.

38 The Winter Olympics of 2014 was the first time that U.S. skaters won gold in the ice dancing competition.

39 THE LONGEST DANCE MARATHON ON RECORD LASTED 131 HOURS.

40 Hoofers are tap dancers that focus on footwork with little arm or upper body movement.

41 Before people could write, they used dance to communicate important events. Dances prepared groups for activities such as harvesting or hunting.

42 Dance/movement therapists use dance to improve the physical, mental, and emotional health of their patients.

43 Indian dancers wear anklets of bells, called *Ghungrus*, to emphasize the rhythm of their footwork.

44 Some NFL players take ballet to strengthen their knees, ankles, and feet. This makes them less likely to be injured when playing football.

75 FACTS ABOUT DANCE

TO KEEP YOU ON YOUR TOES

45 NFL player Steve McLendon says ballet is harder than anything else he does.

46 Women in many Native American tribes do a circular dance wearing dresses with metal jingles as a prayer to heal someone who is ill.

47 Capoeira is a Brazilian martial art form disguised as dance. Slaves created it to practice fighting skills without letting anyone know what they were doing.

48 BIRDS CALLED GREBES PERFORM COORDINATED BEAK-TO-BEAK DANCES WITH THEIR MATES.

49 The moonwalk was originally called the backslide.

50 Dancing provides the same type of workout as bike riding or jogging.

51 A Native American powwow is set up as a series of circles. The innermost circle is the dance arena.

52 Most dances performed at pow-wows come from the Plains tribes of the United States and Canada.

53 Male jumping spiders clap, hum, and tap in an elaborate song and dance when courting females.

54 Although Michael Jackson is best known for the moonwalk, it was performed years earlier by Sammy Davis, Jr., Cab Calloway, and Fred Astaire.

55 DANCING RELEASES BRAIN CHEMICALS THAT MAKE US FEEL HAPPY.

56 The macarena is danced only to the song "Macarena" by Los del Rio. It is the most popular one-hit-wonder of all time.

57 The chicken dance is called the duck dance in Switzerland and Germany.

58 A cockatoo named Snowball was the first nonhuman dancer recognized by scientists as truly dancing (moving to the beat without being trained to do so).

59 Peacock spiders of Australia and freshwater algae are known to dance.

60 A dance party is held in the Dead Sea in Israel each year. In 2014, 13,000 people attended.

61 The Hamster Dance (an animation of hamsters dancing and singing) was created by a college student as part of a dare to see who could get the most online views. (She won.)

62 According to scientists, when we watch someone else dance with sadness or joy we experience the same emotion.

63 When a break-dancer windmills, he spins from chest to upper back using his legs—that are in the air—to propel him in a circle.

64 Morris dancing involves a group of performers who wave handkerchiefs or sticks and wear bells on their legs.

65 At the annual Full-Moon Party in Thailand, enormous sound systems are set up along the beach, so up to 30,000 partygoers can dance the night away.

66 TONY ADAMS, THE WORLD'S FASTEST TAP DANCER, TAPPED 602 BEATS IN JUST 60 SECONDS.

67 Cuban-born Carlos Acosta is regarded as the finest male ballet dancer of recent times.

68 The world's largest line dance involved 25,703 people and took place in China.

69 In Mexico in 2009, almost 14,000 people gathered to show off their zombie moves to Michael Jackson's "Thriller."

70 The boot-scootin' boogie, first performed in 1992, is still the most requested country line dance.

71 The Hawaiian hula dance tells a story. It was originally danced to appease the volcano goddess, Pele.

72 Former U.S. president Gerald Ford danced with Britain's Queen Elizabeth at a White House dinner.

73 ACTION MOVIE ACTRESS MICHELLE YEOH ORIGINALLY TRAINED TO BE A BALLERINA.

74 At the website 24 Hours of Happy, people dance all day and night to Pharrell's hit song "Happy."

75 Bart Simpson has his own dance, called the Bartman. The song "Do the Bartman" was co-written by Michael Jackson.

35 UPLIFTING FACTS ABOUT

1 Even though they are round with SHORT WINGS, bumblebees have enough WING POWER to fly over Mount Everest.

2 An owl's SOFT WING FEATHERS absorb high-frequency sounds, helping it to fly in NEAR SILENCE.

3 Geese fly in a V-formation to REDUCE WIND resistance, which conserves energy so they can fly longer.

4 The least popular days to fly on a COMMERCIAL AIRLINE are Tuesday, Wednesday, and Saturday.

5 A swallowtail butterfly's wings only beat 300 times per minute, THE SLOWEST WING BEAT OF ANY INSECT.

6 A Texas, U.S.A., man once FLEW IN HIS HANG GLIDER—a light, non-motorized aircraft—a record 472.8 miles (761 km). The flight lasted 11 hours.

7 Bats are THE ONLY MAMMALS CAPABLE OF TRUE FLIGHT. Some species can even hover over a flower while eating nectar.

8 Both Union and Confederate SOLDIERS USED HOT AIR BALLOONS during the U.S. Civil War to spy on enemy troops.

9 In the late 15th century, LEONARDO DA VINCI designed—but never built—a HELICOPTER-LIKE MACHINE.

10 A group of 25 parachuters set a record in Dubai, United Arab Emirates, by JUMPING out of a hot air balloon AT THE SAME TIME.

paper kite butterflies

THINGS THAT FLY

11 PAINTED LADY BUTTERFLIES migrate from North Africa to Iceland—that's a trip of about 4,000 miles (6,437 km)!

12 The SpaceX DRAGON is the first commercial free-flying spacecraft designed to deliver goods and people to orbital space.

13 The highest anyone has ever FLOWN A KITE is 14,509 feet (4,422 m) above the point of takeoff. The string was the length of 96 STATUES OF LIBERTY placed on top of one another!

14 A FLYING SQUIRREL doesn't have true powered flight, but it can glide up to 150 feet (46 m), USING ITS LEGS TO STEER AND ITS TAIL TO BRAKE.

15 Dragonflies are the FASTEST FLYING INSECTS. They are known to zip through the air at 35 miles an hour (56 km/h).

16 European airline designers have proposed a plane that runs completely on electric motors, which means NO REFUELING BETWEEN FLIGHTS.

17 The Lockheed Martin P-791 AIRCRAFT COMBINES THE SPEED OF AN AIRPLANE AND THE BUOYANCY OF A BLIMP. It can stay at 20,000 feet (6,096 m) for as long as three weeks!

18 Since flight uses a lot of energy, birds need to be as light as possible. Some of their biggest BONES ARE HOLLOW, but are reinforced with smaller bones that act like supports.

19 DRONES are aircraft that don't have pilots. They are controlled by people—sometimes across the globe—using COMPUTER TECHNOLOGY.

20 When a ROCKET is launched into space it travels at least 30 TIMES FASTER THAN A PASSENGER JET.

21 In 1976, the unmanned Helios 2 orbiter spacecraft became THE FASTEST HUMAN-MADE OBJECT, traveling at 153,800 miles an hour (247,517 km/h).

22 When a type of insect called a MIDGE is in flight, it beats its wings 62,760 TIMES PER MINUTE.

23 Airplanes can only fly forward. But HELICOPTERS can fly up, down, forward, backward, and sideways, and hover!

24 An ENGLISH MAN has racked up more than 15 million frequent flier miles—more than anyone else in the world.

25 In the 1950s, Goodyear, the maker of tires and blimps, made an INFLATABLE AIRPLANE for the U.S. Army. Unfortunately, it could easily be POPPED LIKE A BALLOON!

26 The WRIGHT BROTHERS' father bought them a toy made of cork, bamboo, and paper that FLEW WHEN TOSSED IN THE AIR, sparking their obsession with flight.

27 A dog named Rose CAUGHT SEVEN FLYING FRISBEES, all thrown at the same time, and held them in her mouth at once.

28 A BITING FLY, known as a PUNKIE, is so small that it can fly through the tiny holes of a screen door.

29 The HILLER FLYING PLATFORM, invented in the 1950s, was a platform on which a person could stand and fly, powered by a helicopter blade underneath.

30 During a typical spring or summer month in Britain, there are about THREE BILLION INSECTS within a 0.6-mile (1-km) area flying above your head.

31 BALLOONING SPIDERS release a thread of silk AND HITCH A RIDE ON THE WIND. They have been observed at altitudes of 2.5 miles (4 km) in the sky.

32 The SR-71 BLACKBIRD aircraft once flew from New York, U.S.A. to LONDON, England, in 1 hour and 54 minutes.

33 NASA's experimental jet-flying aircraft is taken high in the sky by ROCKET BOOSTER then its engine kicks in, taking it to a speed of 7,200 miles an hour (11,587 km/h).

34 The GOODYEAR BLIMP, which is filled with helium and CIRCLES ABOVE SPORTS STADIUMS, can only seat seven people!

35 Two British inventors made a flying bicycle that is POWERED BY A GIANT FAN on the back. It can travel up to 25 miles an hour (40 km/h) and reach an altitude of 4,000 feet (1,219 m).

1. Neuschwanstein, the enormous fairy tale–like palace in Bavaria, Germany, that inspired the Sleeping Beauty Castle in Disneyland Park, was built in the late 1800s by King Ludwig II. 2. Pena National Palace in Portugal was built on a rocky peak so it can be seen from anywhere in the forest that surrounds it. 3. Prague Castle, one of the largest castles in the world, was built in about 880. The Czech crown jewels are hidden there. 4. Barbie's Fashion Fairytale Palace includes a V.I.P. drawbridge, a see-through elevator, and a moveable dance floor. 5. Buckingham Palace's 760 windows have to be cleaned every six weeks. The window washer uses a 100-foot (30-m)-long pole with a special brush on the end of it. 6. The gardens at Buckingham Palace include a lake, a tennis court, and a landing pad for helicopters. 7. Neil Armstrong, Wolfgang Amadeus Mozart, Charles Dickens, Mahatma Gandhi, and Nelson Mandela have all visited Buckingham Palace. 8. For more than 200 years a ghost called the Grey Lady has been said to haunt Hampton Court Palace in England and many claim to have seen it. 9. Iolani Palace is the only royal palace in the United States. Located in Honolulu, Hawaii, it was built in the late 1800s for Hawaiian King Kalakaua and Queen Kapiolani. 10. Four palaces make up the Amalienborg palace complex in Copenhagen, home of the Danish royal family. 11. Only kings named "Frederik" have lived in the King Frederik VIII's Palace in Copenhagen, Denmark. 12. The wall surrounding the colorful Grand Palace in Bangkok, Thailand, is more than 1 mile (1.6 km) long. 13. Visitors to the Grand Palace must adhere to a strict dress code or they are not permitted on the grounds. 14. The Temple of the Emerald Buddha on the grounds of the Grand Palace houses a small jade hand-carved Buddha from the 15th century A.D. and is considered priceless. 15. India's Jal Mahal palace sits in the middle of Man Sagar Lake and appears to float—four out of five stories are submerged underwater when the lake is full! 16. The mysterious Amber Room inside Russia's Catherine Palace was decorated with more than six tons (5,443 kg) of amber (worth $142 million today). 17. Built as a summer home in the 17th century, Drottningholm Palace in Sweden sits on an island, about an hour by boat from Stockholm. 18. The Royal Palace of Madrid in Spain has more than 3,000 rooms and covers 1.5 million square feet (140,000 sq m). 19. The Royal Palace is the official residence of the Spanish royal family, but since the 1970s families have chosen to live in the much smaller Zarzuela Palace on the outskirts of Madrid instead. 20. The Palace of Wax in Texas, U.S.A., boasts more than 200 wax figures including Whoopi Goldberg, Johnny Depp, and the cast of *The Wizard of Oz*. 21. The royal residence at Versailles in France was home to three kings, each named Louis, from 1682 to 1789. 22. Louis XIV had the residence transformed into a lavish palace with 700 rooms and more than 2,000 windows. It can hold up to 20,000 people. 23. There are 578 mirrors in the Hall of Mirrors at Versailles. 24. Grigory Rasputin, the "mad monk," was murdered by noblemen at Yusupov Palace in St. Petersburg, Russia, in 1916. 25. Great Britain's King George III frequently took baths in a small tin tub inside a kitchen storage room at Kew Palace in London during the early 1800s. 26. One of the most famous sites in St. Petersburg is the Winter Palace, the official residence for Russian monarchs. It has more than 1,700 doors and 117 staircases. 27. The Palace of Gold glitters on a hill in West Virginia, U.S.A. The Hindu shrine has crystal chandeliers, marble floors, stained glass windows, mirrored ceilings, and gold leaf decorations. 28. The Romanian castle that Bram Stoker used for inspiration for his novel, *Dracula*, went up for sale in 2014 for an estimated $80 million. 29. Fearing assassination, Emperor Paul I of Russia built Mikhailovsky Castle, which was only accessible by a drawbridge. 30. Dragsholm Castle in Denmark, now a luxury hotel, is said to be haunted by many ghosts, including a prisoner from the 1500s. 31. The Summer Palace, built by Peter the Great, was the first palace built in St. Petersburg and had a jail inside where Peter himself would lock up and release prisoners. 32. Nicholas II kept a parrot named Popov in his bathroom in Russia's Alexander Palace. 33. Many believe Ca' Dario palace in Venice, Italy, on the Grand Canal, is haunted because over the years many owners have died shortly after buying the palace. 34. The dungeons and secret passageways inside Scotland's Edinburgh Castle are believed to be some of the most haunted places in the world. 35. There is a secret suite inside Cinderella Castle at Disney World, but you can't book a night's stay there—you have to win it. 36. Scenes for many movies have been filmed at the Palace of Caserta in Italy, including *Star Wars Episode I: The Phantom Menace* and *Mission: Impossible III*. 37. After being recognized as a unique talent, 15-year-old Michelangelo moved into a room in the Medici

Blenheim Palace, Oxfordshire, England

100 FACTS ABOUT ROYAL PALACES

palace in Florence, Italy, so he could focus on his training as an artist. 38. Quirinal Palace sits on the highest hill in Rome and is home to Italy's presidents. 39. The Imperial Palace in Tokyo, Japan, is surrounded by moats. One of the moats, called Chidorigafuchi, has a long walking path lined with cherry blossom trees. 40. Blenheim Palace in England was used for the prince's castle in the 2015 film *Cinderella*. Other films shot there include *Black Beauty* and *Harry Potter and the Order of the Phoenix*. 41. Blenheim Palace bottles and sells its own brand of mineral water. 42. Emperor Domitian had the walls of the Flavian Palace in Rome, Italy, covered in marble because of its reflective surface. He wanted to be able to see if someone was behind him. 43. Singer Castle on Dark Island near Hammond in New York, U.S.A., is a private home chock-full of secret panels and passages. 44. There is a secret door in the wall of the throne room of Buckingham Palace. 45. Rock Palace in Yemen sits high on a giant slab of rock and appears to be growing right out of it. The palace has many narrow stairways and secret passageways. 46. A four-poster bed from the 1600s still sits in Kensington Palace, London. 47. Half of Kensington Palace is made up of royal apartments where the Duke and Duchess of Gloucester currently live, and the other half is occasionally open to the public for tours. 48. One of the most popular tourist attractions in Austria, Schönbrunn Palace in Vienna, has a maze and a labyrinth in its gardens. 49. During select times and special festivals, Mysore Palace in India is lit up with 98,000 light bulbs. 50. Yamashiro restaurant in the Hollywood Hills, California, U.S.A., was modeled after a palace in Japan and offers incredible views of the city. 51. Topkapi Palace in Istanbul, Turkey was once home to a total of 4,000 people. 52. The Château de Chambord in France was built by King Francois I with the help of Leonardo da Vinci in the 1500s. It has 282 fireplaces. 53. The Alhambra palace, meaning "red castle," in Granada, Spain, is named for its reddish walls. 54. At an altitude of 12,000 feet (3,660 m), Potala Palace in Tibet is the highest palace in the world. 55. The Forbidden City palace in Beijing, China, has four "Corner Towers," one on each corner of the city that originally served to house guards as they protected the palace. 56. Researchers found sketches for a palace planned by "Mad" King George III of England that included rooms with no doors and stairways that led nowhere. 57. Henry VII of England began building Nonsuch Palace in 1538. In 1682 the Countess of Castlemaine had it knocked down and sold its parts to pay gambling debts. 58. Within ten years of Emperor Nero's death, every bit of marble, jewels, and ivory were taken from Domus Aurea, his palace, in the center of ancient Rome. 59. When people walked into a room in the center of Domus Aurea, they were showered with flower petals and perfume. 60. One of the rooms in Russia's Winter Palace can hold 10,000 people. 61. The Imperial Palace in Tokyo, Japan, is home to 20 percent of the trees in the city. 62. A crystal chandelier weighing as much as an adult elephant and with 750 lights on it hangs in Dolmabahçe Palace's Ceremonial Hall in Turkey. 63. A high school principal built Bangalore Palace in India for King Chamaraja Wodeyar in 1826. 64. Musicians including Aerosmith and the Rolling Stones have performed on the grounds of Bangalore Palace. 65. There is an amusement park called Fun World on the grounds of Bangalore Palace. 66. Researchers believe that many ancient palaces were used as living quarters for rulers and their families and were also open for the public to use. 67. During the French Revolution in the late 1700s, Luxembourg Palace in France was used as a prison. 68. The Royal Palaces of Abomey, built in the 17th century in West Africa, were surrounded by prickly plants to protect them. 69. The Zulu king, Goodwill Zwelithini, has five royal palaces in South Africa. 70. Three million pebbles cover the courtyard of the Prince's Palace of Monaco in western Europe. 71. Caesars Palace in Las Vegas, U.S.A., is a casino and hotel modeled after ancient Rome. 72. A man in England spent 20 years hand carving his apartment to make it look like the Palace of Versailles. 73. Golestan Palace in Tehran, Iran, has colorful tiled towers that were designed to capture and distribute wind to help keep parts of the palace cool. 74. In 1834 a fire burned the Palace of Westminster in London. When the new palace was built, it had a clock tower that came to be known as Big Ben. 75. Empress Anna Ivanovna created a palace made of ice in Russia during the 1700s, complete with ice furniture. 76. Some cities in North America, including St. Paul in Minnesota, Quebec City in Quebec, and Saranac Lake in New York, build ice palaces every year as part of a winter tradition. 77. An ice palace in Quebec, Canada, was used as inspiration for Queen Elsa's ice palace in the movie *Frozen*. 78. In 2012 an artist made a model of Buckingham Palace out of 3,000 duck spring rolls. 79. A secret tunnel was built inside Mohatta Palace in Karachi, Pakistan, that led to an underground temple. 80. Part of the Royal Palace of Hatfield in England, built in the 1400s, has been used as a setting for many films, including *Batman*. 81. Colonel Muammar Gaddafi kept nine lions as pets on his palace grounds in Libya. 82. Over many years, England's Blenheim Palace has been used as a hospital, a boy's school, and an army training location. 83. King Ludwig II of Bavaria had a special dining table in Herrenchiemsee Palace that sunk down into the room below where servants prepared the table before sending it back up. 84. Ludwig had a porcelain chandelier made for the dining room and insisted the molds be destroyed so that it would be one-of-a-kind. 85. Though nothing remains of China's Weiyang Palace, built in 200 B.C., it remains the largest palace that was ever built, at 1,200 acres (485 ha). 86. The largest residential palace, Istana Nurul Iman, is in Brunei. It has five swimming pools and more than 250 bathrooms. 87. Hawa Mahal is a palace in Jaipur, India, that was built in a pyramid shape and is five stories high. Its name means "palace of the winds." 88. Panels of colorful stained glass in Hawa Mahal create a rainbow of colors on the floor when the sun shines in. 89. In the United Kingdom, the oldest hedge maze—an outdoor maze made of high shrubs—is on the grounds of Hampton Court Palace. 90. In the book *Charlie and the Chocolate Factory*, Grandpa Joe tells about how Willy Wonka built a chocolate palace for a prince who wanted to live inside it rather than eat it. 91. Former royal palace Buda Castle in Budapest, Hungary, hosts festivals in its courtyards including a sausage festival and a chocolate festival. 92. The Ideal Palace was built by a French mail carrier from 1879 through 1912. He collected stones and rocks along his route and built the palace in Hauterives, southern France. 93. A palace in Florida, U.S.A., that was for sale in 2014 had a 22-carat gold leaf front gate, six waterfalls outside, and an IMAX theater with 18 seats. 94. Initially built as a fortress, the Louvre in Paris, France, was rebuilt as a royal palace in the 16th century. In 1793 it changed again, becoming an art museum. 95. Almost 800 people work on staff within the royal household at Buckingham Palace, London, England. 96. Pop singer Madonna is one of the few people who has ever been on the balcony of Casa Rosada, Argentina's "Pink Palace." 97. Campo del Moro, the park behind the Royal Palace in Madrid, Spain, used to be a royal playground. 98. In honor of its 500th anniversary, Hampton Court Palace in London hosted a sleepover party for families. 99. Everything is round in France's Le Palais Bulles, French for "the palace of bubbles." 100. At Legoland in Windsor, England, there is a model of Buckingham Palace built out of 36,000 Lego bricks.

1

TWO TABLESPOONS (14.8 ML) of unpopped kernels creates a whopping FOUR CUPS (0.95 L) of popcorn WHEN POPPED.

2

The kernels burst open when heated. The POPPING SOUND happens when POCKETS OF WATER VAPOR deep inside the kernel explode.

3

Although there are many types of corn, POPCORN is made from the seeds of the maize plant, *Zea mays*, variety *everta*.

4

One EAR OF CORN contains between 400 and 600 KERNELS.

5

Kernels of corn EXPAND UP TO 40 TIMES their original size when popped.

6

Before the hulls of the kernels pop, PRESSURE inside them reaches a level three to four times HIGHER THAN THE PRESSURE OF AIR INSIDE A CAR TIRE.

7

Popcorn was originally eaten by the NATIVES OF NORTH AMERICA.

8

Popcorn (and all other types of corn) is actually a TYPE OF GRASS.

9

The OLDEST EARS of popcorn ever found were about 5,600 YEARS OLD AND TINY—the largest was only TWO INCHES (5 CM) LONG.

10

After popcorn is picked, the EARS MUST BE DRIED until they reach the right level of moisture—13.5 PERCENT.

11

Almost all of the popcorn sold around the world is GROWN IN THE UNITED STATES, more than one-fourth from the STATE OF NEBRASKA.

12

FRENCH EXPLORERS were probably the FIRST EUROPEANS to try popcorn. They learned about it from the IROQUOIS.

13

Native Americans used to believe that SPIRITS LIVED INSIDE kernels of popcorn. They thought heat ANGERED the spirits, causing them to escape AS STEAM.

14

The AZTEC HONORED THEIR GODS by scattering popcorn in front of statues.

15

Aztec also WORE GARLANDS OF STRUNG POPCORN around their necks to honor the gods.

16

ANCIENT TOMBS in Peru, South America, contain kernels of popcorn, SOME OF WHICH STILL POP.

17

During the 1930s, popcorn vendors WALKED WHEELED POPCORN CARTS around cities, stopping wherever they found CROWDS OF PEOPLE.

18

Approximately 2 percent of kernels in any bag of microwave popcorn DO NOT POP, sometimes due to MOISTURE DAMAGE.

19

Americans EAT 16 BILLION QUARTS (15.1 BILLION L) of popped popcorn EACH YEAR.

20

Percy Spencer used popcorn in his EXPERIMENTS as he worked to CREATE THE MICROWAVE OVEN.

21

A whopping 70 PERCENT of popcorn is EATEN AT HOME.

22

A kernel of popcorn can SHOOT THREE FEET (0.9 M) INTO THE AIR when it pops.

23

A MEDIUM POPCORN AND SODA COMBO can contain the SAME FAT AND CALORIES as a huge dish of sausages, bacon, scrambled eggs, and cheese.

24

A MEDIUM BUCKET of popcorn at some movie theaters contains 20 cups of popcorn—the LARGE bucket contains the SAME AMOUNT.

25

Most "BUTTERED" popcorn is actually seasoned with butter-flavored SOYBEAN OIL.

26

CRACKER JACK—a mixture of POPCORN, PEANUTS, AND MOLASSES—was first sold at the Chicago World's Fair in 1893.

27

The world's LARGEST POPCORN BALL was built at the Indiana State Fair in Indiana, U.S.A.—it weighed 6,510 pounds (2,953 kg).

28

The most valuable Cracker Jack prizes were BASEBALL CARDS featuring Joe Jackson, Christy Mathewson, and Ty Cobb. A set of all three sold for $800,000 in 2004.

29

Probably the weirdest flavor of popcorn is the "PREGNANCY MIX." It tastes like dill pickles and ice cream.

30

People in the POPCORN INDUSTRY call the kernels that don't pop "SPINSTERS."

50 BURSTING FACTS ABOUT POPCORN

31
"Hull-less" popcorn has a hull but it simply breaks into **SMALLER PIECES** so the person eating the popcorn **DOESN'T NOTICE IT.**

32
Popcorn comes in two post-pop shapes: **MUSHROOM AND SNOWFLAKE.**

33
Makers of **CARAMEL POPCORN** use mushroom-shaped popcorn because it is **LESS LIKELY TO CRUMBLE.**

34
In 1965 Orville Redenbacher and Charles Bowman created hybrid **SNOWFLAKE** popcorn, which popped up **TWICE AS BIG** as the regular stuff.

35
Popcorn is the **OFFICIAL SNACK FOOD** of Illinois, U.S.A. It became an **ILLINOIS STATE SYMBOL** in 2003.

36
In 2008, a 20-foot (6-m)-tall sculpture of **MICKEY MOUSE** was made entirely of **POPCORN.**

37
ONE CUP of unpopped popcorn contains about **1,600 KERNELS.**

38
QUINOA AND AMARANTH, two grains from the Andes mountains in South America, **ALSO POP WHEN HEATED.**

39
Popcorn kernels can be **YELLOW, WHITE, RED, BLUE, PURPLE,** or **BLACK.** Popcorn may be naturally or artificially colored.

40
Orville Redenbacher was only **12 YEARS OLD** when he **STARTED GROWING POPCORN.**

41
When planted, **ONE HECTARE** (the equivalent of 2.5 soccer fields) of popcorn has nearly **28,000 SEEDS.**

42
People **EAT MORE** popcorn in the **AUTUMN.**

43
Some homes have "**POPCORN CEILINGS**" that are **TEXTURED** to look like popcorn.

44
Ears of popcorn are not **HARVESTED** until the plant has turned **DRY AND BROWN.**

45
Winners of **MTV MOVIE AWARDS** are each given a **GOLDEN POPCORN TROPHY**—a cup of popcorn figurine about 12 inches (30 cm) tall.

46
The **TEMPERATURE INSIDE** a kernel of popcorn reaches almost 350°F (177°C) before it **BURSTS** open.

47
Popcorn stored in a **REFRIGERATOR** will be **LESS LIKELY TO POP** because air inside the refrigerator is **TOO DRY.**

48
ONE-THIRD of popcorn grown in the United States is **SHIPPED TO MEXICO.**

49
The Jelly Belly BeanBoozled Challenge contains buttery popcorn flavored jelly beans—and **IDENTICAL ONES** that taste like **ROTTEN EGGS.**

50
In the early 1900s, movie theaters had signs asking moviegoers to **CHECK THEIR POPCORN WITH THEIR COATS** so as not to make a mess of the theater.

1

WHEN **SUPERMAN** WAS FIRST CREATED, HE WAS A BALD, POWER-HUNGRY BAD GUY.

2 Matter-Eater Lad could **EAT ANYTHING** except food from his **HOME PLANET OF BISMOLL.**

3 **STAN LEE,** creator of many superheroes, put a hyphen in Spider-Man's name because he didn't want people to **CONFUSE THE NEW HERO** with Superman.

4 **SUPERMAN** MAY HAVE SUPERSPEED, BUT **FLASH** IS FASTER, BEATING SUPERMAN IN THREE OUT OF FIVE RACES (THEY WERE TIED IN THE OTHER TWO).

5 UNTIL 2011, THE COMICS CODE AUTHORITY MADE RULES ABOUT WHAT COULD APPEAR IN COMIC BOOKS. WEREWOLVES, VAMPIRES, **AND** ZOMBIES WERE NOT ALLOWED.

6 The publisher of *Spider-Man* comics thought the **IDEA WAS TERRIBLE.** He insisted that kids **HATED SPIDERS.**

7 BATMAN'S SIDEKICK, **ROBIN,** EVENTUALLY GREW UP TO BE A SUPERHERO OF HIS OWN: **NIGHTWING.**

25 SUPER

8 **BOUNCING BOY** TRIED OUT FOR THE LEAGUE OF SUPERHEROES AND WAS **REJECTED—TWICE.**

9 Wolverine's very **FIRST MASK** had a black nose and **WHISKERS.**

10 AQUAMAN'S SIDEKICK AQUALAD HAD A PET WALRUS NAMED TUSKY.

11 **SUPERMAN'S FAVORITE BOOK** is *To Kill a Mockingbird* by Harper Lee.

TO KILL A *Mockingbird*

A NOVEL BY HARPER LEE

12 Marvel Comics shares a trademark on the term **"SUPER HERO"** with DC Comics. Marvel used to own rights to the word **"ZOMBIE"** as well.

13 ARM-FALL-OFF BOY CAN **DETACH HIS ARMS** AND USE THEM AS WEAPONS AGAINST VILLAINS.

14 The man who created **WONDER WOMAN** also created the first **LIE DETECTOR**, not unlike his superhero's LASSO OF TRUTH.

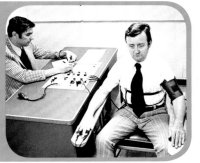

15 When Wonder Woman debuted in 1941, she **WORE A SKIRT.**

16 Wonder Woman **RAN FOR PRESIDENT**— twice —but didn't win.

17 Scientists are working to CREATE ARMORED SUITS that increase the wearer's strength, much like Tony Stark's costume when he becomes IRON MAN.

18 MARVEL COMICS REINVENTED **CAPTAIN MARVEL,** TURNING THE MILITARY CAPTAIN INTO A **TEENAGE MUSLIM GIRL** NAMED KAMALA KHAN.

19 **CAPTAIN AMERICA** was not one of the original Avengers— when he joined, he **REPLACED HULK.**

20 **TONY STARK,** who is also Iron Man, is kept alive by an arc reactor **EMBEDDED IN HIS CHEST.**

21 When **STONE BOY** turned himself to stone, he **COULDN'T MOVE.** Other members of the **LEGION OF SUBSTITUTE HEROES** threw his rocky body at the enemy.

22 Avenger **HAWKEYE DOESN'T ACTUALLY HAVE ANY SUPERPOWERS,** but he is an acrobat and aerialist with world-class archery skills.

23 **GREEN LANTERN'S** super-power is his **IMAGINATION**— he can create anything just by thinking about it.

24 **SQUIRREL GIRL** once defeated Iron Man's nemesis **DOCTOR DOOM** by overwhelming him with **FUZZY-TAILED RODENTS.**

HERO FACTS TO THE RESCUE

25 TEENAGE MUTANT NINJA TURTLES EAT PIZZA WITH SOME **WACKY TOPPINGS:** PEANUT BUTTER, AVOCADO, AND PICKLE; SALAMI AND DOUBLE YOGURT; EVEN **ANCHOVIES AND BANANAS!**

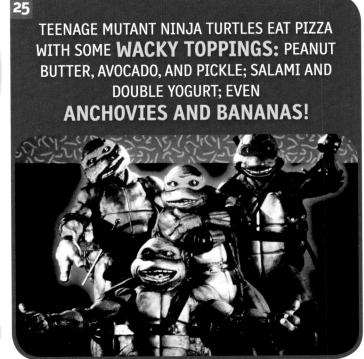

1 More streets are named SECOND STREET in the United States than any other street name.

2 On average, a house on a STREET with a NAME (Duncan Avenue) instead of a NUMBER (Third Street) costs more.

3 Ebenezer Place, a street in Wick, Scotland, is only 6 feet, 9 inches (2.05 m) long. The street runs in front of HOTEL DOORWAY.

4 There are eight hairpin turns in just ONE BLOCK of Lombard Street in San Francisco, California, U.S.A. It's called the CROOKEDEST STREET IN THE WORLD because of these quick, sharp turns.

5 In 1924 drivers traveling on an Italian road connecting Milan to Varese, the Autostrada dei Laghi (Lake Highway), were THE FIRST IN THE WORLD TO DRIVE ON A MOTORWAY connecting two cities.

6 A street in Cary, North Carolina, U.S.A, is JUST PLAIN AWESOME! Literally, it's named Awesome Street.

7 Beijing, the capital of China, has SIX "RING" ROADS THAT CIRCLE THE CITY in wider and wider circles. The outermost road stretches for 117 miles (188 km).

NEAT STREETS

8 A narrow street through the Maeklong Market in Samut Songkhram, Thailand, doubles as a railroad track. **SEVEN TIMES A DAY A TRAIN PASSES THROUGH.**

9 A neighborhood of Zaragoza, Spain, named one of its streets "AVENIDA DE SUPER MARIO BROS" after the video game characters.

10 *Sesame Street* was originally called *1-2-3 AVENUE B.* The TV production company changed the name just before the program was first aired.

11 Duke of Gloucester Street in Williamsburg, Virginia, U.S.A., is known as "DOG" STREET for short (using the first letters of the words in the street name). The street got its name in 1699.

12 The main street of Hershey, Pennsylvania, U.S.A., is **CHOCOLATE AVENUE.**

13 In 1990, after the **AFRICAN COUNTRY OF NAMIBIA** became independent, some high-ranking officials **NAMED STREETS** after themselves.

14 Washington, D.C., U.S.A., has an I Street and a K Street, **BUT NO J STREET.** When the streets were named, the typography for *I* and *J* were interchangeable so they left *J* out to avoid confusion.

15 A street in Reutlingen, Germany, is less than 20 inches (51 cm) at its widest point. The alley between two houses is in danger of **CLOSING UP ENTIRELY** as the houses slump toward each other.

1 One of the oldest things from Earth is no longer on Earth! Early in our planet's history, a body the size of Mars crashed into the planet dislodging a chunk that scientists think created the moon.

2 Leatherback turtles have been around for more than 150 million years—since the time of the dinosaurs.

3 There hasn't always been oxygen in Earth's atmosphere to breathe. It's only been around for about 2.5 billion years.

4 The oldest cat known to have ever lived was Creme Puff, a kitty in Austin, Texas, U.S.A., who lived for 38 years and 3 days.

5 The oldest water on Earth was found 1.5 miles (2.4 km) down in a mine in Canada. It's dated to between 1 and 2.5 billion years old.

6 The Charles William, Jr., house in Somerville, Massachusetts, U.S.A., was the first home to have a telephone line. It was connected to the owner's office. Dial 1 for home and 2 for the office.

7 SCIENTISTS THINK THAT 40,000-YEAR-OLD HAND PRINTS AND CAVE ART IN A CAVE ON AN ISLAND IN INDONESIA ARE THE OLDEST ART IN THE WORLD.

8 A group of quaking aspen trees in Fish Lake, Utah, is 80,000 years old. This colony of trees is called Pando.

9 Yellowstone was the first national park in the U.S. It has petrified trees that were preserved during volcanic eruptions some 50 million years ago.

10 People have been living in the town of Jericho in the Middle East for 11,000 years.

11 Scientists dating rocks from in the Jack Hills of western Australia found that they were the oldest pieces of Earth's crust found to date—about 4.4 billion years old.

12 About 270 million years ago, almost all the land on Earth was contained in one large mass called Pangaea.

13 A science teacher in Maine, U.S.A., kept a Twinkie in his classroom for 30 years. It eventually developed the consistency of Styrofoam.

14 A Norwegian spruce tree in Sweden has roots that have been growing for nearly 10,000 years.

15 SCIENTISTS USE THE MINERAL ZIRCON IN ROCKS TO HELP DATE EARLY EVENTS IN EARTH'S HISTORY BECAUSE ZIRCON IS VERY DURABLE AND DOES NOT CHANGE OR DECAY OVER TIME.

16 The first life on Earth occurred some 3.8 billion years ago with single-celled organisms, such as microscopic bacteria.

17 The Knap of Howar, two stone houses found on the Scottish island of Papay, were built in about 3,600 B.C. and are probably the oldest in northwest Europe. Scientists think they were a house and a barn.

18 A meadow of sea grass between two Spanish islands in the Mediterranean Sea first started to grow 100,000 years ago.

19 Fossilized footprints found in northern Kenya in Africa show that our human ancestors walked upright at least 1.5 million years ago.

20 The first animals on Earth that were made up of more than one cell lived almost 600 million years ago. They are called Ediacarans and they lacked heads or mouths.

21 The Burnt City in what is today's Iran is one of the oldest cities in the world. Founded in 3200 B.C., it was made of mud bricks that were preserved because of the dry desert climate.

22 In the 1930s, a man named George Beauchamp played the first electric guitar. It was called the Frying Pan and was made out of aluminum.

23 Fossils of cells and bacteria found in western Australia are 3.4 billion years old when Earth was much warmer and the oceans were about the temperature of a hot bath.

24 A grape vine growing in Maribor, Slovenia, is more than 400 years old. What's it called? Old Vine, of course!

25 Mummies in northwestern China dating to 1615 B.C. were found with yellowish clumps placed around their chests and neck—the world's earliest known cheese.

26 Gregoire, a chimpanzee, lived to be 66 years old. For decades he lived in a barren cage, but he was rescued. He spent the last 11 years living the good life at a rehabilitation center run by Jane Goodall.

27 A deep-sea microorganism known as sulfur bacteria hasn't changed in more than two billion years.

28 A kind of bacteria found in the permanently frozen ground in Siberia, Russia, has been living for half a million years.

29 Harvard is the oldest university in the United States. It was founded in 1636, and the school was the first to use uniforms to tell players on sports teams apart.

30 The first arthropods (insects with a hard exoskeleton) on Earth lived some 530 million years ago and ate by filtering water through their mouths to get particles of food.

31 Arthropods would give rise to crabs, spiders, and lobsters.

32 SAND HAS BEEN IN THE NAMIB DESERT, AFRICA, FOR SOME 100 MILLION YEARS.

33 Nicknamed the Senator, a pond cypress tree in Florida, U.S.A., lived for 3,500 years before it was intentionally set on fire and died.

34 The first forests on Earth started to grow some 385 million years ago.

35 A piece of birch bark from 5,000 years ago found in western Finland is the oldest piece of chewing gum ever found. It was probably used to treat a gum infection.

36 The first plants on land lived about 475 million years ago; they were similar to today's mosses.

37 Scientists who study prehistoric animals use fossils of their bones and teeth to figure out how they looked.

38 Rocks from the Nuvvuagittuq greenstone belt on the shore of the Hudson Bay in Canada are some of the oldest in the world.

39 The oldest fossil of a jawless fish was found in the Yunnan Province of China. The fossils are more than 500 million years old.

40 One of the oldest birds in the world, an albatross named Wisdom, had a chick when she was 62 years old.

41 Living some two million years ago until the latest ice age, gigantic American ground sloths could stretch 20 feet (6 m) in length—about as long as a killer whale!

42 San Marino, a small country surrounded by Italy, has the oldest constitution in the world. It was written in 1600.

43 A collection of clay tablets written in cuneiform characters from 4,500 years ago from Ebla, in what is today Syria, is the oldest library in the world.

44 AN ANCIENT COIN, MORE THAN 2,600 YEARS OLD, FROM A CITY IN WHAT IS TODAY TURKEY HAS A LION'S HEAD ON ITS FACE.

45 A volcano sponge living in the waters off Antarctica has been living there for some 15,000 years.

46 "Bear-dogs" lived some 15 million years ago and were some of the earliest true carnivores. They looked like a mix between a bear and a dog.

47 Simple sea sponges are some of the oldest types of creatures on Earth. They've been around for almost 600 million years.

48 Yoho National Park in the Canadian Rockies is home to one of the most ancient fossil beds in the world, the Burgess Shale. It contains fossils dated to more than 500 million years ago.

49 The first pair of socks were knitted in Egypt nearly 1,800 years ago. The red socks can be seen in a museum in London, England.

50 Natural hot springs in Japan are a popular attraction. It's thought that the thermal baths at Dogo-onsen hot spring on the island of Shikoku have been in use for 3,000 years.

51 The oldest domesticated animals on Earth were wolves, which were kept as pets and would eventually become dogs.

74 TIME-WARP FACTS ABOUT THE OLDEST THINGS ON EARTH

fossil imprint of a trilobite

52 The oldest mammals lived during the age of the dinosaurs and looked like small mice and rats.

53 The step pyramid of Djoser is the oldest stone pyramid in Egypt. Located in Saqqara, it was built more than 4,500 years ago.

54 BORN APRIL 21, 1926, QUEEN ELIZABETH OF THE UNITED KINGDOM IS THE WORLD'S OLDEST LIVING MONARCH.

55 Some people think Damascus, Syria, is the oldest city in the world. People have been living there for 12,000 years.

56 Baobab trees from South Africa can live for 2,000 years. One of the oldest is as tall as a seven-story building.

57 Some of the oldest life on Earth resembled mats of organisms, like algae, that grew upward in the water to get sunlight for photosynthesis.

58 Scientists can study tree rings to determine what the climate was like in the past.

59 A dinosaur found in Tanzania in 2012 is the oldest dino fossil found so far. Dating back to 240 million years ago and the size of a Labrador dog, scientists are still trying to figure out if it is a true dinosaur.

60 A kind of deep-sea clam called "Ming the mollusc" lived 507 years on the bottom of the Atlantic Ocean near Iceland before scientists dredged it up in 2006 and killed it.

61 The world's oldest bristlecone pine tree was cut down accidently in 1964. It was 5,000 years old.

62 Fossils found in Pakistan show that the first whales had otter-like bodies with short, webbed feet. They lived some 40 million years ago.

63 OSWALD THE LUCKY RABBIT IS THE OLDEST DISNEY CARTOON CHARACTER. THE FIRST CARTOON WAS CALLED *TROLLEY TROUBLES.*

64 Elephant moss on Elephant Island in the south Atlantic has been living for 5,500 years.

65 The oldest geologic time period was the Archean eon, which lasted from 4.5 to 2.5 billion years ago.

66 A university founded in 859 in Morocco by a woman named Fatima al-Fihri is the oldest university that has been continuously in use.

67 THE OLDEST LOVE POEM IN THE WORLD, *THE LOVE SONG FOR SHU-SIN*, WAS WRITTEN IN CUNEIFORM ON A CLAY TABLET IN ABOUT 2000 B.C.

68 A brain coral living on a shallow reef in the Caribbean has been around for 2,000 years. It's 18 feet (5.5 m) wide.

69 A 5,500-year-old shoe—considered the oldest—that looked like a moccasin was found in an Armenian cave. It was made out of leather and stuffed with grasses.

70 The oldest stone tools made by our ancestors date to 2.6 million years ago. Found in Africa, they are known as the Oldowan toolkit and include sharp flakes of stone.

71 The city of Varanasi in India has been lived in for about 3,000 years. Legend has it that it was founded by a Hindu deity known as Lord Shiva 5,000 years ago.

72 A circular plaza in Peru that dates to about 5,500 years ago could be the oldest known urban complex in the Americas. It was found beneath another archaeological site called Sechin Bajo.

73 The Taung Child is the name given to a 2.8-million-year-old fossil of a three-year-old found in Taung, South Africa, that is regarded as the ancestor of all humans.

74 ONE OF THE OLDEST STARS IN THE UNIVERSE IS RIGHT AT HOME IN OUR OWN MILKY WAY GALAXY. IT'S KNOWN AS SM0313 AND WAS BORN 13.6 BILLION YEARS AGO.

35 DECADENT FACTS ABOUT INCREDIBLE DESSERTS

1 Ancient **EGYPTIANS** added honey, nuts, and fruit to bread to make it sweet—a dish thought to be the earliest version of **CAKE**.

2 Dating back thousands of years, **ASHURA**, a sweet Turkish pudding made with fruits, grains, and nuts, is considered the oldest dessert in the world.

3 The term **CUPCAKE** was originally used in the late 19th century for cakes made from ingredients measured by the **CUPFUL**.

4 **CUPCAKES** are called **FAIRY CAKES** in the United Kingdom and are known as **PATTY CAKES** in Australia.

5 A team of bakers once built a **GIANT GINGERBREAD** house almost as big as a tennis court—requiring nearly a **TON (900 KG) OF BUTTER**.

6 One Texas, U.S.A., sno-cone stand offers the "Pick-a-dilly"—a **PICKLE-FLAVORED** version of the frozen treat.

7 An ice cream shop in Dubai, United Arab Emirates, offers a **SUNDAE** made with vanilla scoops sprinkled with flecks of 23-carat **EDIBLE GOLD**.

8 One restaurant in Sri Lanka serves up a $14,500 **FRUIT** and **CHOCOLATE** sculpture that comes with a gigantic gemstone.

9 In **INDIA**, people treat themselves to **GULAB JAMUN**—deep-fried dough balls swimming in sweet **SYRUP** flavored with **ROSE WATER** and **SAFFRON**.

10 To make **MAPLE TAFFY**—a popular sweet in **CANADA**—you pour **BOILING** maple syrup onto fresh **SNOW**, then eat it with a wooden stick.

11 Thirty-five percent of Americans admit to eating **PIE** for **BREAKFAST**.

12 Wealthy Brits used to make "surprise pies" in which creatures like **LIVE BIRDS** would **POP OUT** when the pie was cut open. (The birds usually escaped.)

13 The world's biggest **CHOCOLATE BAR** weighed about as much as an African **ELEPHANT**.

14 At the Tour de Donut **BICYCLE RACE** in Ohio, U.S.A., riders get five seconds taken off of their overall time for every **DONUT** they eat along the way.

15 To honor Canada's 144th birthday, three Toronto bakeries collaborated to make a **255-LAYER** cake—which stood as tall as an **ADULT** woman.

16 Burger King once offered a **SUNDAE** made with vanilla soft serve ice cream, fudge, caramel, bacon crumbles—and a strip of **BACON** on top.

17 A **DAIRY QUEEN** in Canada once made an **ICE CREAM CAKE** wider than a **GARAGE DOOR**, complete with vanilla ice cream, buttercream frosting and a chocolate cookie crumble topping.

18 Dutch settlers are credited for bringing **DOUGHNUTS** to the United States in the 1800s. They were first called olykoeks, or oily cakes.

19 A competitive eater from **CALIFORNIA, U.S.A.**, recently **WOLFED** down 14.5 pounds (6.6 kg) of **BIRTHDAY CAKE** in eight minutes.

20 **BEETS** are sometimes used to give **RED VELVET** cake its crimson color.

21 **LITTLE DEBBIE** snack cakes were originally named for the founder of the company's **FOUR-YEAR-OLD** granddaughter.

22 At one California, U.S.A., restaurant, you can order **CHICKEN** that has been soaked in red velvet **CAKE BATTER**, rolled in toasted red velvet cupcake crumbs, and fried.

23 At least 13 **PEOPLE** in the United States are named "**DONUT**."

24 It wouldn't be unusual to find **EEL-FLAVORED** marzipan served with **DINNER** at 16th-century Italian banquets.

25 A pastry chef in Paris is known for his foie gras macarons—or **GOOSE LIVER** cookies.

26 Legend has it that the **WHOOPIE PIE** got its name from kids who would find the cream-filled chocolate cake in their lunch boxes and excitedly yell "Whoopie!"

27 **BOSTON CREAM PIE** is technically a **CAKE**, not a pie. When it was first introduced in 1856, the words "pie" and "cake" were used interchangeably.

28 You can snack on **FRIED COKE BALLS** at the Texas State Fair—Ping-Pong-ball-size sweets of cola-flavored, deep-fried batter topped with whipped cream, sugar, and a cherry.

29 An Italian gelato shop once created a giant ice cream **CONE** made from **2,000 WAFERS** that stood taller than a **STREET SIGN**.

30 When a **NEW YORK CITY** bakery began selling the **CRONUT**—a hybrid of a croissant and doughnut—some customers camped out overnight to get their hands on one.

31 The average person in the United States **EATS** about **6.86 GALLONS (26 L)** of **ICE CREAM** per year—the most of any country in the world.

32 In 2010, 2,694 people ate **ICE CREAM** together in Illinois, U.S.A.—the biggest-ever gathering of simultaneous ice cream **LICKERS**.

33 A Japanese pastry chef once whipped up a two-layer **FRUITCAKE** decorated with more than 200 **DIAMONDS** worth about $1.7 million.

34 A churro dog is a warm cinnamon **CHURRO** inside a chocolate-glazed **DOUGHNUT** topped with frozen yogurt, caramel, and chocolate sauce.

35 Each year, more than **200 MILLION BOXES** of Girl Scout cookies are sold around the United States—almost enough to give a box to every person in **BRAZIL**.

1. Muscles in your esophagus tighten and relax, which is how food is pushed to your stomach. 2. Even if you were to eat upside down, these muscles would still push food along to your stomach. (But don't try it, you could choke!) 3. Cows, giraffes, and deer have four-chambered stomachs to break down grasses and other plant food. 4. Seahorses don't have stomachs—their food goes straight to their intestines. 5. There are two types of digestion: mechanical, which is digestion by chewing, and chemical, which is when chemicals (called enzymes) break down food into small molecules. 6. Saliva (or spit) in your mouth makes food moist and easier to chew. It also has an enzyme in it that starts to break food down. 7. Once swallowed, it takes about seven seconds for food to move through your esophagus to your stomach. 8. Your stomach can expand to hold 1.6 quarts (1.5 L) of food. 9. The inner walls of your stomach create a special acid that helps kill bacteria. 10. The scientific word for stomach growling is borborygmus. 11. You digest most of your food in your small intestine, not your stomach. 12. On average, women have longer small intestines than men. 13. Your large intestine is shorter than your small intestine. 14. In all, your digestive system has 30 feet (9 m) of "pipes" that converts food into fuel for your body. 15. Your stomach mixes food with enzymes and turns it into a paste called chyme. 16. The small intestine absorbs nutrients from food and sends it into the bloodstream to the liver. 17. Whatever chyme is left after it leaves the small intestine moves to the large intestine where it's eaten by bacteria, mixed with dead cells, and formed into poop. 18. Your pancreas, located behind your stomach, creates a juice that contains enzymes involved in breaking down food in your small intestine. 19. Your gallbladder makes a green-brown bile, a waste material collected from the liver that contains acids that break down fatty matter. 20. Your liver processes nutrients and breaks down unwanted chemicals. 21. Mucus in your esophagus keeps food moving along toward your stomach without it getting stuck. 22. Your stomach is shaped like the letter *J*. 23. No matter what food it is you're eating, your tongue forms it into a ball-shaped form called a bolus before it is swallowed. 24. Sphincters are rings of muscle that control the flow of digested food. 25. Your gallbladder, which is attached to your liver, is green and the size of a plum. 26. Food can stay in your stomach three to four hours before it moves on to your intestines. 27. Digesting food can stay in your large intestine for two days. 28. Large salivary glands make enough saliva to fill up four cans of soda every day. 29. Your esophagus can also be called a gullet. 30. Your liver is the second largest organ in your body after your skin. 31. Your body could still function properly even if a third of your small intestine were removed. 32. Celiac disease is a disorder in which the digestive system is damaged by your immune system's response to gluten, found in wheat, rye, barley, and other plant foods. 33. Your small intestine is 1 to 1.5 inches (2.5 to 3.8 cm) around; your large intestine is 3 to 4 inches (7.6 to 10.2 cm) around. 34. You get diarrhea when germs pass too quickly through your intestines and there isn't time for your intestines to soak up the water. 35. When you swallow, a flap called a soft palate helps to block off the opening between your esophagus and nose. That's why your food doesn't come out your nose! 36. Your esophagus opens into a tube that takes air that you breathe into your lungs. 37. Your epiglottis is like a trapdoor, closing the tube between your esophagus and lungs so food doesn't go into your lungs. 38. Your stomach is

99 FACTS TO SWALLOW ABOUT THE DIGESTIVE SYSTEM

not behind your belly button; it is to the left side of your rib cage. 39. You can get the hiccups by eating too fast. 40. A cheeseburger will stay in your stomach three times longer than pasta before making its way to your intestines. 41. You have millions of pits in your stomach that contain glands that make gastric juice, which helps digest food. 42. Your stomach makes about eight cups (1.9 L) of gastric juice every day. 43. Hydrochloric acid, found in your stomach to break down food, can dissolve metal. 44. The cells in your stomach lining are entirely replaced every three or four days. 45. The inner lining of your small intestine is about 2,700 square feet (251 sq m), almost the size of a basketball court. 46. Your pancreas makes hormones that help regulate your body's energy use and growth. 47. Insulin is one of the hormones your pancreas makes and controls how much sugar your body uses right away and how much is stored for later. 48. If your pancreas doesn't make enough insulin, you can develop diabetes, a disease where blood sugar isn't controlled. 49. Your liver can repair itself: If most of it is injured, a small piece can grow back to a normal-size liver. 50. There are more bacteria in your large intestine than any other place in your body. 51. Since your digestive tract doesn't show up well in an x-ray, you need to drink a substance called barium first that helps your intestines show up. 52. Gallstones are hard lumps that can form in the gallbladder and cause intense pain until they are dissolved or removed by surgery. 53. One of your liver's main jobs is to store carbohydrates when your body's energy levels run low. 54. Your appendix is part of your digestive system, but doesn't have a clear role. It may help babies and kids develop protection against certain diseases. 55. Appendicitis is when your appendix is inflamed or blocked with bacteria. Sometimes people need to have their appendix removed when this happens. 56. The average person gets rid of about a third of a pound (0.15 kg) of poop every day! 57. Bacteria and your large intestine have a partnership: Your intestine provides a warm, nutrient-rich environment for bacteria that break down waste and produce some vitamins. 58. Parasites, like tapeworms, can live in the digestive tract and steal food from their host. 59. Finger-like villi line most of your digestive system and help absorb nutrients. 60. A horse's stomach can hold 35 pints (17 L) of food; a cow's can hold 264 (125 L)! 61. At its fastest, food travels through your digestive system at a rate of 20 inches (51 cm) per second! 62. E. coli is a microbe that lives deep in your guts. Some E. coli produce vitamins, but others can make you very sick. 63. For every hair on your head, there are six million microbes in your mouth. 64. Every time you eat, drink, chew gum, or yawn you let a little bit of air into your stomach. 65. The loudest burp ever recorded was louder than a thunderclap. 66. On average people burp about 15 times a day. 67. People toot an average of 14 times a day. 68. Ninety-nine percent of your toots are made of odorless gas. 69. One percent of your gas is made from bacteria in your gut and sulfides, which gives it the stinky smell. 70. Germs, a virus in your stomach, eating food spoiled with bacteria, or eating too much can cause you to vomit. 71. Vomit is partially digested food mixed with spit, mucus, and the digesting chemical bile. 72. Bile from your stomach gives your vomit a green tinge. 73. The sour taste of vomit and the burning sensation in your throat is the acids in your stomach that help break down food. 74. Bill Gates, co-founder of Microsoft, funded a project that converts human poop and pee into clean drinking water. 75. A survey showed Americans age 15 and over spend an average of 67 minutes a day primarily eating and drinking. 76. Seventy-five percent of your poop is water. 77. Your small intestine is longer than a giraffe is tall. 78. A study found that it's easier to pass gas standing up than lying down. 79. Mucus lining the wall of your stomach prevents your stomach from digesting itself. 80. Toilets on the International Space Station have seat belts to keep astronauts from floating away while going to the bathroom! 81. Drinking a beverage with a straw makes you burp more. 82. Most people make between one and four pints (0.5 to 1.9 L) of gas every day. 83. Certain foods, like eggs, beans, and red meat, make your toots smellier. 84. Scientists are studying cow burps and toots to see how much they are contributing to the world's greenhouse gases. 85. Hookworms can enter people's bodies through their bare feet and then live in their intestines. 86. The Bristol stool scale describes the seven different types of poop people have. 87. Without saliva, you wouldn't be able to taste. 88. The harder you chew, the more saliva you make. 89. Sucking on hard candy helps you make more saliva. 90. Your stomach acid has the same pH level—or acidity—as vinegar and lemon juice. 91. When babies in their mother's womb are just ten weeks old, their intestines and livers are functioning. 92. The world's longest burp lasted 1 minute and 13 seconds. 93. People who have a lot of gas after eating ice cream, yogurt, and milk are lactose intolerant. Lactose is a natural sugar. 94. Indigestion is another name for having an upset stomach. 95. Heartburn doesn't have anything to do with your heart: It's when stomach acid splashes up and irritates your esophagus. 96. You burp more when you drink soda because it is made with carbon dioxide, a gas that can bring up burps. 97. A blue whale's liver weighs as much as a concert grand piano. 98. A blue whale's intestines are up to 500 feet (152 m) long—that's longer than ten school buses! 99. Got a bellyache? Studies have shown that peppermint can improve upset stomach symptoms.

1
A crocodile that lived about **FOUR MILLION YEARS AGO** in what is now Kenya was 27 feet (8.2 m) long and likely **SWALLOWED HUMAN ANCESTORS WHOLE.**

2
The name "crocodile" was first used **2,000 YEARS AGO** by Greek explorers in Egypt. They saw creatures that looked like lizards that they called *krokodeilos*.

3
Up to **200 PEOPLE DIE** each year from being **ATTACKED** by a Nile crocodile.

4
Mummified crocodiles have been found in **EGYPTIAN TOMBS.**

5
Nile crocodiles sometimes **ROLL THEIR EGGS IN THEIR MOUTHS** to help their young hatch.

6
American crocodiles sometimes **REGURGITATE FOOD** in order to attract fish to gobble up.

7
Instead of ear lobes, a crocodilian has **SLITS ON THE SIDE OF ITS HEAD** that lead to an inner ear. The slits close when it dives underwater.

8
Male Nile crocodiles try to get females' attention by **SMACKING THEIR SNOUT** on the surface of the water.

9
SPANISH EXPLORERS in Florida, U.S.A., called American alligators *el lagarto*, or the lizard.

10
Almost all of a crocodile's teeth are on the **OUTSIDE** when its mouth is closed; an alligator's teeth are on the **INSIDE.**

11
Alligators and crocodiles replace lost or **WORN-OUT TEETH.** In a lifetime they may go through as many as 3,000 teeth.

12
NEWBORN Nile crocodiles are one foot (30.5 cm) long.

13
Alligators **DIG HOLES** in the ground and then, after it rains and the holes are filled with water, the alligators **SIT IN THEM.**

14
To stay alive in very cold conditions, American alligators dig a **"GATOR HOLE"** and go into a state of sleep but this is not true hibernation.

15
The alligator is the **OFFICIAL STATE REPTILE** of Florida.

16
Crocodiles kill by **DRAGGING THEIR PREY** into the water and drowning it.

17
Egyptian plovers, a type of bird, can walk right into a Nile crocodile's mouth **WITHOUT GETTING EATEN.** It picks at the croc's teeth to help keep them clean!

18
Crocodiles build nests by **DIGGING A HOLE** and layering their eggs with sand and soil. Alligators build nests above ground and cover them with **LEAVES AND MUD.**

19
Only about 1 out of every **25 HATCHED** crocodiles will live to become adults.

20
Crocodiles **CAN SWIM** 20 miles an hour (32 km/h), and **RUN** for short distances at about half that speed.

21
Crocodilians are **MORE CLOSELY RELATED** to birds and dinosaurs than to most other living reptiles.

22
Crocodiles have special **GLANDS IN THEIR TONGUE** to get rid of extra salt from swallowed salt water.

23
A crocodile can't **STICK OUT** its tongue.

24
Crocodiles can **HOLD THEIR BREATH** for more than one hour.

25
Crocodilians have special **SENSE ORGANS** in their skin that help to detect motion all around them.

26
The **CHINESE NAME** for the Chinese alligator is *Yow-lung*, which means dragon.

27
The slender-snouted crocodile's call sounds like a **CAR BACKFIRING.**

28
One of Earth's **MOST ENDANGERED** species is the Chinese alligator. Less than 200 exist in the wild.

29
Crocodilians can survive **MORE THAN A MONTH** without food.

30
Crocodilians can eat **HALF OF THEIR BODY WEIGHT** in one meal.

31
The world's **LARGEST TOOTHPICK SCULPTURE** was made from more than three million toothpicks and was shaped like an alligator.

32
A group of crocodiles is called **A BASK.**

33
A group of alligators is called **A CONGREGATION.**

34

Crocodiles have **ROAMED EARTH** for more than 200 million years.

35

Crocodilians **SWALLOW ROCKS** to help grind up food in their stomach.

36

Crocodiles' eyes **GET TEARY** when they eat.

37

U.S. president Herbert Hoover's son had two **PET ALLIGATORS,** which sometimes wandered around the White House.

38

Florida's Everglades National Park is the **ONLY ECOSYSTEM** in the world where alligators and crocodiles coexist.

39

When it is chilly out, crocodiles **SLEEP ON THE BOTTOM** of rivers to stay warm.

40

Alligators and crocodiles **CONTINUE TO GROW** their whole lives.

41

Nile crocodiles have **BONY EYELIDS.**

42

When baby alligators are ready to hatch, they make a **BARKING SOUND** from inside the egg.

43

To avoid overheating, crocodiles sometimes **COVER THEMSELVES IN MUD.**

44

Only a crocodile's hind feet are **WEBBED.**

45

Unlike some animals, crocodiles can digest the **HOOVES AND HORNS** of their prey.

46

Crocodiles have **NOSTRILS** on top of their **SNOUT** so they can breathe without their head coming out of water.

47

Claude, a white alligator who lives at the San Francisco, California, Academy of Sciences, is one of only a few dozen **ALBINO ALLIGATORS** that exist in the world.

48

Serum in an American alligator's blood can help fight off **VIRUSES.**

49

Alligators sometimes eat **FRUIT!**

50

Scientists have observed alligators putting **STICKS ON THEIR NOSES** to lure in nesting birds as prey.

American crocodile

50
SNAPPY FACTS ABOUT
CROCS & GATORS

1 French **MIME** Marcel Marceau released an album in 1970. It contained **19 MINUTES OF SILENCE** along with some applause.

2 Studies show that **FOUR SECONDS of AWKWARD SILENCE** in a conversation creates the feeling of **REJECTION** in the human brain.

3 PEOPLE GO ON **SILENT RETREAT** VACATIONS WHERE THEY **UNPLUG** FROM TECHNOLOGY AND SPEND **DAYS** OR **WEEKS IN COMPLETE SILENCE.**

4 The **ZONE OF SILENCE** is a desert in Mexico where local legend says **NO METHOD OF COMMUNICATION** can reach.

Shhh!
25 FACTS ABOUT

5 THE **CONE OF SILENCE** WAS A DEVICE ON THE COMEDY *GET SMART*. IT WAS A PLASTIC COVERING THAT WAS SUPPOSED TO HELP AGENTS SPEAK SECRETIVELY, BUT THEY HAD TO SCREAM TO HEAR ONE ANOTHER.

6 John Cage's **4'33"** also called "silent piece," is a music-less piano solo first **PERFORMED** in 1952. The only sound made was the opening and closing of the lid of the keyboard.

7 On Christmas Day in 1914 during World War I, about **100,000** German and British troops sang "Silent Night" as everyone put down their guns for a holiday truce.

8 A man in **ENGLAND** stayed **SILENT** for **2 MINUTES AND 40 SECONDS** dressed as a knight to earn the record for the **LONGEST SILENT KNIGHT.**

9 **JUKEBOXES** were so **POPULAR** in the 1950s that one record company made a record titled "**THREE MINUTES OF SILENCE**" just so people could play it to get a break from the music.

10 In a 13,000-square-mile (33,670-sq-km) zone of **radio silence** in West Virginia, U.S.A., there is no cell service or Wi-Fi.

11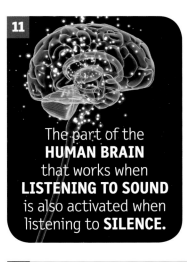
The part of the **HUMAN BRAIN** that works when **LISTENING TO SOUND** is also activated when listening to **SILENCE.**

12
People who take a **VOW OF SILENCE** do not speak to **ANYONE** for an extended period of time, and it is typically used for religious contemplation or meditation. Though rare, some vows are permanent.
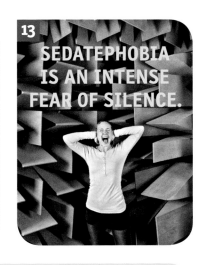

13
SEDATEPHOBIA IS AN INTENSE FEAR OF SILENCE.

14 Even though it appears to us that there is **SILENCE** in space, scientists have detected **SOUND WAVES** there that are not audible to the **HUMAN EAR.**

15 **SILENT MOVIES** weren't completely silent. **MUSIC** was played to accompany them.

Positively NO WHISTLING, STAMPING OR LOUD TALKING Allowed in - This Theatre.

16 30TH U.S. PRESIDENT CALVIN COOLIDGE'S NICKNAME WAS **"SILENT CAL,"** BECAUSE OF HIS CALM, COOL, AND QUIET DEMEANOR.

SILENCE

17
The 1925 film *Ben Hur* was the most **EXPENSIVE** silent film ever made, costing almost **$4 MILLION** ($250 million today).

BEN-HUR LEW-WALLACE THE GREAT FILM TRIUMPH

18
"The Silence" are **VILLAINS** on the BBC series *DOCTOR WHO.* They **HYPNOTIZE** anyone who sees them, which erases any memory of them.

19
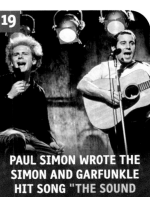
PAUL SIMON WROTE THE SIMON AND GARFUNKLE HIT SONG "THE SOUND OF SILENCE" IN HIS BATHROOM IN THE DARK.

20
In a SOUNDPROOF room, the footsteps of a CENTIPEDE have been recorded.

21
The phrase "silence is golden" dates back to ancient Egypt. A fuller version of the quote is, "Speech is silver, silence is golden."

22
The **QUIETEST PLACE ON EARTH** is inside a chamber in **MINNESOTA,** U.S.A. The longest time any person has stayed inside before wanting to get out is **45 MINUTES.**

23
NASA has used the QUIET CHAMBER in Minnesota to ready astronauts for the SILENCE OF SPACE.

24 **SILENCE** IS A SYNTHPOP, ELECTRONIC MUSIC DUO FROM SLOVENIA. **THE SILENCE** IS A FIVE-PIECE POP/ROCK BAND FROM ENGLAND.

25
Those born in the United States between 1925 and 1945 were called **THE SILENT GENERATION** (first coined by *Time* magazine) because the government of the time was against people voicing their political beliefs.

1 A **FORGER** is someone who imitates or falsifies something and **PRESENTS** it as the **TRUTH**.

2 Two **YOUNG GIRLS** tricked the world with **PHOTOS** of them **POSING** and **PLAYING** with **FAIRIES**. People believed the "Cottingley fairies" photos were real until one of the girls, as an old woman in the 1980s, **ADMITTED** they were **FAKE**.

3 In 1912 a skull and jaw believed to be from a **MILLION-YEAR-OLD HUMAN** was found in England. The Piltdown Man was said to be the **MISSING LINK** between humans and apes. Not until 1953 was the **HOAX** uncovered—the **JAW** of an ape had been connected to the skull of a **MAN**.

4 Counterfeit artist Art Williams, Jr., claimed to have made **MORE THAN TEN MILLION DOLLARS** in counterfeit **CASH**.

5 P. T. Barnum was famous for his circuses but he also presented a **MUMMY** of a **MERMAID** called the Feejee Mermaid. The mummy was soon revealed to be nothing more than a pieced-together creation of monkey and fish bones.

6 In 1947 Han van Meegeren was arrested for having sold a **FAMOUS PAINTING** by Dutch painter **JOHANNES VERMEER** to his country's enemy. He then proved that the painting was a fake by producing another Vermeer imitation. However, it turns out he had gotten rich by selling fakes for years and was found guilty of forgery.

7 A ten-foot (3-m)-tall **STONE MAN** was dug up in Cardiff, New York, U.S.A., in 1869, and people believed it was a petrified **GIANT**. The Cardiff Giant drew crowds even after it was discovered that it was **FAKE**.

FAMOUS FORGERS

8 Before Renaissance artist **MICHELANGELO** became famous, he created a sculpture of a CUPID, buried it in the ground to make it look antique, and SOLD IT as an **ANCIENT** piece.

9 In 1983 a German reporter claimed to have found the diaries of **ADOLF HITLER.** It took only **TWO WEEKS** for the discovery that they were **FAKE** to come out. A famous forger had written them.

10 Famous forger Mark Landis uses a magnifying glass, markers, pens, and frames from Walmart to create the **INCREDIBLE FAKES** of famous works he has been producing for more than 30 years.

11 J.S.G. Boggs is a **FAMOUS ARTIST** who DRAWS MONEY— his fake bills are so good that they often sell **FOR MORE** than their fake amount.

12 In the late 1800s, William Mumler claimed to take PHOTOGRAPHS of people with GHOSTS. His most famous photo is of Mary Lincoln with the ghost of her late husband, Abraham Lincoln.

13 The TOP TEN most commonly **FORGED AUTOGRAPHS** include Elvis, Michael Jordan, and Neil Armstrong.

14 Britain's Royal Mint believes that 1 out of **EVERY 35** £1 coins is **FAKE.**

15 In 2014 teenagers from New Jersey, U.S.A., were caught making **FAKE FIVE** and **TWENTY DOLLAR BILLS** using an ink-jet printer and resume paper. They had spent their fake money mostly on snacks!

1 A SUBMARINE is a special type of NAVAL WATERCRAFT that operates UNDERWATER.

2 SUBMARINE is also used to describe a LARGE SANDWICH, usually with meat on it—also called a HOAGIE, HERO, or SUB.

3 In 1820 a CRIMINAL was hired to help Napoleon Bonaparte ESCAPE from an island PRISON using a homemade submarine.

4 At more than 500 FEET (152 m) long, TYPHOON SUBMARINES are the LARGEST subs in the world.

U.S. Navy nuclear submarine

35
UNSINKABLE

5 The FIRST SUBMARINES carried crews of only ONE or TWO—but today they can carry more than ONE HUNDRED PEOPLE.

6 Submarines were built and used by BOTH UNION AND CONFEDERATE SOLDIERS during the AMERICAN CIVIL WAR.

7 Submarines are typically painted BLACK to help them hide underwater— the color seems to work best in the ocean.

8 NASA is working on a SUBMARINE that can be used to EXPLORE THE LAKES of SATURN'S moon, TITAN.

9 Disneyland Park in California, U.S.A., has a *Finding Nemo* SUBMARINE VOYAGE ride where guests explore a coral reef much like the one in the film.

10 TORPEDOES are EXPLOSIVE DEVICES launched from a submarine that hit underwater targets.

11 Leonardo da Vinci, who lived from 1452 to 1519, DREW detailed PLANS for SUBMARINES long before the craft even existed.

12 EL SUBMARINO is a tasty version of hot chocolate from Argentina where a CHOCOLATE "submarine" is dunked into a cup of steaming HOT MILK.

13 SUBMARINES can stay UNDERWATER for MONTHS at a time.

14 A New Jersey, U.S.A., TEENAGER built a ONE-MAN SUBMARINE using $2,000 worth of parts including an OLD SODA MACHINE, battery sensors, and a CB radio.

15 In 1941 a REINDEER named Pollyanna lived on a British submarine with the crew for SIX WEEKS. It was a gift from the Russians and was eventually given to the LONDON ZOO.

16 A MINIATURE one-person SUBMARINE called the Scubster is powered by pedaling. The sub can go as deep as 20 feet (6 m)! But there isn't any oxygen, so scuba gear is required.

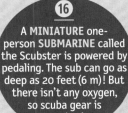

17 An UNDERWATER VOLCANO is also called a SUBMARINE VOLCANO.

18 POOPY SUITS are blue one-piece jumpsuits that submarine crew members wear while AT SEA.

19 In 1915 a German U-BOAT (a type of wartime submarine) sank the passenger ship the *LUSITANIA*, causing the Americans to fight in World War I.

20 An URBAN LEGEND started in the 1970s about a giant GREAT WHITE SHARK named SUBMARINE—a FAKE DOCUMENTARY on the shark was featured in Shark Week 2014.

21 The world's FIRST ATTEMPTED SUBMARINE ATTACK happened in 1776, during the Revolutionary War when the United States tried several times to sink a British ship.

22 The Royal Navy Submarine Museum in ENGLAND is housed within a RESTORED SUBMARINE.

23 U.S. nuclear-powered submarines can go about 25 KNOTS underwater, which translates to about 29 miles an hour (46 km/h) on land.

24 Submarines use a system of sound waves called sonar to hear underwater. Using sonar, technicians can hear other submarines, DOLPHINS, WHALES, and even SHRIMP.

25 There is a SUBMARINE SAUNA in Sweden—guests can sit and relax in the sauna while watching underwater life.

26 PERISCOPES are used in submarines to see above the surface of the water. Modern periscopes have NIGHT VISION, CAMERAS, and MAGNIFYING capabilities.

FACTS ABOUT

SUBMARINES

27 In 1969, the popular music group THE BEATLES released the sound track to *YELLOW SUBMARINE*, an animated film. John Lennon used a straw and a pan of water to make bubbling sounds.

28 The movie *DEEPSEA CHALLENGE 3D* was shot inside a HIGH-TECH SUBMARINE with CAMERAS. The sub was taken SEVEN MILES (11 KM) BELOW the ocean's surface.

29 In 1958 the U.S. submarine *Nautilus* left Alaska and was the FIRST to travel underwater to the NORTH POLE.

30 In the 1950s TOY SUBMARINES came inside some boxes of KELLOGG'S cereal. The submarines were powered with BAKING POWDER and vinegar.

31 A SUBMARINE is one of the FIVE pieces in Hasbro's Battleship game.

32 Some ABANDONED SUBMARINES can be found on the beach. In Aberlady Bay, Scotland, two BRITISH training SUBMARINES lie in the sand, covered in a thick layer of GREEN ALGAE.

33 A FLOATING HOTEL in Liverpool, England, was built to look like the Beatles' YELLOW SUBMARINE. A night's stay can cost £350 (about $600).

34 The COOKIECUTTER SHARK, a small Mexican species known for its sharp TEETH and biting skills, has taken bites out of NUCLEAR SUBMARINES.

35 A Canadian man made the WORLD'S SMALLEST SUBMARINE and named it "Big."

1. The process of computing—using numbers to solve problems—may have begun during the Stone Age, probably using fingers to keep track of numbers. 2. "Digit," the word used to represent a single number, comes from the use of fingers and toes for counting—fingers and toes are also called digits. 3. Many ancient cultures used "talking cords," pieces of leather, vine, or rope that were tied in knots to keep track of numbers. 4. Nearly 5,000 years old, the abacus, a calculating tool, is considered the first step toward the modern computer. 5. In 1821 mathematician Charles Babbage and his team began construction on a primitive computer that required 25,000 parts; it was never completed, and the unused parts were melted down for scrap metal. 6. The amount of money spent on the failed experiment could have paid for 22 brand-new steam locomotives. 7. Countess Augusta Ada Byron, daughter of the poet Lord Byron, was the first computer programmer. 8. To honor Augusta Ada Byron's role in early computing, the programming language Ada was named after her. 9. Hole-punched cards were used to store information for early computers. 10. The hole-punched cards were originally used for weaving; the cards controlled the patterns woven into fabric. 11. The first computer-calculator, invented by IBM, was the size of a room and took up to five seconds to complete one calculation. 12. In 1945 the biggest and most powerful computer, called ENIAC, used so much energy it dimmed the lights of a large section of the city of Philadelphia,

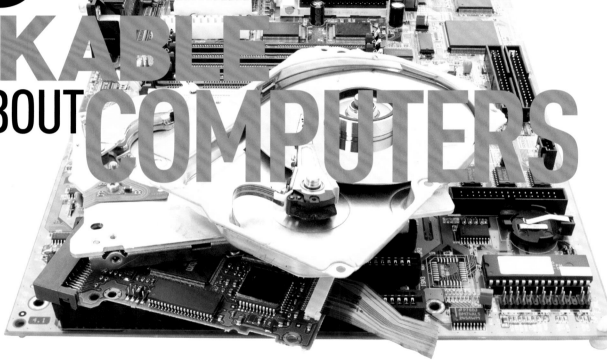

100 CLICKABLE FACTS ABOUT COMPUTERS

Pennsylvania, U.S.A. 13. ENIAC cost $400,000 to build, which would be more than $5,000,000 today. 14. ENIAC could perform up to 5,000 operations each second. 15. The Hewlett-Packard Company (HP) was started in a garage in Palo Alto, California, U.S.A., in 1939. 16. HP's first product was an audio oscillator, which creates pure tones or frequencies. Walt Disney Pictures ordered eight of these oscillators to create sound effects for *Fantasia*. 17. In 1952 scientists used IBM's Selective Sequence Electronic Calculator to calculate the position of the moon in preparation for the Apollo 11 moon landing. 18. Scientists originally used quartz rock to cool computers down. Quartz absorbs excess heat, releasing it to the surrounding air. 19. Computer users once used floppy disks to store information. Computers could get information from the disks but not put new information on them. 20. The original floppy disks were 8 inches (20.3 cm) across and actually floppy. 21. Like computers, floppy disks kept getting smaller: from 8 inches (20.3 cm) to 5.25 inches (13.3 cm) to 3.5 inches (8.9 cm). Only 3.5-inch floppies were not actually floppy. 22. Units of information used by computers are known as bytes; each byte contains eight bits. 23. The first floppy disks stored less than 100 kilobytes (100,000 bytes) of information. 24. Today's flash drives can store up to 128 gigabytes of information—128 million times as much information as the first floppy disks. 25. A one-gigabyte flash drive can store 96 hours of audio books. 26. The first computer network, called SAGE, linked hundreds of radar stations in the United States and Canada. 27. The first computer video game played with a monitor—*SpaceWar!*—was written by hackers at the Massachusetts Institute of Technology in Boston, U.S.A. 28. Before 1974, all computers used lines of text with no images or other graphics. 29. The Alto minicomputer by Xerox was the first to use a graphical interface like those used by most operating systems today. 30. The Xerox Alto was the first minicomputer to use a mouse. 31. Early versions of the computer mouse had a roller ball on the underside to track movement. 32. British computer pioneer Alan Turing was an expert code-breaker during World War II. 33. In 1963 the computer code known as ASCII became the first to allow computers made by different companies to communicate with one another. 34. ASCII uses zeros and ones to represent letters of the alphabet. 35. The amount of energy needed to provide a single Google user with one month of Internet services is equal to the amount needed to drive a car just one mile (1.6 km). 36. In 2014 nearly three billion people had Internet access—that's 40 percent of the world population. 37. Worldwide, one out of every four people uses a social network. 38. In Iceland, 96 percent of all households have Internet access—more than anywhere else in the world. **39.** In 2013, 23 million cars were capable of connecting to the Internet. **40. The phrase "Internet of Things" refers to the interconnectedness of billions of devices, from parking meters to store shelves to car tires. 41. Computers let farmers in the Netherlands know when their cows are sick or about to give birth, thanks to wireless sensors implanted in the animals' ears. 42.** There are more than 300-trillion-trillion-trillion possible Internet addresses—100 for every atom on Earth's surface. **43. A scientist discovered an ancient Egyptian papyrus scroll titled "How to Obtain Information About All Things Dark and Mysterious"; these "dark and mysterious" things included math problems that would be easy for modern sixth-graders. 44.** In 1901 divers discovered a 2,000-year-old mechanical device in a shipwreck that turned out to be an ancient Greek computer used to calculate the position of the sun, moon, and stars. **45.** Emoticons, which use keyboard symbols to make facial expressions, have been around since 1881. **46. After much online discussion in 1982, computer scientist Scott Fahlman suggested today's popular smiley and frowny faces. :-) :-(47.** Scientists using brain scans found that when we see emoticons, our brains respond as if we are viewing faces showing real emotion. **48.** Scientists have created computers using deoxyribonucleic acid (DNA)—the genetic material found in all living cells. **49. DNA computers can perform 330 trillion operations per second—more than 100,000 times faster than the fastest personal computer. 50. DNA computers are not mechanical; rather, they look like water in a test tube. 51.** DNA computers are more than a million times more energy-efficient than personal computers. **52. Scientists think that DNA computers may one day be placed in our bodies, where they will search for and repair damaged and unhealthy tissue. 53. The Game Boy handheld video game device, created in 1989, sold more than 120 million units. 54.** A new cloud server is added for every 120 tablets or 600 smartphones. **55. Computer viruses and other malware (bad software) can damage computers and steal information from them. 56. Almost a third of all computers in the world are infected with some kind of malware. 57.** About 74,000 new viruses are created every day. **58. Just like viruses that infect our bodies, computer viruses can make new copies of themselves to infect new computers. 59. The first computer mouse was made out of wood. 60.** In the movie *Willy Wonka & the Chocolate Factory,* a computer refuses to tell a scientist where to find the remaining golden tickets, saying, "That would be cheating." So far, computers cannot think on their own. A computer would have to be programmed to say this. **61. In New York, U.S.A., it is illegal to throw electronics, including computers, laptops, TVs, and gaming systems into the trash. Instead, they must be recycled. 62.** Recycling one million laptops would save the amount of energy used by 3,657 U.S. homes each year. **63.** China's Tianhe-2 supercomputer performs 33.86-thousand-billion calculations each second. **64. The Tianhe-2 supercomputer has been the world's fastest computer since June 2013. 65.** Wireless Bluetooth technology uses radio waves to send data between devices. **66.** Bluetooth was named after the Danish king, Harald Bluetooth, who helped to unite warring groups of people in what is now Norway, Denmark, and Sweden. **67. A SmartMat yoga mat has built-in sensors and uses Bluetooth technology to tell you how to adjust your yoga pose. 68.** Student Santiago Ambit created WeON Glasses that use Bluetooth technology to connect eyeglasses to the wearer's smartphone. **69.** The island nation of Niue near New Zealand has solar-powered Wi-Fi hot spots in remote locations that don't have electricity. **70. The jungle sometimes grows to completely cover the solar Wi-Fi stations on Niue. 71.** Created in 1958, the very first video game, *Tennis for Two,* was played with an oscilloscope, rather than a screen. Oscilloscopes are used to measure changes in electrical voltage. **72.** Sheep in rural England wear collars that act as Wi-Fi hot spots, so people can connect to the Internet anywhere. **73. The actor who does the voice of J.A.R.V.I.S., Tony Stark's computer in the *Iron Man* movies, used to play guitar for money on the Westminster Bridge in London, England. 74.** The 1982 movie *TRON* was the first to use computer-generated imagery (CGI) throughout a movie; more than 200 scenes were filmed using CGI backgrounds. **75.** Scientists can make bendable computers by printing electric circuits onto flexible strips of plastic or silicon. **76. When researchers fed ten million YouTube images into Google Brain—a group of computers programmed to learn—Brain sorted images into categories (human bodies, human faces, and cats) all by itself. 77.** George Lucas started a company called Industrial Light & Magic, which he used for all of the computer-generated scenery in *Star Wars.* **78.** In the early 1970s, Steve Wozniak and Steve Jobs, founders of Apple, built a blue-box whistle that made a phone-specific sound. The whistle gave them access to phone lines, so they could call anyone they wanted—they used it to call the pope in Vatican City, Rome. **79. By the year 2015, nearly 19 million people worldwide played *Minecraft.* 80.** So many people tried to download *Minecraft* on September 18, 2010, that the server crashed. **81.** A school in Sweden requires students to play *Minecraft* in order to build their thinking skills. **82. In 2015 Intel created the smallest Windows-based personal computer—at only four inches (10 cm) long, it is the size of a pack of gum. 83.** In order to keep track of large projects at the European Organization for Nuclear Research in Geneva, Switzerland, scientist Tim Berners-Lee created the World Wide Web in 1989–1990. **84.** Designers in the Netherlands created "Beauty and the Geek" pants that have a built-in keyboard, speakers, and mouse. **85. In 2015, Apple released the Apple Watch, a miniaturized Mac computer, complete with a watchband. Some Apple Watches cost as much as $17,000. 86.** In 1991, there was just one Internet website, but that number climbed to one billion in just 13 years. **87.** It took computer animators at Pixar more than a year to get Merida's curly hair just right for the movie *Brave.* **88. Computer scientist Simon Colton of the United Kingdom is developing software that creates artwork by itself. 89.** A 3-D printer adds layer upon layer of plastic or other material to build a three-dimensional object. **90.** 3-D printers can use different materials to build objects; this includes plastic, metal, ceramics, living biological tissues, and even food. **91. A company called Natural Machines has created the "Foodini," a 3-D printer that prints actual food that can be cooked and eaten. 92.** In November 2014, astronauts successfully used a 3-D printer to build a wrench and other tools aboard the International Space Station—the wrench was the first tool 3-D-printed in space. **93.** In 2015 a Chinese company used 3-D printing to build an apartment building that is 20 feet (6 m) tall, 33 feet (10 m) wide, and 132 feet (40 m) long. **94. Computer animators created 300 different facial expressions for house elf Dobby for the *Harry Potter* movies. 95.** Recycling one aluminum can saves enough energy to power a computer for three hours. **96.** There is more gold in 1.1 tons (1 MT) of electronics from discarded personal computers than there is in 18.7 tons (17 MT) of gold ore. **97. Computer processing speed doubles every 18 months. 98.** Computers and other electronics are full of toxic metals that can leak out of landfills, which is why they should never be thrown in the trash. **99.** Only about 20 percent of computers in the United States are recycled. **100. Outdated smartphones can be used to control electric equipment in homes.**

* YOU HAVE LEARNED **2,899** FACTS

5,000 AWESOME FACTS 3 **123**

1 The term "THE BIG APPLE" came from a slang term in horse racing, meaning a prize or win. It was first used to describe New York City by a sports reporter in 1921.

2 Albert EINSTEIN'S EYEBALLS are stored in a safe deposit box in New York City.

3 Under the Waldorf Astoria Hotel there is a SECRET UNDERGROUND TRAIN PLATFORM called TRACK 61 that was once used by famous people to sneak into the hotel, unseen.

4 The FIRST New York SUBWAY line opened to the public in 1904 and cost a NICKEL to ride.

5 New York City was home to the first known PIZZERIA in the United States, opened in 1905. LOMBARDI'S PIZZA was opened by an Italian immigrant from Naples.

6 TOILET PAPER was invented by a man named Joseph Gayetty in THE BIG APPLE in 1857.

7 A BABY is born every 4.4 MINUTES in New York City.

8 Each piece of confetti released on New Year's Eve in New York City has a DIFFERENT WISH written on it from PEOPLE AROUND THE WORLD.

9 TIMES SQUARE isn't actually SQUARE-SHAPED. It's TRIANGULAR.

10 Up until 1957, New York City had a special system where you could send mail in TUBES through an underground PIPE—the pipes spanned 27 miles (43 km).

11 Built in the 1880s, THE DAKOTA HOTEL is said to be HAUNTED by several GHOSTS, including John Lennon of the Beatles.

12 The EMPIRE STATE BUILDING has its own ZIP CODE. It was also the tallest building in the world from 1931 till 1972 and the first building to have 100 FLOORS.

13 MICROSCOPIC SHRIMP called copepods have been found in New York City's TAP WATER.

14 A FIRE STATION, Hook and Ladder #8 in Tribeca, New York City, is called the GHOSTBUSTER'S FIREHOUSE because it was used for the film *Ghostbusters*.

15 HOT DOG SELLERS pay vastly different amounts of money to rent a spot for their carts, depending on location. Sellers near CENTRAL PARK pay $289,000 a year.

16 The STATUE OF LIBERTY has a 35-foot (10.7-m) waistline and wears a size 879 SHOE.

17 From 1785 to 1790 NEW YORK CITY was the CAPITAL of the UNITED STATES.

18 A BROWNSTONE building in GREENWICH VILLAGE built in 1856 is called The House of Death because many believe former residents HAUNT the place.

19 The OLDEST ARTIFACT in NEW YORK CITY is 3,500 years old—the 220-ton (200-MT), 70-foot (21-m)-tall sculpture, CLEOPATRA'S NEEDLE, which stands in CENTRAL PARK.

20 New York is home to the OLDEST CONTINUOUSLY PUBLISHED newspaper in the United States: the *New York Post*.

21 It is ILLEGAL to PURPOSELY PASS GAS in CHURCH in NEW YORK CITY.

35 FACTS ABOUT THE BIG APPLE TO TAKE A BITE OUT OF

22 The **WINNIE-THE-POOH** stuffed bear that inspired A. A. Milne to write the stories now lives in the **NEW YORK PUBLIC LIBRARY.**

23 Throughout the 1800s some winters were **SO COLD** that the **EAST RIVER FROZE,** making what people called **ICE BRIDGES** and allowing them to **WALK ACROSS** the river.

24 New York City's **SKINNIEST** house is 9.5 feet (2.9m) **WIDE** and 30 feet (9.1 m) **DEEP.** Its address: 75½ Bedford Street.

25 **HOG ISLAND,** a **ONE-MILE (1.6-KM)-LONG** island, **DISAPPEARED** after the hurricane of 1893.

26 **"URBAN GOLDMINERS"** search the sidewalk in NYC's **DIAMOND DISTRICT** for gold and gems—one man found 800 dollars worth of jewels in **ONE WEEK.**

27 **SOFT WHISPERS** fly across the room like **MAGIC** at the **WHISPERING GALLERY** inside **GRAND CENTRAL STATION** because of the arched ceilings.

28 For **34 YEARS**—between 1942 and 1976—**PINBALL MACHINES** were **BANNED** in New York City.

29 It costs **MORE THAN A MILLION DOLLARS** to get the rights to operate **A NEW YORK CITY CAB.**

30 A street performer known as the **NAKED COWBOY** plays the guitar in **TIMES SQUARE** wearing only cowboy boots and underwear, even on the freezing days of **WINTER.**

31 Every year in the **EMPIRE STATE BUILDING** runners from **ALL OVER THE WORLD** gather to **RUN UP** the 1,576 steps of the building—the **FASTEST** make it up in about **TEN MINUTES.**

32 Since 1916 **NATHAN'S HOT DOG EATING CONTEST** has taken place on **CONEY ISLAND.** The event is broadcast on ESPN every year and about 40,000 fans **ATTEND** to watch **LIVE.**

33 About 1 in **EVERY** 25 residents of New York City is a **MILLIONAIRE.**

34 It is estimated that 800 **DIFFERENT LANGUAGES** are spoken in **NEW YORK CITY.**

35 Many people who go to Times Square on **NEW YEAR'S EVE** wear **ADULT DIAPERS** because of the lack of bathrooms.

1
Mining is the act of removing something valuable from the ground like coal, **DIAMONDS**, or gold.

2
80 percent of the deepest mines in the world are in **SOUTH AFRICA.**

3
A gold mine in South Africa called Mponeng is the **DEEPEST MINE** in the world. It's deeper than 13,000 feet (3.96 km) and its tunnels are **MANY MILES** long.

4
It takes more than an hour to get to the bottom of Mponeg—it's **HOT** and dangerous, with temperatures that get up to 140°F (60°C).

5
The Homestake gold mine in South Dakota, U.S.A., started in 1877 and was the **OLDEST MINE** in North America when it closed in 2002.

6
About 40 percent of all the gold that has been mined in the world comes from **SOUTH AFRICA.**

7
In Poland there is an **UNDERGROUND RESTAURANT** called The Miner's Tavern in a working **SALT MINE.**

8
Most of the world's **PINK DIAMONDS** come from Argyle Diamond Mine in western Australia.

9
Some underground mines have elevators called **CAGES** that lead workers down into the mine.

10
India's diamond mines date back to the **FOURTH CENTURY** B.C., making India one of the first countries to mine diamonds.

11
Having mined more than 6.5 million ounces (185,000 kg) of gold since it opened in 1990, Grasberg Mine in Indonesia is the world's **LARGEST GOLD MINE.**

12
A blue diamond the size of an **ACORN** was found in South Africa in 2014. It is said to be worth between $15 million and $20 million.

13
Someone found a **PAIR OF LEVI JEANS** from the late 1800s in an old mine in Colorado, U.S.A. The Levi Strauss company bought them for $25,000.

14
CULLINAN, the largest diamond ever mined, was cut into **NINE BIG PIECES** and more than 100 **SMALLER ONES.**

15
A **HUGE 100-CARAT DIAMOND** sold at an auction in New York, U.S.A., in 2015 for $22 million.

16
The world's most valuable diamond mine, Jwaneng in Botswana, has been producing up to 15 **MILLION CARATS** of diamonds every year since it opened in 1982.

17
In **SURFACE** mining, workers dig or scrape into the ground's surface. In **UNDERGROUND** mining, workers and equipment go deep beneath the surface.

18
The deepest type of underground mines are called **SHAFT MINES** and are used to mine minerals like copper, zinc, and gold.

19
Crater of Diamonds State Park in Arkansas, U.S.A., has the **ONLY PUBLIC DIAMOND MINE** in the world. Visitors can take home any diamonds they find!

20
Chile's Atacama Desert is home to the **LARGEST COPPER MINE** in the world.

21
OPEN PIT MINING is a type of surface mining often used to retrieve coal, copper, and iron.

22
Since it is so durable and easily recycled, almost **ALL THE NICKEL** ever mined is still around today.

23
Norilsk Nickel mine in Russia is the **TOP NICKEL PRODUCER** in the world.

24
The largest coal mine in the world is an open pit mine in **WYOMING, U.S.A.**

25
In La Rinconada, Peru, miners **WORK FOR FREE** for 30 days and on the 31st they keep whatever they mine that day as their **PAY.**

26
In Disney's *Snow White and the Seven Dwarfs*, the dwarfs work in a **DIAMOND MINE.**

27
Panning involves sifting through gravel, dirt, or sand and is one of the **SIMPLEST FORMS** of **MINING.**

28
Nine miners were rescued after being trapped in a copper mine for **SIX DAYS** in Peru after it collapsed in 2012.

29
The actor who voiced **STINKY PETE**, the old gold miner from *Toy Story 2*, has also voiced Sideshow Bob in *The Simpsons* and Martin the GEICO gecko.

30
In 2010 one miner **BECAME A DAD** while trapped in a Chilean mine for 68 days. His wife named the baby Esperanza, which in Spanish means "hope."

31
A university in Missouri sponsors **EXPLOSIVES CAMP** at their experimental mine for students who want a future career in mining.

32
FRACKING involves drilling into the ground then pumping in **WATER, SAND, AND CHEMICALS** to release natural gas to be used as fuel.

33
Scientists believe the **OLDEST GOLD MINE** in the world is more than 5,000 years old. It's in the country of Georgia.

34
Whether it's salt, gravel, copper, or coal, something is mined from **EVERY STATE** in the United States.

35
Local legends say that a **GHOST** named **DORCAS** haunts a mine in St. Agnes, Cornwall, in England.

36
In 2012 astronomers discovered a planet called 55 Cancri e that is made of **DIAMOND** and is **TWICE AS LARGE AS EARTH.**

37
Over the course of 50 years about 50,000 miners **HAND-DUG** a 42-acre (17-ha), 650-foot (200-m)-deep diamond mine in South Africa.

38
Early miners took canaries in cages into mines to warn them of **POISONOUS GASES.** The birds were affected by poisons in the air quicker than the miners.

39
Less than 20 percent of the diamonds mined in the world are considered **GEM QUALITY.** The other 80 percent are used for things like saws and electronics.

40
90 percent of the **PLATINUM** mined in the world comes from **FOUR MINES;** three are in Africa.

41
The **LARGEST GOLD NUGGET** ever found is called Welcome Stranger. It was discovered in Australia and is 24 by 12 inches (61 by 30 cm)!

42
Three remote Canadian diamond mines must wisely utilize **ICE ROADS** that are only open eight to ten weeks every year.

43
One of the biggest open pit mines is a diamond mine in Russia that is more than **2,000 FEET (610 M) DEEP.**

44
The largest **TIN MINE** is an open pit mine in Namibia.

45
The first diamond mine in Canada didn't open until 1998, but it continues to yield **MILLIONS** of **CARATS** each year.

46
In New Zealand two men shoveled **HALF A TON (508 KG)** of coal in 14.8 seconds—a world record!

47
ASTEROID MINING companies aim to send spacecraft to mine material from asteroids.

48
More than **SIX BILLION POUNDS (2.7 BILLION KG)** of **EXPLOSIVES** are used in mines throughout the United States and Canada every year.

49
All the gold, silver, and bronze used for the 4,700 medals handed out at the **2012 LONDON OLYMPICS** came from the British mining company Rio Tinto.

50
Nine miners were rescued after being trapped for **77 HOURS** in a **FLOODED** Pennsylvania coal mine in 2013. They sold their stories for $150,000 each.

50 DEEP FACTS ABOUT MINES

1 ANCIENT PERSIAN ARMIES USED **WAR ELEPHANTS** TO STAMPEDE THROUGH ENEMY TROOPS DURING BATTLE.

2 Ancient Chinese battle armor was made from **RHINOCEROS** hides.

3 THE **ANCIENT CHINESE CROSSBOW** HAD A MECHANICAL TRIGGER THAT COULD LAUNCH 40 ARROWS IN ONE MINUTE.

25 LETHAL FACTS ABOUT ANCIENT

4 An ancient Greek soldier's weapons and body armor could WEIGH UP TO 60 POUNDS (27 KG).

5 In ancient Greece, soldiers using **SLING-SHOTS** would write messages on the shots such as, "THIS IS FOR DESSERT!"

6 RESIDENTS IN THE ANCIENT CITY OF HATRA, IN MODERN-DAY IRAQ, THREW CLAY POTS FULL OF SCORPIONS AT ATTACKING ROMAN SOLDIERS.

7 **TWO DAGGERS WERE FOUND WRAPPED INSIDE KING TUTANKHAMUN'S MUMMY.** One dagger had a blade made of gold, and the other blade was iron.

8 The Byzantine Empire invented **GREEK FIRE,** a mixture that could even **BURN WHEN FLOATING ON WATER.** Greek soldiers would blast it from tubes mounted on their ships to attack their enemies.

9 IN ASIA, ANCIENT INDIAN WARRIORS HURLED CHAKRAMS—FLAT, RING-SHAPED WEAPONS WITH A SHARP OUTER EDGE—AT THEIR ENEMIES. THE WARRIORS WOULD SPIN A CHAKRAM ON AN INDEX FINGER THEN LAUNCH THE WEAPON.

11 Ancient Turkana tribesmen in Africa used **A SMALL KNIFE THAT WAS HOOKED ON A FINGER** to gouge out the eyes of enemies.

10

A SAMBUCA was a COVERED LADDER that ancient Roman soldiers used to climb the walls of an enemy's city during a siege.

12

Ancient **INCA WARRIORS** who lived in the rain forests used **FLEXIBLE WOOD** to make bows.

13 Some scholars think that early Americans used the **ATLATL** (an ancient throwing weapon) to throw darts so effectively that the weapon may have helped lead to the **EXTINCTION OF WOOLLY MAMMOTHS.**

15 THE 3-BLADE **HUNGA MUNGA** THROWING KNIFE USED BY ANCIENT AFRICAN TRIBES WAS POPULARIZED IN THE TELEVISION SHOW *BUFFY THE VAMPIRE SLAYER.*

14 The **LONG-SWORDS** of ancient Celtic warriors were often **BENT BACKWARD** before being buried in graves with their owners when they died.

16 IN ANCIENT PERSIA (MODERN-DAY IRAN), THE KING WAS ALWAYS PROTECTED BY 10,000 SOLDIERS CALLED THE **TEN THOUSAND IMMORTALS.** IF ONE SOLDIER DIED, HE WAS IMMEDIATELY REPLACED.

17 The largest ancient Greek warships could **HAVE MORE THAN 7,000 CREW MEMBERS**—that's more than on a modern-day aircraft carrier.

18 The **KATANA**, a single-blade, curved sword was used by the **JAPANESE SAMURAI.**

WEAPONS

19 Ancient Chinese warriors would use a large, **HAND-SHAPED CLAW** attached to the end of a long rope or pole to grab an enemy and pull him off his horse.

20 It took a British man just 1 **MINUTE AND 11 SECONDS** to make a boomerang, throw it, and catch it during a 2011 championship. **BOOMERANGS** were used as weapons by the Aboriginal of Australia.

21 According to mythology, **HEPHAESTUS**, the Greek god of fire and blacksmithing, **MADE THE WEAPONS AND ARMOR** for the Greek gods and goddesses.

22 TO DEFEND ITSELF, THE ANCIENT GREEK ISLAND CITY OF SYRACUSE USED **ARCHIMEDES' CLAW**—A LARGE CRANE WITH A HOOK ON IT—TO **LIFT ENEMY SHIPS OUT OF THE WATER.**

23 Contestants in the World Championship **PUNKIN CHUNKIN CONTEST** build large cannons like the ones used in ancient warfare. They are judged on how far the cannon can hurl a pumpkin.

24 The **SCIMITAR** was a sword with a blade that was usually long and thin and always curved. It was often used by warriors in the Middle East in the 14th and 15th centuries.

25 THE **BALLISTA** WAS A POWERFUL WOODEN CROSSBOW INVENTED BY THE ANCIENT ROMANS. IT WAS USED TO SHOOT **IRON-TIPPED BOLTS** THAT COULD PIERCE AN ENEMY SOLDIER'S ARMOR, CAUSING **INSTANT DEATH.**

❶ The recently named rabbit-size dinosaur *Aquilops americanus* had a **FACE** that **RESEMBLED AN EAGLE.**

❷ The remains of a dinosaur the size of a house cat were discovered in South Korea in 2014. Possibly a *Microraptor*, it had **SHARP TEETH** and **CLAWS** and **POSSIBLY FOUR WINGS.**

❸ *Nanuqsaurus hoglundi*, a dinosaur half the size of *T. rex*, was recently **DISCOVERED** in what is today the **ARCTIC.** Seventy million years ago, when it roamed, the region was warm and covered in forest.

❹ Since the 1993 release of the movie *JURASSIC PARK*, there has been increased interest in dinosaurs, which has led to **MORE FUNDING** for paleontologists and **MORE DISCOVERIES.**

❺ The fossil of *Dreadnoughtus*—**PERHAPS THE LARGEST DINOSAUR** to have ever walked Earth—was recently found in Patagonia. The dinosaur would have **WEIGHED AS MUCH AS A DOZEN AFRICAN ELEPHANTS.**

❻ A hunting guide in Canada found **THREE SETS OF *T. REX* TRACKS,** indicating these school bus–long dinosaurs **TRAVELED IN PACKS.**

❼ A new dinosaur found in southern Chile was **A COUSIN OF *T. REX*,** but it wasn't a fierce meat-eater, it was **VEGETARIAN.** Its name, *Chilesaurus diegosuarezi*, honors a **SEVEN-YEAR-OLD BOY** named Diego who **FIRST SPOTTED THE BONES.**

❽ *Spinosaurus aegyptiacus*, a 49-foot (15-m) dinosaur recently discovered in Morocco, was **BIGGER THAN *T. REX*.** It used its **FLAT HIND FEET** for **SWIMMING** through water.

DINO DISCOVERIES

9 With those big teeth, one would assume *T. REX* had a big bite, and scientists studying *T. rex* skulls recently reported that its **BITE WAS FOUR TIMES STRONGER THAN ONCE THOUGHT**— making it ten times as forceful as a modern **ALLIGATOR'S.**

10 Increased **COMMERCIAL FLIGHTS** to the **GOBI** desert and the **HIGH ARCTIC** have made more dinosaur discoveries possible since paleontologists have better access.

11 What was once a **PIT OF QUICKSAND** has led to a trove of discoveries in Utah, U.S.A., where paleontologists have uncovered six **UTAHRAPTOR,** cousins of *VELOCIRAPTOR.*

12 A researcher discovered **TWO NEW SPECIES** of dinosaurs after studying fossils that had been **STORED IN A CANADIAN MUSEUM FOR 75 YEARS.**

13 Paleontologists recently found **FEATHERS** on a turkey-size, plant-eating dinosaur. Prior to this they thought only meat-eating dinosaurs had feathers. The new discovery raises the **POSSIBILITY THAT ALL DINOSAURS HAD FEATHERS.**

14 A new type of tyrannosaur with a very LONG, SLENDER SNOUT and a row of horns on top has been nicknamed *PINOCCHIO REX.*

15 An 11-foot (3.4-m), 500-pound (225-kg) oviraptorosaur named *Anzu wyliei* was recently named as a new species after three skeletons were found in South and North Dakota, U.S.A. The **TWO-LEGGED FEATHERED DINOSAUR** had a birdlike beak.

1 Historians believe the first weddings occurred more than 4,000 years ago in Mesopotamia, which is modern-day Iraq.

2 ANCIENT WEDDING CEREMONIES HAD TO INCLUDE A FEAST IN ORDER TO BE CONSIDERED LEGITIMATE.

3 Women in ancient Egypt were the first to wear wedding bands, which were made of plants twisted into small circles.

4 Wedding bands for men did not become popular until World War II, when soldiers started wearing rings as a reminder of their wives at home.

5 Researchers believe that cavemen had prehistoric engagement rings—cords of braided grass tied around their chosen mate's wrists, ankles, and waist.

6 The word "wedding" comes from the Anglo-Saxon *wedd,* meaning a symbolic pledge.

7 Prior to the 2011 wedding of British Prince William and Catherine Middleton, 1,800 guests of the royal family received handwritten, gold-decorated invitations.

8 Before their wedding, traditional Japanese brides fold 1,001 white-paper origami cranes as a symbol of a long and happy marriage.

9 The first royal wedding in Westminster Abbey in England was between King Henry I and Princess Matilda of Scotland in 1100.

10 In Victorian England, women began sporting wedding rings designed like a snake with ruby eyes, its coils winding into a circle to symbolize eternity.

11 Ancient Romans believed that diamonds were sparkly splinters from heavenly stars.

12 Britain's Queen Victoria started the trend of brides wearing a white dress, at her wedding in 1840. Until then, brides just wore their best dress in any color.

13 A bride traditionally wears a veil because ancient Greeks and Romans believed it protected her from evil spirits.

14 A man from California, U.S.A., was married a total of 29 times before he passed away at age 88.

15 In Korea, brides wear bright shades of red and yellow to take their vows.

16 During the Roman Empire, wedding guests ate bread, not cake—and they traditionally broke the loaf over the bride's head.

17 Queen Victoria's wedding cake weighed 300 pounds (136 kg) and was nine feet (2.7 m) across.

18 Chefs at a hotel in Connecticut, U.S.A., once whipped up a gigantic wedding cake weighing more than 15,032 pounds (6,818 kg).

19 The term "tying the knot" comes from a tradition in many cultures where the hands of the bride and groom are tied together to symbolize the couple's bond.

20 Princess Mary, daughter of Henry VII of England, is said to have received an engagement ring from the Dauphin of France when she was just two years old.

21 From ancient times until the 1800s, brides carried bunches of herbs such as garlic and dill to ward off evil spirits.

22 In 2003, a bride in Ontario, Canada, was given a bouquet made from 1,500 flowers, weighing 203 pounds (92 kg). It was carried by the bridesmaids and groomsmen.

23 IN INDIA, TOE RINGS ARE SOMETIMES WORN INSTEAD OF FINGER RINGS TO SHOW MARITAL STATUS.

24 In 1908, the daughter of a mining tycoon received a diamond, emerald, and pearl necklace as a wedding gift—valued at an amount equal to about $3.6 million today.

25 Greek wedding culture says that brides who tuck a sugar cube into their glove will sweeten their marriage.

26 At Czech weddings, peas are thrown at the newlyweds as they leave the ceremony, not rice.

27 About 34,000 pounds (15.4 MT) of gold are made into wedding rings each year in the United States.

28 In the 1920s, a jeweler in the United States launched an unsuccessful campaign for men's engagement rings.

29 English lore says that finding a spider in your wedding dress is a sign of good luck.

30 The 1981 wedding between the Prince and Princess of Abu Dhabi lasted for seven days, was held in a stadium built for the festivities, and cost $100 million.

31 In India, some grooms ride into their wedding ceremonies on elephants, a symbol of luck in Indian culture.

32 According to Hindu tradition, rain on the wedding day brings good luck to the married couple.

33 ON VALENTINE'S DAY IN 2001, 34 COUPLES GOT MARRIED TOGETHER UNDERWATER.

34 In 2015, 11 couples from around the world braved temperatures as low as −4°F (−20°C) to say "I do" at an ice festival in China.

35 In Hong Kong, couples can get married at McDonald's. The package includes balloon wedding rings and an apple pie display.

36 The host of more than 100,000 weddings a year, Las Vegas, Nevada, U.S.A., is the world's most popular spot to tie the knot.

37 The longest bridal wedding veil was made for a wedding show in Sharjah in the United Arab Emirates in 2014. It measured 5,124 yards (4,685 m) in length.

38 In Morocco, a bride will bathe in milk before the wedding to purify herself.

39 In 2011, 187 groomed horses marched in the procession leading to Buckingham Palace for the wedding between Prince William and Catherine Middleton.

40 A 1995 wedding in India welcomed 150,000 guests. The total cost was more than $23 million!

41 For good luck, Egyptian women pinch the bride on her wedding day.

42 In 1659 Charles II of England was given the cities of Tangier and Bombay as a wedding gift from Queen Luisa of Portugal.

43 The popularity of June weddings is linked to Juno, the Roman goddess of marriage and childbirth.

44 In early U.S. history, Wednesday was considered the luckiest day for weddings. Now, Saturdays are the most popular.

45 THE OLDEST BEST MAN WAS 96 YEARS OLD.

46 It costs the average couple around $76,000 to have a wedding in New York City—the most expensive place to get married.

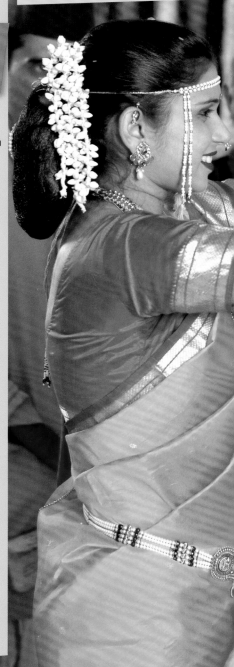

47 The most affordable places to get married in the United States? Arkansas and Utah, where weddings usually cost under $19,000.

48 A designer once made a wedding gown with 150 carats' worth of diamonds priced at $12 million!

49 MORE THAN 9,000,000 WEDDINGS TAKE PLACE IN CHINA EVERY YEAR.

50 In Venezuela, the families of the bride and groom exchange 13 gold coins to symbolize wealth.

51 Two billion viewers tuned in to watch the 2011 British royal wedding on TV, with another 600,000 spectators lined up on the procession streets from Westminster Abbey to Buckingham Palace.

52 ONE CELEBRITY COUPLE SENT INVITATIONS WRITTEN IN INVISIBLE INK AND HOLOGRAMS TO THEIR GUESTS.

53 Brides in the Middle East, Pakistan, India, and some parts of Africa paint henna on their hands and feet to protect themselves from bad fortune.

54 A couple in Mexico was engaged for 67 years before they finally married—the longest engagement on record.

55 A bride in the Netherlands wore a wedding dress with a train measuring 8,164 feet, 10 inches (2,489 m)—longer than the length of 25 soccer fields!

56 One couple—both scuba diving instructors—tied the knot nearly 430 feet (130 m) underwater in a cave at Song Hong Lake, Trang, Thailand.

57 In February 2012, a 95-year-old woman married a 98-year-old man—one of the oldest couples to get hitched.

58 In Illinois, U.S.A., couples can get married on a 1940s fire truck that's been converted to a rolling mobile chapel.

59 IN 2007, 178 CANINE COUPLES SEALED THEIR MARRIAGE WITH A BARK AT A MASS DOG "WEDDING" IN COLORADO, U.S.A.

60 A giant book measuring 13 feet (3.96 m) wide and 17 feet (5.2 m) long featuring snapshots of more than 250 Indian couples is said to be the largest wedding photo album ever.

61 The 2012 wedding between pampered pooches Baby Hope Diamond and Chilly Pasternak in New York City cost more than $270,000.

62 A dance instructor had all 110 of her students serve as bridesmaids at her 2010 wedding.

63 Five couples got hitched in the aisle of a Fiji Airways flight while flying at 41,000 feet (12,497 m) in 2013.

64 A woman wearing a wedding dress ran the 2014 London Marathon in 3 hours, 16 min, 44 seconds.

65 A man also ran the 2014 London Marathon while donning a wedding dress—in 3 hours, 16 minutes, 44 seconds.

66 In 1922, a prince in India threw a lavish, three-day party to celebrate the wedding of his pet dog Roshanara to a local governor's dog named Bobby.

67 British royal brides do not toss their bouquet—they leave them at the grave of the unknown warrior at Westminster Abbey in London.

68 The bells of Westminster Abbey ring for three hours after a royal wedding.

69 In ancient times, guests would tear off part of the bride's gown as a token of good luck.

70 At Walt Disney World in Orlando, Florida, U.S.A., couples can get married 400 feet (122 m) in the air while floating in a gondola attached to a giant tethered helium balloon.

71 SUPERSTITIOUS SWEDISH BRIDES STASH A COIN IN EACH OF THEIR SHOES TO GUARANTEE WEALTH IN THE FUTURE.

72 A couple from North Carolina, U.S.A., was married for a grand total of 86 years, 9 months, and 16 days. When they died, both the husband and wife were 105 years old.

73 Facebook founder Mark Zuckerberg's announcement of his marriage set the record for most "likes" on Facebook—more than one million.

74 With a combined height of 13 feet, 5 inches (4.09 m), a husband and wife in Essex, England, are the world's tallest living couple.

75 One couple in Tennessee, U.S.A., have renewed their wedding vows more than 100 times—after being married for only 27 years.

75 ENGAGING FACTS ABOUT WEDDINGS

YOU HAVE LEARNED **3,099** FACTS

1
A **NAKED RUNNER** named Coroebus was the first ever **OLYMPIC CHAMPION** in 776 B.C., winning a sprint footrace known as the **STADE**.

2
A **FRENCHMAN** swam 3,700 miles (5,955 km) from **MASSACHUSETTS**, U.S.A., to Brittany, **FRANCE**, to become the first swimmer to cross the **ATLANTIC OCEAN** without a **KICKBOARD**.

3
Runner Michael Covert was the very first person to cross a finish line wearing a pair of **NIKE SHOES** when he completed the 1972 U.S. Olympic Trials **MARATHON**.

4
BOXER Jack Johnson became the first African American to win boxing's world heavyweight championship after **KNOCKING OUT** his opponent in 1908.

5
New York City **FIREMEN** raising money for **CHARITY** invented running **RELAY** races in the late 19th century, passing **RED FLAGS** instead of a baton.

6
In 2015 teams from the National Basketball Association (NBA) played a tournament in Johannesburg, **SOUTH AFRICA**—the first ever game for the league in Africa.

7
Major League Baseball's Colorado Rockies is the first **PRO** sports **TEAM** to use **SOLAR ENERGY** in its stadium.

8
During the summer of 1936, **GERMANS** gathered in social halls to watch the 1936 Summer Olympics in **BERLIN**—the first **LIVE TELEVISED** sporting event.

9
The first **SUPER BOWL**—held in January 1967—had about **50 MILLION** television viewers. The 2015 championship drew a historic TV audience of 114.5 million.

10
A **POOL** was first used for **OLYMPIC** swimming events in 1908. Before that, swimmers competed in **RIVERS**.

11
Baseball great **LOU GEHRIG** was the first athlete to appear on a **WHEATIES** cereal box in 1934.

12
For the 2016 Olympic Games, **BRAZIL** became both the first **HOST** country in the **SOUTHERN** hemisphere and the first to have **PORTUGUESE** as its national language.

13
American Eddie Eagan became the first athlete to **WIN GOLD** at both the summer and winter Olympic Games, taking medals in **BOXING** in 1920 and **BOBSLEDDING** in 1932.

14
Long-distance runner Dan Berlin became the first **BLIND** athlete to criss-cross the **GRAND CANYON** in 2014, completing the trek in 28 hours.

15
In 2009, **BASKETBALL** star Michael Jordan became the first athlete to reach **BILLIONAIRE** status. Golfer Tiger Woods has since earned more than $1 billion as well.

16
The first **WOMAN** on the front of a **WHEATIES BOX**? **GYMNAST**—and Olympic gold medalist—Mary Lou Retton in 1984.

17
The year 1908 was the first time a **BROTHER AND SISTER DUO** won Olympic medals: Charlotte "Lottie" and William Dod won the women's and men's **ARCHERY** contests, respectively.

35 WINNING FACTS

18
Brit Roger Bannister was the first runner to crack the **FOUR-MINUTE** barrier in the **MILE** (1,609 m) at a **TRACK** race in Oxford, England, in 1954.

19
The first **INDOOR** baseball game was played on April 9, 1965, in the **ASTRODOME** in Houston, Texas, U.S.A.—then known as the "**EIGHTH WONDER** of the world."

20
Slugger **BABE RUTH** became the first baseball player to hit 500 **HOME RUNS** in his career in 1929. To date, more than 20 players have reached that mark.

21
In 1994, a **STRIKE** over **BASEBALL** players' salaries led to the first ever **CANCELLATION** of the **WORLD SERIES**.

22
Olympic fans accessed **LIVE** streaming **VIDEO** on their mobile **PHONES** for the first time during the 2006 games in **TURIN, ITALY**.

ABOUT SPORTING FIRSTS

23 In 1960, the first **PARALYMPICS** were held in **ROME** as a sporting event for **WORLD WAR II** victims with **SPINAL CORD** injuries.

24 **BASKETBALL** player Bob Kurland is credited for the sport's first ever **SLAM DUNK** in 1944—a feat he claims was done **BY ACCIDENT.**

25 At more than 130 years old, the Argentine Open championship is one of the longest-running **COMPETITIVE POLO** matches in the world.

26 In 1998, **JAMAICA** became the first **ENGLISH-SPEAKING** Caribbean country to qualify for the **SOCCER WORLD CUP** finals. The team went on to finish 22nd that year.

27 Australian track star Cathy Freeman was the first athlete to **LIGHT** the **OLYMPIC TORCH** during the opening ceremony and win a gold medal at the **SAME** games, achieving the feat in 2000.

28 At the 2012 Olympic Games in **LONDON**, England, the **UNITED STATES** sent more **FEMALE** athletes than **MALES**—a first for the country.

29 Disguised as a boy, a 12-year-old named Kathryn Johnston became the first **GIRL** to **SUCCESSFULLY** try out for a **LITTLE LEAGUE** baseball team in 1950.

30 When ice climber **WILL GADD** scaled to the top of the **FROZEN** Niagara Falls in 2015, he became the first person to ever go **UP** the famous waterfall.

31 It's believed that the "STAR-SPANGLED BANNER" began being played **REGULARLY** at the **START** of sporting events in the early 1900s.

32 A **TURKISH** man spent five years **WALKING** and **ROWING** around the world—the first **SOLO** person to travel around the **GLOBE** using only **HUMAN POWER.**

33 In 1993, **ROCK CLIMBER** Lynn Hill was the first person to **FREE-CLIMB** the nose route of mountain El Capitan in Yosemite National Park in California, U.S.A.

34 **WOODROW WILSON** was not only the first **U.S. PRESIDENT** to attend a **WORLD SERIES** baseball game in 1915, but he was also the first president to throw out the **FIRST PITCH.**

35 The world's first flying disc—now registered as a **FRISBEE**—was invented in 1955. It went by the name "Pluto Platter" and was modeled after a **CAKE PAN.**

e are more than one billion passenger cars driving around the planet, which is one car for every seven people! 2. The United States has the ...st rate of cars per person: There are three cars for every four residents. 3. You can buy a car air freshener that smells like toast. 4. A single ...s about 30,000 parts. 5. In parades across the United States, members of the Shriners, an organization that helps sick children, have beer ...g around in tiny cars since the 1970s to bring attention to the charity. 6. In Japan, 13,800 cars are made every day. 7. Italian car manufacture ...rghini makes the world's most expensive road cars—the Veneno Roadster sells for more than $4.5 million. 8. It takes a total of about 18 hours ...ke a car. 9. "Bass Battles," which are competitions to see which car has the loudest car stereo, often sees winners with stereos as loud as 16C ...ls, which is louder than a jet at takeoff. 10. Seat belts don't ever rip because they are made from special fibers that can support more than two ....8 MT) of force! 11. One of the first crash test dummies was an actual person, a university professor nicknamed Crash, who tested safety ...es on cars himself! 12. In Brazil, most cars built to run on ethanol fuel made from sugarcane. 13. Los Angeles, California, drivers spend about ...rs a year stuck in traffic—that's the same as 15 days of school! 14. The world's first car accident occurred in 1881 when a car hit a bump and ...ed into a hitching post. 15. After car radios were introduced in 1920, several states proposed a ban stating that they distracted drivers ...Russia, you can get a ticket for driving a dirty car. 17. From 2008 to 2014, citizens of Turkmenistan were given a monthly allowance of 32 gallons ...) of free gas for their cars. 18. There are more cars than people in Los Angeles, California. 19. In the United States cars are driven an average of 13,476 miles (21,688 km) each year. 20. Honking your car horn unless it is an emergency is illegal in New York City. (Although many drivers ignore the rule.) 21. About 95 percent of a car's lifetime is spent parked (not driving). 22. The first parking meter was installed in Oklahoma City, Oklahoma, U.S.A., in 1935 and named Park-O-Meter No. 1. It is now on display at the city's history center. 23. The first asphalt roads were made for cyclists, not cars. 24. Motorists in China can pay to have someone wait in their car in a traffic jam while they are whisked away in a motorcycle. 25. In 2010 a traffic jam in Beijing, China, lasted for 12 days. 26. In some European countries, the cost of a speeding ticket is based on how much money you make. 27. A car's engine body is made by pouring molten iron into a mold that is made of sand, which is called casting. 28. In-the-know mechanics can play the video game *Pong* on the onboard computer in a Saab when they plug in a device to check the car's diagnostics. 29. British police keep teddy bears in their cars to comfort people who have been in a traffic accident. 30. At least 56 percent of drivers admit to singing while in the car, a study found. 31. The study also reported that the most popular song to sing while in the car is "Don't Stop Believin'" by Journey. 32. The world's fastest monster truck, which can go 99 miles an hour (159 km/h), only travels 264 feet (80 m) per

100
CAR FACTS
TO GET YOUR
MOTOR RUNNING

1963 Ferrari 250 GTO

gallon (3.8 L) of gas? 33. Half of all drivers report that they eat while driving. 34. If you were able to fly your car at 60 miles an hour (97 km/h), 24 hours a day, it would take you six months to reach the moon. 35. **The fastest tire change on a regular car was 1 minute, 23 seconds.** 36. In 2013, a 1963 Ferrari sold for $52 million, making it the world's most expensive car. 37. A North Carolina, U.S.A., man set a record in 2013 for pushing a car 50 miles (80 km) in 24 hours. 38. **A man in the United Kingdom holds the world record for having a collection of more than 400 cars that are powered by pedaling.** 39. Two 200-foot (60-m)-tall glass storage towers at a factory in Germany hold 800 new Volkswagen cars. The cars are parked by special elevator. 40. You can buy a toaster shaped like a Volkswagen van that toasts bread with the Volkswagen symbol on it. 41. **A street-legal, grown-up version of the Little Tikes Cozy Coupe was auctioned on eBay with bids starting at $33,000.** 42. A "Carstache" is a fuzzy mustache you attach to the front of your car. 43. In Finland in 2002 a man had to pay a $103,000 speeding ticket. 44. **You can buy a special french fry holder that sits in your car's cup holder to secure your container of fries.** 45. Hyundai means "modernity" in Korean. 46. Volkswagen is German for "people's car." 47. **In German, Passat means "trade wind" and Jetta means "jet stream."** 48. Prius is Latin for "to go before." 49. A public vote for what the plural of Prius should be was decided in favor of "Prii." 50. **The Corvette car was named after a small, fast, sailing warship of the 17th century.** 51. **The first monster truck is considered "Bigfoot," which was created in the 1970s. Today, monster truck tires are more than ten feet (3 m) high.** 52. The Pontiac car company originally made covered wagons. 53. **Volvo means "I roll" in Latin.** 54. In Japanese the name for the Pleiades constellation is Subaru. 55. The symbol of Volvo—a metallic-gray circle with an arrow on the right—is intended to be the Roman symbol of the planet Mars, with the suggestion of iron standing for strength. 56. **Since 1968, more than four billion Hot Wheels toy cars have been made.** 57. A special edition Hot Wheels car covered in 1,388 blue diamonds, 988 black diamonds, 319 white diamonds, and 8 rubies was auctioned in 2008 for $60,000. 58. A teenager from Romania designed a life-size Lego car from more than 500,000 Lego pieces. Its top speed is 19 miles an hour (31 km/h). 59. **The nickname for Henry Ford's Model T, first produced in 1908, was "Tin Lizzie."** 60. On the Model T, there wasn't a gas pedal—just a handle on the steering wheel that you pull to adjust the car's power. 61. You have a better chance of avoiding carsickness if you face forward in a car to keep the motion sensed by your eyes and ears the same. 62. **The little bumps in the road that divide lanes are called Botts' dots, named after the man who invented them in the 1950s.** 63. AeroMobil is a prototype car that can fly. Its lightweight wings collapse, so after landing, it can drive around like any other car. 64. Driverless cars—that use computer technology to navigate without the help of humans—can be programmed to avoid cows that are on the roadway. 65. **A car company in San Francisco, California, has invented an electric car that rides on two wheels and self-balances.** 66. **A stretch of road in the Netherlands uses glow-in-the-dark painted street lines instead of streetlights to light the way for drivers.** 67. A Czech company is developing a way to make car tires out of dandelions, which have roots that produce milky rubber particles. 68. **In an electric Tesla car, there is a button labeled "insane" that, when pressed, gives you 50 percent more power.** 69. One car company printed the shell of a car using a 3-D printer in 44 hours. 70. The "Tweel" is a tire that never goes flat. It doesn't have air in it, but rather a beam that's steel on the outside and rubber on the inside. 71. **Scientists created a robot that can drive a car using cameras and "obstacle avoiding sensors."** 72. Scientists are working to develop "smart seat belts" that monitor drivers' heart rates and breathing to see if they are asleep at the wheel. If they are, an alarm of some sort will sound to perk them up. 73. Ford Motor Company is exploring ways to use unused tomato parts from a ketchup company and turn them into materials for cars! 74. **Because electric cars are so quiet, pedestrians and cyclists can't hear them, even when they're very close. One company is working on a way to add sound effects to the cars to make them noticeable.** 75. A prototype of a smart rearview mirror "sees through" clutter that is in the back of your car by communicating with a live-feed camera placed on the back window so the driver can still see out. 76. The first passenger-carrying car ran in 1801 and was powered by steam. 77. **In Italy, you can buy a Fiat car with a built-in espresso machine.** 78. An Australian man built a street-legal Batmobile. He uses it to cheer up children who have illnesses and are fans of the *Batman* movies and comic books. 79. Britain's "Red Flag Act" of 1865 stated that cars must have two drivers and a third person was to walk in front with a red flag during the day or a lantern at night. 80. **Henry Ford's moving assembly line invented to make the Model T is still used today, but robots are generally used instead of people.** 81. Four Formula One racing car tires can be changed out in as few as two seconds at a pit stop. 82. Formula One cars use tires without tread, called slicks, but only in dry weather because treads help the tires grip in wet conditions. 83. **Some of the first car tires were solid rubber, which meant they never popped, but also gave passengers a rougher ride.** 84. In 1948, In-N-Out Burger became the first drive-thru where customers could stay in their car and place an order using a two-way speaker system. 85. The first drive-in movie theater opened in 1933 and charged 25 cents per car, as well as 25 cents per person. To penny-pinch, people sometimes hid passengers in the trunk and snuck in! 86. **A recent study found that people's faces tend to resemble the appearance of the fronts of their cars.** 87. NASCAR drivers can lose five to ten pounds (2.3 to 4.5 kg) of sweat in one race! 88. Seat belts fitted to the front seats of cars weren't standard until 1966. 89. **Barbie's first car was a 1962 Austin Healey roadster.** 90. In 1903 Massachusetts became the first U.S. state to require license plates. 91. In the movie *Cars*, Luigi's license plate number is 445-108, which is the latitude and longitude (44.5 N, 10.8 E) for a Ferrari car factory in Italy. 92. **The "Popemobile" is any car specially designed for the pope—the head of the Roman Catholic Church. The car often has a bubble top so the pope can see and be seen easily by the crowds.** 93. Eighteen Australians set a world record by squeezing into one Smart Car. 94. One man racked up more than three million miles (4.8 million km) on his Volvo—a world record for distance covered by a car. 95. **The Ford Anglia used in *Harry Potter and the Chamber of Secrets'* flying car scenes temporarily went missing from the film studio, but was recovered at a castle six months later.** 96. Sports cars used by police officers of Dubai, United Arab Emirates, can reach speeds of more than 190 miles an hour (306 km/h). 97. L. L. Bean has a "Bootmobile"—a truck that looks like a rubber boot. If it were a real boot, its size would be 747. 98. **The band One Direction has a Scooby-Doo-themed tour bus. The outside is painted like the Mystery Machine.** 99. Since 1995, the fast food restaurant Jack in the Box has sold or given away more than 22 million antenna balls—decorations that fit on the tip of a car's antenna. 100. The smallest road car in the world is just 25 inches (64 cm) high and 50 inches (127 cm) long. It can travel at 33 miles an hour (53 km/h).

YOU HAVE LEARNED **3,234** FACTS

5,000 AWESOME FACTS 3 **137**

1

Star Wars' creator **GEORGE LUCAS** based the story behind the original film on fairy tales, Western movies, and early **SCI-FI MOVIES.**

2

All of the first seven episodes of the *STAR WARS* movies start with the line, "A long time ago, in a galaxy far, far away."

3

With more than **$4.4 BILLION** in worldwide box office sales, more people have seen the *STAR WARS* movies than any other franchise in history.

4

Every May the 4th (which sounds like **"MAY THE FORCE,"** a famous tag line), Star Wars Day is marked by fans around the world with parties and movie screenings.

5

YODA was originally named **"BUFFY"** and then **"MINCH YODA"** before Lucas shortened it to just Yoda.

6

The **PHRASE** "I have a bad feeling about this" is used in **EVERY** *Star Wars* movie.

7

The fictional planet **TATOOINE** was mostly filmed in southern Tunisia.

8

You can stay in **LUKE SKYWALKER'S** house in *Star Wars,* now a hotel in the **MIDDLE** of the Tunisian desert.

9

The barren **DEATH VALLEY** in California, U.S.A., was also used as a **BACKDROP** in the original movies.

10

Sandstorms in **TUNISIA** destroyed several sets and **DELAYED** filming during the original *Star Wars* film in 1976 and again on the set of *The Phantom Menace* in 1999.

11

The 2015 *THE FORCE AWAKENS*, the seventh episode in the *Star Wars* saga, is actually a **SEQUEL** to *Return of the Jedi*, which was released in 1983.

12

George Lucas initially wanted Yoda to be played by a **MONKEY** wearing a **MASK** before deciding to use a **PUPPET.**

13

Yoda's **PUPPETEER** was the same person behind the *Muppets'* **MISS PIGGY** and *Sesame Street'*s **COOKIE MONSTER, BERT,** and **GROVER.**

14

It took two hours every day on the *Star Wars* film set to create **PRINCESS LEIA'S** famous buns.

15

To create the sound of the *Star Wars'* **TIE STARFIGHTER ENGINES,** producers altered the recording of an **ELEPHANT'S** bellow.

16

Every **CLONE TROOPER'S** costume in the *Star Wars* films was created with **CGI**— there were no actual outfits made.

17

More than **250 MILLION** *Star Wars* action figures were sold between **1978** and **1986** alone—making it the most successful movie-related toy line ever.

18

The shape of the **MILLENNIUM FALCON** was inspired by the shape of a half-eaten hamburger with an olive in its side.

19

Nearly **200** films and countless **TV SHOWS** have direct references to the *STAR WARS* series.

20

George Lucas based the idea of friendly wookie **CHEWBACCA** on his pet dog, an Alaskan **MALAMUTE** named Indiana.

21

The actor who has played **CHEWBACCA** in every single episode of the *Star Wars* series is **7 FEET, 3 INCHES (2.2 M)** tall.

22

Chewbacca's garbled voice is a blend of **BEAR, LION, WALRUS,** and **BADGER VOCALIZATIONS.**

23

A man in **CALIFORNIA** has amassed more than **300,000** unique *Star Wars*-themed items—the largest known collection in the **WORLD.**

24

You can check out **LIFE-SIZE WAX** figures of 16 *Star Wars* characters— including Yoda, Luke Skywalker, and Darth Vader—at a museum in London, England.

25

The squishy sound of **JABBA THE HUTT'S** slither in *RETURN OF THE JEDI* is actually a recording of someone running his hands through cheese casserole.

26

Star Wars-related books have brought in more than **$100 MILLION** of sales—and **80** have made the *New York Times* best seller list.

27

An **88-SECOND CLIP** of *Star Wars: The Force Awakens* notched more than **60 MILLION** views in a week when it was posted on YouTube in 2014.

28

The **ASTEROIDS** zooming across space in *The Empire Strikes Back* are actually **SPRAY-PAINTED POTATOES** filmed against a blue screen.

29

The iconic sunset over *Star Wars'* fictional planet Tatooine—showing **TWO SUNS**—predicted the existence of planets orbiting **BINARY STARS.**

30

For about **$100,000,** you can buy your own *Star Wars* battle pod **ARCADE GAME** with leather seats and plush carpeting.

31

In 2012 Disney bought **LUCASFILM,** the maker of *Star Wars* movies, from its founder George Lucas for **$4.05 BILLION.**

32

There's an artificial pond called **LAKE EWOK** at the **SKYWALKER RANCH** in California, the home of George Lucas's archives.

33

The language spoken by the **JAWAS** in the original film was created by recording speakers of the **AFRICAN ZULU** language, then speeding it up electronically.

37
The **EWOK** language is a combination of **TIBETAN** and **NEPALESE**.

34
YODA'S bulging eyes were inspired by **ALBERT EINSTEIN'S** similarly bug-eyed features.

35
The word "**JEDI**" is said to be linked to Japanese *JIDAIGEKI* or "period dramas"—the type of movies that influenced the early career of George Lucas.

38
The **SNOW** in some of the *The Empire Strikes Back* scenes was created using a **BLEND OF FLOUR** and a special type of glue.

39
JABBA THE HUTT was controlled by a team of at least **SIX** puppeteers.

36
Parts of *THE EMPIRE STRIKES BACK* were filmed at the Hardangerjøkulen Glacier in **NORWAY**.

40
The giant **BANTHA CREATURE** in *Star Wars Episode IV: A New Hope* is actually an **ELEPHANT** wearing a furry costume.

41
DARTH VADER'S heavy breathing was recorded by putting a microphone inside a regulator on a **SCUBA TANK**.

42
The eyepieces on **C-3PO'S** costume were made of **REAL GOLD** to prevent corrosion.

43
"**LEIA**," a new 3-D technology that lets you beam images and video from a mobile phone, was inspired by **HOLOGRAPHIC IMAGERY** in *Star Wars*.

44
Luke Skywalker's **LIGHTSABER** from *Return of the Jedi* flew to the International Space Station in **2007**.

45
A **RECENT SCREENING** of the six *Star Wars* movies in **SHANGHAI** marked the first time the original trilogy was ever shown in a movie theater in China.

46
Star Wars has inspired more than **300 STAR WARS** video games.

47
Star Wars III: Revenge of the Sith was initially more than **4 HOURS LONG**. (It was eventually cut to 2 hours, 20 minutes.)

48
R2-D2'S "voice" was created with actual **BLEEPS** and **BLOOPS** vocalized by a sound designer on a digital **SYNTHESIZER**.

49
The *Star Wars* movie *The Force Awakens* was filmed in **IRELAND**, **THE UNITED KINGDOM**, and **ABU DHABI**.

50
The tiny **SOUTH PACIFIC ISLAND OF NIUE** accepts limited edition *STAR WARS* collectible coins as legal tender.

50
INTERGALACTIC
FACTS ABOUT
STAR WARS

R2-D2 and C-3PO

1

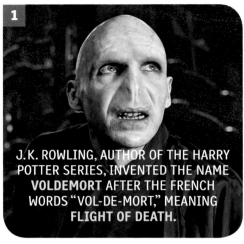

J.K. ROWLING, AUTHOR OF THE HARRY POTTER SERIES, INVENTED THE NAME **VOLDEMORT** AFTER THE FRENCH WORDS "VOL-DE-MORT," MEANING **FLIGHT OF DEATH.**

2

NOTORIOUS GUNFIGHTER BILLY THE KID FELL INTO THIEVERY AND LAWLESSNESS IN THE AMERICAN SOUTHWEST IN THE LATE 1800s BEFORE HE WAS SHOT BY A SHERIFF.

4

SHREDDER, THE VILLAIN IN *TEENAGE MUTANT NINJA TURTLES*, WAS DESIGNED AFTER A CHEESE GRATER.

3

IN THE MOVIE *JAWS*, THE SHARK DOESN'T FULLY APPEAR ON SCREEN UNTIL **1** HOUR AND **21** MINUTES INTO THE 2-HOUR MOVIE.

25 MISCHIEVOUS FACTS ABOUT VILLAINS

5

In the original Brothers Grimm's *Snow White and the Seven Dwarves*, THE QUEEN tries to kill Snow White with a SHARP CORSET, a POISONED BRUSH, and finally with a poisonous APPLE.

6

According to *Star Wars* creator George Lucas, **DARTH** is a variation of the word **"DARK"** and **VADER** is a variation of **"FATHER"** in some languages, so Darth Vader can mean **DARK FATHER.**

7

English captain **WILLIAM BLIGH** was so disliked by his crew for being **HARSH AND CRITICAL** that, in April 1789, there was a rebellion on his ship *BOUNTY* and he was sent off in a lifeboat.

8

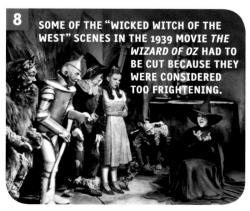

SOME OF THE "WICKED WITCH OF THE WEST" SCENES IN THE 1939 MOVIE *THE WIZARD OF OZ* HAD TO BE CUT BECAUSE THEY WERE CONSIDERED TOO FRIGHTENING.

9

Though never named in the 1953 film *PETER PAN*, the **CROCODILE** who ate Captain Hook's hand is known as **TICK TOCK** in a spin-off TV series.

11

BELLATRIX, the Slytherin witch in the Harry Potter books, means **FEMALE WARRIOR** in Latin.

10

THE JOKER was supposed to appear only in the first two comics of *BATMAN*, but the writers thought he was too interesting to kill off.

12 THE DREADED PIRATE **BLACKBEARD,** WHO LIVED DURING THE 18TH CENTURY, **BRAIDED HIS BEARD** AND TIED THE BRAIDS WITH BLACK RIBBONS!

13 A 43-foot (13-m) version of **GOLLUM,** the **MISERABLE CREATURE** of *The Lord of the Rings* and *The Hobbit*, is on display at New Zealand's Wellington airport.

14 LAWYER-TURNED-VILLAIN **TWO-FACE,** FROM THE *BATMAN* COMICS, WAS INSPIRED BY THE 1932 FILM VERSION OF **THE STRANGE CASE OF DR. JEKYLL AND MR. HYDE.**

15 RUSSIAN TSAR IVAN IV GOT HIS NICKNAME **"IVAN THE TERRIBLE"** FOR RUTHLESSLY ACQUIRING LAND BY **DISPLACING AND DESTROYING NOBLE FAMILIES** TO CREATE A CENTRALLY CONTROLLED GOVERNMENT.

16 Before he assassinated President Lincoln at Ford's Theater in Washington, D.C., John Wilkes Booth was a well-known actor.

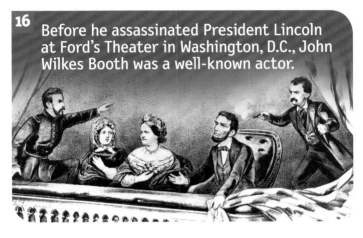

17 THE CO-CREATOR OF *CAPTAIN AMERICA* SAID HE CAME UP WITH THE VILLAIN'S RED SKULL WHILE LOOKING AT A **HOT FUDGE SUNDAE.**

18 The main character in the 1897 novel *DRACULA* was inspired by characters of folktales of the "UNDEAD," along with a 15th-century prince madman, **VLAD THE IMPALER.**

19 In Disney's **SNOW WHITE,** the real name of the evil queen is **QUEEN GRIMHILDE.**

20 THE EVIL SITH, LORD DARTH MAUL, HAS ONLY THREE LINES IN *STAR WARS EPISODE I: THE PHANTOM MENACE.*

21 **GENGHIS KHAN** CONQUERED HALF OF THE KNOWN 13TH-CENTURY WORLD AND IS CONSIDERED BY SOME TO BE A **BLOODTHIRSTY WARRIOR,** BUT TO OTHERS HE WAS A HERO WHO **LED HIS PEOPLE** TO GREATNESS.

22 **BLACK BART** was believed to have **ROBBED 28 STAGECOACHES** between 1875 and 1883 in California, U.S.A. He was finally caught when his dropped handkerchief was identified by the company who had recently cleaned it.

23 Stan Lee, the co-creator of *SPIDER-MAN*, originally planned on the **GREEN GOBLIN** not being a human, but rather a **MYTHICAL MONSTER** that came from a **SARCOPHAGUS.**

24 In Marvel's movies, **LOKI,** the mischievous trickster, is **THOR'S ADOPTED BROTHER.** In Norse mythology, Thor's father found Loki after he killed his **GIANT FATHER,** but he never adopted Loki.

25 IN *MALEFICENT*, THE CHILD WHO PLAYS YOUNG AURORA IS **THE DAUGHTER** OF THE ACTRESS ANGELINA JOLIE, WHO PLAYS THE CHARACTER MALEFICENT.

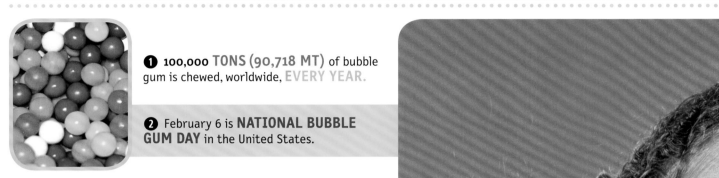

1 **100,000 TONS (90,718 MT)** of bubble gum is chewed, worldwide, EVERY YEAR.

2 February 6 is **NATIONAL BUBBLE GUM DAY** in the United States.

3 The roseate spoonbill, a colorful bird found in Florida, U.S.A., is said to have **BUBBLEGUM PINK FEATHERS**.

4 Bubble gum comes in many flavors and some are pretty weird: MEATBALL, **COCKTAIL WIENIE**, GRAVY, and **PICKLE**.

5 Bubble gum was included in **RATION KITS** given to U.S. soldiers during World War II. It served a dual purpose: a stress reliever when chewed and a patch for things such as tires and gas tanks.

6 The longest GUM WRAPPER CHAIN was almost **1.5 MILES (2.4 KM) LONG.**

7 A 15-foot (4.6-m)-tall, 70-foot (21-m)-long alley in California, U.S.A., known as BUBBLEGUM ALLEY is covered entirely in chewed-up bubble gum.

8 **BUBBLE GUM** is mass-produced in factories from a mixture of **CHEMICALS** and **FRUIT AND VEGETABLE EXTRACTS** prepared in laboratories.

BUBBLE GUM

9 A type of **BUBBLE-GUM CORAL** has grape-size soft parts that expand during the day to allow photosynthetic **ALGAE** inside to get more light.

10 Humans aren't the only ones who love bubble gum—some animals like the sugary taste. Bubble gum can be used as **BAIT** to **CATCH CATFISH** and **CRABS.**

11 Walter E. Diemer, the **INVENTOR** of **BUBBLE GUM,** lived to be **93 YEARS OLD.**

12 A man in the United States snagged the record for the **BIGGEST HANDS-FREE BUBBLE GUM BUBBLE** in 2004. The bubble was 20 inches (51 cm) in diameter—about twice as big as a basketball.

13 Duck brand introduced the very first scented tape using **BUBBLEGUM SCENT.**

14 In 2014 McDonald's created **BUBBLE GUM–FLAVORED BROCCOLI.** It tested so poorly that it never made it onto the menu.

15 In Germany in 2014, a group of artists decorated the outside of a house with **COLORFUL KNITTED BALLS** to look like a coating of giant bubble-gum balloons.

1 A custom or tradition is something that is done by a large group of people regularly or habitually over a long period of time.

2 On Groundhog Day in the United States, Americans rely on a groundhog named Phil to predict when spring will arrive. If he sees his shadow, there will be six more weeks of winter. If not, spring will come early. Phil is right about 39 percent of the time.

3 In Spain, a popular New Year's Eve tradition is to eat 12 grapes at midnight. In Peru, good luck will turn up only if you eat 13 grapes.

4 THE WHITE HOUSE IN WASHINGTON, D.C., U.S.A., HOSTS AN EASTER EGG ROLL EACH YEAR.

5 Because magpies (a type of bird) are bad luck in British folklore, many Brits ward off bad luck by saying, "Hello Mr. Magpie, and how is your lady wife today?" if they see one.

6 At mealtimes in Japan, never lick the ends of your chopsticks, cross them when they're resting on the table, or use them to take food from a plate that is being shared.

7 Brides in China traditionally are expected to cry for a whole month before getting married.

8 Loudly slurping noodles is completely appropriate in Japan.

9 Most people find passing gas in the presence of others rude, but in some Inuit cultures, tooting after a meal is a sign that you really enjoyed the food.

10 Mexican birthday traditions include smashing the birthday boy or girl's face in their cake.

11 Ancient Romans had a tradition where they would "feed the dead" by pouring wine and food into graves through a pipe.

12 In China, painting your door red is said to bring good luck.

13 Kids in Greece throw their baby teeth on the roof of their house for good luck and wish for healthy, strong adult teeth.

14 It was traditional in ancient Greece to exercise naked in public.

15 In the state of Puebla in Mexico, the fifth of May, Cinco de Mayo, is traditionally celebrated with parades, music, and street parties. The holiday is now celebrated in New York, too.

16 Buddhists in Japan annually set out offerings to "feed the hungry ghosts."

17 Hogmanay is the Scottish celebration of the last day of the year. Many Hogmanay traditions are done to bring good luck, like the "first foot" to enter a house after the clock strikes 12 should be a dark-haired male.

18 La Tomatina, the biggest tomato fight in the world, is held every year in Buñol, Spain, on the last Wednesday of August. One of the messiest traditions, 240,000 pounds (108,900 kg) of tomatoes are thrown at anything that moves.

19 In France, Spain, and Colombia, the Tooth Fairy is a mouse.

20 Sticking out your tongue is considered rude in many places.

21 Since medieval times, the English have celebrated May Day by dancing to music around a maypole with colorful ribbons.

22 Kids in some countries in the Middle East, such as Jordan and Egypt, throw their baby teeth to the sky for good luck.

23 Many people in India celebrate a spring festival called Holi, during which celebrants dance, sing, and throw colorful paint at one another.

24 Some people see the face of a man in the moon, but in Japan they see a rabbit.

25 EVERY SEPTEMBER IN LONDON ABOUT 100,000 RUBBER DUCKS RACE DOWN THE THAMES RIVER IN THE GREAT BRITISH DUCK RACE.

26 Every January in Maryland, U.S.A., people jump into the freezing waters of the Chesapeake Bay in the annual Polar Bear Plunge.

27 In the cheese-rolling tradition in Gloucester, England, a cheese is rolled down the hill and the contestants chase it in an attempt to outrun— and get to keep—the cheese.

28 Dia de los Muertos is a colorful two-day holiday that celebrates life and honors the dead. The tradition comes from the Aztec and continues today in Mexico.

29 Turkey has had a tradition of camel wrestling—watching specially trained camels wrestle one another.

30 Dating back to 1890, the Rose Parade in Pasadena, California, U.S.A., takes place every year on New Year's Day. The parade features floats made with millions of flowers.

31 A Christmas tradition in the Catalonian region of Spain involves a log that is kept as a pet. Children "feed" it and, once Christmas comes, the kids sing and hit the log with a stick until it "poops out" candies and presents.

32 In Greece during New Year's, they serve a cake called *vassilopita* that has a coin baked inside. The person who gets the slice with the coin should have good luck all year.

33 A DEVILISH BEAST CALLED KRAMPUS WITH HORNS AND FANGS IS A SORT OF ANTI-SANTA THAT SCARES GERMAN CHILDREN INTO BEING GOOD EVERY YEAR IN EARLY DECEMBER.

34 Dyngus Day is a Polish holiday, celebrated every year on the Monday after Easter, during which people throw water at one another.

35 Once a year, on Shrove Tuesday, people in the United Kingdom celebrate Pancake Day with pancake-flipping races.

36 Each year, the new lord mayor of London must travel from the City to Westminster to swear loyalty to the monarch—a tradition that has been repeated for more than 800 years.

37 Since 1952, the Detroit Red Wings hockey team of Michigan, U.S.A., has had a tradition where fans throw octopuses onto the ice rink at games.

38 The city of Lopburi in Thailand has an annual celebration called the Monkey Buffet Festival where a huge feast is set out for thousands of local monkeys and everyone watches them eat it.

39 The tradition of throwing coins into fountains and making a wish has been around since ancient times. It is believed that originally it was a way to offer something to gods so that they would offer luck or protection.

40 Bhangra is a form of dance from Punjabi culture in Southeast Asia. Like many older traditions, younger generations have created fusion styles merging Bhangra and hip-hop.

41 Cricket fighting is a tradition in China that has been around for thousands of years.

42 According to Japanese tradition, when it thunders children who are not wearing clothes must cover their stomachs and hide their belly buttons so a monster doesn't eat them.

43 The tradition of shaking hands dates back to ancient times when people did it to ensure the other person didn't have a weapon.

44 Traditions for a child's first haircut vary from culture to culture. Muslims cut a baby's hair when he is seven days old. Orthodox Jews wait three whole years.

45 About 3,000 euros are collected from the Trevi fountain in Rome, Italy, every day.

46 It's customary in Russian small towns for dating teenagers to meet around a fountain.

47 Putting candles on a cake is something most Western cultures do to celebrate birthdays. Many believe the tradition started in ancient Greece—the cake represents the moon and the candles its glow.

48 Some Sufi believers perform a traditional dance involving dancers spinning or whirling around. The idea started during the 13th century and is considered a form of meditation.

49 FOR GREEKS, SPITTING THREE TIMES IS SAID TO KEEP BAD LUCK AWAY.

50 Removing shoes before entering a home is a popular Asian tradition. It is found in Hawaii and Alaska, too.

51 For the past 200 years, on the first day of school German children are given a giant cone full of sweets and supplies called a *Schultüte*.

52 EACH YEAR NORWAY SENDS ENGLAND A GIANT CHRISTMAS TREE TO STAND IN TRAFALGAR SQUARE, LONDON, IN THANKS FOR HELP DURING WORLD WAR II.

53 Ancient Egyptians may have started the tradition of wearing wedding rings on the third finger of the left hand. They believed the vein in that finger led directly to the heart.

Indian woman covered in colored dye in celebration of Holi

54 Dressing in costume on Halloween comes from an ancient Celtic tradition but, back then, people dressed in costumes to keep evil ghosts away.

55 Eating kosher is traditional for many Jewish people across the world. On a kosher diet, certain foods cannot be eaten, such as shellfish and pork, and meat and dairy foods may not be mixed.

56 IN SOME COUNTRIES IT IS CONSIDERED AN INSULT TO LEAVE A TIP AFTER A MEAL AT A RESTAURANT.

57 Covering your mouth when you yawn is a tradition that stems from the ancient idea that demons could enter a person's soul through a wide-open yawning mouth.

58 Pope Innocent III started the tradition of engagement rings when he introduced a waiting period between engagement and marriage in the Middle Ages.

59 Bowing and not handshaking is the traditional greeting in many Asian cultures.

60 In most Arab countries, all people eat with the right hand as the left is viewed as unclean.

61 Tea time in the United Kingdom is traditionally four o'clock in the afternoon.

62 If you want to wish an actor luck before a show it's tradition to say "Break a leg." Theater tradition and superstition says it's bad luck to say "good luck."

63 YODELING IS A SWISS TRADITION OF SINGING WITHOUT WORDS THAT ORIGINATED IN THE ALPS AS A WAY OF COMMUNICATING FROM MOUNTAIN TO MOUNTAIN.

64 The Boat Race is an annual British tradition involving rowing teams from Oxford and Cambridge universities racing together on the Thames River in London.

65 Tailgate parties—where people grill and party outside the stadium before a sporting event—are such a popular American tradition that there is an American Tailgater Association.

66 In Finland it's rude to eat everything on your plate, but in the Philippines it's rude to leave something uneaten.

67 Children in Egypt have to eat with both feet on the floor to avoid showing the bottom of their shoes to anyone—a sign of disrespect.

68 DURING *SIESTA*, THE COUNTRY OF SPAIN TAKES A BREAK OR NAP EVERY DAY AND EVERYTHING SHUTS DOWN FROM 2 P.M. UNTIL 5 P.M.

69 Since 1896, it is an American tradition to place a garland of roses around the neck of the winning horse at the Kentucky Derby.

70 Chewing gum in public is considered rude in New Zealand, France, Germany, and Poland.

71 The story of Cinderella is a tradition across many cultures, with different versions of the story dating back to the first century B.C.

72 Many cultures place babies in cradles or rockers, but Swiss babies nap in a little hammock called a *hangemette*.

73 In Brazil, people greet one another with multiple kisses and hugs while in England people simply smile or shake hands.

74 For Brazilians it is customary to shower multiple times a day. On average they shower 12 times a week!

75 In both England and Sweden it is a tradition for brides to have coins in their shoes on their wedding day.

75 BY-THE-BOOK FACTS ABOUT CUSTOMS AND TRADITIONS

1 About one percent of people have 20/10 VISION, meaning that they can see something TWICE AS FAR away as someone with 20/20 eyesight.

2 Your eyeball size determines your vision: People with LONGER eyeballs have trouble seeing items that are far away, while people with SHORTER eyeballs are farsighted.

3 About 6 in 1,000 people have *heterochromia iridis*—or two DIFFERENT COLOR eyes.

4 Your eyeballs GROW in diameter just about 0.2 inches (0.5 cm) from when you're BORN to the time you're an ADULT.

5 Doctors are developing a BIONIC EYE that sends messages from the RETINA to the BRAIN, allowing some blind people to make out basic SHAPES and to see LIGHT.

6 An octopus can "see" with its SKIN as it's embedded with special proteins that are able to perceive LIGHT.

7 PHANTOM EYE is a phenomenon that happens to BLIND PEOPLE who experience a sense of VISION or still feel able to see COLORS or SHAPES.

8 Some people suffer from OMMETAPHOBIA—or the FEAR of eyes.

9 Your eyes are QUICK HEALERS—most minor cuts on the cornea repair themselves in just ONE or TWO days.

10 You BLINK about 17 times every minute—and about 5.2 MILLION times every year.

11 BABIES blink at a much slower rate than adults, typically only ONCE or TWICE a minute.

12 Your eyes are extremely sensitive to ULTRAVIOLET (UV) RAYS and you can get a SUNBURN.

13 Human eyes are slightly smaller than a GUM BALL. Colossal squids have eyes the size of DINNER PLATES.

14 The LENS of each of your eyes, which sits right behind the pupil, is almost the exact SAME SIZE as a plain M&M.

15 Your PUPIL responds to EMOTION and can change size when you're ANGRY, SCARED, or looking at someone you LOVE.

16 All BABIES are born with eyes that are a shade LIGHTER than they will be as ADULTS since PIGMENTATION isn't fully developed at BIRTH.

17 CUTTLEFISH are the only animals in the world with W-SHAPED pupils.

18 There's a rare GENETIC condition that allows some people to distinguish between 100 MILLION COLORS. Most people can see only 10 MILLION hues.

19 If you lined up all of the EYELASHES you lose in a LIFETIME, they'd be longer than the length of a BASKETBALL court.

20 A **CHAMELEON'S** eyes can move in almost **ANY DIRECTION** independently of each other, giving the lizard **360-DEGREE** vision.

21 The first **BLUE-EYED** person lived about 10,000 **YEARS** ago. Before then, all humans had **BROWN** eyes.

22 Each of your eyes has **TWO MILLION** working parts—plus 110 **MILLION** light-sensitive **CELLS**.

23 **CAMELS** have extra-long eyelashes to keep their eyes protected during fierce **SAND STORMS**.

24 **CORNEAS** are the only **TISSUES** in your body that don't have **BLOOD VESSELS**.

25 Research suggests that regular **EXERCISE** may help to **PROTECT** your eyes as you get older by reducing the risk of **DISEASES** that deteriorate vision.

26 Great white **SHARKS** have an almost **IDENTICAL** eye structure to human's—and their corneas may one day be used as **HUMAN TRANSPLANTS**.

chameleon

27 Your **IRIS** has 256 unique characteristics—six times as many as a **FINGERPRINT**.

28 **BOX JELLYFISH** have **COMPLEX** eyes similar to human's but their vision is permanently out of **FOCUS** because they don't have a **BRAIN**.

29 The ancient **MAYA** found **CROSSED EYES** attractive and would even suspend a wax ball from a **NEWBORN'S** hair to make their eyes go inward.

30 Researchers are developing a **HIGH-TECH** lens that can be implanted into the eye and allow you to have **THREE TIMES** better vision than 20/20.

31 Scientists are studying **MANTIS SHRIMP'S** eyes—that are sensitive to polarized light—in the hopes of developing a tiny camera that can detect **CANCER**.

32 Many animals have a **HAW**—or a third, transparent **EYELID**—that helps to keeps the eye extra-protected in the wild.

33 Your eyes are constantly moving in **RAPID, TWITCHY** movements. The brain works to stabilize this motion so you can see **CLEARLY**.

34 Contrary to popular belief, sitting **TOO CLOSE** to the TV will not damage your **EYESIGHT**.

35 Because they contain vitamin A, eating **CARROTS, APRICOTS, ASPARAGUS,** and **NECTARINES** can help improve your vision.

35 EYE-POPPING FACTS ABOUT PEEPERS

1. The word "Lego" is a combination of the first two letters of the Danish words *"leg godt,"* which mean "play well." 2. The number of Lego bricks sold in a year would stretch around Earth more than 18 times. 3. When the first LEGOLAND in Billund, Denmark, opened in 1968, it was estimated that 200,000 people would go to the park—instead more than 625,000 visited in the first year. 4. Lego bricks are interchangeable—a brick made in 1958 would still connect with one made today. 5. One of the first toys the Lego Group sold wasn't a plastic brick—it was a wooden duck. 6. *The Lego Movie* was the fifth top gross-earning movie in the United States in 2014—it made $258 million. 7. Lego artist Nathan Sawaya will create a life-size replica of you made out of Lego bricks, if you happen to have $60,000 lying around. 8. In 1947, Kiddicraft, a toy company in the United Kingdom, started selling plastic toys called Self Locking Bricks—two years before Lego sold its first brick. 9. Thirty-six billion Lego elements are produced in a year. That's 68,000 pieces per minute or 1,140 elements every second! 10. The "clutch power" of Lego bricks is what makes them snap together tightly, but pull apart easily. 11. To manufacture Lego bricks, plastic is heated to between 446 and 590°F (230 and 310°C) and then injected into the molds at a pressure of 25 to 150 tons (23 to 136 MT). 12. During a Lego wildlife exhibition at the Bronx Zoo in New York City, U.S.A., visitors could view giant Lego wildlife creations along with the real animals at the zoo. 13. The Lego Group started manufacturing Automatic Binding Bricks in 1949— the

100 FACTS ABOUT LEGO TO BUILD ON

forerunner to today's Lego bricks. Automatic Binding Bricks had small slits on the sides and were hollow underneath. 14. How many clicks does it take before two Lego bricks won't snap together? 37,112 tries according to a Lego fan who built a robotic machine that snapped them together and pulled them apart for ten consecutive days. 15. Lego pieces have been washing up on the shores of Cornwall, England, after a container with 4.8 million Lego toy parts fell off a ship near the coast in 1997. 16. Lego bricks are made from durable ABS (acrylonitrile-butadiene-styrene) plastic that is scratch and bite resistant. 17. The Lego manufactories are so accurate that only 18 out of 1 million elements produced are considered defective. 18. An artist in Wuppertal, Germany, painted a plain street overpass to look like it was made out of gigantic Lego bricks. 19. It would take a giant column of 40 billion Lego bricks to reach the moon. 20. The Lego Group has manufactured more than 4.4 billion Lego minifigures. That's more than the populations of China, Europe, India, and the United States combined! 21. If Lego continues to make minifigures at the current rate, by 2019 there will be more minifigures in the world than humans. 22. The Lego Group first worked with the Massachusetts Institute of Technology (MIT) in Cambridge, Massachusetts, U.S.A., to develop Lego MINDSTORMS—a product that allows users to build programmable robots. 23. Six 2 x 4 Lego bricks can be combined in more than 900 million different ways. 24. A Lego version of British Queen Elizabeth's great-granddaughter, Princess Charlotte, was added to the Miniland Royal Family at LEGOLAND in Windsor, England, just three days after she was born. 25. A Lego toy train track measuring 2.5 miles (4 km) long was built using 93,000 Lego bricks. The toy train took two hours to complete one loop. 26. It took a little over a month for 1,000 volunteers to build a life-size house in Surrey, England, using 3.3 million Lego bricks. 27. The Lego Group built the first LEGOLAND theme park in 1968 because so many people visited their factory to look at the Lego models that were on display. 28. The Lego Group doesn't just produce bricks; it is also the biggest tire manufacturer in the world. More than 650 million tires were produced in a year. 29. Except for a few unique pieces such as President Business's hair, all of the minifigures and other Lego elements in *The Lego Movie* can be found in existing Lego sets. 30. The Lego Group's motto is *"Det bedste er ikke for godt,"* which means "Only the best is good enough" in Danish. 31. "L'eggo my Lego Eggo!" In 2007, Kellogg's produced a special line of Eggo waffles shaped like Lego bricks. 32. Built with more than two million Lego bricks, "Bronty the Brontosaurus" is the largest model at LEGOLAND in Carlsbad, California, U.S.A. 33. The word "Lego" is never said throughout *The Lego Movie.* 34. *Arrrgh!* All Lego minifigures had smiley faces until the Lego pirates line was introduced in 1989. 35. The first licensed Lego theme sets were based on *Star Wars* and Winnie-the-Pooh. 36. A Lego collector paid $15,000 for a platinum Lego BIONICLE mask that had been given out during a promotion by Cartoon Network. 37. The wall behind the registration desk at the LEGOLAND Hotel in Orlando, Florida, U.S.A., has 5,000 Lego minifigures on display. 38. An oversize replica of the *Star Wars* X-wing Starfighter was built following the Lego set. It was 42 times as large as the regular model and used five million bricks. 39. The son of the Lego Group's founder started working at the company when he was only 12 years old. 40. If your mom or dad likes Lego, you can call them an AFOL (Adult Fan of Lego). 41. The staff Vitruvius holds in his hand in *The Lego Movie* is a chewed-up lollipop. 42. In 2014 the Lego Group became the top-selling toy company in the world, making more money than both Mattel and Hasbro. 43. A teenager from Alberta, Canada, raised thousands of dollars to build wells in Tanzania by auctioning off Lego creations he made. 44. There are 4,200 different Lego elements, and they come in a range of 58 different colors. 45. The Lego Taj Mahal has the highest number of pieces of any other set—5,922 pieces. 46. The first minifigure with a two-sided face was Professor Quirrell from Lego *Harry Potter*. When you turn its head around, Lord Voldemort's face appears. 47. At the LEGOLAND in Billund, Denmark, the Miniland trains, cars, and aircraft travel a total of more than 72,700 miles (117,000 km) in a year. 48. The helmet that Benny the "1980-something space guy" wore in *The Lego Movie* had a crack in it because the real Lego piece often broke in that exact spot. 49. Kellogg's created fruit-flavored snacks in the shape of 2 x 2 Lego bricks that could connect to the bottom of a real Lego brick. 50. A Romanian man built a real-size car using more than 500,000 Lego bricks. The car can go 20 miles an hour (32 km/h) and uses a compressed air–powered engine. 51. The hairpiece that the Lego Shakespeare minifigure wears is usually placed on female minifigures. 52. The FIRST Lego League (FLL) competition was founded in 1998. Teams, composed of kids ages 9 to 14, created robots using Lego MINDSTORMS to compete against one another. 53. Artist Sean Kenney built a seven-foot (2-m)-wide sculpture of a Nintendo DSi using 51,324 Lego pieces—it took him 200 hours to build it. 54. The co-founders of Google used Lego bricks to build storage cases for all the hard drives they used while developing the Google search engine. 55. The original *Star Wars* voice actor for C-3PO and the actor who played Lando Calrissian supplied the voices for their characters in *The Lego Movie*. 56. Lego's best-selling product is the Lego MINDSTORMS Robotics Invention System. 57. The worst-selling Lego product was Galidor, a series of action figures sold in 2002 that were based on a kids' television show. 58. On the "Super-Fan Builds" web series, set designers built a life-size double-decker couch just like the one featured in *The Lego Movie*. They gave it to a family of Lego fans. 59. At a Lego factory, bricks are tested for their durability by machines that drop, squeeze, and even "bite" the bricks. 60. A machine made out of 7,000 Lego pieces folds paper into paper airplanes and then launches them! 61. A music and Lego fanatic made Lego replicas of his favorite bands. He also created a Lego version of Michael Jackson's "Thriller" video. 62. Godtfred Kirk Kristiansen, son of Lego founder Ole Kirk Kristiansen, was appointed a Knight of the Order of Dannebrog of Denmark in 1979. 63. Soccer superstar David Beckham is a Lego fan. He has worked on the Lego London Tower Bridge and Lego Taj Mahal sets. 64. At the 87th Academy Awards ceremony, dancers handed out Lego Oscar statues to celebrities in the audience during the performance of the "Everything Is Awesome" song from *The Lego Movie*. 65. Anyone too afraid to ride the 168-foot (51-m)-tall waterslide at the Schlitterbahn Waterpark in Kansas City, Kansas, U.S.A., can visit a 4-foot (1.2-m)-tall Lego model of it instead. 66. It took two months to create the end credits for *The Lego Movie*. Sometimes as many as 150 Lego pieces had to be moved for each stop-animation frame. 67. There are four Lego factories in the world—in Denmark, Hungary, the Czech Republic, and Mexico. A fifth Lego factory is scheduled to open in Jiaxing, China. 68. The NBA Lego minifigures were the first minifigures to have spring-loaded arms and legs—all the better to dunk with! 69. The Lego Group released its first video game, *Lego Island,* in 1997. 70. To celebrate the 30th anniversary of *Star Wars,* Lego created 10,000 gold and chrome C-3PO minifigures and randomly put them in Lego Star Wars sets. 71. One of the rarest minifigures is Boba Fett from the Lego *Star Wars* Cloud City set. It was the first to have printed writing on its arms and legs. 72. A limited edition Lego set featuring three female scientists sold out in just a few days. 73. Instead of a business card, some senior Lego employees pass out a minifigure with their name on it. 74. In 2016, with the new addition of LEGOLAND Dubai, there will be seven LEGOLAND parks in the world. 75. With a few Lego molds, gelatin, and corn syrup, you can make your own Lego gummy candy. 76. In May 2015, visitors at the LEGOLAND resort in Windsor, United Kingdom, constructed a Lego mosaic of singing superstar Taylor Swift. 77. A BURP is a Big Ugly Rock Piece in Lego terminology. 78. To maximize the number of Lego bricks you can put in a Pick-a-Brick cup at Lego stores, place the elements in a way that leaves the fewest air pockets. 79. You could start a Lego rock band with playable instruments that have all been constructed with Lego bricks. 80. All male Lego minifigures wore hats until 1979 when Lego created the first hairpiece. 81. Lego bricks have been inducted in the U.S. National Museum of Play National Toy Hall of Fame. 82. A contestant in a Lego MINDSTORMS competition built a robot that could ski on its own using an internal sensor and motor. 83. It took three years to build some of the well-known Asian landmarks, such as the Taj Mahal and the Petronas Twin Towers, in Miniland at LEGOLAND in Johor Bahru, Malaysia. 84. Using a homemade weather balloon, two teenagers from Toronto, Canada, launched a Lego minifigure 15 miles (24 km) into space. 85. *The Lego Movie* was Morgan Freeman's first animated role. He played the character Vitruvius. 86. The actual Lego set in Finn's basement at the end of *The Lego Movie* was put on display at LEGOLAND in Carlsbad, California. 87. In the year 2000, both *Fortune* magazine and the British Toy Retailers Association named Lego "The Toy of the Century." 88. At the LEGOLAND in Günzberg, Germany, a Lego sculpture of Einstein's head weighs 4,334 pounds (1,966 kg). 89. Stepping on a Lego hurts because Lego bricks can support the weight of an adult—so the piece doesn't bend, but digs into your skin. 90. At the Lego factory in Billund, Denmark, computerized robots move up and down 65.5 square miles (170 sq km) of shelves selecting the boxes of Lego bricks needed for production. 91. The Lego Ninjago minifigure Kai has scars around his left eye, even though his character on the television show doesn't have them. 92. In 2014 the Lego *Batman* video game was officially recognized as the top-selling superhero game of all time by the *Guinness Book of World Records.* 93. The small hole on the top of a minifigure's head is to prevent choking if a child accidentally swallows the piece. 94. Lego DUPLO bricks are eight times larger than regular Lego bricks but they all can still connect with one another. 95. To celebrate the 50th anniversary of Lego in Australia, 13-foot (4-m)-tall Lego pine trees and flower sets were "planted" in the Australian outback. 96. In 1973 two cousins from Denmark made the oldest known stop-animation film using Lego bricks. 97. The Lego Group has created a program that helps companies develop their employees' creative thinking and collaboration skills using Lego bricks. 98. If you have an idea for a Lego set, upload a picture of your creation on the Lego Ideas website. If it receives enough votes, Lego may make it into an actual set. 99. The musician Fergie wore a dress made out of Lego bricks to the 24th annual Nickelodeon Kids' Choice Awards. 100. A working Lego foosball table features *Star Wars* minifigures—the Empire versus the Republic—as opposing teams.

1
In 1898 more than 1,000 fans showed up to watch pro baseball player **LIZZIE ARLINGTON,** who pitched a game in black stockings and a knee-length skirt.

2
Women competed in the Olympic Games for the first time at the 1900 games in Paris, France. Out of 997 **ATHLETES,** less than **3 PERCENT WERE WOMEN.**

3
During a 16½ month period in **1930–1931,** American swimmer **HELENE MADISON** held 16 freestyle swimming world records.

4
In 1901 **ANNIE TAYLOR** was the first person to successfully go over **NIAGARA FALLS**—in a pickle barrel.

5
British rowing pair **HELEN GLOVER** and **HEATHER STANNING** were unbeaten in 28 contests over **4 YEARS.**

6
American **TENNIS PLAYER** Marion Jones Farquhar became the first non-British woman to compete in **WIMBLEDON** in 1900.

7
American sprinter **WILMA RUDOLPH** ran into the record books by becoming the first **AMERICAN WOMAN** to win three golds in a single Olympic Games in 1960.

8
In 1936 Babe Didrickson—who also won two **OLYMPIC GOLDS** in track and field—was the first woman to play in the men's PGA golf tournament.

9
FIFTY-EIGHT years after Didrickson's PGA debut, Swedish golfer **ANNIKA SÖRENSTAM** repeated that feat, playing at an event in Texas, U.S.A.

10
Lasting from 1943 TO 1954, The All-American Girls **PROFESSIONAL BASEBALL LEAGUE** was made up of ten teams and drew nearly a million fans at its peak.

11
Today, women still compete in the **BASEBALL WORLD CUP,** which happens every other year.

12
In 1958 Italy's **MARIA TERESA DE FILIPPIS** became the first woman to compete in **FORMULA ONE** world championship races.

13
By taking the title at the **INDY JAPAN 300** in 2008, American driver **DANICA PATRICK** was the first woman to win a major auto race.

14
In 1804 Alicia Meynell, a 22-year-old **BRITISH JOCKEY,** became the first female ever to race horses in England.

15
In 1993 American jockey Julie Krone led her colt, **COLONIA AFFAIR,** to a Belmont Stakes title— the first time a female jockey had won a major horse race.

16
With her Wimbledon win in 1957, American tennis pro **ALTHEA GIBSON** became the famous event's first **AFRICAN-AMERICAN CHAMPION.**

17
After scoring **3,649 POINTS** playing at college, **LYNETTE WOODARD** became the first woman to play for the Harlem Globetrotters basketball team.

18
In 1972 tennis star **BILLIE JEAN KING** made headlines as the first athlete to be named Sportsperson of the Year by *Sports Illustrated* magazine.

19
In 1976 14-year-old Romanian gymnast **NADIA COMANECI** nabbed the first ever perfect score in Olympic gymnastics.

20
American **ASHLEY MARTIN** made history in 2001 as the first woman to **SCORE POINTS** in a collegiate football game by kicking three extra points for her team.

21
Ultrarunner **PAM REED** once logged 300 miles (483 km) straight **WITHOUT STOPPING TO SLEEP**—the first person to ever do so.

22
TENNIS PLAYER CHRIS EVERT won 125 straight matches on a clay court between 1973 and 1979.

23
KELLY KULICK, a bowler from New Jersey, U.S.A., became the first woman to win the **PROFESSIONAL BOWLERS** Association tournament in 2010.

24
As a 19-year-old, swimmer **GERTRUDE EDERLE** became the first woman to cross the **ENGLISH CHANNEL** in 1926—taking nearly two hours off the record.

25
In 2013 American swimming superstar **MISSY FRANKLIN** became the first woman to win **SIX GOLD MEDALS** at a single world championship.

26
Women's ice hockey hit the **OLYMPIC GAMES** in 1998, with the United States winning **GOLD** over Canada, 3–1.

27
At the 1996 Olympics, American gymnast **KERRI STRUG** landed her final vault attempt on a **SPRAINED ANKLE** to seal the U.S. team's gold medal.

28
In 2005 **SARAH REINERTSEN** became the first female above-the-knee amputee to complete the **HAWAII IRONMAN TRIATHLON.**

29
ILA BORDERS, the first woman to earn a baseball scholarship to college, also became the **FIRST WOMAN** to pitch in a minor league baseball team in 1997.

30
At the 2014 Little League World Series, 13-year-old baseball phenom **MO'NE DAVIS** pitched a no-hitter—a first for a girl at the championships.

31
In 2002 **LISA LESLIE** of the **LOS ANGELES SPARKS** became the first player to dunk in a women's professional basketball game.

32
British-German cyclist **JULIANA BUHRING** biked around the world in 2012, covering **18,063 MILES (29,070 KM)** in an unprecedented 152 days.

50 FACTS ABOUT AWESOME FEMALE ATHLETES

33 JOHANNA QUAAS of Germany competed in events such as the parallel bars and balance beam when age **87**, making her the world's oldest active gymnast.

34 German tennis star **SABINE LISICKI'S** serve has been clocked at 131 miles an hour (210.8 km/h)—that's faster than a **SPEEDING TRAIN!**

35 In 2010, 16-year-old **AUSTRALIAN JESSICA WATSON** completed a **SOLO BOAT VOYAGE** around the globe—the youngest ever person to do so.

36 In 2012, a female Nepali climber named **CHHURIM** climbed 29,035 feet (8,850 m) to summit **MOUNT EVEREST** twice in one week.

37 92-year-old **HARRIETTE THOMPSON** completed a marathon in California, U.S.A, in just under 7.5 hours—the oldest woman ever to do so.

38 After signing with the U.S. Basketball League in 1986, **NANCY LIEBERMAN** became the first woman to play in men's professional basketball.

39 In 2010, **35,681** fans watched Belgium's **KIM CLIJSTERS** defeat Serena Williams in Brussels, Belgium—the most attended tennis match ever.

40 At the 2012 Olympics, 16-year-old **GABBY DOUGLAS** became the first **AFRICAN-AMERICAN GYMNAST** in Olympic history to win the all-around title.

41 Pro basketball player **MAYA MOORE** is the first woman to get her own **SIGNATURE SHOE** from Nike.

42 Canadian **CLARA HUGHES**, a speed skater and cyclist, is one of **FOUR ATHLETES** to have won Olympic medals in both winter and summer sports.

43 At 11 years old, American golfer **MICHELLE WIE** became the youngest player ever to qualify for a major amateur golf championship.

44 In **SNOWBOARDING**, American **ELENA HIGHT** became the first person to land a double backside alley-oop rodeo during a halfpipe competition.

45 Track star **JACKIE JOYNER-KERSEE**—who won six medals over the span of **FOUR OLYMPICS**—was also a basketball standout.

46 Having earned some **$27 MILLION** during her career, Russian tennis star **MARIA SHARAPOVA** is widely considered the world's richest female athlete.

47 Probably the best female soccer player in history, U.S. star **MIA HAMM** scored 158 goals in her 17-year career.

48 In 2013 **DIANA NYAD** swam 103 miles (166 km) from **CUBA TO FLORIDA** without a protective cage from sharks—the only person to dare to do that feat.

49 Canada's **MANON RHÉAUME** became the first and only woman to ever play in an **NATIONAL HOCKEY LEAGUE (NHL) GAME** in 1992.

50 When video of **9-YEAR-OLD** football ace **SAMANTHA GORDON** went viral in 2012, she became one of the most Googled female athletes of the year.

Teenager Jessica Watson heads off on her solo global circumnavigation.

1
There are 660,000 gallons (2,498,372 L) of water in an **OLYMPIC-SIZE POOL**—that's the same as **6.6 MILLION CANS OF SODA!**

2
When swimmers compete in the butterfly and breaststroke, **IF THEY DON'T TOUCH THE WALL** at the end of the pool **WITH BOTH HANDS** at the same time, they're **DISQUALIFIED.**

3
HOME SWIMMING POOLS became popular in the United States **AFTER WORLD WAR II**, when movies showed people swimming in their private pools.

4
When the movie *Titanic* was filmed, the **ICY SCENES** of Rose and Jack overboard in the ocean were filmed in a **HEATED SWIMMING POOL.**

5
An indoor swimming pool at the White House is now **COVERED BY A FLOOR** and used as a **PRESS BRIEFING ROOM.**

6
When it opened in 1925, the Fleishhacker Pool, located next to the **SAN FRANCISCO ZOO**, was so big that **LIFEGUARDS PATROLLED IT USING ROWBOATS.**

7
A pool's **LANE LINES** are designed to **SCATTER ENERGY** from waves to keep them from getting into another competitor's lane.

8
The **FLAGS** at the end of a competition swimming pool tell backstrokers that they have 16 feet (5 m) before they **REACH THE WALL.**

9
One in five Americans **ADMIT TO PEEING IN THE POOL**, according to a survey.

10
Nearly 100 percent of **ELITE COMPETITIVE SWIMMERS** admit to peeing in the pool regularly.

11
There are **10.4 MILLION RESIDENTIAL** and more than 300,000 **PUBLIC** swimming pools in the United States.

12
U.S. PRESIDENT GERALD FORD had the outdoor swimming pool built at the White House in 1975. **AN UNDERGROUND PASSAGE** lets people travel from the house to the pool.

13
MANATEES can swim up to 45 miles (72 km) a day—that's **1,350 LAPS** in an Olympic-size pool.

14
THE *TITANIC* had a heated swimming pool onboard that was filled with sea water!

15
At certain angles, swimmers in the 500-foot (152-m)-long infinity pool on the **55TH FLOOR** of a Singapore skyscraper look as though they will slip off the edge of the building.

16
The **AVERAGE AMERICAN HOUSEHOLD** uses enough water to fill up an Olympic-size pool about **EVERY SIX AND A HALF YEARS.**

17
Yellowstone's **MORNING GLORY POOL** was once **BRIGHT BLUE**, but it is now more yellow and green from tourists throwing in coins and other trash, changing the color.

18
Diving from the ten-meter **DIVING BOARD** into a pool is the same as diving off a **THREE-STORY BUILDING.**

19
The bottom of the 2012 London Olympics swimming pool has **A MOVABLE FLOOR**, which can make the pool deeper or more shallow.

35 SPLASHY FACTS ABOUT SWIMMING POOLS

20 A SHIPPING CONTAINER was turned into a swimming pool on Berlin's Spree River.

21 Golden Nugget Casino in Las Vegas, Nevada, U.S.A., has a swimming pool that WRAPS AROUND A GIANT FISH TANK, which lets you feel like you're SWIMMING WITH SHARKS.

22 A resort in THAILAND has a BLOOD-RED pool, but it's not the result of dye. Tiles on the bottom make the water appear red.

23 Pamukkale, a SACRED POOL in Turkey, is warmed by hot springs and filled with COLUMNS AND OTHER RUINS from the ancient city of Hierapolis.

24 A lodge in Tanzania, Africa, has a pool where you can swim while WATCHING ELEPHANTS at a nearby WATERING HOLE.

25 HAVASU FALLS, located on the Havasupai Indian Reservation in Arizona, U.S.A., flows over a 100-foot (30-m) cliff into a BLUE-GREEN POOL at the bottom.

26 A pool at a Hawaiian resort is CARVED OUT OF LAVA ROCK and features 3,000 TROPICAL FISH and a SPOTTED EAGLE RAY.

27 In Africa, Victoria Falls' DEVIL'S POOL is located at the top of the falls and it LOOKS LIKE SWIMMERS COULD EASILY BE PULLED OVER, but a rock wall keeps everyone safe.

28 The WORLD'S LARGEST FRUIT SALAD ever made—that contained 11,197 pounds (5,079 kg) of fruit—was served in a LARGE, INFLATABLE SWIMMING POOL.

29 On a Disney CRUISE SHIP, there is a pool shaped like MICKEY MOUSE'S HEAD.

30 At a resort in India, guests can SWIM IN THE POOL DIRECTLY FROM THEIR ROOM.

31 Sacred Blue Cenote in Mexico is a pool located 82 feet (25 m) BELOW THE GROUND and surrounded by WATERFALLS that swimmers can take a dip in.

32 The WORLD'S DEEPEST SWIMMING POOL is 137 feet (42 m) deep and used for dive training and scientific research.

33 Some cruise ships have WAVE POOLS onboard that you can surf in.

34 SWIMMING IS NOT ALLOWED in the pools at the Roman-inspired Hearst Castle in California, U.S.A., which was once home to a rich newspaper owner.

35 Japanese macaques, also called SNOW MONKEYS, have thick fur to keep them warm in the frigid northern highlands, but they also TAKE BATHS IN HOT SPRING POOLS.

1

Mekong **giant catfish** can reach ten feet (3 m) long and **weigh** up to 650 pounds (295 kg)—about the size of a large black bear.

2 THE **GOLIATH TIGERFISH** OF THE CONGO RIVER BASIN HAS **14 LONG, SHARP** TEETH—AS LONG AS A GREAT WHITE SHARK'S TEETH—TO ATTACK PREY.

3

The **GREAT WHITE SHARK**—the **LARGEST** **PREDATORY FISH** on Earth—can swallow an adult person whole.

25 MONSTER FISH FACTS

5 **VAMPIRE FISH IMPALE PIRANHAS WITH THEIR SHARP FANGS,** which can grow up to six inches (15 cm) long.

6 The aggressive snakehead fish—an invasive species in North America—can **BREATHE AIR** and **SURVIVE OUT OF WATER** for **4 days.**

4 A **VENOMOUS** stonefish is camouflaged **TO LOOK LIKE ROCK,** and its dorsal fin spines can inject a deadly poison.

7 **PIRANHAS** sometimes eat one another **IF FOOD IS SCARCE.**

8  PREHISTORIC MEGAPIRANHA, A RELATIVE OF TODAY'S PIRANHA, HAD A BITE FORCE THREE TIMES MORE POWERFUL THAN THE AMERICAN ALLIGATOR.

9 TORPEDO-SHAPED **YELLOWFIN TUNA,** ALSO KNOWN AS AHI, WEIGH UP TO 450 POUNDS (204 KG) AND SOMETIMES SWIM WITH DOLPHINS.

10

Whale sharks—the BIGGEST FISH IN THE OCEAN—weigh as much as FIVE ADULT male African ELEPHANTS

11 A fangtooth fish has such **LONG TEETH** that when it closes its jaws the lower teeth fit into **SPECIAL POCKETS** in the roof of the mouth on either side of its **BRAIN.**

12 FRILLED SHARKS HAVE **300 ROWS** OF **NEEDLE-LIKE** TEETH.

13 **HATCHETFISH** get their name from their hatchetlike shape.

14 Sloane's viperfish are only 12 inches (30 cm) long, but their **FANG-LIKE TEETH** are half the size of their head, allowing them to impale fish swimming by.

15 PREHISTORIC-LOOKING **GOBLIN SHARKS**—WHICH LIVE IN THE PITCH-DARK DEPTHS OF THE OCEAN—HAVE RAZOR SHARP TEETH AND A **LONG SNOUT** THAT POINTS OFF THE TOP OF ITS HEAD.

TO REEL IN

16 Deep sea anglerfish—which **LIVE IN TOTAL DARKNESS**—have teeth that angle inward so when they catch prey, their victims can't escape.

17 **LIVERFISH**— WHICH LIVE ON THE OCEAN FLOOR—HAVE **TEETH ON THEIR TONGUES!**

18 King mackerel, the **LARGEST MACKEREL**, can grow to **THREE FEET** (0.9 m) long and weigh **100 POUNDS** (45 kg).

19 The coelacanth fish is called a "LIVING FOSSIL" because its LOBE FINS look like LEGS as seen in early types of fish.

20 6.5-FOOT (2-M)-LONG **LAKE STURGEON** CAN LIVE FOR *150* YEARS.

21 **GIANT FRESHWATER STINGRAYS**, which are 16.5 feet (5 m) long including the tail, **PROWL** river bottoms in Thailand, Borneo, New Guinea, and northern Australia.

22 Weighing more than 80 pounds (36 kg), wolffish have large teeth and strong jaws that can **CRUSH CLAMS.**

23 AFRICAN VUNDU CATFISH ARE AIR-BREATHING AND CAN SURVIVE LONG PERIODS OUT OF WATER.

24 Bluefin tuna can **RETRACT** their dorsal and pectoral fins to swim through the water **MORE EFFICIENTLY.**

25 A restaurant owner in Japan paid **$1.76 MILLION** for a bluefin tuna that he served as sushi.

❶ Before she became **NANCY DREW**, some of the other names suggested for the young female detective were **STELLA STRONG**, **NELL CODY**, **HELEN HALE**, and **DIANA DARE**.

❷ **MORE THAN 2.2 MILLION COPIES** of *The Tower Treasure*, the first book in the **HARDY BOYS** detective series, have been sold.

❸ The creators of the canine detective Scooby-Doo had considered making him a **LARGE SHAGGY SHEEPDOG** instead of a **GREAT DANE.**

❹ Jena, an eight-year-old German shepherd **POLICE DOG** for the Escondido Police Department in California, U.S.A., was **PROMOTED TO THE RANK OF DETECTIVE.**

❺ British detective **SHERLOCK HOLMES,** who is the most-filmed fictional character, appearing in **226 MOVIES**, had his office at 221b Baker Street, London, England.

❻ By going undercover as a rich lady, **KATE WARNE**, the **FIRST FEMALE DETECTIVE** in the United States, helped to **UNCOVER THE ASSASSINATION PLOT** to kill Abraham Lincoln on his trip through Baltimore, Maryland, to his inauguration in Washington, D.C.

❼ The board game **CLUE**, in which players are detectives, has been sold in nearly **50 COUNTRIES.** In Portugal it is called *DETETIVE.*

❽ In 1850 Allan Pinkerton formed the **FIRST DETECTIVE AGENCY** in the United States. The Pinkerton National Detective Agency slogan was "We never sleep," and it used the **IMAGE OF AN EYE** for a logo—the origins of the term "**PRIVATE EYE.**"

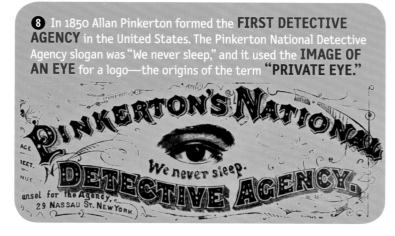

9 Detectives are sometimes called GUMSHOES because they have to act stealthily, as if they were WEARING SOFT, QUIET shoes made of rubber.

10 Detectives are trying to capture the "PINK PANTHERS," a group of thieves named after the Pink Panther movies. These thieves have stolen some $500 MILLION WORTH OF JEWELS in 35 cities, including Dubai, United Arab Emirates, and London, England.

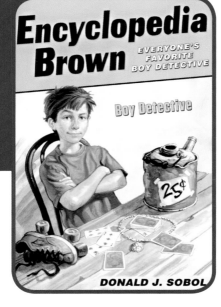

11 Even after 40 YEARS of solving mysteries, Leroy Brown, the boy detective from the *Encyclopedia Brown* series, never raised his fee—it always remained 25 CENTS A DAY, PLUS EXPENSES.

Encyclopedia Brown EVERYONE'S FAVORITE BOY DETECTIVE

Boy Detective

DONALD J. SOBOL

12 There are some 30,000 PRIVATE INVESTIGATORS in the United States. They HELP FIND missing persons and INVESTIGATE crimes.

13 The children's book *Harriet the Spy* by Louise Fitzhugh was BANNED IN SCHOOLS when it was first published because adults thought Harriet's actions would be a BAD INFLUENCE on children.

14 The first private detective agency in FRANCE was created in part by A FORMER CRIMINAL, Eugène François Vidocq, who had worked for NAPOLEON BONAPARTE.

15 The United States Department of Agriculture's (USDA's) Agricultural Research Service has two "detective" dogs named Opal and Tig, who use their KEEN SENSE OF SMELL to locate pesky STINK BUGS so they don't keep eating up crops.

1. Natural rubber comes from the white latex that flows from rubber trees.

2. People tap rubber trees by making a slit in the bark. The latex drips into a bucket hung just below the bottom end of the cut.

3. Rubber trees are tapped every two days. Each time, about one cup (237 ml) of latex is collected.

4. People who are allergic to latex need to avoid balloons and rubber gloves made from natural latex.

5. People with latex allergies need to avoid avocados, bananas, kiwis, and chestnuts because those foods contain proteins that are similar to those in latex.

6. Korean artist Yong Ho Ji makes sculptures of people and animals using strips of recycled tires.

7. A company in Michigan, U.S.A., turns old motorcycle and bicycle parts into chairs and tables.

8. **RUBBER BALLOONS MADE FROM LATEX ARE COMPLETELY NATURAL AND BREAK DOWN ABOUT AS QUICKLY AS AN OAK LEAF.**

9. When helium balloons are released, they rise as high as five miles (8 km) above the ground before freezing and bursting. (Animals can eat the pieces, though, so you shouldn't do this.)

10. According to Spanish explorers, the Aztec wore sandals made of rubber.

11. The Aztec added juice from morning glory vines to make the rubber bouncier, making the first rubber balls.

12. Researchers who re-created Aztecan rubber discovered that they had to be in the tropics for it to work—their air-conditioned labs were too cold.

13. After mixing the latex and juice, the Aztec had to work quickly—they had only a few minutes to shape the rubber before it hardened.

14. Rubber today is heated and mixed with sulfur. This makes rubber less sticky and more durable.

15. The process of adding sulfur is called vulcanization after Vulcan, the Roman god of fire.

16. **RUBBER GOT ITS NAME WHEN AN ENGLISH SCIENTIST REALIZED IT COULD BE USED TO RUB OUT PENCIL MARKS.**

17. "Rubber" is the slang term for "eraser" in Australia and the United Kingdom.

A spaniel cross jumps for a tennis ball.

75 BOUNCING FACTS ABOUT RUBBER

18 Before rubber, people used bits of bread to erase pencil marks.

19 Pencils in Europe usually don't have an eraser at one end.

20 The Australian slang term for rubber rain boots is "gumboots."

21 Most rubber ducks are not made of rubber. They are made of plastic.

22 A 2,500-pound (1,100-kg) ball of rubber bands was dropped from a plane to see how high it would bounce. It didn't.

23 There is a rubber duck that looks like Queen Elizabeth. People can also buy rubber ducks that look like Robin Hood, Captain Hook, and the main characters from *The Wizard of Oz*.

24 Children in Thailand can play on a rubber tree with long, sprawling roots that was made entirely from recycled tires.

25 When dropped from the same height, a piece of steel will bounce higher than a rubber ball of the same size.

26 A glass ball will bounce higher than a rubber one of the same size—as long as it doesn't break.

27 Tennis balls were originally made of just rubber. The felt covering came later.

28 To make tennis balls, a sheet of rubber was originally stamped into the shape of a three-leaf clover. The "leaves" were then stitched together to make a ball.

29 Tennis balls are now made of two rubber half-shells that are sealed with a rubber seam.

30 Until 1972 tennis balls were black or white, not yellow.

31 A WHOPPING 290 MILLION TENNIS BALLS WOULD FIT IN WIMBLEDON'S CENTER COURT (WITH THE ROOF CLOSED).

32 Bowling balls were first made of wood, then rubber, and now polyester and a stretchy plastic-like material called urethane.

33 Even though rubber trees are native to South America, most of the natural rubber used today comes from Southeast Asia.

34 Most rubber used today is synthetic (manufactured). It is made from petroleum oil.

35 Most car and truck tires are a mix of natural and synthetic rubber.

36 About seven gallons (26.5 L) of oil are needed to make an average tire.

37 A German company is working on making car tires out of the white latex that oozes from dandelions.

38 Dandelion latex tires would be better for the environment because dandelions can be locally grown.

39 Worldwide, about 1.5 billion tires are thrown away each year.

40 People in Kenya make "thousand-miler" sandals out of old car tires. Maasai tribesmen have been known to wear them for decades as they walk with their herds through the grasslands of Tanzania.

41 A Swedish company uses a mix of old tires and recycled plastic to make tough, recyclable floors.

42 STRETCHING A RUBBER BAND ADDS ENERGY TO IT, CAUSING IT TO HEAT UP (BUT ONLY SLIGHTLY).

43 Hockey pucks are now made of rubber, but when the game first started, players reportedly used frozen cow dung.

44 Hockey pucks are frozen before games and between periods to keep them from being too bouncy.

45 NASA trains astronauts how to move massive objects in space with their "two-ton hockey pucks" that float on a layer of air, much like a giant air hockey table.

46 The world's largest rubber duck is 61 feet (18.6 m) tall and has traveled around the world.

47 In 1983 seven million old tires caught fire in Virginia, U.S.A. They burned for nine months, creating a 3,000-foot (914-m)-high plume of smoke and polluting three states.

48 British artist Susie MacMurray made a wedding gown out of 1,400 inside-out rubber gloves.

49 The first Koosh ball was made out of rubber bands. It was named for the sound it makes when it hits your hand.

50 The biggest rubber band ball contained 700,000 rubber bands. It weighed more than 9,000 pounds (4,000 kg) and was taller than most adult men.

51 DURING WORLD WAR II, SCIENTISTS TRIED TO MAKE A REPLACEMENT FOR HARD-TO-FIND RUBBER—AND WOUND UP MAKING SILLY PUTTY.

52 Jean Lussier, the third person to go over Niagara Falls, did so in a six-foot (2-m)-wide rubber ball lined with rubber tubes. Lussier later sold off the rubber tubes for extra cash.

53 The longest rubber band chain stretched 1.32 miles (2.12 km).

54 Some golf balls have a liquid center surrounded by a layer of rubber.

55 The dimples (indentations) on a golf ball help the ball fly farther.

56 When introduced in the 1960s, the bounciest ball wasn't made of rubber—it was made of Zectron, a material used to cap oil wells.

57 Zectron balls bounced six times higher than rubber balls. They were later sold as toys called Super Balls.

58 Some toy cars can be powered by winding a rubber band around the axle (the shaft that runs between the wheels).

59 The Wright brothers, who built the first airplane, were inspired by a rubber-band-powered helicopter given to them by their father.

60 The molecules in rubber bands are long and stringy, like spaghetti. That's what makes them so stretchy.

61 When most things warm up, they expand, but when rubber bands are heated, they shrink.

62 People have built houses out of dirt-filled tires.

63 The song "Rubber Duckie" from *Sesame Street* has been recorded in French, German, Spanish, Dutch, Hebrew, and Chinese.

64 According to rumor, England's Queen Elizabeth II has a rubber duck in her bathroom. It wears an inflatable crown.

65 After falling one mile (1.6 km), a massive rubber band ball created a three-foot (0.9-m)-deep crater and burst into pieces. Some pieces flew the length of almost two football fields before landing.

66 Bungee cords used for bungee jumping have cloth wrapped around one or more strings of rubber.

67 Bungee cords were originally made for the U.S. military to soften the blow when parachutes open.

68 The first bungee jumpers leaped from a bridge on April Fools' Day in 1979.

69 Bungee cord strength differs from person to person. The cord must be matched according to body weight.

70 A bungee cord can stretch up to four times its original length.

71 THE LIGHTSUITS WORN BY ACTORS IN THE MOVIE *TRON: LEGACY* WERE MADE OF FOAM LATEX. THE LATEX WAS POURED INTO MOLDS TO EXACTLY FIT EACH ACTOR'S BODY.

72 Natural rubber is flammable.

73 Tire fires are hard to put out because the inside keeps burning. The best way to extinguish a tire fire is to cover the tires with sand.

74 In 1992, 28,000 rubber bath toys fell off of a ship in the Pacific Ocean. Most washed up on the shores of Australia and North and South America, but some reached the Arctic and Atlantic Oceans.

75 84: The most rubber bands stretched over a person's forehead in one minute.

1 A **GOLEM** is said to be a creature made from clay and **BROUGHT TO LIFE** by its creator.

2 According to myth, some golems **NEVER STOP GROWING** and can become **DANGEROUS** once they get too big.

3 The **LEVIATHAN** was said to be a sea monster with glowing eyes. It breathed fire and was so big, it made the water seem to **BOIL WHEN IT SWAM ON THE SURFACE.**

4 The leviathan was **FIRST MENTIONED** in the book of Genesis in the **BIBLE.**

35 MYSTIFYING FACTS ABOUT

5 Stories of **DRAGONS** are thought to be based on **DINOSAUR BONES.** One fossil looks so much like a dragon, it was named *Dracorex hogwartsia* **IN HONOR OF J. K. ROWLING.**

6 In *The Hobbit*, the dragon Smaug gives off **SO MUCH HEAT** that he can be felt before he can be seen.

mythical Chinese dragon

7 The **STORY OF THE PHOENIX**—a bird that bursts into flame and is reborn from the ashes— was common in **CHINA, JAPAN, ARABIA,** and **ANCIENT EGYPT.**

8 During the Middle Ages, people believed that drinking from a **UNICORN-HORN CUP** protected them from poison. The cup was actually made from a **NARWHAL TUSK** or **RHINO HORN.**

9 Explorer **MARCO POLO** saw a herd of **RHINOS** and thought they were **UNICORNS.** He called them **UGLY.**

10 Due to a mistranslation, **UNICORNS** are mentioned **NINE TIMES** in the King James Bible. In current versions, they are called **OXEN.**

11 Many North American native tribes believed in a **THUNDERBIRD**—an eagle with thunderous wing-beats and **FLASHES OF LIGHTNING** that shot from its eyes.

12 Ancient Greeks probably created stories of the **ONE-EYED CYCLOPS** after finding the **SKULLS OF ELEPHANT-LIKE ANIMALS.** The single eye-like opening is actually for the **NOSE.**

13 According to Greek mythology, **THREE CYCLOPS** created **ZEUS'S THUNDERBOLT.**

14 The Zulu people of Africa believed in **TIKOLOSHE**— mischievous **WATER SPRITES** that could become **INVISIBLE** by swallowing a pebble.

15 In West Africa, **TIKOLOSHE** were said to have the head of a dog and the body of a worm.

16
According to legend, a tikoloshe is **STRONG ENOUGH** to knock over an ox by **BUTTING THE ANIMAL WITH ITS HEAD.**

17
A **MANTICORE** was said to have the head of a human, the body of a lion, and a **STINGING SCORPION TAIL.**

18
MANTICORES GET AROUND. They have been reported in Persia (now Iran), Brazil, and Indonesia, and occasionally in North America and Europe, as well.

19
Many cultures have stories of **WEREWOLVES,** but in Ethiopia they tell of people turning into **HYENAS.**

MYTHICAL CREATURES

20
Psychologists have a **SPECIFIC WORD— LYCANTHROPY**—for people who think they **ACTUALLY TURN INTO A WOLF.**

21
A Japanese **KAPPA** has the body of a tortoise and legs of a frog. The top of its head is shaped like a **SHALLOW BOWL.**

22
The bowl on a Kappa's head holds **WATER.** Legend says that if the water is spilled, the Kappa **LOSES ITS SUPERNATURAL POWERS.**

23
According to legend, the easiest way to **CALM A KAPPA** is to give it a **CUCUMBER.**

24
GENIES (also called Djinn) first appeared in Arabian stories. According to tales, the mischievous creatures were **BORN FROM FIRE** and could take any shape they wanted.

25
Genies were said to live inside **ALL KINDS OF NONLIVING THINGS,** from trees to stones to air.

26
According to legend, genies would **CAUSE DISEASES AND ACCIDENTS** for people who crossed them.

27
The monster **NIAN** was said to terrorize villages in China until a beggar **FRIGHTENED IT AWAY** with fire, explosions, and **THE COLOR RED.** Red is now considered lucky.

28
NAGA were half-human, half-cobra creatures from Hindu mythology. Supposedly, they would **ONLY BITE PEOPLE WHO WERE TRULY EVIL.**

29
RULING FAMILIES in ancient Asia claimed to have **NAGA ANCESTORS.**

30
The **ILLINOIS TRIBE** of Native Americans told tales of the **PIASA BIRD,** a deer-tiger-man-bird that killed and ate warriors.

31
The Piasa bird's tail was said to be two to three **TIMES THE LENGTH OF ITS BODY.**

32
If **KING KONG** were real, he wouldn't actually be able to climb— **OR EVEN WALK**— due to his massive size.

33
The **AZTEC GOD** Cipactli was said to have a mouth at each joint of its body and **EAT EVERYTHING HE ENCOUNTERED.**

34
According to the Aztec creation stories, when the other Aztec gods destroyed Cipactli, they **USED HIS BODY TO CREATE THE WORLD** and everything in it.

35
People once thought the mythical **BASILISK** could kill all living things with a look or breath. Only **WEASELS** could escape its **DEATH-STARE.**

50 FACTS ABOUT INSTRUMENTS THAT STRIKE A CHORD

1
The oldest found **BRASS INSTRUMENTS**, called lurs, were **FOUND IN A PEAT BOG** in Zealand, Denmark, in 1797. They are more than 3,000 years old.

2
A **TRUMPET** contains 6.5 feet (2 m) of tubing.

3
When someone blows through the holes of a three-foot (0.9-m)-tall **STONE** in Oxfordshire, England, the **SOUND** can be heard six miles (9.7 km) away.

4
According to legend, King Alfred used a **BLOWING STONE**—a sandstone filled with holes—to summon soldiers to **FIGHT OFF A VIKING ATTACK.**

5
STEINWAY grand pianos have 12,116 **INDIVIDUAL PARTS.**

6
It takes 57 **INDIVIDUAL PARTS** for a Steinway piano to make just **ONE MUSICAL NOTE.**

7
A piano can play both **HIGHER AND LOWER NOTES** than any other instrument in a traditional orchestra.

8
Traditionally, people used a special form of **CHANTING** when they learned to play the **BAGPIPES.** A different consonant or vowel was used for each note.

9
Some **BAGPIPES** are played by blowing into a **"BLOWSTICK."** Others must be **SQUEEZED** under the arm to force air through the pipes.

10
Bagpipes were used to **RALLY WARRIORS** of the Scottish Highlands as they prepared for **BATTLE.**

11
VIOLIN STRINGS can be made of silk, steel, nylon, or **ANIMAL GUT** and may be wrapped in silver, gold, or aluminum.

12
"Cat gut" violin strings are **NOT ACTUALLY MADE FROM CAT GUTS.**

13
Scientist Mark Whittle found a way to **LISTEN TO THE UNIVERSE** by turning **PRESSURE WAVES** from deep space into **SOUND** using a computer program.

14
More kids in the United Kingdom play **ELECTRIC GUITAR** than violin.

15
The world's biggest harp, called the **EARTH HARP,** has 400-foot (122-m) strings that can be connected to **BUILDINGS** or **MOUNTAINS.**

16
The record for **MOST INSTRUMENTS** used to play a piece of music: 315.

17
Benjamin Franklin invented the **GLASS HARMONICA.** Spinning a set of **GLASS DISKS** and holding his fingers against the rims, he made musical sounds.

18
A **STREET PERFORMER** in Old Town Alexandria, Virginia, U.S.A., plays Mozart using **WATER-FILLED GLASSES.**

19
The **OCTOBASS,** which looks like a giant cello, is so big it requires **SPECIAL FOOT PEDALS** to play.

20
The Madison Symphony Orchestra in Wisconsin, U.S.A., has an organ with more than **1.5 MILES (2.4 KM) OF PIPES.**

21
The **BLUE MAN GROUP** plays the **DRUMBONE**—a collection of PVC pipes that are beaten with **DRUMSTICKS.**

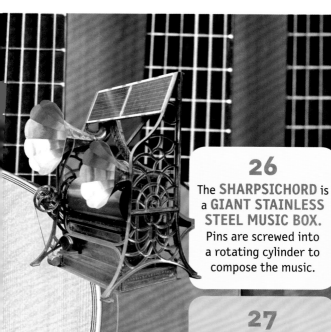

38
The **REED** in a woodwind instrument **VIBRATES** when a player blows across it. It is the vibration that makes the sound.

32
A **NORMAL GUITAR** has 1 hole, 1 neck, and 6 strings. The **PIKASSO GUITAR** has 2 holes, 4 necks, and 42 strings!

45
Actor **SAMUEL L. JACKSON** played the **FRENCH HORN** from elementary through high school.

26
The **SHARPSICHORD** is a **GIANT STAINLESS STEEL MUSIC BOX.** Pins are screwed into a rotating cylinder to compose the music.

39
FRICTION HARPS are not plucked. Instead, the player wears **GLOVES COATED WITH ROSIN (PINE RESIN)** to rub the strings.

33
The **SINGING RINGING TREE** is a curved tower of pipes in Burnley, England. When the **WIND BLOWS THROUGH THE PIPES,** it creates eerie music.

46
PERCUSSION INSTRUMENTS make a sound **WHEN HIT, SHAKEN, OR SCRAPED.** They include the xylophone, maracas, drums, and cymbals.

27
The Midmer-Losh pipe organ is the **BIGGEST PIPE ORGAN** in the world with **7 KEYBOARDS AND 33,110 PIPES.**

22
A **PYROPHONE** is an organ-like instrument that uses **COMBUSTION—** explosions of gas—to force air through the pipes.

40
Celebrity chef **EMERIL LAGASSE** used to be a **DRUMMER** in a high school band.

34
Each year at Christmas, carols are played on an **OLD FACTORY WHISTLE** in York, Pennsylvania, U.S.A. They can be **HEARD** from 12 miles (19.3 km) away.

47
A **MELODICA** is a cross between a **RECORDER** and a **PIANO.**

28
Leonard Solomon's **MAJESTIC BELLOWPHONE** contains an orchestra in one instrument. It was built with a spinning wheel, pipes, and bottles.

41
To play a **BRANCHING CORRUGAHORN,** you blow into one end of a flexible tube; the tone changes depending on **HOW HARD YOU BLOW.**

48
The first **ELECTRONIC SYNTHESIZER** (a machine that electronically produces and controls sounds) was made in 1905.

23
Musicians play the Pyrophone Juggernaut by **FLAMING THE ENDS OF ORGAN PIPES** with propane torches.

35
The **HYDRAULOPHONE** uses water to power a massive outdoor organ. It is played by blocking **THE FLOW OF WATER** through a pipe with holes in the side.

29
To play a **NOSE FLUTE** involves breathing out through the nose.

42
The **ZEUSAPHONE** uses electricity to make music. It is named after the **GREEK GOD OF THE SKY,** whose weapon was a lightning bolt.

49
Stradivarius violins, which are **FAMOUS FOR THEIR SOUND,** are hard to imitate because the wood used to build them grew during **THE LITTLE ICE AGE.**

24
People have created trombones and tubas that **SPOUT FLAMES** when played.

36
A cajón is a **SIX-SIDED BOX** with a hole on one side; players sit on top and **DRUM THE SIDES** with their hands. It was originally created by **SLAVES IN PERU.**

30
Singer Björk had a **UNIQUE** instrument built for her to play. It looks like a piano, but the hammers inside hit the **METAL PLATES** of a xylophone, not strings.

43
The **HARDANGER FIDDLE** has two sets of strings. When the upper strings are played with a bow, the lower strings vibrate, creating a **DRONING SOUND.**

25
In a cave in Virginia, U.S.A., **GREAT STALACPIPE ORGAN** players strike stalactites with soft rubber mallets to make musical sounds.

37
DIDGERIDOOS used by Australian aboriginals were created when **TERMITES HOLLOWED OUT** the inside of eucalyptus plants.

50
ELECTRIC VIOLINS come in all kinds of crazy shapes, including **S, ANCHORS,** and **HORSESHOES.**

31
The **HOLOPHONOR** is a clarinet modified to **SHINE PATTERNS OF LIGHT** from the instrument's bell.

44
Scientists found a 40,000- to 60,000-year-old **FLUTE** they believe was made by **NEANDERTHALS.**

1 INSIDE A STANDARD TELESCOPE TUBE, A SERIES OF LENSES MAGNIFY OBJECTS TO MANY TIMES THEIR ACTUAL SIZE. EACH LENS CURVES LIGHT, MAKING IMAGES APPEAR BIGGER THAN THEY REALLY ARE.

2 ACCORDING TO LEGEND, A GROUP OF KIDS ACCIDENTALLY CREATED THE FIRST TELESCOPE IN 1605 WHILE PLAYING WITH LENSES FROM SPECTACLES.

3

Through GALILEO'S TELESCOPES people saw that stars and planets move in patterns, which helped them figure out that EARTH ORBITS THE SUN, rather than the other way around.

4 Different telescopes can "see" DIFFERENT TYPES OF ENERGY from space: radio waves, visible light, x-rays, gamma rays, and other high-energy particles.

25 UP CLOSE AND PERSONAL FACTS ABOUT

5 Astronomers' high-power telescopes USE CURVED MIRRORS TO FOCUS LIGHT FROM DISTANT SPACE onto a small area we can see.

6 The Spitzer Space Telescope is SUPERCOOL—literally! It's kept at minus 450°F (−268°C).

7 A TELESCOPE LEFT ON A PATIO IS BELIEVED TO HAVE STARTED A HOUSE FIRE IN SUNNY ARIZONA, U.S.A.

8 Some of the FIRST TELESCOPES weren't used to look at the stars. They were used to SPOT ENEMY SHIPS.

9

ONE OF THE BIGGEST TELESCOPE MIRRORS IS 330 INCHES (8.4 M) ACROSS. TO MAKE THE MIRROR, A REFLECTIVE METAL SURFACE IS LAID ON A GIANT, SOLID-GLASS BASE.

10

ALMA, the world's biggest radio telescope observatory, has 66 MOVEABLE RADIO ANTENNAS.

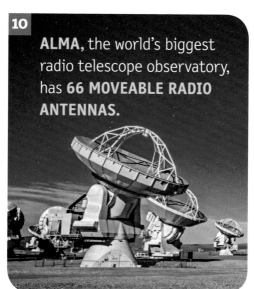

11

NASA's NuSTAR TELESCOPE observes X-RAYS—the same thing doctors use to SEE YOUR BONES.

12 GAMMA-RAY TELESCOPES have to be in orbit to work, because EARTH'S ATMOSPHERE ABSORBS the high-energy rays. Bursts of gamma rays from distant galaxies give off MORE ENERGY IN TEN SECONDS than our sun will in its ENTIRE LIFETIME.

13 The Hubble telescope is SO ACCURATE it could shine a laser on a dime 200 MILES (322 KM) AWAY.

15 An inventor created a telescope that CONVERTS LIGHT INTO SOUND, giving viewers a multi-sensory experience.

16 CELL PHONES AND CAMERAS can be clamped to the eyepiece of a telescope to take PHOTOS OF SPACE.

17 GALILEO used his telescope to observe the sun at sunrise and sunset. He later WENT BLIND, but not from LOOKING AT THE SUN.

14 WHEN THE GIANT MAGELLAN TELESCOPE IS BUILT in 2021, IT WILL HAVE MIRRORS MADE OF HOLLOW GLASS AND VIEW OBJECTS SUCH AS THESE "PILLARS OF CREATION."

TELESCOPES

18 A chemist built the world's WEIRDEST TELESCOPE by using a tub of DRY-CLEANING FLUID to catch high-energy particles from the sun. He later won the NOBEL PRIZE for his unusual experiment.

19 THE HUBBLE TELESCOPE HAS TRAVELED MORE THAN THREE BILLION MILES (4.8 BILLION KM).

20 The telescope mirror at Mount Wilson Observatory, in California, U.S.A., took 200 MEN to put into place. It was carried to the mountaintop on a truck that traveled just ONE MILE AN HOUR (1.6 KM/H). THE TRIP TOOK EIGHT HOURS.

21 The ALMA observatory is located in Chile's Atacama Desert because there is ALMOST NO HUMIDITY THERE to block light from deep space. Some places in the Atacama are SO DRY anything that dies there turns into a MUMMY.

22 The NuSTAR allows astronomers to see the X-RAY-LACED WINDS blasting out of SUPERMASSIVE BLACK HOLES. The winds come out in the SHAPE OF A SPHERE.

23 RADIO TELESCOPES USE MASSIVE ANTENNAS THAT LOOK LIKE SATELLITE DISHES TO "SEE" RADIO WAVES FROM DEEP SPACE.

24 The SPITZER SPACE TELESCOPE has found Neptune-size planets surrounded by CLOUDS OF HELIUM.

25 NASA'S KEPLER TELESCOPE zooms through the MILKY WAY GALAXY in search of other Earth-like planets. It has discovered HUNDREDS OF POSSIBLE PLANETS in our galaxy alone.

1 A **WEDDING RING** hanging from a string and held over a pregnant woman's belly is often said to **PREDICT** the sex of a baby.

2 Some people believe that if you catch a **FALLING LEAF** on the first day of autumn you will go all winter without catching **A COLD.**

3 **BANANAS** and **SUITCASES** are not allowed onboard most crab-fishing boats because they are believed to bring bad luck.

4 A Nigerian superstition says that if you **KISS A BABY** on the lips it will **DROOL** as an adult.

5 The **EARLIEST** ideas of superstitions date back to **ANCIENT GREECE.** An early idea was to cross one's fingers for luck, as a cross marks the coming together of **GOOD SPIRITS.**

6 The idea that **BRIDES** should be **CARRIED** over the **THRESHOLD** dates back to medieval Europe and is said to prevent **EVIL SPIRITS** from entering the house.

7 It is supposedly bad luck to **SPILL SALT** but, if you throw a pinch of salt over your **LEFT SHOULDER,** you can reverse the bad luck.

8 An old superstition says that opening an **UMBRELLA** indoors will bring a **STORM** of bad luck.

9 The **NUMBER 13** is notoriously believed to bring **BAD LUCK.** Many hotels and apartments skip number 13 when numbering floors, going from 12 to 14.

10 **TRISKAIDEKAPHOBIA** is a fear of the number 13. Black Friday—a Friday that falls on the 13th day of a month—is considered by many to be an unlucky day.

11 At least **10 PERCENT** of **AMERICANS** have a fear of the number 13.

12 A scientist once proved that 75 percent of a study group of **PIGEONS** became superstitious, believing that nodding their head a certain way meant they would get fed.

13 Ancient Greeks believed that **ROSEMARY** helped keep away **EVIL SPIRITS** and **HEATHER** is meant to bring good luck.

14 Many believe you should **HOLD YOUR BREATH** when passing a **CEMETERY** to keep **SPIRITS** from entering your body.

15 An old superstition states that **WEEDS** grow on the graves of **EVIL PEOPLE** and flowers grow on graves of the **GOOD.**

16 In Turkey, some people believe if you chew **GUM** at **NIGHT** you are chewing a **DEAD BODY.**

17 Researchers say that **WOMEN** are **MORE SUPERSTITIOUS** than **MEN** and as people age they become **LESS SUPERSTITIOUS.**

18 Fifteen percent of **AMERICANS** read their **DAILY HOROSCOPE.**

a four-leaf clover

19 Shakespeare's play *Julius Caesar* refers to the superstition that **ITCHY PALMS** suggest **MONEY** is about to be lost or won.

20 **NAPOLEON BONAPARTE** was superstitious and had a fear of cats—believing them to be **BAD LUCK.** Black cats are often associated with luck—good and bad.

21 A JAPANESE superstition states that if you HICCUP 100 times in a row you will DIE.

22 A woman in Florida, U.S.A., held onto a TOASTED CHEESE SANDWICH for TEN YEARS because she believed it brought her LUCK. Then she SOLD it online for $28,000.

23 Whistling or saying the word "PIG" on a ship is believed to bring BAD WEATHER.

24 Some FRENCH believe that STEPPING in DOG POOP with your LEFT foot brings good luck, while a poopy RIGHT FOOT means BAD LUCK.

25 You CANNOT get your HAIR CUT on a TUESDAY in INDIA because a HINDU superstition considers it BAD LUCK.

26 In CHINA, 8 is the luckiest number—the Beijing Olympics Opening Ceremony started at 8:08 and 8 seconds on August 8, 2008.

27 A company called KNOCK ON WOOD sells wooden blocks so that believers of the superstition can always have a piece of wood handy.

28 A Japanese superstition says that the person in the middle of a PHOTOGRAPH will have bad luck and possibly DIE YOUNG.

29 According to TRADITION a four-leaf clover brings GOOD LUCK to its finders, especially if found accidentally.

30 Some superstitious Koreans believe that writing a name in RED INK means that person will DIE.

31 A superstition dating back to ANCIENT TIMES says that you will stay young if you CARRY ACORNS in your pockets.

32 A RUSSIAN superstition says that if a woman drops her knife on the floor a MALE visitor will COME.

33 Some FRENCH CANADIANS believe that if a pregnant woman does not eat fish, her baby will be born with a FISH HEAD.

34 Many actors never want to hear the word "MACBETH" uttered inside a theater due to a supposed CURSE.

35 Some believe keeping GOATS close helps keep EVIL away.

35 GOOD AND BAD FACTS ABOUT SUPERSTITIONS

1 For 30 years leading up to the U.S. Civil War, the Underground Railroad was a **NETWORK OF PEOPLE** that helped take slaves from the southern states to find freedom in the northern states and Canada.

2 The Underground Railroad **WASN'T UNDERGROUND.** Escaping slaves and the people helping them were breaking the law at that time and had to be **SNEAKY,** or go "underground."

3 **HARRIET TUBMAN,** a slave who escaped from a plantation in eastern Maryland, **HELPED GUIDE 50 TO 70 SLAVES** to freedom in her lifetime. She went on to serve as a **NURSE** for the Union army.

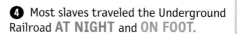

4 Most slaves traveled the Underground Railroad **AT NIGHT** and **ON FOOT.**

5 Some slaves **ESCAPED INSIDE WAGONS** that had hidden bottom compartments in them.

6 One man helped 28 slaves escape in Ohio by **RENTING A HEARSE** and making people think it was a **FUNERAL PROCESSION.**

7 Henry "Box" Brown, a slave from Richmond, **PUT HIMSELF IN A WOODEN BOX** and had himself **SHIPPED** to Philadelphia.

8 People who went south to help find slaves were called **PILOTS.** People who guided the slaves north to freedom were called **CONDUCTORS.** The slaves themselves were called PASSENGERS.

9 Along the way from the South to the North, some people and businesses offered "passengers" and "conductors" a place to stay. These places were called **STATIONS.**

10 Slaves who were caught escaping were returned to their owners and faced **HARSH PUNISHMENT.**

$200 Reward.

Ranaway from the subscriber, last night, a mulatto man named FRANK MULLEN, about twenty-one years old, five feet ten or eleven inches high. He wears his hair long at the sides and top, close behind, and keeps it nicely combed; rather thick lips, mild countenance, polite when spoken to, and very genteel in his person. His clothing consists of a variety of summer and winter articles, among which are a blue cloth coat and blue casinet coatee, white pantaloons, blue cloth do., and a pair of new ribbed casinet do., a blue Boston wrapper, with velvet collar, several black hats, boots, shoes, &c. As he has absconded without any provocation, it is presumed he will make for Pennsylvania or New-York. I will give one hundred dollars if taken in the State of Maryland, or the above reward if taken any where east of that State, and secured so that I get him again, and all reasonable expenses paid if brought home to the subscriber, living in the city of Washington.

THOS. C. SCOTT.

October 21, 1835.

11 **BOUNTY HUNTERS** made a living catching slaves and returning them to their owners.

12 Anyone caught helping a slave escape could be **ARRESTED** and sent to JAIL.

13 Most slaves who were successful at REACHING THE NORTH were from states in the upper south, like Kentucky, Maryland, and Virginia. Few were from the **DEEP SOUTH** because it was far to travel without being caught.

14 John Rankin, considered Ohio's first and most active "conductor," helped hundreds of slaves escape. He put a **CANDLE IN THE WINDOW** of his home as a SIGN THAT IT WAS SAFE to cross the Ohio River.

15 **ABOLITIONISTS**— people who wanted to end slavery—sometimes had **ROOMS HIDDEN** behind cupboards and false walls in their houses and even **SECRET TUNNELS.**

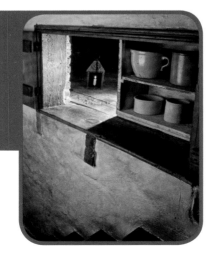

1 In 1876 Alexander Graham Bell made the first telephone call ever. He called his assistant in an adjoining room and said, "Mr. Watson, come here—I want to see you."

2 You can buy an iPhone 6 with pink diamonds for $48.5 million. Matching EarPods go for $300,000.

3 DynaTAC was the first portable phone. The original model had 20 to 35 minutes of battery life, weighed 2.5 pounds (1.13 kg), and sold for $4,000.

4 THE FIRST PRACTICAL SMARTPHONE, IBM'S "SIMON," LAUNCHED IN 1993. ABOUT 50,000 WERE SOLD FOR $899 A POP.

5 A company in California, U.S.A., is developing the first round smartphone called a "Runcible."

6 Some criminals have been caught after accidentally calling the police. In Florida, U.S.A., a car burglary was stopped after one of the thieves "pocket-dialed" the police.

7 Apple's iPhone launched in June 2007. Since then, more than 700 million have been sold.

8 A study found that the average cell phone has more bacteria than kitchen counters, dog bowls, doorknobs, and public toilets.

9 The phone number 666-6666 was sold in Qatar at a charity auction, for $2.7 million.

10 A phone from the late 1800s hangs on a wall inside a shop at Disneyland, U.S.A. When guests pick up the phone they are surprised to hear an old recorded conversation.

11 An artist used old rotary phones to create sculptures of sheep. The exhibit, called "Telephone Sheep," was displayed in Germany.

12 Alexander Graham Bell thought people should say "Ahoy" when they picked up the phone, but Thomas Edison won out with "Hello."

13 The Sonim phone holds the Guinness World Record for being the toughest mobile phone—it still makes calls after being frozen, thrown against a brick wall, and dropped 12 stories into the street.

14 TODAY'S CELL PHONES HAVE MORE POWER THAN THE COMPUTERS NASA USED FOR THE 1969 APOLLO 11 MOON LANDING.

15 A phone booth shaped like a Mercury spacecraft from NASA's Kennedy Space Center at Cape Canaveral Florida, U.S.A., is on display in the Smithsonian.

16 When Apple co-founders Steve Jobs and Steve Wozniak were students they were hackers called "phone phreaks." They built a device that allowed them to make long-distance calls on pay phones for free.

17 Many of the calls made with the "phone phreak" device were pranks, including one by Steve Wozniak to the Vatican to speak to the pope.

18 A new iPhone feature called Live Photo allows photos to "come alive" and move, like the portraits hanging on the walls of Hogwarts School in *Harry Potter*.

19 A phone booth in the middle of the Mojave Desert, U.S.A., from the 1960s (originally put there for miners) became a legend and functioned until it was made obsolete and torn down in 2000.

20 Dogs can learn to dial the phone: A rottweiler in the United States called the police when his owner fell out of her wheelchair. He also unlocked the door for the police.

21 In the late 1950s there was a fad called "phone booth stuffing" where college students tried to see how many people they could fit into a phone booth.

22 There's gold in mobile phones—recycling 35 to 40 phones can recover about one gram of gold.

23 "Fake cell towers" have been discovered in China and the United States that are said to be part of government secret programs to track and intercept cell phone calls.

24 Ninety percent of mobile phones in Japan are waterproof. Many people even use them while showering.

25 Artist Salvador Dali created ten working sculptures of a lobster on a telephone called "Lobster Telephone" in 1936.

26 At the 1964 World's Fair in New York, U.S.A., AT&T introduced the world's first "videophone," where people could see the people they were talking to.

27 There is a phone booth on the roof of City Hall in Lincoln, Illinois, U.S.A., that was put there in the 1950s to help with communication when spotting tornadoes.

28 Clark Kent often uses a phone booth to change into Superman.

29 A study showed that almost half of the cell phones damaged by water in Britain were accidentally dropped into the toilet.

30 The fear of being without your cell phone or mobile device is called nomophobia.

31 MORE THAN 8.6 TRILLION TEXT MESSAGES ARE SENT EVERY YEAR THROUGHOUT THE WORLD.

32 The world record for fastest text, involving the following message, took 25.94 seconds: "The razortoothed piranhas of the genera *Serrasalmus* and *Pygocentrus* are the most ferocious freshwater fish in the world. In reality they seldom attack a human."

33 A 17-year-old boy in Wisconsin, U.S.A., won the National Texting Championship two years in a row. He received $50,000 for each win.

34 Two guys in California made a makeshift telephone using a piece of string 650 feet (198 m) long and two cans.

35 Fisher-Price has been making the Chatter Telephone since 1962. It is one of the few phones with a rotary dial on the shelves today!

36 The first telephone directory (or phone book) created was in Connecticut, U.S.A., in 1878. It was one page long.

37 A company made working cell phones out of old parts and grass from Twickenham Stadium in the U.K.

38 Scientists invented a way to charge a cell phone using urine.

39 A study showed that the average cell phone user checks his or her phone about 110 times a day.

40 Some companies sell new telephones made to look like old ones—like rotary dial or crank phones, and even 1950s-style pay phones.

41 In 2011 a 13-year-old Norwegian boy played rock music on his cell phone to scare away wolves.

42 Using an online trading portal, a 15-year-old in California started with an old cell phone and continually traded up until he had a Porsche.

43 An Australian scientist is working on creating a working shoe phone that can be used for monitoring vitals, especially with elderly patients.

44 The smallest phone in the world is made to look like a key chain.

45 A town in Maine, U.S.A., used old-fashioned crank-powered phones 55 years longer than any other city in the United States. They recently put up a 3,000-pound (1,361-kg) giant crank phone statue to honor it.

46 Scientists in Hawaii had a mother and baby dolphin talk to each other over the telephone to study dolphin language.

47 The first coast-to-coast telephone line was 3,400 miles (5,472 km) and stretched across the United States in 1914.

48 A 12-year-old girl invented a device called iCPooch to let pet owners video chat with their pets and even give them treats.

49 OLD PHONE BOOTHS HAVE BEEN TURNED INTO EVERYTHING FROM AQUARIUMS TO COMMUNITY LIBRARIES.

50 One of the most famous phone conversations ever was in 1969 when American astronauts landed on the moon and President Nixon called to congratulate them.

51 Even though Alexander Graham Bell is considered the "father of the telephone," inventor Antonio Meucci was the first to design a telegraph or telephone in 1849 and had to stop developing it because of financial troubles.

52 One in every five people check their cell phone every ten minutes.

53 At first, telephone operators were teenage boys, but in 1878 they began hiring young girls.

54 SOMEONE BUILT A WORKING PHONE BOOTH OUT OF ICE IN ALASKA.

55 When telephones were first invented a switchboard was used to connect calls. The people who worked at the switchboard were called operators.

56 China has more cell phones than any other country in the world, but United Arab Emirates claims more than two cell phones per person.

57 According to one British study, almost one in ten children get their first cell phone by the age of five.

58 A study found that 84 percent of people across the world say they're unable to go a day without their mobile phone.

59 When Alexander Graham Bell died in 1922, the telephone lines in the U.S. and Canada were shut off for one minute.

60 MORE PEOPLE IN THE WORLD HAVE ACCESS TO CELL PHONES THAN TOILETS.

61 An audience member watching a Broadway production in New York City, U.S.A., jumped on stage to plug in his cell phone to a socket moments before the play started.

1970s telephones

62 THE PHILIPPINES IS THE TOP COUNTRY WHEN IT COMES TO TEXT MESSAGES, SENDING 1.4 BILLION TEXTS A DAY.

63 Fishermen in Malaysia used pay phones as bait: They connected the phones to a battery and sent out high-pitched sounds to attract fish.

64 The world's largest conference call, in 2012, included 16,972 participants

65 In the 1970s, more Americans knew the bell logo from Bell System (a now defunct phone service) than the name of the U.S. president.

66 If you ask Siri, the voice command system for iPhone, which flights are overhead, she can tell you.

67 Even though many owners try to use FaceTime with their dogs, some dogs cannot recognize them because the screen is so small.

68 A small town in Louisiana, U.S.A., changed its area code in the 1960s, swapping out "666," often associated with evil, for "749."

69 Researchers from a university in England launched a cell phone into space to test the theory that "in space no one can hear you scream."

70 There are some funny answers you can get if you ask Siri certain questions. A popular one is "What is zero divided by zero?" Her response includes a comment about *Sesame Street*'s Cookie Monster.

71 You can teach iPhone's Siri how to pronounce words and names.

72 As a joke, Thomas Edison told a magazine he was working on a "spirit-phone," a device to hear the voices of the dead.

73 Ninety percent of people from the ages of 18 to 29 sleep with their mobile device.

74 In 2015 Motorola introduced the Droid Turbo 2, the first shatterproof smartphone.

75 A city in China, Chongqing, set up two separate lanes in the sidewalk— one for those using smartphones and one for those who are not.

75 TELEPHONE CALL HOME ABOUT

FACTS TO

35 RADICAL FACTS

1 A **REVOLUTION** is a dramatic event, often ending the rule of a government, which **COMPLETELY CHANGES** the way people live and work.

2 French Queen Marie Antoinette, who was overthrown and killed in 1793 during the **FRENCH REVOLUTION**, ordered 300 **GOWNS A YEAR.**

3 When Mohamed Bouazizi was stopped from **SELLING VEGETABLES** in Tunisia in 2010, he set off demonstrations that forced the country's president to **RESIGN.**

4 A band from Czechoslovakia, called **THE PLASTIC PEOPLE OF THE UNIVERSE**, helped inspire that country's Velvet Revolution of 1989.

5 About 2,700 years ago the **INCA OF SOUTH AMERICA** started growing corn, which began an **AGRICULTURAL REVOLUTION** that allowed their civilization to flourish.

6 The **WEST FLORIDA REBELLION** in September 1810 lasted for less than **A MINUTE.** At the end, Florida, U.S.A., was independent but this status lasted for less than two months.

7 British celebrity chef Jamie Oliver started a **FOOD REVOLUTION DAY** in May 2015 to help teach kids to grow and cook healthy food.

8 During the "Orange Revolution" in 2004 in Ukraine, protestors wore **ORANGE**, the color of the opposition party, **TO PROTEST** the result of the election.

9 The Russian **OCTOBER REVOLUTION** happened in November 1917 according to the calendar used in Russia at the time, which was 12 days behind the European one.

10 In 1896 a revolution in **ZANZIBAR**, Africa, to overthrow British colonial rule lasted for less than **ONE HOUR.** Great Britain won.

11 In 1804, during the Industrial Revolution, an Englishman invented a **STEAM ENGINE TO POWER TRAINS** that soon replaced horses to transport goods over long distances.

12 After the 1959 **CUBAN REVOLUTION** overthrew dictator Fulgencio Batista, the United States closed its embassy in Havana, Cuba. It **OPENED AGAIN** in July 2015.

13 During the Industrial Revolution, **KIDS WORKING IN FACTORIES** after the American Civil War toiled for up to **14 HOURS A DAY.**

14 About **ONE-THIRD** of American colonists remained loyal to Great Britain during the American Revolution. They were known as **LOYALISTS OR TORIES.**

15 During China's Cultural Revolution in the late 1960s, **SCHOOLS AND UNIVERSITIES** were closed so students could devote themselves to "REVOLUTIONARY STUDY."

16 The 1688 revolution that brought **KING WILLIAM III AND QUEEN MARY** to the throne in England is also known as the **GLORIOUS REVOLUTION** because there was little bloodshed.

17 Norman Borlaug, the father of the "Green Revolution" that **INCREASED THE AMOUNT OF FOOD** that could be grown on an area of land, grew up **ON A FARM** in Iowa, U.S.A.

18 Starting in December 2010, people in Arab countries including Tunisia and Egypt started protesting their harsh governments in what is called the **ARAB SPRING.**

19 The French Revolution started a trend for **SIMPLE FLAG DESIGNS**, and in 1794 a flag with **VERTICAL STRIPES OF BLUE-WHITE-RED** was made the national flag of France.

Storming of the Bastille on July 14, 1789, the start of the French Revolution

ABOUT REVOLUTIONS

20 Indians protesting British rule revolted during 1857 and 1858. When the United Kingdom regained **CONTROL**, it agreed to keep some **TRADITIONS** of Indian society.

21 In 1773, before the American Revolution started, **COLONISTS DRESSED** as Native Americans dumped 342 chests of tea into **BOSTON HARBOR** to protest a tea tax.

22 It's said that when her husband **COLLAPSED AT HIS CANNON** during the Battle of Monmouth during the American Revolution, Molly Pitcher took over **CANNON DUTIES**.

23 During the **AMERICAN CIVIL WAR**, 11 Southern states tried to leave the **UNITED STATES** to set up their own government.

24 The Beatles song "REVOLUTION," recorded in August 1968, was inspired by student protests a few months earlier in **FRANCE, GREAT BRITAIN**, and the **UNITED STATES**.

25 The **INDUSTRIAL REVOLUTION** brought people to cities. In 1750 only 15 out of 100 people in the United Kingdom lived in towns, but by 1900 it was 85 out of 100 people.

26 When government forces in **IRAN FIRED ON PROTESTORS** in Tehran in September 1978, killing hundreds, the day became known as **BLACK FRIDAY**.

27 Two researchers found that between 1900 and 2006, **NONVIOLENT RESISTANCE** to a dictatorship was **SUCCESSFUL TWICE AS MANY TIMES** as those using violence.

28 **NIKE** used the Beatles song "Revolution" from 1968 nearly 20 years later in an advertisement for **RUNNING SHOES**.

29 **LEXINGTON**, Massachusetts, U.S.A., the town where the first shots were fired in the American Revolution, has a "Revolutionary Revelry" **SCAVENGER HUNT**.

30 The 2000 revolution to overthrow the Yugoslavian president is sometimes called the **BULLDOZER REVOLUTION** after a protestor bulldozed a government building.

31 During the American Revolution, George Washington had his troops inoculated against **SMALLPOX**. This **GREATLY REDUCED** the number of deaths from the disease.

32 During the French Revolution, the **PRICE OF BREAD INCREASED**, which was a staple food for the **WORKING CLASSES**.

33 In 1811, after a bloodless revolution in **PARAGUAY** in South America, the Spanish government was overthrown and independence granted **WITHIN DAYS**.

34 About 12,000 years ago when humans started farming, people could live in **PERMANENT VILLAGES** instead of traveling to follow food sources. This is called the **NEOLITHIC REVOLUTION**.

35 A revolution in the Eastern European country of **GEORGIA** in 2003 is called the **ROSE REVOLUTION** because protestors gave roses to government soldiers.

100 FACTS ABOUT ANTS TO BUG OUT ABOUT

1. Ants are small insects. They can be found everywhere on Earth except around the Poles and on super-icy lands. **2.** Scientists in New Zealand observed yellow jacket wasps picking up ants and moving them to a new location so that they couldn't compete for the same food. **3.** Followers of the 1980s rock group Adam and the Ants called themselves "Antpeople." **4.** There are 39 species of leafcutter ant. They live in American tropical forests and use leaves to grow fungus gardens to feed on. **5.** It may be small, but the bulldog ant in Australia can kill a human within 15 minutes with its venomous sting. **6.** Specialized birds will follow masses of army ants when they set out to attack a tarantula or scorpion. The birds pick up and eat the bugs as they flee the attack. **7.** Ants don't communicate using words or vision—they use chemicals to leave trails and communicate with fellow nest-mates. **8.** Ant brains weigh one-millionth as much as human brains. **9.** In 2008 a blind, pale ant was discovered living in the Amazon rain forest. It's in exactly the same form as early ants that lived more than 100 million years ago. **10.** Leafcutter ants can carry 50 times their body weight. Their muscles are thicker relative to their body size, which gives them superstrength. **11.** Ant candy comes in apple and cherry flavors. It's a sweet ribbon of candy with real black ants included. **12.** There are some 12,000 different species of ants, but that's still less than 2 percent of all insect species in the world. **13.** Ants usually come in four colors: red, black, yellow, and brown. **14.** Ants in the Sahara are able to remember how many steps they take, and this helps them figure out where to find their nests. **15.** In the Australian outback a 62-year-old man who was lost for days survived by eating ants. **16.** A group of ants carrying a heavy load will change direction based only on the subtle tug by one of the ants in the team. **17.** Ant Flat Road goes through Ant Valley in Cache County, Utah, U.S.A. **18.** Ancient pictures on rocks in the American southwest show creatures with antennae and large heads on tiny bodies. They are called the "ant people." **19.** Giant, black ant sculptures crawl up a building in Philadelphia, Pennsylvania, U.S.A. It used to be the location of a clothing store called Zipperhead. **20.** Ants have been on Earth since the time of the dinosaurs—for some 140 million years. **21.** Leafcutter ants can live in giant nests that are the size of a small car. **22.** Ants range in length from about 0.08 inch (2 mm) to 1 inch (25 mm). That's pretty small! **23.** Anteaters use their tongue to lap up some 35,000 ants and termites a day. Since anteaters lack any teeth, they just swallow their meal whole. **24.** One scientist looks at the structure of ant underground nests by pouring molten aluminum into the nests to preserve the shape. **25.** The "Big Ant" sculpture in Broken Hill, Australia, looks like a giant ant rising from giant scaffolding on the ground. **26.** African driver ants in their nomadic stage move to a new nest site every day. **27.** Ant queens spend their whole lives laying eggs. **28.** Ants look different from termites; they have a narrower waist. **29.** The Marvel Comics Ant-Man can shrink from a six-foot (1.8-m)-tall man into an ant-size superhero that can punch with as much strength as a human. **30.** Most ants seen by humans are wingless female worker ants. They are the worker ants that protect the nest and forage for food. **31.** Leafcutter ants chomp into leaves and carry them above their heads, so they are sometimes called parasol ants. **32.** The antennae on ants are used to smell different things, which means ant antennae are like their noses. **33.** When yellow crazy ants were introduced on Christmas Island in the South Pacific, they started to threaten the local crab population by taking over their burrows and killing the crabs. **34.** Some honeypot ants stuff their nest-mates with nutritious liquid, and during the rainy season these ants swell up so much they become living food stores for the colony. **35.** In Hasbro's game Ants in the Pants, kids try to get as many plastic ants into a giant pair of overalls as they can. **36.** To kill household ants, some homeowners make a solution of borax mixed with apple mint jelly. The borax kills the ants but is safe for humans. **37.** Fire ants in Texas, U.S.A., cause $1.2 billion worth of damage every year. **38.** Ants in the sandbox? One way to keep them out is to spray white vinegar throughout the sand. **39.** Talk about only liking one thing: some ant species have been growing the same type of fungus for five million years. **40.** When a ton of ants run around, a scientist in India found that they run in straight lines and keep a constant speed. Studying this behavior may help better understand human traffic jams. **41.** Some leafcutter ant nests can have more than 1,000 chambers. **42.** Ant colonies are usually divided into three different classes (or castes): queen, males, and workers. **43.** Ants use chemical signals to communicate with each other; that's how they know to follow each other on long trails through the forest. **44.** There's a software program called Apache Ant. The "ant" stands for "another neat tool." **45.** All the ants in the world weigh about the same as all the people in the world. **46.** Red fire ants first came to the United States in the 1930s, probably from a ship from Brazil. For humans, their super-painful stings feel like an attack by fire. **47.** The chemical ants used to communicate is known as a pheromone. **48.** Some ants will send older ants into battles so that the younger ants have a better chance of surviving. **49.** Ant cows are a kind of bug called an aphid that lives on plants. Ants cultivate aphids because they make honeydew, which the ants eat. **50.** Ants are different from termites in that the antennae on ants are always bent, just like your elbow. **51.** Carpenter ants are large black ants that like to live in old logs and timber. So instead of building things out of wood like carpenters do, they live in it. **52.** The study of ants is known as myrmecology (mur-meh-CAH-leh-gee). **53.** Researchers are studying ants on the International Space Station to see if the way they search changes in space. **54.** A study found that worker fire ants had about 250 sleep episodes every day. But each episode only lasted for about 1.1 minutes! **55.** One species of leafcutter ants from Costa Rica is a picky eater! The ants eat only 17 out of 332 plant species available to them. **56.** Worker driver ants are blind—they don't have eyes. **57.** In the nursery rhyme "The Ants Go Marching," the ants are marching to get out of the rain. **58.** In Japanese, the word "ant" uses two characters: one for "insect" and the other for "loyalty." Ants will indeed go to great lengths to protect their nests. **59.** Only male ants are called drones. They live for a brief time—just a few months— and live solely to fertilize a princess ant. **60.** The word "ant" comes from an Old English word "aemette," which means to cut away. This probably came from the supreme ability of ants to chomp things. **61.** Black garden ants, which are often found in Europe and the United States, will make trash piles outside of their nests, full of dead ants and leftover food. **62.** In the 1950s, people in the United States started serving chocolate-covered ants as a surprise for dinner guests. **63.** Ants that have lost a leg or two can still live for several more weeks. **64.** Ants have four life cycles that each last for about ten weeks. The stages are egg, larva, pupa, and adult. **65.** Ant farms, where you can observe ants in their underground nests, have the scientific name *formicarium*. The word comes from two Latin words that mean "a place for you." **66.** French scientist Charles Janet, who studied ant anatomy, created the first ant farm in 1900. **67.** Red ants have high levels of protein and low levels of fat. Yum! **68.** A group of ants can be called an army or a colony. **69.** Army ants got their name from how they move in a line, killing anything that gets in the way. They are also called driver ants. **70.** Female mud dauber wasps lay an egg in a mud cylinder. Scientists think these wasps are the closest living relatives to the ants we see today. **71.** Ants belong to the same group of animals (called an order) as wasps and bees. **72.** Ants in the Sahara can handle temperatures of 140°F (60°C) for a short time. Their long legs let the ants keep their bodies above the blazing hot sand. **73.** In the 1998 animated movie *Antz*, some 60,000 ants made up the army of the bad guy, General Mandible. **74.** Some leafcutter ants send only special garbage workers to go into chambers where they put their ant trash. **75.** Texas leafcutter ant nests can stretch 20 feet (6 m) deep into the ground. That's as tall as a two-story building. **76.** Chimpanzees will craft different tools to fish for ants. They use thin twigs for the so-called ant dip that lets them feast on army ants and not get bitten. **77.** Fire ants have a unique way of dealing with floods. They lock claws to build a raft that can have thousands of ants. The ants then take turns being under the water. **78.** An artist has created a necklace showing an ant lifting a log, encouraging the wearer to accomplish even the most challenging goals. **79.** A French researcher noted that after he cut the head off of an ant it lived for 19 days. **80.** The "ant" in the Dutch line of clothing known as A.N.T. Origins stands for "a native tourist." **81.** A colony of leafcutter ants in tropical forests can turn over as much moist soil as about nine African elephants! **82.** Giant underground ant colonies contain tunnels, fungus gardens, waste pits, and dens. **83.** In trees, weaver ants make nests the size of soccer balls by weaving leaves together. **84.** Black garden ants go to the bathroom only at specific spots in their nests. **85.** Black bears in Colorado's Rocky Mountain National Park eat a diet that contains a lot of ants. Why? The ants are high in calories, which the bears need. **86.** Scientists have found only one kind of snail that lives in ant colonies. The snails use chemicals to camouflage themselves so the ants don't know they are there. **87.** If you are unlucky enough to get bitten by an ant, try putting a tea bag on the bite. The tannic acid in the tea helps neutralize the acid ants produce. **88.** A beetle that lived 52 million years ago lived among ants, eating their eggs and maybe even a liquid that the ants produced. **89.** Some people make a paste of clay and water to put on ant bites to help them stop itching. **90.** Scientists in the United States are using phorid flies that attack ants to control invasive fire ants. **91.** Leafcutter ant jaws can vibrate 1,000 times per second. **92.** From 2011 to 2014 Disney showed a TV show called *A.N.T. Farm*. It featured a talented singer named Chyna who went to school in the Advanced Natural Talents program. **93.** A species of ant from Ecuador uses mud held in place by hairs on their bodies as camouflage. Snails are their favorite food. **94.** For every person on Earth there are about one million ants! **95.** Some maggots live in underground ant colonies. A tough shield on their backs protects them from the ants so they can eat their fill of ant eggs. **96.** The jaws of the trap-jaw ant snap shut faster than any animal. They can go from 0 to 143 miles an hour (230 km/h)—2,300 times faster than the blink of an eye! **97.** One species of ants in the Amazon builds a trap with holes in it from plant fiber. When another insect steps on the trap, hundreds of ants use their jaws to seize it. **98.** For insect species, ants can live a long time. One queen ant in Idaho, U.S.A., lived for 30 years. **99.** *The Ant and the Grasshopper* is one of Aesop's Fables. In the story, the ant prepared for the winter by storing corn, but the grasshopper wasted his time and was not prepared for the winter. **100.** Army ants, because they attack in mass, can work together to kill small mammals.

1

In 1913 Pedro Lascuráin was president of Mexico for **LESS THAN AN HOUR.** He ruled during the Mexican Revolution when a military coup overthrew his office.

8

The constitution of the United States is the **SHORTEST CONSTITUTION OF ANY GOVERNMENT IN THE WORLD.**

14

Switzerland's government is made up of seven elected officials who **ROTATE THE RESPONSIBILITY** of being the federal president **EACH YEAR.**

21

The National Geographic Society recognizes **195 INDEPENDENT COUNTRIES** in the world.

27

The small African country of Eritrea has had only **ONE PRESIDENT, ISAIAS AFWERKI.** He has been president since 1993.

2

The U.S. Federal government **OWNS APPROXIMATELY** 28 percent of the 2.27 billion acres (918,600,000 ha) of land in the United States.

9

In the film series *STAR WARS,* the **GALACTIC REPUBLIC** was a democratic union for **1,000 YEARS.** The Jedi Knights served as the peacekeepers.

15

Argentina once had **FIVE PRESIDENTS OVER A SPAN OF TWO WEEKS.** That would be hard to remember on a history test!

28

Voters in ancient Greece cast their votes by placing **A PEBBLE IN ONE OF TWO URNS,** marking their choice. The winner was the person with the most pebbles.

3

The president of the United States may live in the White House, but the president of Argentina works in **LA CASA ROSADA,** the Pink House.

10

One of the main rules of the Antarctic Treaty, which governs Antarctica, is that **ANTARCTICA SHOULD BE USED ONLY FOR PEACEFUL PURPOSES.**

16

Rwanda has **THE HIGHEST NUMBER OF WOMEN** serving in their government. In 2015, women made up 64 percent of the members in the lower house.

22

Countries can only claim rights to the ocean waters **200 NAUTICAL MILES (370 KM)** off their shores. The rest of the ocean is governed by international laws.

29

China's National People's Congress has 3,000 members. It's the **WORLD'S LARGEST PARLIAMENT.**

4

Dating back to more than 2,500 years ago, the **IMPERIAL FAMILY OF JAPAN** is the longest reigning dynasty in the world.

11

The peacekeeper troops of the United Nations are nicknamed the **"BLUE HELMETS"** because of the sky-blue color helmets they wear.

17

In the 1950s, a **SECRET NUCLEAR FALLOUT SHELTER** was built for Congress **UNDERNEATH THE GREENBRIER RESORT** in West Virginia, U.S.A.

23

A ten-foot (3-m)-tall replica of the **U.S. CAPITOL BUILDING** was made out of **LEGO BRICKS** for the **LEGO AMERICANA ROADSHOW.**

30

Government leaders speak for about 15 minutes during the **UNITED NATIONS GENERAL ASSEMBLY.** In 2009 Libya's leader talked for 96 minutes!

5

There are 34,801 words in the **CONSTITUTION OF THE SMALL ISLAND COUNTRY OF TUVALU**—that's seven times longer than the U.S. Constitution!

12

Everything is bigger in Texas, U.S.A.! The **STATE CAPITOL BUILDING** in Austin has the largest gross square footage of any state capitol building in the U.S.

18

India has the **LONGEST CONSTITUTION** of any country in the world.

24

U.S. President William Henry Harrison gave the **LONGEST INAUGURATION SPEECH** of any president, but he held office **FOR ONLY 32 DAYS!**

31

The **GAVEL USED IN THE U.S. SENATE** is a small ivory gavel given to the U.S. by the vice president of India in 1954.

6

During the U.S. president's State of the Union address, one Cabinet member **DOES NOT ATTEND** in case a catastrophe happens to the president.

13

NEARLY HALF of the 566 federally recognized American Indian tribes in the United States **ARE IN THE STATE OF ALASKA.**

19

The two red lines that run on both sides of the floor of United Kingdom's Commons Chamber are said to be **TWO SWORD LENGTHS APART.**

25

In 1997 the small town of Talkeetna, Alaska, **APPOINTED A CAT NAMED STUBBS** to be their mayor.

26

The capitol building of Australia was designed in the **SHAPE OF A BOOMERANG.**

32

Small nations not recognized by world governments hold a **MICROLYMPIC GAMES** for the micronations of the world.

7

A **TECHNOCRACY** is a type of government led by experts in science and technology.

20

The Iroquois Great Law of Peace united the Five Iroquois Nations more than **1,000 YEARS AGO,** making it North America's **OLDEST CONSTITUTION.**

33

THE PRINCIPALITY OF SEALAND is built on an **ABANDONED WORLD WAR II MILITARY PLATFORM** off the coast of Great Britain.

34

In 1982 residents of the Florida Keys jokingly **FORMED THEIR OWN GOVERNMENT,** and they called it the **CONCH REPUBLIC.**

35

In April 2015, the mayor of San Juan, Puerto Rico, **BANNED HORSE-DRAWN CARRIAGES** in the capital city by executive order.

36

Is it a filibuster or a bladder buster? In 1957, U.S. Senator Strom Thurmond gave a speech lasting **24 HOURS AND 18 MINUTES** to delay a vote.

37

The **OLMEC CIVILIZATION** had the earliest government in the **AMERICAS.** They lived in what is today **MEXICO** beginning in 1200 B.C.

38

Canada has **TWO TWITTER ACCOUNTS** focused on giving its citizens **TRAVEL INFORMATION.** One is in English and the other in French.

39

The word **"GOVERNMENT"** was first used in the 1300s.

40

Peru's president lives in the **GOVERNMENT PALACE** in downtown Lima. The city's last Inca chief lived on the same spot in the early 1500s.

41

King Oyo rules over more than two million people in western Uganda. He was crowned in 1995 when **JUST THREE YEARS OLD.**

42

It is **ILLEGAL TO WEAR A SUIT OF ARMOR** into the United Kingdom's Houses of Parliament.

43

A dog, **DUKE**, was voted mayor of Cormorant, Minnesota, U.S.A., in 2014.

44

At a small camp in Alabama, U.S.A., known as **ALAPINE VILLAGE, WOMEN CONTROL** everything. Men are not allowed in the village.

45

During the 20th century, the Soviet Union paid people to move to **COLD AND REMOTE** towns in Siberia.

46

Since 2007 people in the small European country of Estonia **CAN VOTE FOR THEIR LEADERS** from their computers.

47

The European Union is made up of 28 countries but has **LESS THAN 7 PERCENT** of the world's population.

48

In 2010 Iraq was **WITHOUT A GOVERNMENT** for 289 days—the longest time in modern history.

49

In 2005 President Mahinda Rajapaksa of Sri Lanka **APPOINTED 52 CABINET MEMBERS** to help him lead his country—the highest number in the world.

50

In 1979 a 14-year-old boy in the United States **DECLARED HIS BEDROOM** a sovereign nation called **THE KINGDOM OF TALOSSA.**

50 GOVERNMENT FACTS THAT RULE

United Nations building in New York City

1 DESERTS are usually thought to be HOT PLACES, but there are COLD DESERTS too. A DESERT is a place that gets little or NO RAINFALL.

2 The world's LARGEST DESERT is ANTARCTICA. It is a POLAR DESERT that covers 5.4 million square miles (14 million sq km). It gets as little as TWO INCHES (51 mm) of rain each year.

3 SOME PEOPLE THINK THEY COULD SURVIVE IN THE DESERT BY DRINKING CACTUS WATER BUT IT'S NOT A GOOD IDEA—ACIDS INSIDE CACTUS CAUSE DIARRHEA.

4 The Sahara in North Africa, spanning 3.5 million square miles (9.1 million sq km), is the LARGEST HOT DESERT on Earth, with temperatures that can reach 136°F (58°C).

5 MORE THAN ONE BILLION PEOPLE IN THE WORLD LIVE IN DESERTS.

25 BLAZING
FACTS ABOUT

6 A BEETLE that lives in the hot NAMIB DESERT uses its SHELL to collect water in the morning. Later in the day the water drips down into its MOUTH.

7 One of the tracks in the video game *Mario Kart* is called the KALIMARI DESERT because it was modeled after the Kalahari Desert.

8 DESERTIFICATION is when semi-arid areas, which experience an average of 27.6 inches (701 mm) of rainfall each year, TURN INTO DESERTS over time.

9 THE NAMIB IN AFRICA IS THE OLDEST DESERT IN THE WORLD, HAVING BEEN DRY FOR 55 MILLION YEARS.

10 The Uyuni Desert in Bolivia is the SALTIEST desert, containing ONE BILLION TONS (907 MILLION MT) OF SALT.

11 There are MUSICAL SAND DUNES in the Mojave Desert, U.S.A. KELSO DUNES make a tuba-like honking or booming sound when the sand slips down over the dunes.

12 The world's **SMALLEST DESERT** is the Atacama Desert in Chile. It spans only 40,600 square miles (105,200 sq km).

13
EXTRATERRESTRIAL DESERTS are deserts **OUTSIDE EARTH**—they have been discovered on **MARS.**

14 In 2012 scientists found **WATER RESERVES** underneath the deserts of Africa—including the **SAHARA,** which was thought to be one of the driest places on Earth.

15
The Atacama Desert in Chile, South America, is the **DRIEST DESERT** on Earth. It usually gets less than 0.04 inch (1 mm) of rain per year.

16 In 1979 and 2012, **SNOW FELL** on parts of the **SAHARA.**

17 **CHUCKWALLAS** ARE LIZARDS THAT LIVE IN THE DESERTS OF MEXICO AND THE UNITED STATES OF AMERICA. WHEN IN DANGER, THEY CAN **PUFF THEMSELVES UP,** WEDGING THEMSELVES INTO ROCK CREVICES TO PROTECT THEMSELVES.

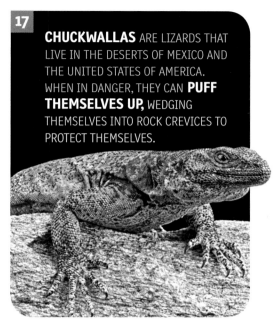

18
SAND DUNES are a common sight in deserts. They are created by WIND pushing GRAINS OF SAND into large hills.

DESERTS

19 About ONE-THIRD of EARTH'S surface is DESERT.

20 There is a **PUBLIC SWIMMING POOL** in the **MOJAVE DESERT.** It is an art installation, found using a **GLOBAL POSITIONING SYSTEM (GPS) LOCATION** unlocked from a special website.

21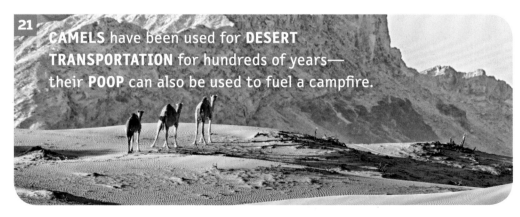
CAMELS have been used for DESERT TRANSPORTATION for hundreds of years— their POOP can also be used to fuel a campfire.

22 AN ENDANGERED CACTUS KNOWN AS THE **BASEBALL PLANT** IS FOUND ONLY IN THE **DESERTS** OF **SOUTH AFRICA.** IT LOOKS LIKE A BASEBALL.

23 **PLANTS** THAT LIVE IN DESERTS CAN **STORE WATER,** HAVE **DEEP ROOTS** THAT REACH WATER SOURCES, OR GO **WITHOUT WATER FOR YEARS.**

24
The DORCAS GAZELLE lives in the Sahara and doesn't drink ANY WATER. It also DOESN'T EVER PEE.

25
The MARATHON DES SABLES is an annual six-day MARATHON through 150 miles (241 km) of the SAHARA. Competitors have to carry everything they need except water.

15 SPROUTING FACTS

1 **SEEDS** are how many (but not all) plants **REPRODUCE.** The outside of the seed protects its insides—the embryo (a tiny baby plant) and endosperm (food for the baby plant before leaves develop).

2 A typical **POMEGRANATE** has between 600 and 1,000 bright red **EDIBLE SEEDS.** Pomegranate seeds are highly nutritious.

3 In 1963 a **2,000-YEAR-OLD SEED** was discovered in Israel. In 2005, inside a lab, the seed was planted and it grew into a four-foot (1.2-m)-high plant named "Methuselah."

4 The **SEEDS** of the **BURDOCK PLANT** stick to fur and socks. They were the inspiration for the invention of **VELCRO** in the 1940s.

5 One **DANDELION PLANT** makes up to 2,000 seeds, with between 54 and 172 on each flower head.

6 Very small amounts of **CYANIDE,** a **DEADLY POISON,** are found in **APPLE SEEDS.**

7 **EVERY** part of a **WATERMELON** is **EDIBLE**—including the seeds.

8 The **BIGGEST SEED** comes from the plant that also has the **LONGEST LEAVES**—the coco de mer palm. It grows naturally on only two islands on Earth.

9 **ANIMALS** that eat seeds help the seeds **GROW** when they **POOP** them out. Once they hit the ground, the seeds are instantly planted and **FERTILIZED!**

10 **ANCIENT SEEDS** that had been **BURIED** by an **ICE AGE SQUIRREL** 32,000 years ago were germinated and grew into a chickweed-like plant.

11 At **SPITSBERGEN**, Norway, is a **VAULT** where seeds from all over the world are **KEPT** and **STORED**.

12 Some seeds from South African plants called proteas will only grow after being exposed to **SMOKE** and **FIRE**.

13 In the game *MINECRAFT*, the CODES that the game uses for different worlds are called SEEDS because they "grow" those worlds.

14 **SEEDS** from the *Moringa oleifera* tree can be used to **KILL BACTERIA** in water, making it safe to drink.

15 Seed and bean beetles are **BUGS** that damage crops by **BORING INTO SEEDS.**

75 WHEEL-TURNING FACTS ABOUT BIKES

1 Bicycles are defined as human-powered land vehicles driven by foot pedals.

2 Before they were known as bicycles, people called them velocipedes.

3 Orville and Wilbur Wright ran a bicycle repair shop in Dayton, Ohio, U.S.A., before they started building airplanes.

4 THE TINIEST ADULT BIKE EVER BUILT USED SILVER DOLLARS FOR WHEELS.

5 Tsugunobu Mitsuishi of Japan set an odd record in 1965 for staying completely still while balanced on a bike for 5 hours and 25 minutes.

6 The first bicycle ride in space took place in 1973 when Mission Commander Alan Bean rode a stationary bike aboard Skylab (the first U.S. space station).

7 The world record for deepest underwater cycling is held by a man in Italy—he pedaled a distance of 213 feet (65 m) underwater at a depth of 92 feet (28 m).

8 The world's largest bicycle (that a person can ride) is more than 25 feet (7.6 m) long and 12 feet (3.7 m) high.

9 Extreme biking involves off-road racing, acrobatics, and stunts.

10 The first mountain bike was built in 1977 in California, U.S.A. It was called the Breezer 1.

11 At $51,000, Moynat Malle Bicyclette is one of the most expensive bicycles—it comes with a fancy picnic trunk basket in the front.

12 There is an average of 100 million bikes made in the world each year. Most of them are made in China.

13 Bike messengers—people who deliver and pick up packages on their bikes—have been around since the late 1800s and are still common in large cities.

14 A bike-sharing program in the center of London, England, was so popular that in the first six months of service users rode the equivalent of 13 round trips to the moon.

15 You can buy a mountain bike covered in 24k gold, with a logo made of gems, and an alligator skin seat, for $500,000 in California, U.S.A.

16 IN NEW YORK CITY, U.S.A., MORE THAN 200,000 PEOPLE BIKE EACH DAY.

17 In China, some people use bikes to spin fibers for cotton candy.

18 The 1926 Tour de France was the longest ever, spanning 3,570 miles (5,745 km). The average Tour de France route is around 2,300 miles (3701 km).

19 In 1985 John Howard set the world record for fastest speed on a standard bicycle, reaching 152.2 miles an hour (244.9 km/h). He rode in the slipstream of a car.

20 There are more than 500 million owners of bicycles in China. In Shanghai 60 percent of people bike to work.

21 A penny-farthing, also known as a high-wheel, was a kind of bike popular in the late 1800s. It had one giant wheel in the front and a much smaller one in the back.

22 A MAN WHO BUILT ONE OF THE WORLD'S BIGGEST PENNY-FARTHING BIKES ALSO BUILT THE WORLD'S SMALLEST VERSION FOR HIS TWO-YEAR-OLD SON.

23 Sam Wakeling in Wales, United Kingdom, set a world record when he rode a one-wheeled cycle—also called a unicycle—more than 281 miles (452 km) in a 24-hour period.

24 Students in France made electricity-generating stationary bikes out of trash. Three of these bicycles were used to power film projectors for 54 minutes.

25 IN STANFORD, ENGLAND, A MAN BUILT A BICYCLE WITH WHEELS MADE OF SOLID ICE.

26 Americans average 25 miles (40 km) a year bicycling whereas Europeans cycle an average of 117 miles (188 km) a year.

27 Atari's *Paperboy* was a video game in which the user plays a newspaper delivery boy trying to deliver papers on a bicycle while avoiding obstacles.

28 Norman, a six-year-old briard, is the fastest dog to pedal 98 feet (30 m) on a bicycle. He did it in 55 seconds.

29 A 13-year-old Australian boy rode his bike home after being bitten by a shark. Then he made toast before being taken to the hospital.

30 Lance Armstrong's "butterfly bike" had real butterfly wings on the frame and was ridden during the Tour de France in 2009. It sold at auction for $500,000.

31 Two teenagers with one bike started a United Parcel Service (UPS) delivery service after borrowing $100 from a friend in the 1900s.

32 THE BICYCLE FROM THE FILM *PEE-WEE'S BIG ADVENTURE* SOLD IN 2014 FOR $36,600.

extreme sports mountain biking

33 In France, François Gissy used a rocket-powered cycle to reach 207 miles an hour (333 km/h).

34 THERE ARE MORE BIKES THAN PEOPLE IN COPENHAGEN, DENMARK.

35 In 2014, 880 people set the world record for most riders in a bicycle bus in Australia. (A bicycle bus is when cyclists ride together, picking up more cyclists along the way.)

36 During the Tour de France, taking pee breaks is handled differently for riders—some simply go on themselves.

37 An American composer wrote a "Symphony of Spokes" using only sounds from bicycle parts.

38 A bike seat made from carbon fiber, Kevlar (the same material as bulletproof vests), and gold retails for $2,000.

39 The Cycling Messenger World Championships is an annual cycling competition that includes a race with packages to be picked up and dropped off along the way.

40 In 2011 a 16-year-old "popped a wheelie"—coasting on his back wheel a whole 686 feet (209 m)—to set a world record.

41 A 99-year-old women's bicycle lost 50 years ago was found wedged in the trunk of a tree that had grown around it.

42 Throughout a Tour de France race all the riders together sweat enough to flush a toilet 39 times.

43 The Draisine, created by Karl von Drais in 1817, had no chains or pedals and became the model on which most bicycles were designed.

44 You can buy a bike-powered generator and pedal to power things such as laptops and cell phones.

45 Washington, Delaware, Utah, and Maryland are in the top ten "most bike-friendly" states in the U.S.

46 In California, riding a bicycle in a swimming pool is against the law.

47 The Australian motorbike frog gets its name from the sound it makes—the animal sounds like a motorbike changing gears.

48 The lightest bike in the world weighs only six pounds (2.7 kg) and sells for $45,000.

49 In 1904 Henri Cornet became the youngest person ever to win the Tour de France—he was 19 years old.

50 The Olympic bicycle motocross event first started in the 2008 Olympic Games, in Beijing, China. Motocross is cross-country racing on motorcycles.

51 A FIVE-SEATER BIKE IS FOR FIVE RIDERS AND IS CALLED A "QUINT."

52 In Connecticut, U.S.A., it's against the law to ride your bike more than 65 miles an hour (105 km/h).

53 A company makes bike gloves with light-emitting diode (LED) turn signals on them. A flashing orange arrow shows which way the rider is turning.

54 A treadmill bike rolls down the street like a bike while the rider walks or runs on the tread belt.

55 "Tall bikes" are bicycles with multiple frames welded together. The Eiffel Tower Bicycle created in the 1890s stood almost 13 feet (4 m) tall.

56 The world's loudest bicycle horn is on the Hornster. It has a modified freight train horn.

57 A Japanese company invented a poop-powered motorbike that has a toilet-shaped seat. It runs on biofuel from farm animal waste.

58 The Michaux-Perreaux steam velocipede was the first steam-powered bicycle, built between 1867 and 1869. It's considered to be the first motorcycle.

59 A man in Minnesota, U.S.A., made a bicycle with square wheels that rides smoothly over bumpy surfaces.

60 People riding bikes instead of driving cars saves about 238 million gallons (901 million L) of gasoline each year.

61 A Solarbike is an electric bicycle with solar panels. The panels collect the sun's rays, which in turn power the bike's motor.

62 John Boyd Dunlop used air-filled tires in 1887 for the bicycle. The tires were later adapted for automobiles.

63 New technology is being developed that can keep a bike balanced even when it is stopped. The idea is that the balance system can be used instead of training wheels on a child's bike.

64 An Austrian cyclist rode a bicycle down the side of a volcano at speeds of more than 100 miles an hour (160 km/h).

65 During the 1930s, Fred A. Birchmore from Athens, Georgia, U.S.A., rode his bike around the world, racking up more than 25,000 miles (40,234 km) over two years.

66 Travis Pastrana of Maryland, U.S.A., back-flipped into the Grand Canyon on a dirt bike in 2002.

67 In Albuquerque, New Mexico, U.S.A., you can take a haunted bicycle tour on Halloween.

68 Muhammad Ali took up boxing seriously at a gym after his new bicycle was stolen.

69 Roboticist Masahiko Yamaguchi created a remote-controlled robot that can ride a tiny bike.

70 The California Science Center has a high-wire bicycle that visitors can ride while suspended 43 feet (13 m) above the ground.

71 American daredevil Nik Wallenda holds the world record for the highest bicycle ride on a wire, riding 260 feet (79 m) in the air.

72 An Israeli engineer designed a cardboard bicycle called the Alfa Bike. It cost less than $12 to make and won the 2013 Invention Award with *Popular Science* magazine.

73 THERE IS A TOWN IN CENTRAL ETHIOPIA CALLED "BIKE." BIKE HAS A POPULATION OF JUST OVER 9,000 PEOPLE.

74 A motorcycle was the largest object ever pulled from the Los Angeles sewer system.

75 The World Naked Bike Ride is an international bicycle ride where clothing is optional. It has annual events in major cities across the globe including London, U.K.; Seattle, U.S.A.; and Auckland, New Zealand.

1
Visitors to President Abraham Lincoln's tomb in Springfield, Illinois, U.S.A., rub the nose on a bronze replica of his head **FOR GOOD LUCK.**

2
In 2015 food company Tombstone came out with two limited-edition flavors for their pizzas: **BRATWURST AND DIABLO,** the Spanish word for "devil."

3
In ancient times, some royalty were **BURIED WITH SERVANTS.** The idea was that the servants could continue to **SERVE THEIR MASTER** in the afterlife.

4
The tomb of **SCIENCE-FICTION WRITER JULES VERNE** in Amiens, France, includes a sculpture of him emerging from the grave.

5
The tomb of St. Erkembode in Saint-Omer, France, is always **COVERED IN TINY SHOES.** People leave them in the hope that the saint will bless kids who can't walk.

6
People of the Hindu faith **CREMATE THEIR DEAD** as a way to purify the corpse.

7
Most people in the village of Sagada in the Philippines bury their dead in coffins, but then **THEY NAIL OR TIE THE COFFINS** to a cliff face.

8
A cemetery in the **ANCIENT CITY OF UR** in modern-day Iraq contains some 1,800 graves that date back **4,600 YEARS.**

9
In 2013 a robot found mysterious spheres of a gold-like material in a possible burial chamber in the **TEMPLE OF THE FEATHERED SERPENT** in Teotihuacan, Mexico.

10
The **EGYPTIAN TOMB BAT** lives in parts of Africa, the Middle East, and India. It roosts during the day in stone buildings or rocky places.

11
During the **QINGMING FESTIVAL** in China, people take a day off to sweep their **ANCESTORS' GRAVES.**

12
A Spanish man has collected more than 2,380 items related to the **VIDEO GAME** *TOMB RAIDER.*

13
Benjamin Franklin and **FOUR OTHER PEOPLE** who signed the **DECLARATION OF INDEPENDENCE** are buried in Christ Church Burial Ground in Philadelphia, Pennsylvania, U.S.A.

14
MICHAEL JACKSON'S GRAVE in Forest Lawn Memorial Park in California, U.S.A., is carefully watched over by guards to make sure nobody tries to steal his remains.

15
In Edinburgh, Scotland, you can find a memorial to a **LOYAL DOG NAMED BOBBY.** For 14 years after his master died in 1858, the Skye terrier watched over his grave site.

16
The 2014 movie *Night at the Museum: Secret of the Tomb* was filmed at the **BRITISH MUSEUM** in London, United Kingdom.

17
The Wadi Al-Salam cemetery in Najaf, Iraq, includes **MILLIONS OF GRAVES.** It covers 2,266 acres (917 ha) of the city.

18
More than 100,000 pets are buried at a pet cemetery in Hartsdale, New York, U.S.A. It even includes a grave for **A PET LION NAMED GOLDFLECK** who died in 1912.

UNEARTHING
35 FACTS ABOUT

19
In 1939 an 89-foot (27-m)-long ship was unearthed in England. Known as **THE SUTTON HOO SHIP BURIAL**, it contained the remains of an Anglo-Saxon man from about 1,400 years ago.

20
In the 1970s, you could buy sweet-tart tasting candy that came in **A LITTLE, PLASTIC COFFIN.** Now some come in wooden coffins.

21
Since April 6, 1948, the 3rd U.S. Infantry Regiment has guarded the **TOMB OF THE UNKNOWN SOLDIER** all day, every day, in Arlington National Cemetery, Virginia, U.S.A.

22
In 1978 two men stole the remains of **FILM STAR CHARLIE CHAPLIN** from his grave in Switzerland. They asked for a ransom but were soon caught.

23
Both explorer Sir Walter Raleigh, who died in 1618, and scientist Sir Isaac Newton, who died in 1717, are buried in **WESTMINSTER ABBEY** in London, U.K.

24
In the 3rd century, people in Japan started burying their dead in large mounds known as *kofun*. This period of the Yamato kingdom is known as the **TUMULUS, OR TOMB, PERIOD.**

25
A gravestone in Key West, Florida, U.S.A., says: "**I TOLD YOU I WAS SICK.**"

26
In China, **LAND IN CITIES CAN BE HARD TO FIND**, so government officials are offering financial incentives for people to bury their loved ones at sea.

27
Jewish tradition holds that to honor the dead, loved ones **PLACE STONES** on the grave site.

28
Moviegoers can watch outdoor movies from a **GRASSY FIELD SURROUNDED BY THE GRAVES** of Hollywood Forever Cemetery in Los Angeles, California.

29
In the **CORNER OF A PARKING LOT** in Sand Springs, Oklahoma, U.S.A., sits a cemetery of about 40 Creek Indian graves. The Creek were buried from 1883 to 1912.

30
Most **TOMBSTONES** today are made out of granite, marble, or bronze.

31
Human bones from 9,500 to 5,500 years ago have been found mysteriously in tidy piles **SCATTERED AROUND ARCHAEOLOGICAL SITES** in what is today Serbia.

32
The Toraja people of South Sulawesi, Indonesia, **DIG UP THE MUMMIES OF THEIR LOVED ONES** every 3 years to give them new clothes. They believe this helps honor their spirits.

33
High in the Andes, in Uyuni, Bolivia, there is a **GRAVEYARD FOR OLD TRAINS.** The trains rust quickly from the salty air.

34
A small stone marker in Makanda, Illinois, U.S.A., supposedly marks the grave site of a three-legged dog **NAMED BOOMER WHO COULD RUN AS FAST** as the train his master worked on.

35
The village of **STONEGRAVE IN NORTH YORKSHIRE, U.K.**, contains a church that is more than 1,200 years old.

TOMBS AND GRAVES

1. John Adams, the second U.S. president, was the first to live in the White House, moving there in 1800. 2. Irish-born architect James Hoban won a competition to design the White House, basing his blueprint on a building in Dublin. 3. It cost about $230,000 to build the original White House—the equivalent of $4,380,000 in today's dollars. 4. The White House is valued at about $300 million today. 5. From the time it was built until the 1860s, the White House was the largest home in the United States. 6. Thomas Jefferson had a pet mockingbird that flew freely around the White House. 7. During the early 1800s, First Lady Abigail Adams would hang out her laundry in the East Room of the White House. 8. Until 1901, the White House was known as the President's Palace, the President's House, or the Executive Mansion. 9. Today the East Room is used for special events such as concerts. 10. During the War of 1812, British troops set fire to the President's House, while then president, James Madison, fled safely to Maryland. 11. The British troops who invaded the President's House during the War of 1812 reportedly feasted on the president's leftovers before setting the mansion ablaze. 12. When the War of 1812 ended, the badly damaged President's House was rebuilt and painted white to cover the smoke marks. People began calling it the White House. 13. Theodore Roosevelt officially named the building the White House in 1901. 14. The White House has undergone two major renovations: once during President Theodore Roosevelt's term, and again while President Harry S. Truman lived there. 15. Theodore Roosevelt had the West Wing built onto the White House, then moved his office there so he could have a quiet place to work. 16. Harry S. Truman had central air-conditioning installed in the White House during the renovation in 1952. 17. The White House did not have running water until 1833. 18. It took until the 1850s for the presidential family to have running water in their upstairs bathroom. 19. Without running water, James Madison bathed in a tin tub filled with steaming hot water. 20. A Christmas Eve fire in 1929 gutted the White House's West Wing. 21. During the 1929 fire, Herbert Hoover had to leave his Christmas party to oversee the removal of important papers from the Oval Office. 22. There are 27 wood-burning fireplaces located throughout the White House. 23. There are 35 bathrooms, 132 rooms, and 6 levels in the White House. 24. There are also 412 doors, 147 windows, 8 staircases, and 3 elevators. 25. Revelers at a raging White House party during Andrew Jackson's term broke dishes and stood on furniture in their muddy boots. 26. James K. Polk's wife was so strict, she did not allow any dancing or card playing in the White House while they lived there from 1845 to 1849. 27. Until Millard Fillmore built the first White House library in the early 1850s, there was no permanent collection of books in the home. 28. Grover Cleveland is the only president to have had his wedding inside the White House. 29. In 1893 Grover Cleveland's daughter Esther became the first child born in the White House. 30. John Tyler once served turtle soup at a Fourth of July dinner at the White House. 31. Benjamin Harrison had the White House wired for electricity in 1891, but never touched a switch. He was afraid of being electrocuted. 32. Dwight D. Eisenhower was the first president to use a helicopter that took off and landed on the White House lawn. 33. A stolen helicopter, a drone, and an airplane have all crashed on the White House lawn. 34. Herbert Hoover's son's pet alligators crawled around the White House grounds. 35. Calvin Coolidge's pets included dogs, a donkey, a bobcat, lion cubs, a bear, a wallaby, and a pygmy hippo. 36. The White House's first telephone was installed in 1877. The phone number was just "1." 37. Theodore Roosevelt's children roller-skated on the newly installed wood floors of the East Room. 38. A quote spoken by John Adams in 1800 is carved in the large stone mantelpiece in the State Dining Room. 39. Andrew Jackson once invited friends over to help him eat a 1,400-pound (635-kg) block of cheese he received as a gift. They trampled so much cheese into the carpet, it took months to remove the smell. 40. Upon her death in 1842, Letitia Tyler, John Tyler's wife, became the first president's wife to pass away in the White House. 41. First Lady Jacqueline Kennedy won an Emmy for her televised tour of the White House. 42. Richard Nixon's wife, Pat, created tours of the White House for the blind and deaf. 43. The south side of the White House is about six inches (15.24 cm) taller than the building's north side. 44. The White House is the only private residence of a head of state that is open to the public free of charge. 45. The White House kitchen has five full-time chefs who may serve dinner to as many as 140 guests at a time. 46. The White House requires 570 gallons (2,158 L) of paint to cover its outside surface. 47. There is both a floral shop and a chocolate shop on the ground floor of the White House. 48. The White House's Map Room was once used as a war room by Franklin D. Roosevelt during World War II. 49. The White House stables, big enough to house 25

100 WOW-WORTHY WHITE

horses, were demolished in 1911. 50. The wallpaper in the Meeting Room was selected by First Lady Jacqueline Kennedy in 1962. 51. A full-length portrait of First Lady Grace Coolidge wearing a red dress and posing with her dog hangs in the China Room. 52. The White House's Red, Green, and Blue Rooms are all named for the color of the carpet, walls, and furniture in each room. 53. The Blue Room was not always blue—it was red until Martin Van Buren changed the color scheme in 1837. 54. Each year, the official White House Christmas tree is placed in the Blue Room. 55. There are more than 50 other live Christmas trees found throughout the house during the holiday season. 56. Woodrow Wilson kept a flock of more than 40 sheep on the White House lawn to eat the grass. He also sold their wool for charity. 57. The souvenir White House Easter Egg Roll eggs are made out of wood and are signed by the president and the first lady. 58. The White House's family theater seats 42 people. 59. In 1865 Andrew Jackson greeted the Washington Nationals and the Brooklyn Atlantics—the first known meeting between a president and a pro baseball team at the White House. 60. The White House sits on 18 acres (7.3 ha) of land with a tennis court, a swimming pool, and other leisure facilities. 61. George H. W. Bush invited tennis champions to play with him on the White House courts. 62. Barack Obama added removable basketball hoops to the tennis court so he could practice shooting hoops. 63. There's also a smaller indoor basketball court found inside the White House. 64. The White House grounds and the surrounding parkland are known as President's Park. 65. There is a dentist's and a doctor's office in the White House basement. 66. Harry S. Truman officially opened the first White House bowling alley in 1947. 67. A putting green, first installed by Dwight D. Eisenhower in 1954, sits on the lawn outside the Oval Office. 68. Jimmy Carter had computers and printers installed in the White House in 1978. 69. George H. W. Bush sent the first email as a sitting president from the White House in 1992. 70. The White House website went live in 1994. 71. The White House receives more than 100,000 emails and 3,500 phone calls a day. 72. Bill Clinton had a hot tub installed on the White House South Lawn. 73. The White House's hot tub, outdoor shower, and pool are heated by solar energy. 74. A jogging track around the driveway of the South Grounds was built during Bill Clinton's first term. 75. The Secret Service is making plans to build an $8 million replica of the White House for security training. 76. A wealthy businessman has built a $20 million home in Iraq that looks almost exactly like the White House. 77. Mary Lincoln, Abraham Lincoln's wife, held séances to channel spirits in the White House. 78. Legend has it that the ghost of Abraham Lincoln haunts the White House. 79. In 1913 First Lady Ellen Wilson planted the first roses outside the White House. 80. Today, the Rose Garden is the site for bill signings, press conferences, and diplomatic receptions. 81. Richard Nixon's daughter Tricia was married in the Rose Garden. 82. At least 30 weddings have taken place at the White House. 83. Every day, about 7,000 people visit the White House. 84. First Lady Mamie Eisenhower would wrap green ribbons around the White House's columns on St. Patrick's Day. 85. A large château outside of Paris, France, bears a striking resemblance to the White House. 86. The White House has more than six million Twitter followers. 87. The presidential family must pay for their own food, plus toilet paper and toothpaste. 88. You can tour an upside-down White House in a Wisconsin Dells amusement park. 89. Each year, the White House hosts the 3D Printed Ornament Challenge. The winners go on display at the Smithsonian's Natural History Museum. 90. Before moving out of the White House, Ronald Reagan left a note for George H. W. Bush in the drawer of his desk in the Oval Office. 91. A staff of 95 has just five hours to clean up the White House between the departure of one first family and the arrival of the next. 92. In case of emergency, a fire truck is always on hand anytime a helicopter takes off or lands at the White House. 93. Eleanor Roosevelt was the first first lady to hold press conferences in the White House. 94. A curious four-year-old child once caused the White House to go into temporary lockdown after climbing under a bike rack in front of the house. 95. The fence surrounding the White House is topped with supersharp steel spikes to keep intruders out. 96. On June 26, 2015, the White House was lit in multicolored lights to honor the Supreme Court decision to allow gay marriage. 97. Every year, there's a nationwide contest to select the official White House Christmas tree. 98. After a 40-year ban on cameras in the White House, guests are now allowed to snap pics while touring the home. 99. As a security precaution, there's a round-the-clock team of snipers positioned on the White House roof. 100. In 2015, 50 Girl Scouts were invited to pitch tents, stargaze, and camp out on the White House lawn. After a few hours, a severe storm forced them to evacuate.

HOUSE FACTS

50 GROSS FACTS ABOUT YUCKY STUFF

1 MITES LIVE ON ADULTS' FACES, buried head-down in their HAIR FOLLICLES.

2 Skin mites don't live long because they CAN'T POOP—they die when their bodies fill up with feces. Then they DECOMPOSE ON YOUR BODY.

3 Many people with INDOOR ALLERGIES are reacting to DUST MITE POOP.

4 Dust mites particularly like LIVING IN PILLOWCASES, mattresses, and carpeting.

5 The DUST in your home is made up of flakes of dead skin, sand, flour, dirt, and INSECT exoskeletons and droppings.

6 Your body makes 1.5 quarts (1.5 L) of MUCUS EVERY DAY.

7 Most of that mucus WINDS UP IN YOUR STOMACH after you swallow.

8 You produce the SAME AMOUNT of snot when you are sick or have allergies as you do when healthy. It's just THICKER, so you NOTICE IT MORE.

9 Boogers are DRIED CHUNKS OF MUCUS, and the majority of people PICK THEM OUT OF THEIR NOSES.

10 Your snot is CLEAR when you're healthy, YELLOW-GREEN when you're sick, and can turn BLACK if you have a fungal infection in your nose.

11 Dead cells, mucus, and other debris can get caught in tonsils and lump together. Bacteria feed on those TONSIL STONES and cause BAD BREATH.

12 A typical person PASSES GAS as much as 20 times each day.

13 Most digestive gas DOESN'T SMELL, unless it contains SULFUR. Only tiny amounts of sulfurous gases are needed to create a BIG STINK.

14 The stinky sulfur part of digestive gas can PROTECT CELLS FROM DISEASE.

15 Researchers studying digestion COLLECTED DIGESTIVE GAS from 16 people then asked others to judge HOW BAD EACH ONE SMELLED.

16 Digestive gas comes from TRILLIONS OF BACTERIA that live in our guts. They break down food WE CAN'T.

17 People DON'T MIND the smell of their own gas because they get used to the specific BOUQUET OF ODORS created by their gut bacteria.

a head louse clinging to a strand of hair

When most people eat **ASPARAGUS,** their pee starts to **SMELL FUNNY** because it contains **AN ACID** found **ONLY** in asparagus.

NOT EVERYONE produces smelly asparagus-pee. And some people aren't able to **SMELL IT.**

The stinky compound that causes **GARLIC BREATH** travels through the body **TO THE LUNGS,** where the garlic eater **BREATHES IT OUT.**

A woman who **WORE HER CONTACTS** for six months straight went **BLIND** because amoebas **ATE HER CORNEA**— the front-most layer of the eye.

People with **CHOCOLATE ALLERGIES** may actually be allergic to the **COCKROACH BODY PARTS** found in the sweet treat.

The U.S. government allows up to 10 **RODENT HAIRS** per 1.8 ounces (50 g) of **CINNAMON,** and up to 225 insect parts per 8 ounces (227 g) of pasta.

Insect parts are in almost **ALL OF OUR FOOD.** You would have to **STOP EATING** to avoid them entirely.

People probably first got **BEDBUGS** while **SHARING CAVES WITH BATS.**

A single pregnant female **BEDBUG** can infest an **ENTIRE HOUSE.**

GAS GANGRENE is death and rotting of flesh and formation of gas in a wound caused by an **INFECTION** of bacteria found in soil. It can prove fatal.

After having an operation to remove **EXTRA FAT** from his body, an artist in Florida, U.S.A., turned that fat **INTO SOAP** that sells for $1,000 a bar.

An Australian man uses his **OWN BLOOD** to **PAINT PICTURES.**

Doctors once removed a **TUMOR** that weighed **50 POUNDS (23 KG)**—about ten times more than such tumors typically weigh.

A Japanese man **SCARFED DOWN** 18 pounds (8 kg) of **COW BRAINS** in 15 minutes.

COMPETITIVE EATERS don't digest faster than other people. Their **STOMACHS** blow up like **BALLOONS.**

Using **LEECHES** in medicine was an outdated practice until doctors began using suckers again to **REDUCE SWELLING AFTER SURGERY.**

A **LEECH** can go up to **SIX MONTHS** without eating.

When they get too hot, some vultures and storks **SHOWER THEIR LEGS** with a mix of pee and poop—as it evaporates, it **COOLS** the birds down.

An Australian boy spent nearly a minute in a box with **125 GOLDEN ORB SPIDERS.**

A **PORK TAPEWORM** (that usually lives in the intestines) made its way into a woman's **BRAIN.**

A British man **USED HIS MOUTH** to move 37 pounds (17 kg) of **MAGGOTS** from one tub to another.

To cover the body's odors, people have long used **PERFUMES;** some of the most expensive ones use **SPERM WHALE VOMIT** called ambergris.

Rabbits **EAT THEIR OWN POOP** to get the **BACTERIA AND FUNGI** in it. If they don't, they can get very sick.

Watch out for **HOUSEFLIES** on your food. First they **SPIT SALIVA** to break down the food, then they **SOP UP THE GOO** with their sponge-like mouth parts.

BOTFLY LARVAE, found in Central and South America, **BURROW INTO MAMMAL SKIN,** where they grow to be half as long as a quarter.

When a botfly larva is ready to change into an adult, it **WIGGLES THROUGH ITS BREATHING HOLE** and crawls out.

STINKHORN MUSHROOMS earn their name—they can smell like dog feces or **ROTTEN MEAT.**

A woman who tested shoe deodorizers **SNIFFED** approximately **5,600 FEET.** She also smelled lots of **ARMPITS.**

Athlete's foot and ringworm are caused by a **FUNGUS** that thrives in warm, wet areas—like **LOCKER ROOMS AND GYM MATS.**

NAIL FUNGUS can cause toenails to turn yellowish brown, flaky, and **SMELLY.**

The **LOUDEST BURP** ever recorded matched the sound from a **STEREO AT TOP VOLUME.**

The "natural" **VANILLA FLAVORING** in your favorite food may actually be **GOO FROM A BEAVER'S REAR END.**

L-cysteine, which is added to **MANY FOODS** for freshness, comes from **DUCK FEATHERS** and **HUMAN HAIR.**

1 STEVE JOBS was fired by the board of Apple in 1985, but later FOUNDED PIXAR, and then RETURNED TO APPLE to make it the world's most valuable company.

2

Introduced to the world in 1980, the RUBIK'S CUBE was a MAJOR FAD. Now, THANKS TO SPEED CHALLENGES, the toy is popular again. A teen recently SET A RECORD SOLVING it in 5.25 seconds.

3 THE WOOLLY MAMMOTH has been extinct for 4,000 years, but scientists are considering ways to BRING BACK A VERSION OF ONE THROUGH DNA CLONING.

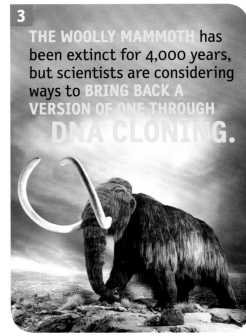

25 FAMOUS COME-

4 IN 1968, AFTER A STRING OF HO-HUM FILMS AND RECORDINGS, SINGER ELVIS PRESLEY TAPED A COMEBACK SPECIAL, GIVING A PERFORMANCE THAT REBOOTED HIS CAREER.

5 Before iPods and CDs, music was listened to on VINYL RECORDS. Sales of those records have SUDDENLY SKYROCKETED, partly because some people think THE SOUND FROM THEM IS BETTER.

6 BASKETBALL STAR MICHAEL JORDAN RETIRED THREE TIMES FROM THE NBA, EVEN THOUGH AFTER THE SECOND RETIREMENT HE SAID HE WAS 99.9 PERCENT SURE HE WOULDN'T COME BACK.

7 After BEING HUNTED NEARLY TO EXTINCTION, only a few WILD EUROPEAN BISON were living in zoos in the early 1900s. Today, 2,300 ROAM FREE, thanks to conservation efforts.

8 IN 1994 GEORGE FOREMAN BECAME THE WORLD'S OLDEST HEAVYWEIGHT CHAMP AFTER TAKING YEARS OFF FROM BOXING TO BECOME A PREACHER AND FOUND A YOUTH CENTER.

9 A MONTH AFTER BEING ATTACKED BY A SHARK WHILE SURFING AND LOSING HER ARM, PRO SURFER BETHANY HAMILTON WAS BACK HITTING THE WAVES AGAIN.

10 PRZEWALSKI'S HORSE IS THE LAST REMAINING BREED OF WILD HORSE. MADE EXTINCT IN THE WILD IN THE 1900S, IT HAS BEEN BRED IN CAPTIVITY. ABOUT 250 HAVE BEEN RELEASED INTO GRASSLANDS IN MONGOLIA.

11

ULYSSES S. GRANT HAD QUIT THE U.S. ARMY BEFORE THE CIVIL WAR BEGAN, BUT THEN ASKED TO REJOIN. HE WAS PROMOTED TO THE TOP GENERAL OF THE UNION FORCES.

12

GROVER CLEVELAND WAS THE 22ND U.S. PRESIDENT, LOST THE ELECTION FOR A SECOND TERM, AND THEN WON FOUR YEARS LATER TO BE THE 24TH PRESIDENT!

14

In a wild card NFL play-off game, the **BUFFALO BILLS** were down 28–3 at the half, but then **BEAT THE HOUSTON OILERS** 41–38 in overtime, known to fans as "**THE COMEBACK.**"

13

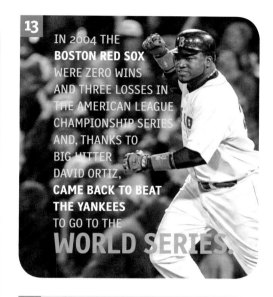

IN 2004 THE **BOSTON RED SOX** WERE ZERO WINS AND THREE LOSSES IN THE AMERICAN LEAGUE CHAMPIONSHIP SERIES AND, THANKS TO BIG HITTER DAVID ORTIZ, **CAME BACK TO BEAT THE YANKEES** TO GO TO THE **WORLD SERIES.**

15

After a 1966 injury from a tackle in the **WORLD CUP,** many thought Brazilian soccer star **PELÉ'S CAREER WAS DONE,** but he came back in 1970 and **BRAZIL WON** the competition.

BACKS TO RECALL

16

Nearly extinct in the 1800s, the **SOUTHERN WHITE RHINO** is now the **MOST ABUNDANT** rhino species in the world thanks to **CONSERVATION EFFORTS.**

17

After being attacked by a spectator during a tennis match in 1993, TENNIS STAR MONICA SELES recovered and, on her return, WON HER FIRST TOURNAMENT.

18

In 1995 TENNIS STAR ANDRE AGASSI was ranked number 1, but INJURIES AND POOR PERFORMANCES dropped him 140 notches. After a comeback in 2002, he became the oldest player to reach number 2.

20

Before he became what many consider the **GREATEST PRESIDENT IN U.S. HISTORY,** Abraham Lincoln **LOST** a bid for **CONGRESS** and two bids for **SENATE,** as well as losing the **VICE PRESIDENTIAL RACE.**

21

BOXER MUHAMMAD ALI WAS STRIPPED OF HIS WORLD TITLE WHEN HE REFUSED MILITARY SERVICE. HE APPEALED, WON, AND CAME BACK TO WIN TWO MORE WORLD BOXING TITLES.

19

In 2002 there were fewer than 100 SANTA CRUZ ISLAND FOX left living on the island off of California, U.S.A. THANKS TO A BREEDING PROGRAM, there are now more than 1,000.

23

In 2012, when the company that made TWINKIES went bankrupt, many thought the sweet treat was gone forever. But a new company took over and MORE THAN ONE MILLION are made every day.

24

IN 1901, ONLY ONE PAIR OF ATLANTIC PUFFINS NESTED IN THE UNITED STATES DUE TO PEOPLE TAKING THEIR EGGS OR HUNTING THE BIRDS FOR THEIR MEAT AND FEATHERS. TODAY, THERE ARE **600** NESTING PAIRS.

22

In the United States, CLEAN AIR has made a comeback after the passage of the 1970 CLEAN AIR ACT, which called for BETTER POLLUTION CONTROL. Carbon monoxide pollution from cars and factories has been cut almost in half.

25

In some parts of the United States there are **MORE FORESTS TODAY THAN THERE WERE 100 YEARS AGO** thanks to legislation that helped bring forests back **AFTER MAJOR HARVESTING** in the 1800s.

15 ADORABLE

1 Puppies of large breeds have **BIG, OVERSIZE PAWS** that they have to grow into.

2 Abraham Lincoln was given **TWO KITTENS** when he became president. He fed one during an **OFFICIAL DINNER,** using a **GOLD FORK.**

3 When a mother carries her puppy or kitten by the **SCRUFF OF ITS NECK,** the baby stops moving. This helps the mother **MOVE HER LITTER** to a safe place **MORE QUICKLY.**

4 A puppy's **NOSE-PRINT** can be used to identify it, in the same way **WE USE FINGERPRINTS.**

5 The paws of puppies and dogs sometimes have bacteria on their feet that make them **SMELL LIKE STALE CORN CHIPS,** a condition called **"FRITO FEET."**

6 Although kittens and cats **CAN'T TASTE SWEETNESS,** they are able to taste other flavors that **WE CAN'T.**

7 **NEWBORN** kittens are both **DEAF AND BLIND.** It may be **TWO WEEKS** before they can hear and see properly.

8 Filmmakers needed **230 DALMATIAN PUPPIES** to make the movie *101 Dalmatians* because the puppies **GOT TOO BIG.** Younger dogs were brought in **EVERY TWO WEEKS.**

PUPPIES AND KITTENS

9 Young kittens sleep a whopping **16 HOURS A DAY.**

10 Puppies and kittens have a special **REFLECTIVE LAYER** in the eye to help them see at night. The layer is the reason their eyes **SEEM TO GLOW.**

11 People in New York, San Francisco, and Seattle can call up a pet taxi service and have a **KITTEN DELIVERED** for 15 minutes of **CUDDLING.**

12 Each year puppies play in the **PUPPY BOWL** and kittens in the **KITTEN BOWL**— pet-owners' versions of the **SUPER BOWL.**

13 A kitten that **WENT MISSING** in New Mexico, U.S.A., mysteriously **TURNED UP** in Maine—2,300 miles (3,700 km) away.

14 **KOKO,** the sign-language **GORILLA,** has two pet **KITTENS.**

15 **PUPPY LOVE** is a real thing—when you look a puppy in the eyes, its brain releases a "love hormone."

1 Colonization is when a country establishes control in a new land by sending people to settle and rule over those already living there. The new settlers are known as colonists.

2 At an auction in 2013, a copy of the *Bay Psalm Book*, printed in 1640 by the Massachusetts Bay Colony—an early English colony— sold for $14.2 million dollars. There are only 11 copies in the world.

3 A timber-frame house in Dedham, Massachusetts, U.S.A., built in early colonial times, is thought to be the oldest standing building made out of wood in North America.

4 If you were an orphan living in England during colonial times, there was a good chance you would be sent to a new home in the New World.

5 THE AMERICAN COLONISTS HARDLY EVER BATHED. TO GET CLEAN THEY WOULD USE A WET RAG AND WIPE OFF *JUST* THEIR HANDS OR FACE!

6 European colonial administrators in tropical Africa and Asia in the 1800s often wore pith helmets— cloth-covered hats made of soft wood (or pith)—to keep the sun off their heads and faces.

7 During the colonization of Africa, Ethiopia kept its monarchy and its freedom except for a brief occupation by the Italians from 1936 to 1941.

8 In 1858 the British government established colonial rule over most of India. That period was known as the British Raj since "raj" means "to rule" in the Indian language of Hindi.

9 In colonial America, colonists drank a beverage made from molasses, ginger, water, and vinegar—known as switchel—as a tonic or pick-me-up. It originated in the Caribbean.

10 Pleasant Rowland, creator of the line of American Girl dolls, got the idea for the historic dolls after visiting Colonial Williamsburg, Virginia, U.S.A.

11 Pilgrim farmers at Plymouth Plantation grew a new kind of corn called Indian corn. It had red, yellow, black, and white kernels all on the same ear.

12 An average American colonial household would use between 200 and 400 candles in one year.

13 GEORGE WASHINGTON'S DENTURES WERE MADE FROM IVORY FROM A HIPPOPOTAMUS TUSK.

14 Most American colonial children did not pack a lunch to take to school. They would walk home from school to eat an afternoon meal with their families.

15 In 1621 the Virginia Company of London sent a ship full of single women to the colony of Virginia in North America. A male colonist had to pay the company 120 pounds (54 kg) of tobacco if he wanted to marry one of the women.

16 The first textbook printed in colonial America, *The New England Primer*, used rhymes based on biblical stories to teach children how to read.

17 Now a living history museum, El Rancho de las Golondrinas, the Ranch of the Swallows, located near Santa Fe, New Mexico, U.S.A., was an actual resting stop for travelers on a Spanish colonial trade route during the 1700s.

18 Boys in school in colonial America were taught how to use the stars to navigate ships.

19 The oldest wooden schoolhouse in the United States, built more than 200 years ago, is located in St. Augustine, Florida, U.S.A.

20 A favorite colonial desert was a type of fruit cobbler called slump or grunt. Yum!

21 After researching the history of chocolate, the Mars candy company developed American Heritage Chocolate—chocolate made using the same ingredients as those used in colonial times.

22 Colonial children were not allowed to sit down during dinner. They had to stand at the table without making any noise—even while eating!

23 Students at Wellesley College in Wellesley, Massachusetts, still play a colonial children's game. Every April, seniors at the college hold a hoop-rolling contest.

24 IF YOU WERE A COOPER IN AMERICAN COLONIAL TIMES, YOUR JOB WAS TO MAKE WOODEN BARRELS.

25 Instead of using dinner plates, American colonists ate off of square pieces of carved wood called trenchers.

26 A few Norse explorers from Europe colonized North America more than 1,000 years ago at L'Anse aux Meadows, Newfoundland, Canada.

27 In colonial America kids would make dolls from corn husks, using charcoal or berry juice to color their faces.

28 In the 1680s, France started sending children punished by their parents to the French colonies in the West Indies.

29 IN COLONIAL TIMES, BOYS WORE DRESSES UNTIL ABOUT AGE THREE TO SEVEN. THEN THEY SWITCHED FROM SKIRTS TO PANTS.

30 From 1659 until 1681 it was illegal to celebrate Christmas in the Colony of Massachusetts. If you were caught celebrating, you would be fined five shillings.

31 It was illegal to kiss your wife in public in some parts of colonial America.

32 A shoebox found in 2012 in the United Kingdom contained nearly 200 photographs of daily life in colonial India.

75 YE OLDE FACTS ABOUT COLONIAL TIMES

33 The Arch of Colonial Trees in San Francisco, California, U.S.A., contains 13 trees representing the original 13 colonies. They were planted in October 1896.

34 THE FIRST THEATER IN NORTH AMERICA WAS BUILT IN 1716 IN COLONIAL WILLIAMSBURG, VIRGINIA.

35 One of the oldest sewer systems in the Americas dates back to colonial times. It was built in 1502 underneath a part of Santo Domingo, in the Dominican Republic in the Caribbean.

36 El Camino Real de Tierra Adentro, "The Royal Road of the Interior," was a 1,600-mile (2,575-km)-long trading route between Mexico City, Mexico, and San Juan Pueblo, New Mexico, U.S.A. Spanish conquistadores and colonists traveled on it for more than 300 years.

37 To cure a fever, a colonial doctor would make patients drink a liquid made from boiled toads or have sliced herrings tied to their feet.

the Governor's Palace in Colonial Williamsburg, Virginia, U.S.A.

38 The American colonists followed the European tradition of eating tomatoes from pewter plates. If placed on lead plates, the acid in tomatoes would create a chemical reaction that could cause illness or even death.

39 In 2010 the remains of a wooden ship from the colonial era was found underneath the ground at the World Trade Center construction site.

40 Double Dutch jump rope was named after Dutch colonists who introduced the game to North America.

41 The phrase "goody two-shoes" comes from a colonial children's story about a girl named Little Goody Two-Shoes, who, of course, never did anything wrong!

42 The first European settlement in the New World wasn't Jamestown—it was the city of St. Augustine, Florida—established by the Spanish in 1565.

43 Of the first 104 colonists that came to Jamestown in 1607, only 38 survived the first nine months there.

44 The American game of baseball has roots that go back to colonial times. Early settlers played bat-and-ball games as far back as the 1600s.

45 Portugal was the first country to establish a global empire through colonization. It established colonies in South America, Asia, and Africa.

46 In colonial America, three friends could play a game called "honey pots." Two would link arms to form a chair to carry around the third friend.

47 CLOCKS DURING COLONIAL TIMES HAD ONLY AN HOUR HAND.

48 Colonial Americans may have referred to someone who had died as "kicking the bucket," which may have come from how a person was hanged.

49 Children in early America used a hornbook to learn their ABCs. A hornbook was a wooden paddle with a piece of parchment paper attached to it, covered by a clear, protective layer shaved off an animal's horn.

50 Mary Kingsley, a British explorer and critic of colonialism, trekked across Africa wearing a long dress and corset.

51 Hurricanes struck in colonial times, too. Jamestown and the Massachusetts Colony were hit by one in August of 1635.

52 Before New York City became New York City, it was a Dutch colony called New Amsterdam.

53 Don't like brushing your teeth? Try brushing them with powdered chalk and pumice, or a chewed twig, as colonial children did.

54 Native Americans taught early colonists how to plant the "Three Sisters"—corn, beans, and squash together— a successful farming technique that had been used for more than 300 years prior to European contact.

55 COLONISTS WHO CAME TO THE NEW WORLD SAILED NOT ON FANCY CRUISE SHIPS BUT ON SEAFARING VESSELS MADE MOSTLY TO CARRY CARGO.

56 In 1460 Portugal was the first European country to claim a region of Africa that lies south of the Sahara. Today that region is known as Sierra Leone.

57 In the early 1800s, the American Colonization Society sent free black people from the United States to Africa. The colony they established became the nation of Liberia in 1847.

58 Colonial America supplied "raw" goods such as timber and tobacco to Great Britain, and the Brits sent back finished goods such as clothing and furniture.

59 The territory of Western Sahara is the only colonial remnant in Africa. It was a Spanish colony but is now ruled by Morocco.

60 In colonial America, if you had a sore throat you would say you "caught the pip."

61 In 1647 the Massachusetts Colony established the first public school when it passed a law requiring every township with 50 or more families to hire a teacher to teach children.

62 Mulligatawny soup can trace its history back to British colonization of India. It is a soup made with chicken and its Indian name means "pepper water."

63 In 1519 the Spanish conquistador Hernán Cortés arrived in what is today Mexico. He soon conquered the Aztec who lived there.

64 The three-cornered hats men wore during colonial times were often made out of beaver felt.

65 As Europeans colonized Africa, the conquest became known as the "scramble for Africa." The scramble was for cultural influence.

66 Colonial Williamsburg, in Williamsburg, Virginia, is the largest living history museum in the United States.

67 If you were a pilgrim, instead of saying "hello" you would have said, "good morrow" or "what cheer." The English word "hello," which is often credited to Thomas Edison, wouldn't be around for several hundred years.

68 Since both milk and water could carry diseases in colonial times, colonists would drink tea or cider with their meals.

69 Because there was a lack of British currency during colonial times, colonists would barter for services or would trade wampum— tubular shell beads used by Native Americans as a form of exchange.

70 In colonial times people did not eat with forks: They either used their hands or a spoon.

71 AS OF 2015, THERE WERE 16 TERRITORIES IN THE WORLD STILL CONSIDERED TO BE COLONIES.

72 Since the United Nations was formed in 1945, 80 former colonies have become independent nations.

73 The British brought the game cricket to India and Pakistan, where it is now a popular sport.

74 In Spanish colonial Central and South America, towns would often be built around a central square or plaza in the city center.

75 Historians can tell when the Vikings colonized an area because they find Viking brooches, which are oval pieces of jewelry about four inches (10 cm) long.

35 BRIGHT FACTS ABOUT CONSTELLATIONS

1
Constellations are **GROUPS OF STARS** that, from the point of view of Earth, form a certain pattern. There are **88 CONSTELLATION BOUNDARIES AND NAMES.**

2
ANCIENT GREEKS described more than half of the official constellations recognized today.

3
The constellation Scorpius gets its name from the Latin word for **SCORPION.** The red star **ANTARES** is placed where the scorpion's heart should be.

4
Some names for newer constellations come from **MODERN INVENTIONS:** Telescopium is named after the **TELESCOPE.**

5
A 17,300-year-old painting **FOUND IN A CAVE** in France is believed to be a **MAP OF THE STARS.**

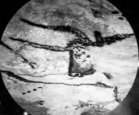

6
When the night sky is viewed from Earth, the **LARGEST CONSTELLATION** is Hydra—the water snake. It extends over 3 percent of the sky.

7
Centaurus—the Centaur—has **101 VISIBLE STARS,** more than any other constellation.

8
The Zodiac is a family of constellations that lie on the plane of the path our sun takes across the celestial sphere. They make up the **12 ZODIAC SIGNS** used in **ASTROLOGY.**

9
In the **CANCER** constellation, there is a huge group of stars in the center of its shell called the **BEEHIVE CLUSTER.**

10
CETUS CONSTELLATION, located in the northern sky, is known as the Whale. It is named after Cetus, the **SEA MONSTER** from Greek mythology.

11
In the original **PLANET OF THE APES** movie, three astronauts land on a planet 320 light-years from Earth in the constellation Orion.

12
The **PAC-MAN NEBULA** is named after the dot-eating video game character and located in the **CASSIOPEIA** constellation.

13
The constellation Cepheus—named after King Cepheus of Greek mythology—is **SHAPED LIKE A HOUSE.**

14
The Andromeda galaxy, which lies in the **ANDROMEDA** constellation, is 2.5 million light-years from Earth and is **THE FARTHEST OBJECT** that can be seen with the naked eye.

15
Crux—the Southern Cross—is the **BRIGHTEST CONSTELLATION** in the sky. The main stars of the cross are featured on the **NEW ZEALAND FLAG.**

16
The constellation **LEO**—which is Latin for "lion"—is one of the **FIRST** recorded constellations. It was written about in Babylonia, more than 2,500 years ago.

17
The Pollux star in Gemini is **NINE TIMES LARGER** than the sun.

18
ASTRONOMY is the oldest science. From as long ago as when people lived in caves, **STAR FORMATIONS** were written down. Telescopes were first used in the 1600s.

19
Unlike other ancient constellations, **LIBRA** is not connected to Greek mythology. In Latin, "LIBRA" MEANS SCALES, which represent balance, harmony, law, and fairness.

20
Lyra, **ONE OF THE SMALLEST CONSTELLATIONS**, has one of the brightest stars: Vega. It's the fifth brightest star in the night sky.

21
Vega, Deneb, and Altair, the brightest stars in each of the constellations of Lyra, Cygnus, and Aquila, form the **SUMMER TRIANGLE** seen in the mid-northern latitudes.

22
The constellation Orion is made up of bright blue supergiant stars and **ONE RED SUPERGIANT STAR** named Betelgeuse, which is at Orion's shoulder.

23
Rigel, the brightest star in Orion, is **40,000 TIMES BRIGHTER THAN THE SUN** and emits 100,000 times its energy!

24
The constellation Lyra is associated with the Greek mythological character Orpheus, a **TALENTED MUSICIAN** who could charm Nature.

25
The constellation Gemini, which is **LATIN FOR "TWINS,"** has two stars that are named after the Greek mythological characters **POLLUX** and **CASTOR**.

26
Three stars that run through the middle of the Orion constellation are known as **ORION'S BELT**. They align with Sirius, **THE BRIGHTEST STAR** in the night sky.

27
The constellation **LEO** was named for one of the lions that Hercules killed. He was said to have placed it in the heavens **AS ONE OF HIS CONQUESTS**.

28
Located in Sagittarius, which is often depicted as a teapot on star maps, is a **SUPERMASSIVE BLACK HOLE**, Sagittarius A, that is four million times the mass of our sun.

29
Pegasus—recognized as a constellation more than 2,000 years ago—was considered a **COMPANION** to two mortals in Greek mythology, **PERSEUS** and **BELLEROPHON**.

30
The annual Perseid **METEOR SHOWER**—where up to 100 meteors can be seen from Earth in an hour—originates from the constellation **PERSEUS**.

a huge cloud of gas where stars are being born in the zone of the constellation Orion

31
Pisces is one of the **TRICKIEST** constellations to see because it doesn't have any bright stars in it. It is best seen in places that **LACK LIGHT POLLUTION**.

32
The Sagittarius constellation, which lies near the center of the Milky Way, represents a centaur, which is **HALF HUMAN AND HALF HORSE**.

33
The constellation Pegasus can be found by the bright group of stars that form the **GREAT SQUARE OF PEGASUS**.

34
Virgo, the second largest constellation, is home to **GALAXY CLUSTERS**, each of which might hold hundreds or even thousands of galaxies.

35
URSA MAJOR, the constellation that includes the Big Dipper, is Latin for **"GREAT BEAR."** Native Americans also considered the pattern of stars to be a bear.

1
It's believed that a goat herder in what is now Ethiopia DISCOVERED COFFEE 1,200 years ago when his goats got an energy boost after eating some red berries.

2
Each flower on a coffee tree produces a SMALL RED FRUIT known as a coffee cherry or berry with two green coffee beans inside.

3
Ancient African tribes MADE ENERGY BALLS from coffee berries and animal fat.

4
After coffee was discovered in Ethiopia, ancient MUSLIM people soon began boiling the berries to make a drink they called AL-QAHWA.

5
Coffee was brought to Europe from the MIDDLE EAST in 1615.

6
The world's first COFFEE SHOP opened in Venice, Italy, in 1645. By 1700 there were hundreds of coffeehouses in London, England, alone.

7
People didn't start ADDING CREAM to their cups of coffee until the 17th century.

8
Some people sip sweet coffee out of a "WAFFEE"— a chocolate-lined crunchy waffle cup.

9
COFFEE TREES can grow as tall as a three-story building.

10
Before roasting, coffee beans are SPONGY and smell GRASSY—it's the roasting process that brings out the familiar strong scent of coffee.

11
It takes approximately 2,000 coffee cherries—4,000 BEANS—to produce one pound (454 g) of roasted coffee.

12
Researchers estimate that there are more than 100 known species of COFFEE PLANTS.

13
It takes up to four years for a coffee SEED to grow into a TREE that produces coffee beans.

14
The area known as the "BEAN BELT"— covering parts of North America, South America, Africa, and Asia—is where all the coffee of the world is grown.

15
Coffee harvested from COFFEE BEANS FOUND IN ELEPHANT DUNG has been known to sell for $500 a pound.

16
CAPPUCCINO coffee gets its name from the color of the ROBES worn by Christian Capuchin monks in Italy.

17
Americans spend $40 BILLION on coffee each year, according to a study.

18
In England in the 1700s, "PENNY UNIVERSITIES" were coffee shops where you could listen to scholars for a penny, the price of a cup of coffee.

19
For about $27, you can BATHE IN COFFEE at a spa in Japan.

20
MOCHA—a chocolate-coffee blend—gets its name from the town in Yemen where the coffee beans were originally traded from.

21
Coffee was brought to the United States by DUTCH TRADERS in the mid-1600s.

22
In the 1700s, COFFEE surpassed TEA as the FAVORITE DRINK in the original United States colonies.

23
Coffee loses 70 percent of its FLAVOR within minutes after brewing.

24
Researchers are developing a method to turn used coffee grounds in to BIODIESEL fuel.

25
There are more than 100,000 COFFEE FARMS in Mexico alone.

26
Thanks largely to their RICH SOIL and TROPICAL CLIMATES, Hawaii and Puerto Rico are the only places in the United States where coffee can be grown.

27
Forty percent of the world's coffee is PRODUCED BY BRAZIL AND COLOMBIA.

28
Astronauts can drink COFFEE IN SPACE thanks to a high-tech, gravity-defying machine.

29
A cat named CREME PUFF, who lived to be 38 years old, had a breakfast of coffee, eggs, bacon, and broccoli each morning.

30
Some coffee trees live for longer than 200 YEARS.

31
It takes approximately 37 GALLONS (140 L) OF WATER to make just ONE CUP OF COFFEE if you factor in what it takes to grow and process the beans.

32
Coffee is grown in more than 50 COUNTRIES and across four continents.

33
A car that runs on coffee known as the CAR-PUCCINO is said to reach 60 miles an hour (97 km/h) and can travel 1 mile (1.6 km) per 56 cups of espresso.

50 BUZZ-WORTHY FACTS ABOUT COFFEE

39
You can munch on **DEEP-FRIED** coffee at a fair in San Diego, California, U.S.A.

40
A British chemist named George Washington invented an early version of **INSTANT COFFEE** in 1906.

36
The world's **LARGEST CUP** of coffee contained 3,758.7 gallons (14,228.1 L) of the drink—that's more than 50 BATHTUBS FULL.

34
One third of the **TAP WATER** consumed each day in North America is used to **BREW** pots of coffee.

37
Mixing coffee grounds into your conditioner can make your hair **SHINIER AND SOFTER.**

35
You can repurpose used coffee grounds to **DEODORIZE** a stinky car, keep slugs out of gardens, and **EXFOLIATE** your skin.

38
One company has come up with **CHEWY COFFEE CUBES,** each equivalent to half a cup of coffee.

43
An 18-year-old invented an alarm clock that can wake you up with the **SMELL** of coffee.

41
Today more than **TWO BILLION CUPS** of coffee are consumed around the world every day—enough to fill more than 300 Olympic-size **SWIMMING POOLS.**

42
President Teddy Roosevelt is said to have drunk about a gallon (3.8 L) of coffee a day—and put as many as **SEVEN LUMPS OF SUGAR** into each cup.

44
Since caffeine is toxic to most insects, it serves as a **NATURAL BUG REPELLENT** that protects the coffee tree.

45
Just the smell of coffee can **PERK YOU UP,** a study shows.

46
Coffee with **CREAM** added stays warmer for longer than plain black coffee.

47
You can sip coffee from 20 feet (6 m) above the ground in a diner built into a **TREE** in Okinawa, Japan.

48
In Norway, coffee is traditionally made with a **RAW EGG** and boiling water.

49
A brand of high-energy coffee known as **BULLETPROOF** is made with a blend of unsalted **GRASS-FED BUTTER** and coconut oil.

50
Some businesses **PUMP THE SMELL** of coffee into their shops to trigger customers to crave a cup.

1
A spacecraft—also known as a spaceship—is a **VEHICLE** or **MACHINE** designed to **FLY** in outer space.

2
Before they were **RETIRED** in 2011, NASA's fleet of five space shuttles traveled a total of 513.7 million miles (826.7 million km). That's 1.3 times the distance between **EARTH AND JUPITER.**

3
SINCE 1957, SOME **7,000 SPACECRAFTS** HAVE BEEN LAUNCHED INTO SPACE. **THE FIRST** WAS SPUTNIK, A **SATELLITE** SENT INTO ORBIT BY THE RUSSIANS.

4
A SPACECRAFT **GLOWS RED HOT** AS IT RETURNS TO EARTH FROM SPACE—WITH ITS EXTERIOR TEMPERATURE RISING TO MORE THAN 3,000°F (1,650°C).

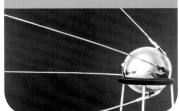

25 FACTS ABOUT SPACECRAFT TO LAUNCH INTO

5
FAMOUS ASTRONAUTS Neil Armstrong and Buzz Aldrin took a small space capsule called *EAGLE* to the **MOON in 1969.** They landed with just **25** seconds of fuel left!

6
THE COMPUTER ABOARD *EAGLE* WAS ABOUT AS POWERFUL AS A **DIGITAL WATCH.**

7
Between 1961 and 1983, the Soviet Union sent probes to **VENUS**—the **FIRST** human spacecraft ever to land on **ANOTHER PLANET.**

8
Before they sent **PEOPLE** into orbit, NASA used an "ASTROCHIMP" named **HAM** to test the shuttle. His successful trip into space and back lasted 16 minutes, 39 seconds.

9
IN 1995 A RECORD-SETTING 13 PEOPLE WERE IN SPACE SIMULTANEOUSLY AS BOTH AN AMERICAN AND A RUSSIAN SPACE SHUTTLE WERE IN ORBIT AT THE SAME TIME.

10
A SPACECRAFT GRAVEYARD filled with space stations, some 160 SATELLITES, and cargo crafts lies 2,500 miles (4,023 km) off the coast of New Zealand in the Pacific Ocean.

11
The space shuttle *ENTERPRISE* was originally called the *CONSTITUTION* until *STAR TREK* fans successfully campaigned to have the name changed to honor the popular TV SHOW.

12 Astronauts will soon be able to take a high-tech **"SPACE TAXI"**—complete with leather seats and a tablet-like computer—to and from the **INTERNATIONAL SPACE STATION**.

13 THE UNMANNED SPACECRAFT *NEW HORIZONS* TRAVELED NEARLY TEN YEARS AND ABOUT 750,000 MILES (1,207,008 KM) PER DAY TO REACH **PLUTO** AND TAKE **CLOSER-THAN-EVER** PHOTOGRAPHS OF THE DWARF PLANET.

14 In 1981 **NASA** launched the space shuttle *Columbia*, the first reusable, **HUMAN-CARRYING** spacecraft designed to **ORBIT** around **EARTH**.

15 Scientists are developing a gas-filled **SPACE BALLOON** set to orbit around **SATURN'S** biggest **MOON,** Titan.

16 The United States **AIR FORCE** has designed a **ROBOTIC** space shuttle that runs on **SOLAR POWER** and can stay in orbit for more than **200 DAYS**.

17 On the space shuttles *Gemini* and *Apollo*, astronauts had to **RELIEVE THEMSELVES** in plastic bags. Today's space shuttles are equipped with narrow **SPACE TOILETS**.

18 NASA launches spacecraft from Cape Canaveral, Florida, U.S.A., because it's **CLOSER** to the **EQUATOR** where Earth **ROTATES FASTER**, giving rockets a better **BOOST** as they **BLAST OFF**.

19 NASA's *JUNO* PROBE TO JUPITER INCLUDED **LEGO** FIGURES IN THE LIKENESS OF **GALILEO** AND THE ROMAN GODS **JUNO** AND **JUPITER**.

20 A **MISSING** European spacecraft was recently found on the surface of **MARS** after it **VANISHED** from contact 11 years earlier.

21 With the help of the world's **LARGEST WIND TUNNEL, NASA** is able to test the **PARACHUTES** used to bring certain spacecraft back to **EARTH**.

22 One scientist raised **$500,000** in an online campaign so that he can build his own **SOLAR-POWERED** spacecraft.

23 A **RUSSIAN ROCKET** once delivered a **THIN-CRUST PIZZA** to the International Space Station. The **PRICE TAG** on that pizza? **$1 MILLION.**

24 Scientists are working on building a spacecraft made of graphene, a **SUPERTHIN,** lightweight material that's **200 times STRONGER** than **STEEL.**

25 THE UNMANNED *MESSENGER* SPACECRAFT TRAVELED ABOUT FIVE BILLION MILES (8 BILLION KM) AND FLEW BY THREE PLANETS BEFORE IT WAS PURPOSELY CRASHED INTO MERCURY IN 2015.

35 GLITTERING FACTS ABOUT JEWELRY

1 A fashion designer in Utah, U.S.A., sells "LIVE JEWELRY"—giant Madagascar hissing COCKROACHES bejeweled with Swarovski crystals. Prices range from $60 to $80.

2 Queen Elizabeth II's Imperial State CROWN weighs THREE POUNDS (1.36 kg), is 177 years old, and contains the world's fourth largest polished diamond.

3 The NECKLACE ABOARD the R.M.S. *TITANIC* that is said to have inspired the famous necklace in the movie *Titanic* was known as the Love of the Sea.

4 A jeweler in Ukraine holds the world record for MOST DIAMONDS set in ONE RING—the Tsarevna Swan has 2,525 diamonds in it and is valued at $180,000.

5 A designer in New York, U.S.A., creates jewelry from BARBIE DOLLS, incorporating parts of the dolls into pins, necklaces, and earrings.

6 The LARGEST GOLD RING in the world, the Star of Taiba, is on display in Dubai, U.A.E. It weighs 141 pounds (64 kg) and is worth more than $3 MILLION.

7 A jeweler in Amsterdam makes jewelry that HOUSES living animals — such as a cage-like necklace with a MOUSE running inside and a headband that holds a BIRD.

8 The MOST EXPENSIVE piece of jewelry ever made for a movie was worn by actress Nicole Kidman. It was a necklace worth about $1 MILLION.

9 THE ALFRED JEWEL is an Anglo-Saxon artifact made of gold, enamel, and quartz for KING ALFRED THE GREAT OF WESSEX. It was rediscovered in England in 1693.

10 Disney fans can buy ENGAGEMENT RINGS based on their favorite DISNEY PRINCESS. Each ring is in the color scheme of that princess and has a unique engraving.

11 The OLDEST PIECES OF JEWELRY are three pierced SHELLS that look like BEADS. They were found in Israel and are said to be 90,000 to 100,000 years old.

12 For hundreds of years it was popular to wear JEWELRY MADE OUT OF HUMAN HAIR. The trend stopped in about the mid-1920s.

13 The world's LONGEST CANDY NECKLACE was made in Maryland, U.S.A., and was 3,744 feet (1,141 m) long.

14 In ancient Egypt, special rings called SIGNET RINGS were engraved with the owner's unique seal and were used to SIGN and SEAL legal documents.

15 A sculptor in Australia uses TRASH found in the OCEAN to make beautiful JEWELRY.

16 An 11-year-old girl in Hawaii started a business making RINGS out of LEFTOVER SURFBOARD RESIN.

17 A special-edition BARBIE DOLL was created by a famous Australian designer with a BARBIE-SIZE DIAMOND NECKLACE and RING. The necklace alone was worth $300,000.

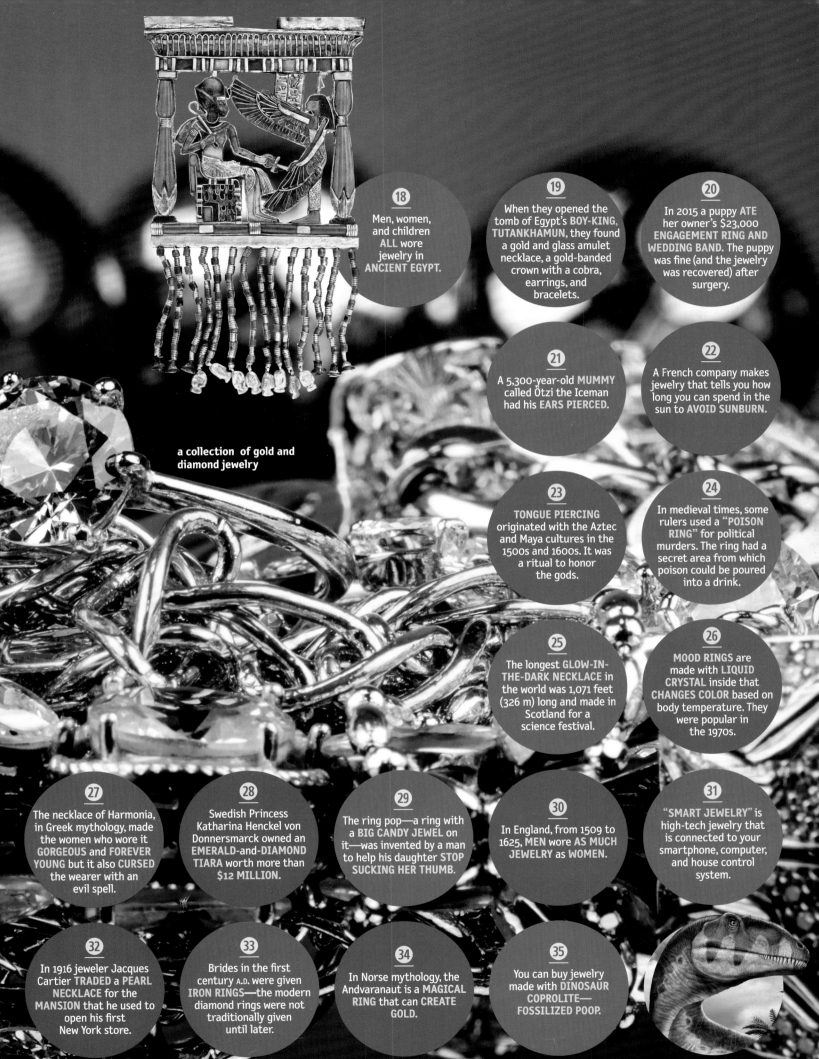

18 Men, women, and children ALL wore jewelry in ANCIENT EGYPT.

a collection of gold and diamond jewelry

19 When they opened the tomb of Egypt's BOY-KING, TUTANKHAMUN, they found a gold and glass amulet necklace, a gold-banded crown with a cobra, earrings, and bracelets.

20 In 2015 a puppy ATE her owner's $23,000 ENGAGEMENT RING AND WEDDING BAND. The puppy was fine (and the jewelry was recovered) after surgery.

21 A 5,300-year-old MUMMY called Ötzi the Iceman had his EARS PIERCED.

22 A French company makes jewelry that tells you how long you can spend in the sun to AVOID SUNBURN.

23 TONGUE PIERCING originated with the Aztec and Maya cultures in the 1500s and 1600s. It was a ritual to honor the gods.

24 In medieval times, some rulers used a "POISON RING" for political murders. The ring had a secret area from which poison could be poured into a drink.

25 The longest GLOW-IN-THE-DARK NECKLACE in the world was 1,071 feet (326 m) long and made in Scotland for a science festival.

26 MOOD RINGS are made with LIQUID CRYSTAL inside that CHANGES COLOR based on body temperature. They were popular in the 1970s.

27 The necklace of Harmonia, in Greek mythology, made the women who wore it GORGEOUS and FOREVER YOUNG but it also CURSED the wearer with an evil spell.

28 Swedish Princess Katharina Henckel von Donnersmarck owned an EMERALD-and-DIAMOND TIARA worth more than $12 MILLION.

29 The ring pop—a ring with a BIG CANDY JEWEL on it—was invented by a man to help his daughter STOP SUCKING HER THUMB.

30 In England, from 1509 to 1625, MEN wore AS MUCH JEWELRY as WOMEN.

31 "SMART JEWELRY" is high-tech jewelry that is connected to your smartphone, computer, and house control system.

32 In 1916 jeweler Jacques Cartier TRADED a PEARL NECKLACE for the MANSION that he used to open his first New York store.

33 Brides in the first century A.D. were given IRON RINGS—the modern diamond rings were not traditionally given until later.

34 In Norse mythology, the Andvaranaut is a MAGICAL RING that can CREATE GOLD.

35 You can buy jewelry made with DINOSAUR COPROLITE— FOSSILIZED POOP.

50

SEACRAFT
TO KEEP YOU AFLOAT

1 The **PIRATE SHIP** *Whydah* is believed to have had the treasure of over 50 ships on board when it sank off Cape Cod, Massachusetts, U.S.A., in 1717.

2 America's Cup—a series of international races between **YACHTS**— is named after the boat that won the inaugural race, held in 1851.

3 *Steamboat Willie*— starring **MICKEY MOUSE**—was released in 1928 and was the first **DISNEY CARTOON** with sound.

4 A **SCUTTLEBUTT** is a drinking fountain on a ship.

5 Since 1997 **LEGO PIECES** have been washing up on England's beaches. They come from a container that fell off a ship at sea.

6 When New York's Hudson River freezes over, people often bring out **ICE YACHTS**— special boats that travel across the ice using a sail.

7 **DRAGON BOATING**— in which 20 rowers paddle in unison in a narrow boat with a dragon head—originated in China 2,000 years ago.

8 As many as **100,000** people live on houseboats in the rivers and canals of London.

9 State officials in the U.S. state of Washington plan to **TURN OLD WARSHIPS INTO BRIDGES** for cars.

10 You can sightsee New York Harbor aboard *THE BEAST,* a jet-powered speedboat with teeth painted on the sides that travels at 45 miles an hour (72 km/h).

11 A U.S. company made a **KAYAK THAT FOLDS UP** like origami so that it can be carried in a case over your shoulder.

12 A Norwegian man designed the HotTug, a **HOT TUB BOAT** with a wood-fired stove on board that heats the water up for a crew of eight!

13 You can buy a two-person **SUBMARINE SHAPED LIKE AN ORCA** for $90,000.

14 For $2 million you can drive a sports car that can also **CRUISE UNDERWATER.** Built-in scuba tanks let you stay underwater for an hour.

15 A boat race held in Key West, Florida, U.S.A., only allows participants to use **BOATS MADE OF PLYWOOD AND DUCT TAPE.**

16 A **TUG BOAT** towed a 68-foot (21-m) floating **WOODEN HIPPO** up London's River Thames as an art installation project.

17 For $5,000 you can buy a **DRAGON PEDAL BOAT,** which is like a regular pedal boat except it's shaped like a sea serpent!

18 To race in a **PUMPKIN REGATTA,** you carve out a giant pumpkin, sit in it, and use a paddle to get around.

19 Competitors in North Yorkshire, England, gather annually to **RACE BOATS MADE OF YORKSHIRE PUDDING.**

20 45,000 students **FOLDED** 230,000 **BOATS** that together created an **IMAGE OF A DOVE** to make the world's largest display of origami boats.

21 A British man sailed from San Francisco, U.S.A., to Australia in a 60-foot (18-m)-long boat made from **12,500 PLASTIC WATER BOTTLES.**

22 In 2012 a **SOLAR-POWERED BOAT** finished circling the globe after 587 days.

23 An airplane designer created plans for a YACHT OF THE FUTURE that transforms into a seaplane.

24 BULK CARRIER SHIPS can hold 220,000 tons (199,580 MT) of cargo—that's the same as 31,000 African elephants!

25 A CORACLE is a ONE-PERSON BOAT.

26 Ancient Egyptians made boats by BUNDLING PAPYRUS REEDS that grew along the banks of the Nile River.

27 In Belgium, you can race in a BATHTUB REGATTA. Prizes are based on speed and creativity.

28 In Bangkok, Thailand, you can shop for fruits and vegetables at FLOATING MARKETS, where venders sell their produce from boats.

29 The Inuit hunted from KAYAKS made out of driftwood and covered with seal skins.

30 At the National Concrete Canoe Competition engineering students must make A CONCRETE BOAT THAT FLOATS.

31 A QUFFA is a circular riverboat used in Iraq to carry about 20 people. It is made as a tightly woven BASKET OF REEDS covered in tar.

32 Musicians PLAYED FLUTES on ancient Greek WARSHIPS so the rowers could keep time with one another.

33 Sailors who worked on WHALING BOATS that set sail from New England were sometimes called "blubbers" after the word for whale fat.

34 WAR CANOE RACES, a popular sport in Canada, involve 15 paddlers per boat racing in lanes against other teams for up to 1,094 yards (1,000 m).

35 British sailors earned the nickname LIMEYS because they ate limes to WARD OFF SCURVY, a disorder caused by lack of vitamin C.

36 The Maori of New Zealand used STONE TOOLS to make canoes from hollowed trees.

37 Aboriginal people in Australia made boats out of the BARK OF EUCALYPTUS TREES.

38 The novel MOBY-DICK; OR, THE WHALE was INSPIRED BY A REAL BOAT, the *Essex*, that had been attacked and sunk by a sperm whale.

39 Sailing ships often have FEMALE NAMES and, in many cultures, boats are referred to as female. Early ships were often dedicated to goddesses.

40 The *AMERICAN QUEEN*, the largest steamboat ever built, is 418 feet (127 m) long and can hold 436 passengers.

41 The R.M.S. *Titanic* was POWERED BY THREE PROPELLERS that were each as tall as a giraffe!

42 In 2012 a man on a fishing boat FOUND A BOTTLE with a note in it that had been adrift at sea for 99 YEARS.

43 IN ALASKA, crab fishermen wear SURVIVAL SUITS that prevent them from getting hypothermia in the icy cold water.

44 When a ship is first launched, a bottle of champagne is often SMASHED OVER ITS BOW for good luck and safe travel.

45 FIREBOATS are large tugboats equipped with POWERFUL PUMPS that can shoot out streams of water to fight a fire.

46 A LIGHTSHIP is a floating lighthouse that warns passing ships of UNDERWATER HAZARDS, such as sandbars.

47 In 2014, as part of Malaysia Day celebrations, 1,180 boats gathered for the WORLD'S LARGEST PARADE OF BOATS.

48 The FASTEST SPEED anyone has traveled on a boat is 317 miles an hour (510 km/h).

49 The LARGEST FOLDED PAPER BOAT was 33 feet (10 m) long and weighed 60 pounds (27 kg).

50 The record number of WATER-SKIERS pulled behind a single boat is 145.

an ocean-going oil tanker ship

※ YOU HAVE LEARNED **4,764** FACTS

1 Dippin' Dots **ALIEN VANILLA CRUNCH** flavor is green vanilla ice cream topped with chocolate **"SPACE ROCKS."**

2 UFO stands for unidentified flying object. The Mutual UFO Network, which **COLLECTS REPORTS OF UFO SIGHTINGS,** usually receives between 500 and 1,000 sightings every month.

3 In 2013 the U.S. government officially announced that **AREA 51**—an Air Force base located in the Nevada desert—**DOES EXIST** and was used to test spy planes, not UFOs.

4 **"ALIEN" CAN MEAN FOREIGN OR FROM ANOTHER PLANET. ACCORDING TO SOME SPACE ALIEN EXPERTS, ALIENS CAN BE CATEGORIZED INTO THREE MAIN KINDS: GREYS, REPTILIANS, AND NORDICS.**

5 THE MCDONALD'S RESTAURANT IN **ROSWELL, NEW MEXICO, U.S.A.,** IS THE WORLD'S ONLY UFO-THEMED MCDONALD'S.

25 OUT-OF-THIS-WORLD FACTS ABOUT

6 SOME PEOPLE REFER TO THE **STUDY OF UFOs** AS UFOLOGY.

7 Two astronomers from the Carnegie Institution in Washington, D.C., U.S.A., have compiled a list of more than 17,000 **NEARBY STARS** that are likely to have **PLANETS THAT COULD SUPPORT COMPLEX LIFE.**

8

9 The city of Vulcan in Canada wasn't named after the **ALIEN RACE OF VULCANS** from the *Star Trek* TV show and movies, but a **REPLICA OF THE STARSHIP *ENTERPRISE*** can be found outside its visitor center.

10 After the **UFO-SIGHTING** craze of the 1950s and 60s, the **CENTRAL INTELLIGENCE AGENCY (CIA)** announced that most of the sightings were **U-2 SPY PLANES** flying at 60,000 feet (18,288 m).

When the citizens of Green River, Wyoming, U.S.A., started to worry about **ALIENS FROM JUPITER** being hurt when a comet hit the planet in 1994, they **BUILT A SPACEPORT** to welcome them.

11 The English word "alien" comes from the **LATIN WORD** *alienus*, which means **FOREIGN.**

12 FOR ALIEN LIFE TO **CONTACT EARTH,** IT WOULD NEED TO EVOLVE FROM SIMPLE, **ONE-CELLED ORGANISMS** TO COMPLEX LIFE. SCIENTISTS DON'T KNOW HOW EASY IT IS FOR THAT TO HAPPEN.

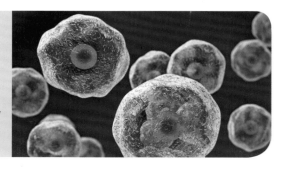

13

Brazilian artist Henrique Alvim Corrêa drew **GIANT ALIEN PODS** on **STILT LEGS** in 1906 to illustrate H. G. Wells's book *The War of the Worlds* about Martians invading Earth.

14

The French National Center for Space Studies (CNES) beamed a television show called *Cosmic Connexion* to a sunlike star that may have **EXTRATERRESTRIAL LIFE.**

15

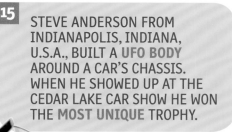

STEVE ANDERSON FROM INDIANAPOLIS, INDIANA, U.S.A., BUILT A **UFO BODY** AROUND A CAR'S CHASSIS. WHEN HE SHOWED UP AT THE CEDAR LAKE CAR SHOW HE WON THE **MOST UNIQUE** TROPHY.

16

American pilots during WWII thought the **MYSTERIOUS BALLS OF LIGHT** that sometimes followed their planes were aliens. It's possible they were seeing **BALL LIGHTNING** or the after-images from explosions.

ALIENS

17

THE OWNER OF THE FARM WHERE THE *TELETUBBIES* TV SHOW WAS FILMED DEMOLISHED THE HILL THAT HOUSED THE LOVABLE ALIENS. SHE WAS TIRED OF FANS **TRESPASSING** ON HER LAND.

18

IN THE 1982 FILM *E.T. THE EXTRA-TERRESTRIAL*, A BOY HELPED A FRIENDLY ALIEN RETURN TO ITS HOME. ACCORDING TO THE FILM'S NOVELIZATION, *"E.T."* IS MORE THAN TEN MILLION YEARS OLD.

19

MANY PEOPLE WHO CLAIM TO HAVE SEEN A UFO ALSO MENTION A VISIT BY **MEN IN BLACK.** THESE STRANGE VISITORS ARE BELIEVED BY CONSPIRACY THEORISTS TO BE **GOVERNMENT SECRET AGENTS.**

20

Dogs strut their stuff catching flying discs at the UFO WORLD CUP SERIES annual event. In a separate challenge, a dog caught a **FLYING DISC** thrown 402 feet (122.5 m).

21

At the **UFO MUSEUM** at Roswell, New Mexico, you can see representations of the **ALIENS** believed to have landed on Earth near the town in July 1947.

22

AT THE ANNUAL ALIEN FESTIVAL IN **ROSWELL** YOU CAN ENTER YOUR PET IN THE **ALIEN COSTUME CONTEST.**

23

Scientists are actively debating whether we should send **SIGNALS INTO SPACE** to try to contact aliens. Some think that could be **DANGEROUS** if the alien civilization is unfriendly.

24

In 1960 astronomer Frank Drake used a **TELESCOPE** at the National Radio Astronomy Observatory in West Virginia, U.S.A., to try to listen to signals from aliens coming from two **SUNLIKE STARS.**

25

Want some beef jerky that tastes like it's from another world? Try some ALIEN FRESH JERKY from a California, U.S.A., company with flavors like BBQ ON THE MOON.

1. A young turkey is called a poult. 2. Of all farm animals, pigs have the stinkiest manure—and the best sense of smell. 3. Chickens will lay eggs even if a rooster is not around. 4. When Abraham Lincoln created the U.S. Department of Agriculture in 1862, 90 out of every 100 Americans was a farmer. 5. Today, just 2 out of every 100 Americans farm. 6. Corn and soybeans are grown on more than half of farmland in the United States. 7. There are 25 billion chickens in the world—more than any other species of bird. 8. Some farmers rent beehives because bees pollinate their crops. 9. One-third of the food that we eat is pollinated by bees and other animals. 10. Animals allowed to roam freely in pastures are called free-range. 11. One acre (0.4 ha) of soybeans can be used to make 82,368 crayons. 12. There are more than 200 breeds of goat. 13. Farmers measure milk by the pound (kg), not the gallon (L), because it's easier to keep track of it that way. 14. Meat from grass-fed cattle has less fat than meat from cattle raised on feedlots. 15. Female chickens are called pullets until they are old enough to lay eggs. Then they are called hens. 16. Eighty percent of the corn grown in the United States is used to feed livestock, not people. 17. Farmers store harvested grain in towering buildings called silos. "Silo" means cellar; the first ones were just pits in the ground. 18. Silos can be dangerous: The air inside can be filled with toxic gases capable of killing a person within minutes. 19. The dust from grain catches fire easily. Sparks or flame near a silo could cause it to explode. 20. Holy cow! A dairy cow eats about 100 pounds (45 kg) of food each day. 21. When viewed from above, fields of crops in the central United States look like green circles. 22. Pigs can get bad sunburns. 23. More than 90 percent of the water you consume each day was used to grow the food you eat. 24. Nearly half of the grains grown in the world are used to feed farm animals. 25. Roosters attract hens by "tidbitting," pretending to pick up food over and over while giving food calls. 26. A dairy cow needs to drink 4.8 gallons (18 L) of water in order to make 1.2 gallons (4.5 L) of milk. 27. "Smart" tractors sense which nutrients are needed in the soil and only add what is needed to fertilize crops. 28. Worldwide, more people drink goat milk than any other kind of milk. 29. Farmers in Japan use remote-control planes to tend hard-to-reach plants. 30. Chickens create a pecking order (show the others who's in charge) by literally pecking at one another. 31. Some farmers use self-driving tractors that follow a path through the fields without needing someone on board to steer. 32. Sheep can recognize human faces (but they're better at recognizing other sheep). 33. Sheep can recognize up to 50 sheep faces, even when seen from the side. 34. Cows that are milked more often make more milk. 35. Combine harvesters cut crop plants, beat them to separate the grains, and clean the grain before storing it in a bin. 36. Farmers have barn cats to cut down on the mice and rats that steal food from livestock. 37. German shepherds were originally bred to protect flocks of sheep. 38. Farmers in the United States tend between two and four million goats. 39. Farmers often plant different crops on a field from one year to the next. This helps keep crop-eating pests from coming back and replenishes nutrients in the soil. 40. The red fleshy wattle beneath a rooster's chin attracts hens. 41. Beans and peas don't need to be fertilized. Their roots have special fungi that do the job for them. 42. "Flerd" combines the words for flock and herd and is used for a group of different species that graze together. 43. Sheep can see almost all the way around without turning their heads. 44. Goat milk changes flavor depending on what the goat has been eating—and even smelling. 45. There are 62 different breeds of chickens. 46. Sheep have a split upper lip that they use to grab leaves when munching on plants. 47. Some farmers use llamas to protect their flocks from predators. 48. Donkeys respond to threats by kicking, biting, slashing, and chasing the intruders away. 49. Pigs don't graze like cows or sheep. Instead they eat just about anything, including meat. 50. Chickens can fly, but not very far. The longest recorded flight lasted a whopping 13 seconds. 51. Roosters don't just crow at dawn—they start even before the sky begins to brighten. 52. Until the 1930s, tractors had metal wheels. 53. When a cow chews its cud, it re-chews food it already swallowed (and brought back up)! 54. About 22 million ducks are raised on farms in the United States each year. 55. As recently as the early 1800s, pigs were allowed to wander the streets of New York City. 56. Goats and sheep have eyes with rectangular pupils. 57. Although there are many breeds of beef cattle, the most common breed in the United States is black angus. 58. An average dairy cow produces 7.1 gallons (27 L) of milk a day. 59. The amount of fleece a sheep grows in one year provides about 8 pounds (3.6 kg) of wool. 60. One pound of wool can make ten miles (16 km) of yarn. 61. A single baseball contains 219

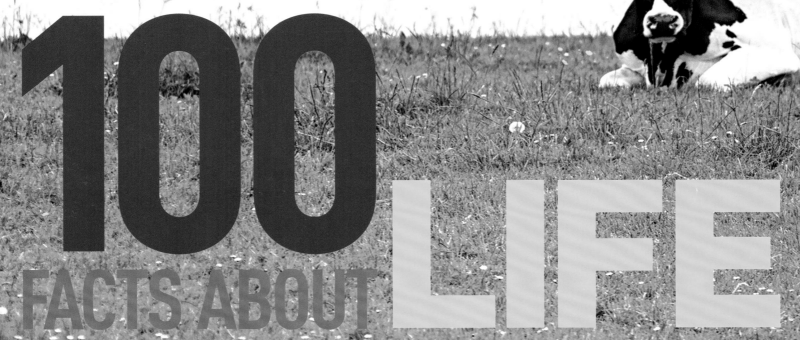

100
FACTS ABOUT LIFE

yards of wool yarn. **62. Chickens, like pigs, eat all kinds of things, from seeds and insects to mice and lizards.** 63. Corn plants can have several ears of corn, but most plants grow just one. **64. Turkeys less than a week old need 16 to 18 hours of sleep each day.** 65. Just 2.5 pounds (1.1 kg) when they are born, piglets double their weight within a week. **66. Most full-grown pigs weigh somewhere between 300 to 700 pounds (135 to 320 kg).** 67. An egg shell can have up to 17,000 tiny holes, or pores, that allow gases like oxygen to move in and out of the egg. **68. About 75 percent of people in the world eat goat meat.** 69. A hen can lay only one egg a day. **70. Male pigs are called boars; females are sows.** 71. Cows at a farm in England are milked by a laser-guided robot, called an "automated milk harvester," that runs 24 hours a day. **72. The cows enter the automated milk harvester on their own when they are ready to be milked.** 73. The milk harvester calculates the amount of milk in a cow's udder before milking. If the cow has less than 2.6 gallons (10 L) of milk, the harvester doesn't milk it. **74. A turkey raised for food weighs twice as much as a wild turkey.** 75. Farm chickens are the many-greats-grandchildren of Asian red jungle fowl. **76. Red jungle fowl weren't chickens' only ancestors. They got their yellow legs from gray jungle fowl.** 77. Sheep milk has lots of calcium and vitamins that makes it great for cheese. **78. Australian cattle dogs herd cattle by gently but firmly nipping at their legs—just hard enough to get the cows to move.** 79. Turkeys and chickens pant when they get too hot. **80. Pigs use their snouts to root in the dirt in search of food.** 81. Alpaca farmers raise these small relatives of llamas for their soft wool. The most common type of alpaca has dense, spongy wool. **82. There are nearly 900 breeds of sheep in the world, about 40 of which can be found in the United States.** 83. One bushel (35 L) of wheat contains one million kernels. Wheat kernels are actually dry fruits, each of which contains a single seed. **84. Farmers can get 40 bushels (1,410 L) of wheat from a single acre of farmland.** 85. Despite a reputation for eating anything, goats are actually fairly picky, going for the best quality food available. Nibbling on cans and shirts is just a sign of curiosity. **86. A duck waterproofs its feathers by rubbing oil from a gland near its tail all over its body. It does this using its head.** 87. Only female ducks quack. **88. Plows (or ploughs) chop up the ground in preparation for planting seeds.** 89. Bird flu is so contagious—and deadly—it can kill 90 to 100 percent of the birds in a flock of chickens in 48 hours. **90. A grain drill, used to plant seeds, does not drill holes for the seeds. It just leaves them in nice, evenly spaced rows.** 91. Farmers that raise livestock can use the poop to fertilize crops. **92. Pigs raised on farms in the United States eat mostly corn. Those raised on European farms eat mostly barley.** 93. Turkeys grow bigger when they are trained to eat many small meals. **94. A cow must have a calf in order to produce milk.** 95. A one-year-old sheep is called a hogget. A two-year-old is called a two-tooth. **96. A typical ear of corn has kernels arranged in 16 rows.** 97. George Washington considered himself first and foremost a farmer. **98. Turkeys raised on farms cannot fly.** 99. Hens turn their eggs up to 50 times a day to prevent the yolk from getting stuck in one spot. **100. President Woodrow Wilson had a flock of sheep that nibbled** the White House lawn to keep the grass trimmed.

ON THE FARM

1. An ancient Babylonian plaque, dating more than 5,000 years ago, shows two figures fighting in a martial arts style.

2. In the early sixth century, a monk named Bodhidharma traveled from India to the Shaolin Temple in the Henan Province, China, and taught martial arts to the Buddhist monks. To many, the Shaolin Temple is the birthplace of kung fu.

3. A martial arts instructor is called a *sensei* or master.

4. The name tae kwon do means "the way of kicking and punching." Tae kwon do has been the national martial art of South Korea since 1955. It is now an international sport.

5. The colored belt ranking system—called *Dan*—in martial arts was first created in the 1880s by Dr. Jigoro Kano for the sport of judo. It was later accepted into karate and tae kwon do.

6. The Japanese word *karate* means "empty hand."

7. **THE FURIOUS FIVE CHARACTERS IN THE MOVIE *KUNG FU PANDA* (TIGRESS, MONKEY, MANTIS, CRANE, AND VIPER) EACH REPRESENT A KUNG FU STYLE BASED ON THE MOVEMENTS OF THAT ANIMAL.**

8. Kendo is based on sword-fighting techniques used by Japanese samurai. Instead of a real sword, participants use a sword made out of bamboo called a *shinai*.

9. Cowabunga! The first *Teenage Mutant Ninja Turtles* comic book written in 1984 is now worth $20,000.

10. Karate originated on the island of Okinawa, Japan, in the 17th century when people were not allowed to carry weapons. They had to learn to fight using their hands, feet, knees, and elbows.

11. Each of the four "benders" on the Nickelodeon cartoon *Avatar: The Last Airbender* were based on actual martial arts styles—Hung Ga, Northern Shaolin, Tai Chi, and Ba Gua Zhang.

12. Elvis Presley had a black belt in karate.

13. Judo was founded by Dr. Jigoro Kano in the 1880s—but its origins come from jujitsu—the technique Japanese samurai used when engaged in hand-to-hand combat.

14. In 1964 judo became the first martial arts to be included in the Olympic Games. In 2000 tae kwon do became the second.

15. In karate, the *gohon nukite* (five-finger, spear-hand punch) is usually delivered to an opponent's face. Ouch!

16. **A TAE KWON DO SPINNING BACK KICK CAN CARRY MORE THAN 1,500 POUNDS (680 KG) OF FORCE.**

17. Capoeira is a form of martial arts that combines kicking, aerobatics, and dance. It originated in Brazil by African slaves who practiced it for self-defense but disguised it from their owners as a dance.

18. In the 2010 movie *The Karate Kid*, the main character, Dre, learns kung fu, not karate.

19. Aikido is used for self-defense—there are no offensive moves. In a competitive version, shodokan aikido, two opponents alternate trying to hit each other with a rubber or wooden knife to earn points.

20. The visual effects team for the movie *Teenage Mutant Ninja Turtles* modeled ninja turtle Donatello's face after Leonard Nimoy, the actor who played Spock in *Star Trek*.

21. A martial artist with a black belt in karate hit a board at a rate of 46 feet (14 m) per second—enough force to break a solid concrete slab.

22. In 2012 a young woman from the Netherlands performed a martial arts jumping front kick that reached 7 feet 8 inches (2.35 m) high.

23. The actor Jason David Frank, who plays Tommy Oliver in the *Mighty Morphin Power Rangers* series, has developed his own form of martial arts that he calls "tose kune do."

24. Russian President Vladimir Putin has a black belt in judo.

25. Before a match, sumo wrestlers raise their legs and stomp down on the ground to scare away any demons. They also throw salt in the air to purify the ring.

26. Muay Thai, the national sport of Thailand, is referred to as the "art of eight limbs" because eight points of contact (hands, elbows, knees, and shins) can be used against an opponent.

27. Ziggy Trixx, a Staffordshire bull terrier from Southend-on-Sea, Essex, England, can ride a skateboard and perform martial arts tricks!

28. "Wushu" is the term used for all the martial arts that originated and developed in China. It standardizes all the different forms and provides a way for practitioners to compete against one another.

29. The martial arts actor Jet Li was vacationing in the Maldives when a tsunami struck the island. After this experience, he created a foundation to help disaster victims.

30. In the 1982 kung fu movie *Dragon Lord*, Jackie Chan shot more than 2,900 takes of one scene trying to get the action just right.

31. Yum! A line of 1,288 noodle bowls, like ones served in Mr. Ping's noodle shop in *Kung Fu Panda*, were placed along a street in Chinatown in London, U.K., to celebrate the 2011 release of *Kung Fu Panda 2*.

32. The 1970s song "Kung Fu Fighting" by Carl Douglas was recorded in just ten minutes. It ended up becoming a hit song that sold ten million copies worldwide.

33. **IN A RESEARCH STUDY, A MUAY THAI MARTIAL ARTIST KICKED THE CHEST OF A CRASH TEST DUMMY WITH THE SAME FORCE AS A CAR TRAVELING AT 35 MILES AN HOUR (56 KM/H).**

34. Ninjas in ancient Japan practiced *yoko aruki*—sideways walking—so their footprints wouldn't reveal which direction they were going.

35. A *ronin* is a Japanese samurai without a master.

36. Eagle claw kung fu focuses on a strong gripping technique and striking an opponent's pressure points, such as their wrist and neck.

37. In just one minute, a tae kwon do practitioner from India kicked 57 plastic cones off two people's heads.

38. In conjunction with the 2014 movie release of *Teenage Mutant Ninja Turtles*, Pizza Hut sold Cheesy Bites Pizza made with topping combinations favored by the "heroes in a half shell."

39. When measured by an accelerometer, a martial arts expert struck an object at a speed of 40 feet (12 m) per second. In comparison, snakes lash out at an average of 8 to 10 feet (2.4 to 3 m) per second.

40. In 2011 martial artists from Maryland, U.S.A., wore LED lights while performing martial arts stunts in a darkened theater—some described the show as *The Karate Kid* meets *Stars Wars*.

41. Michelle Yeoh, a famous female martial arts movie star, was a former ballerina and beauty pageant queen.

42. A sandwich shop in Scotland, U.K., serves the Jackie Chan sandwich—marinated chicken thighs, kimchi, pickled carrot, sprout and cucumber salad with sour cream and lots of hot sauce.

43. Movie star and martial arts expert Bruce Lee developed his own style of kung fu called "jeet kune do."

44. **BRUCE LEE COULD DO A TWO-FINGER PUSH-UP USING JUST HIS THUMB AND FOREFINGER TO HOLD HIM UP.**

45. Martial arts tricking is an extreme sport that combines martial arts kicks, gymnastics flips, and break-dancing moves. It is used in music videos and fight scenes in films.

46. In 1998 filmmakers collaborated with DJs to create *Hop-Fu!*—a live performance where DJs spin hip-hop beats for the sound track to kung fu movies playing on a big screen.

47. In the early 1990s, Hostess sold Teenage Mutant Ninja Turtles pudding pies—green sugar crust with vanilla puddin' power inside!

48 The Asian Games are the second largest multi-sports event after the Olympic Games. It is held every four years and includes the martial arts of judo, wushu, tae kwon do, and karate.

49 Judo has been an official sport of the Paralympic Games since 1988. To become a part of the U.S. team, visually impaired or blind judo athletes must often play against sighted players.

50 The uniform worn in karate is called a *gi*, pronounced "gee"—in tae kwon do it is a *dobok*, pronounced "doh-bohk."

51 POLICE OFFICERS IN JAPAN PRACTICE JUDO AND KENDO AS PART OF THEIR POLICE TRAINING.

52 In the 1998 Disney movie *Mulan*, the scene in which Mulan disarms her enemy using a handheld fan is based on an actual martial arts technique.

53 According to legend, the wing chun style of kung fu was developed in the early 1700s by a female Buddhist nun living at the Shaolin Temple in China.

54 At a ceremony in 2013, 2,000 Chinese students performed a choreographed martial arts display near the Shaolin Temple on Song Shan mountain, in Dengfeng, China.

55 Sir Arthur Conan Doyle's Sherlock Holmes character practiced a form of martial arts called bartitsu—a mix of Japanese jujitsu and boxing developed by E.W. Barton-Wright in England in the early 1900s.

56 A 28-foot (8.55-m)-tall judo uniform was made to celebrate the 2010 Judo World Championships—that's about the same height as five rhinos stacked on top of each other.

57 The drunken monkey style of kung fu imitates the actions of a monkey that has eaten fermented fruit. The wobbling moves are used to surprise an opponent.

58 In kendo, when opponents strike one another they let out a loud shout to focus their mind on the strike.

59 Of the 3,000 people living in Chen Village in rural China, all but 500 practice tai chi. More than 400 years ago, the Chen style of tai chi was founded there.

60 A karate student in Texas, U.S.A., smashed 62 walnuts in one minute using nunchucks—two sticks joined by a short rope or chain.

61 A *TESSEN* IS A FOLDABLE, HANDHELD, IRON FAN USED BY JAPANESE SAMURAI. THE ART OF FIGHTING WITH ONE IS CALLED *TESSENJUTSU*.

62 Some of tai chi's poses include "white crane spreads its wings" and "embrace the tiger and return to the mountain."

63 The flying leaps seen in karate were originally used as tactics to kick enemies off their horses.

64 At a resort in China, visitors can perform kung fu fights over a lake while suspended from a high-tech wiring system.

65 The yellow jumpsuit worn by Bruce Lee in his final movie was sold at an auction in Hong Kong, China, for $100,000.

66 In Chinese lion dance competitions, martial artists have to leap on tall stilts while wearing a heavy lion costume.

67 A video of Claude, the "kung fu bear" at a zoo in Hiroshima, Japan, spinning a five-foot (1.5-m)-long stick has received more than five million views on the Internet.

68 As a part of their training, Shaolin monks must stand on their heads for long periods of time. They also thrust their hands into containers of packed sand to strengthen all their muscles.

69 THE NBC SHOW *AMERICAN NINJA WARRIOR* IS BASED ON THE JAPANESE TELEVISION SHOW *SESUKE*, WHICH HAS ONLY HAD THREE WINNERS AFTER 30 SEASONS ON AIR.

70 Since the 1920s, 40 members of the Gracie family have participated in Brazilian jiu-jitsu—making it the largest family of athletes of different generations in the world.

71 Seventy million people in 188 different countries participate in tae kwon do—making it one of the most popular martial arts in the world.

72 Even though there is no official ranking system in muay Thai, some schools use color-coded armbands to rank students' progress.

73 Kendo participants wear a long pleated skirt called a *hakama*. The hakama has seven pleats to represent the seven samurai virtues: goodwill, honor, courtesy, wisdom, truth, loyalty, and devoutness.

74 RAY PARK, THE ACTOR WHO PLAYED DARTH MAUL IN THE MOVIE *STAR WARS: EPISODE 1—THE PHANTOM MENACE* HAS A BLACK BELT IN WUSHU.

75 In a *shuriken* "ninja throwing-star" contest in Iga, Japan, contestants aim throwing stars at a target 19.7 feet (6 m) away. The top three winners receive a shuriken made out of gold, silver, or bronze.

75 KICKIN' FACTS ABOUT MARTIAL ARTS

35 FESTIVE CELEBRATIONS

1 In German Bavaria, villages celebrate spring by putting up **DECORATED TREE TRUNKS CALLED MAYPOLES.** They also steal maypoles from other villages.

2 During the **BOYEONG MUD FESTIVAL** in South Korea, people **SWIM, SLIDE,** and **WRESTLE** in mud, then kick back and relax to music and fireworks.

3 People in Basel, Switzerland, **DRESS IN MASKS AND COSTUMES** for a three-day Fasnacht celebration that begins **PROMPTLY AT 4:00 A.M.** the day after Ash Wednesday.

4 In Ivrea, Italy, people **CELEBRATE FREEDOM** by reenacting a battle—**BY THROWING ORANGES.**

5 At the **ICE AND SNOW FESTIVAL** in Harbin, China, visitors can walk among **MASSIVE BRIGHTLY COLORED ICE SCULPTURES.**

6 The **COLORFUL FESTIVAL** of Holi in India represents **GOOD OVERCOMING EVIL.**

7 St. Petersburg, Russia, celebrates the summer solstice with the **SCARLET SAILS CELEBRATION,** complete with a red-sailed ship straight out of a Russian fairy tale.

8 **ST. PATRICK'S DAY,** the celebration of all things Irish, was actually **INVENTED IN THE UNITED STATES.**

9 **DRAGON COSTUMES** made to celebrate the Chinese New Year usually have 9, 11, or 13 joints, because **ODD NUMBERS ARE CONSIDERED LUCKY.**

10 During the Hindu festival **DIWALI,** people clean their homes, light clay lamps, and create patterns on the floor using **COLORED SAND.**

11 During the **FIRE FESTIVAL** in Shetland, U.K., 800 men dress as **VIKINGS** and **BURN A SHIP** built just for the occasion, then dance the night away.

12 During the two-day Jarramplas Festival in Piornal, Spain, **PEOPLE PELT COSTUMED CHARACTERS** with as many as 14,000 **TURNIPS.**

13 The night sky is **DOTTED WITH 100,000 to 200,000 LANTERNS,** not stars, during the Pingxi Sky Lantern Festival in Taiwan.

14
During the Jewish holiday of **PURIM**, people eat triangle-shaped **COOKIES**, hold beauty **CONTESTS**, and perform **PLAYS**.

15
Two million people visit the **SAPPORO SNOW FESTIVAL** in Japan each year.

16
DRUMMERS KEEP THE BEAT as their canoes glide among **THOUSANDS OF MEN NETTING FISH** during the Argungu Fishing Festival in Nigeria.

AROUND THE WORLD

Rio de Janeiro Carnival, Brazil

17
During the Balls of Fire celebration in El Salvador, people **THROW FLAMING BALLS OF CLOTH AT ONE ANOTHER**, in memory of a past volcanic eruption.

18
Long ago, Norwegians believed witches would **STEAL BROOMS TO RIDE** on Christmas Eve. People still **HIDE ALL THE BROOMS** in the house before going to bed on Christmas Eve.

19
During the Japanese festival of **HADAKA MATSURI**, men wearing only loincloths **COMPETE FOR A PAIR OF SACRED STICKS**.

20
People fling **MUDDY RAGS** and **FIRE ANTS** at passersby during the Entroida festival in Galicia, Spain. Tradition says that **CAUSING DISCOMFORT** purifies participants' souls.

21
On Guy Fawkes Day, British people light **BONFIRES** and fireworks and make **"GUYS"**—crudely made effigies of historical bad-guy Guy Fawkes—to burn.

22
Every November, young German children celebrate the **LANTERN FESTIVAL** by making lanterns and **PARADING** through town with their **BEACONS OF LIGHT**.

23
People play a snowy version of **HUMAN FOOSBALL** at the **FROZEN DEAD GUY DAYS** celebration in Nederland, Colorado, U.S.A.

24
People in **THAILAND** wash away the old year with **SCENTED WATER**. Ceremonial **ELEPHANTS** spray water during the three-day Songkran **NEW YEAR'S FESTIVAL**.

25
On **CHILDREN'S DAY**, the Turkish president, prime minister, and other politicians **TURN THEIR JOBS OVER TO CHILDREN** to celebrate the fact that children are the future.

26
EEYORE may have been a mopey donkey in the *Winnie-the-Pooh* series, but people in Austin, Texas, U.S.A., throw a **BIG BASH** to celebrate his **BIRTHDAY** each spring.

27
At the Cheung Chau Bun Festival in Hong Kong, **PEOPLE SCALE 60-FOOT (18-M) TOWERS OF BUNS**, trying to grab as many lucky ones as possible.

28
Mexicans **MAKE SKULLS OUT OF SUGAR** and decorate them with colorful icing as part of their **DAY OF THE DEAD** celebration.

29
For three days, Muslims **SHARE FEASTS AND SWEET TREATS** to celebrate the end of their month of fasting, called **RAMADAN**.

30
During the festival of San Fermín, **PEOPLE RUN ALONGSIDE BULLS** through the streets of Pamplona, Spain.

31
Until the Moose Dropping Festival got too large, people in Talkeetna, Alaska, U.S.A., **BAKED AND VARNISHED MOOSE DROPPINGS** before using them in various **GAMES**.

32
At the Australian **TUNARAMA FESTIVAL**, people **TOSS WHOLE TUNA FISH** to see how far they will go.

33
In the Festival of **NEAR-DEATH EXPERIENCES** in Las Nieves, Spain, people who have almost died are **CARRIED AROUND IN COFFINS**.

34
The **CARNIVAL IN RIO DE JANEIRO**, Brazil, is the biggest pre-Lent celebration in the world, with more than **HALF A MILLION** foreigners joining the locals each year.

35
People in Caracas, Venezuela, **ROLLER-SKATE TO CHURCH** during the two weeks before Christmas. Streets are even **CLOSED TO TRAFFIC** to let everyone through!

FACT

5,000

ABOUT
100,000,000,000,000
INTESTINAL MICROORGANISMS
HELP YOU DIGEST
YOUR FOOD,
WHILE ABOUT
100,000,000,000
brain cells help
you digest
the facts
in this
BOOK.

BEHIND THE
FAcTS

Just how did we get **5,000** awesome facts about everything into this book? First, we came up with a list of the coolest stuff there is—stuff we knew kids would really care about. Like ugly animals and popcorn. Rockets, eggs, and teeth. Superheroes. Mega-vehicles. Bubble gum. Everything. Then we looked at how to fit the most facts about all this cool stuff on the pages of this book. Some of the subjects have 15 facts. Some have 25. Some even have 100! We carefully researched each and every fact to make sure it's absolutely true. And we illustrated and designed the pages so well that you'll never get bored looking at them. Then we added up all the facts with the fact ticker to get to 5,000. It didn't take 5,000 people to make this awesome book—but it did take a crew of writers, a gang of editors and photo editors, and a slew of designers—the most awesome book team around!

ILLUSTRATION CREDiTS

CO: Corbis; DR: Dreamstime; GI: Getty Images; SS: Shutterstock

COVER: (UP LE), Jagodka/SS; (UP RT), Curtis Johnson/GI; (CTR LE), StevenRussellSmithPhotos/SS; (LO LE), OlegDoroshin/SS; (LO RT), evantravels/SS; (LO CTR), M. Unal Ozmen/SS; Back Cover (UP LE), ericfoltz/GI/iStockphoto; (UP RT), GI; (LO RT), Anna Kucherova/SS

INTERIOR: 1 (CTR), Arnaud Weisser/DR; 2-3 (Background), Andrey Armyagov/SS; 4 (UP), Ginosphotos/DR; 5 (LO), Dlrz4114/DR; 5 (UP), Len Green/DR; 6-7 (Background), Matthias Kulka/CO; 8-9 (Background), Supparuj Taechatanont/DR; 8 (LO), Olga Buiacova/DR; 8 (CTR), Reuters/CO; 8 (UP), Roger-Viollet/TopFoto; 9 (UP), Christopher Elwell/DR; 9 (CTR), Ints Vikmanis/DR; 9 (LO), Pavol Kmeto/DR; 10-11 (Background), Huguette Roe/DR; 12-13 (Background), Roman Krochuk/DR; 12 (LO), Aurinko/DR; 12 (UP), Bigrock/DR; 13 (CTR LE), Tischenko Irina/SS; 13 (UP), MarcelClemens/SS; 13 (LO LE), Chilkoot/DR; 13 (LO RT), Sergey Kichigin/DR; 13 (CTR RT), Kirkgeisler/DR; 14-15 (Background), Thomas Barrat/SS; 16-17 (Background), Achimdiver/SS; 16 (UP), Kjersti Joergensen/DR; 16 (LO), Flip Nicklin/Minden Pictures/CO; 17 (CTR), Konstantinos Moraitis/DR; 17 (LO), Bennymarty/DR; 17 (UP LE), Volodymyr Sergeiev/DR; 17 (UP RT), Ivkovich/DR; 18 (1), Ahmet Gündogan/DR; 18 (2), Subbotina/DR; 18 (3), Michael Jenner/Robert Harding; 18 (4), The Granger Collection/TopFoto; 18 (6), Jevgenija Pigozne/Robert Harding; 18 (7), Jrtmedia/DR; 18 (8), Ttatty/DR; 18 (9), David Wood/DR; 18 (10), Sebalos/DR; 18 (11), Davidmartyn/DR; 18 (CTR LE), Falk66/DR; 18 (CTR RT), Sergio Alejandro Rodriguez Hernández/DR; 19 (12), Aleksander Kovaltchuk/DR; 19 (13), Amattel/DR; 19 (14), Rodrigo Reyes Marin/AFLO/Nippon News/CO; 19 (15), Clark Sorensen; 19 (18), NASA/Science Photo Library; 19 (20), Gave White/GI; 19 (22), Tifonimages/DR; 19 (23), Dean Bertoncelj/SS; 19 (24), underworld/SS; 19 (CTR), Les Palenik/DR; 20 (CTR LE), irin-k/SS; 20 (UP), Aetmeister/DR; 20 (LO), Iryna Rasko/DR; 20-21 (CTR), Anders Ryman/CO; 20 (CTR RT), VOISIN/phanie/Phanie Sarl/CO; 21 (LO), Kenshin2/DR; 21 (CTR), Jamesbox/DR; 21 (UP), Catherine Karnow/CO; 23 (Background), Dhoxax/SS; 24 (UP RT), brackish_nz/SS; 24 (CTR), Emilia Stasiak/DR; 24 (LO), Alberto Dubini/DR; 24 (UP LE), Kelvintt/DR; 24-25 (Background), Maxim Golubchikov/DR; 25 (CTR), Jeff Schultes/DR; 25 (UP), Shawn Hempel/DR; 25 (LO), Svetlana Foote/DR; 26 (UP), Steve Bower/SS; 28-29 (Background), Sakarin Sawasdinaka/SS; 28 (LO LE), Photographerlondon/DR; 28 (LO RT), Eun Jin Ping Audrey/DR; 28 (UP LE), Selensergen/DR; 28 (UP RT), Srlee2/DR; 29 (UP), Ernst Daniel Scheffler/DR; 30 (2), The Granger Collection/TopFoto; 30 (3), Elkeflorida/DR; 30 (4), Michael Dykstra/DR; 30 (5), Cheryl Forbes/GI; 30 (7), Bruce Jenkins/DR; 30 (10), Angelo Merendino/CO; 30 (12), Samson Kwong; 30 (CTR), Putu Gede Putrayasa/DR; 31 (13), Subbotina/DR; 31 (14), Jim Bennett/CO; 31 (15), Khellon/DR; 31 (16), Lee Snider/DR; 31 (17), Fotofermer/DR; 31 (18), Lana Langlois/DR; 31 (20), Oliver Suckling/DR; 31 (22), Erica Schroeder/DR; 31 (25), Igorr/DR; 32 (UP), Rares Pulbere/DR; 32-33 (CTR), Travelstock44/LOOK/Robert Harding; 32 (LO), Aurora Photos/Robert Harding; 33 (UP), Radin Myroslav/SS; 33 (LO), Joe McBride/CO; 34-35 (Background), Kristian Bell/DR; 36 (LO RT), Graphic Compressor/SS; 36 (UP LE), Dimbar76/DR; 36 (UP RT), Jorg Hackemann/DR; 36-37 (Background), Mikephotos/DR; 36 (LO LE), Lebrecht Authors/Lebrecht Music & Arts/CO; 37 (UP), Sovfoto/GI; 37 (LO), Dean Conger/CO; 38-39 (Background), photolinc/SS; 38 (LO), Dave Bredeson/DR; 40 (CTR), Horia Vlad Bogdan/DR; 40 (LO RT), Dennis Dolkens/DR; 40 (UP), Sofiaworld/DR; 40 (LO LE), Serg_dibrova/DR; 40-41 (Background), Agap13/DR; 41 (UP), CM Dixon/Heritage Images/TopFoto; 41 (LO RT), Basslinegfx/DR; 41 (LO LE), Werner Forman/GI; 42 (1), Isselee/DR; 42 (2), Eric Isselee/SS; 42 (3), Janossy Gergely/SS; 42 (4), Karelgallas/DR; 42 (6), Gerard Lacz/Okapia/Robert Harding; 42 (7), Eric Isselee/SS; 42 (9), Treviso Photography/SS; 42 (10), r.classen/SS; 42 (11), Vrabelpeter1/DR; 43 (14), Arthur Franklin/DR; 43 (15), C. Johnson/Still Pictures/Robert Harding; 43 (16), Hotshotsworldwide/DR; 43 (17), Brandon Seidel/DR; 43 (19), Mikelane45/DR; 43 (20), Jaime Chirinos/Science Photo Library; 43 (21), Inga Locmele/SS; 43 (22), Hotshotsworldwide/DR; 43 (24), Anekoho/DR; 43 (25), Jeffreystudio/DR; 44 (LO), Corey A. Ford/DR; 44-45 (CTR), George Tiedemann/CO; 44 (CTR), Matauw/DR; 44 (CTR), Joseph Gough/DR; 45 (UP), Tomas Griger/DR; 45 (CTR), Mark Thiessen/National Geographic Creative/CO; 45 (LO), Aleksandr Stennikov/DR; 46-47 (Background), Ipadimages/DR; 48 (UP), Julie Clopper/SS; 48 (CTR), Edyta Pawlowska/DR; 48-49 (Background), antpkr/SS; 48 (LO), Alan Root/Okapia/Robert Harding; 49 (UP), Andrey Davidenko/DR; 49 (LO), Selenka/DR; 50 (UP), Steve Collender/SS; 50 (LO), Johnfoto/DR; 50-51 (Background), Vlad Limir Berevoianu/DR; 51 (CTR LE), Brent Hathaway/DR; 51 (UP), Flynt/DR; 51 (CTR RT), Sheila Fitzgerald/SS; 51 (LO), Murray Cooper/Minden Pictures/CO; 52 (UP), Somchai Rak-in/DR; 54 (LO), Andreevaee/DR; 54 (UP), Jon Helgason/DR; 54 (Background), David Lomax/Robert Harding; 54-55 (Background), Tomas Griger/DR; 55 (CTR), Gaja/DR; 55 (LO), Copora/DR; 55 (UP), Alfredo Dagli Orti/The Art Archive/CO; 56 (1), James Davidson/DR; 56 (3), Wim van Egmond/Visuals Unlimited/CO; 56 (4), Darrenw/DR; 56 (5), Sonke Johnsen/Visuals Unlimited/CO; 56 (6), Norbert Wu/Minden Pictures; 56 (7), Laurent Laveder/Science Photo Library; 56 (9), Richard Mcmillin/DR; 56 (11), John Wollwerth/SS; 56 (12), Visuals Unlimited/CO; 57 (13), Jurgen Freund/Nature Picture Library/CO; 57 (14), Doug Perrine/Nature Picture Library/CO; 57 (15), Dmitry Zhukov/DR; 57 (16), Norbert Wu/Science Faction/CO; 57 (19), Catmando/SS; 57 (21), Norbert Wu/Minden Pictures/CO; 57 (22), British Antarctic Survey/Science Photo Library; 57 (23), Thomas Marent/Minden Pictures/CO; 58 (LO), OlegDoroshin/SS; 58-59 (CTR), urbanbuzz/SS; 58 (UP), Gabe Ginsberg/GI; 59 (UP), Gabe Ginsberg/GI; 59 (LO), Bo Li/DR; 60 (CTR), Pat Doyle/CO; 62 (CTR), Konstantin Markov/DR; 62 (LO LE), Leisuretime70/DR; 62 (LO RT), Nanantachoke/DR; 62 (UP LE), Ron Chapple/DR; 62 (UP RT), TMarchev/DR; 62-63 (Background), Lane Erickson/Dreamstime; 63 (CTR RT), Dan Van Den Broeke/Dreamstime; 63 (LO), Alexandr Mitiuc/Dreamstime; 63 (UP RT), Rodriguesjo/Dreamstime; 63 (CTR LE), YONHAP/epa/Corbis;; 64-65 (Background), Ginosphotos/DR; 66 (LO LE), oksana2010/SS; 66 (UP RT), Vinicius Tupinamba/SS; 66 (LO RT), Nevinates/DR; 66 (UP LE), Elena Elisseeva/DR; 66-67 (Background), bitt24/SS; 67 (CTR), Ilyarexi/DR; 67 (UP), Margouillat/DR; 67 (LO), Anick Kiskas/SS; 68 (2), Joseph Sohm/SS; 68 (4), Benkrut/DR; 68 (5), James L. Amos/CO; 68 (6), catwalker/SS; 68 (7), Vaynerbrother/DR; 68 (8), CO; 68 (9), James L. Amos/CO; 68 (10), Julia Gatewood/DR; 68 (12), 2003 Topham Picturepoint/TopFoto; 68 (13), The Granger Collection/TopFoto; 69 (14), World History Archive/TopFoto; 69 (15), rck_953/SS; 69 (16), The Granger Collection/TopFoto; 69 (17), The Granger Collection/TopFoto; 69 (18), Kulsawasd Sawasdee/DR; 69 (19), Margiew/DR; 69 (21), The Granger Collection/TopFoto; 69 (22), James L. Amos/CO; 69 (24), NAWROCKI/Classic-Stock/TopFoto; 69 (CTR RT), Rambleon/DR; 70 (CTR), Irina Kozhemyakina/DR; 70 (LO), Hotshotsworldwide/DR; 70 (LO), Derek Holzapfel/DR; 70 (UP), Cary Kalscheuer/SS; 70-71 (CTR), Jones/Shimlock-Secret Sea Visions/Photodisc/Ocean/CO; 71 (LO), Jim Hughes/DR; 71 (CTR), Francofirpo/DR; 72-73 (Background), Suranga Weeratunga/DR; 74-75 (Background), Lanaufoto/DR; 74 (LO LE), Arthur Morris/CO; 74 (LO RT), Gordon Wiltsie/GI; 74 (UP LE), Irochka/DR; 74 (UP RT), TopFoto; 75 (CTR), Exinocactus/DR; 75 (LO), Daisy Gilardini/GI; 75 (UP), Marketa Jirouskova/GI; 76 (LO), Scanrail/DR; 77 (CTR), Sebalos/DR; 78 (UP), The Granger Collection/TopFoto; 78 (CTR), Nico Smit/DR; 78 (LO), Nastiakru/DR; 78-79 (Background), mkrberlin/SS; 79 (LO), Tsekhmister/DR; 79 (UP), Johan63/DR; 80 (2), CO; 80 (6), Dimaberkut/DR; 80 (9), Halil I. Inci/DR; 80 (11), Tatiana Belova/DR; 81 (12), Wrangler/DR; 81 (13), Salih Külcü/DR; 81 (15), Vladimirnenezic/DR; 81 (16), Bruce Chambers/ZUMA Press/CO; 81 (21), Kim Kulish/CO; 81 (22), Ford Prefect/SS; 81 (23), mrfiza/SS; 81 (25), Nikkytok/DR; 82-83 (CTR), Petra Wegner/Nature Picture Library/CO; 82 (UP), Dante Fenolio/Science Photo Library; 82 (CTR), Tom McHugh/Science Photo Library; 82 (CTR), Kjersti Joergensen/SS; 83 (LO), NASA/Science Photo Library; 83 (UP), Frans Lanting/Robert Harding; 84-85 (Background), Ixuskmitl/DR; 86 (CTR), Oksun70/DR; 86-87 (Background), James Balog/GI; 86 (LO), Andrey_Kuzmin/SS; 86 (UP), Blend Images/SS; 87 (UP), NBC NewsWire/GI; 87 (LO), Imaginechina/CO; 87 (CTR), Claudio Divizia/SS; 88 (LO), Wolf/CO; 90 (CTR), Chingyunsong/DR; 90 (LO), Lance Bellers/DR; 90 (UP), Viorel Dudau/DR; 90-91 (Background), Søren Sielemann/DR; 91 (UP), Iuyeaa/DR; 91 (LO), Vitalii Nesterchuk/SS; 92 (2), 2003 Charles Walker/TopFoto; 92 (4), Anthony Brown/DR; 92 (5), Alexandre Fagundes De Fagundes/DR; 92 (8), The Granger Collection/TopFoto; 92 (9), Ann Ronan Picture Library/HIP/TopFoto; 92 (10), Dave Bredeson/DR; 93 (11), Evgeny Baranov/DR; 93 (13), Fine Art Images/HIP/TopFoto; 93 (15), The Granger Collection/TopFoto; 93 (17), Halpand/DR; 93 (20), Oksanabratanova/DR; 93 (25), British Library Board/TopFoto; 94-95 (CTR), Lindsay Hebberd/CO; 94 (LO), Thomas Peter/Reuters/CO; 94 (UP), Eugene Berman/SS; 95 (CTR LE), Alexander Popov/DR; 95 (LO), Igor Dolgov/DR; 95 (UP), Artzzz/DR; 95 (CTR RT), Tobias Arhelger/SS; 96-97 (Background), Jack.Q/SS; 98 (UP LE), Viter8/DR; 98 (UP RT), Charles Melton/Visuals Unlimited/CO; 98-99 (Background), Juriah Mosin/SS; 99 (CTR), Steve Mann/DR; 99 (UP), Gsrethees/DR; 99 (LO), Keith Tarrier/SS; 100 (Background), Leonid Andronov/DR; 100 (LO), Rusu Eugen Catalin/DR; 102-103 (Background), Kts/DR; 102 (CTR), Tyler Olson/DR; 102 (LO), Photographerv8/DR; 102 (UP LE), Dimakp/DR; 102 (UP RT), Homydesign/DR; 103 (LO), Jose Antonio Nicoli/DR; 103 (UP), 145/Carl Pendle/Ocean/CO; 104 (1), Topham Picturepoint/TopFoto; 104 (3), Monika Graff/The Image Works/TopFoto; 104 (5), Lana Stem/SS; 104 (7), TopFoto; 104 (11), The Granger Collection/TopFoto; 105 (14), The Granger Collection/TopFoto; 105 (17), Norman Chan/DR; 105 (19), World History Archive/TopFoto; 105 (25), United Archives/TopFoto; 106 (LO), Jason Lee/Reuters/CO; 106 (CTR), World History Archive/TopFoto; 106-107 (UP), Fumio Okada/Robert Harding; 106 (UP), Richard Cummins/GI; 107 (CTR), Lee Snider/DR; 107 (UP), Eugenesergeev/DR; 107 (LO), Lee Snider Photo Images/SS; 108-109 (Background), Merlin74/SS; 110 (LO), Dejan Vekic/DR; 110-111 (Background), Ivonne Wierink/SS; 110 (CTR), Ruth Black/SS; 110 (UP), M. Unal Ozmen/SS; 111 (LO), Imagestore/DR; 111 (UP RT), Boarding1now/DR; 111 (UP LE), Sheila Fitzgerald/SS; 112-113 (Background), Skylines/SS; 114 (LO), Liuqf/DR; 114 (UP RT), Amwu/DR; 114 (UP LE), Sandro Vannini/CO; 115 (UP), Philip Gould/CO; 115 (CTR), Kamonrat/SS; 115 (Background), Norbert Probst/Robert Harding; 116 (1), Colette Masson/Roger-Viollet/TopFoto; 116 (7), Topham Picturepoint/TopFoto; 116 (9), Frank Oppermann/SS; 117 (11), Sebastian Kaulitzki/SS; 117 (12), Jake Warga/CO; 117 (13), Henrik Sorensen/GI; 117 (15), The Granger Collection/TopFoto; 117 (17), World History Archive/TopFoto; 117 (19), Photoshot/TopFoto; 117 (20), Dave Bredeson/DR; 117 (22), Jeff Corwin/GI; 117 (25), Jeff Corwin/GI; 118-119 (CTR), Charles O'Rear/CO; 118 (UP), 2004 Fortean/TopFoto; 118 (LO), 2004 The Image Works/TopFoto; 119 (UP), Richard Baker/CO; 119 (LO), National Pictures/TopFoto; 120 (UP), Michael Flippo/DR; 120 (LO), Topham Picturepoint/TopFoto; 120-121 (Background), David Lomax/Robert Harding; 121 (CTR), Steve Kaufman/CO; 121 (UP), Eric Gaillard/Reuters/CO; 121 (LO), DEA/A. Dagli Orti/GI; 122 (UP), Serkan Yıldırım/DR; 122 (LO), Radius Images/CO; 124 (LO), Valentina Razumova/DR; 124 (UP), Dmitrii Kiselev/DR; 124-125 (Background), Songquan Deng/SS; 124 (CTR), Lebendkulture/SS; 125 (LO), Dan Heighton/DR; 125 (UP), Jimbophotoart/DR; 125 (CTR), 2004 UPP/TopFoto; 126 (CTR), Alexander Levchenko/DR; 126 (LO LE), Artur Marciniec/DR; 126 (LO RT), Paisan Homhuan/SS; 126 (UP), 2ndpic/DR; 127 (Background), TTstudio/SS; 127 (LO), Nomadsoul1/DR; 127 (UP), Ognyan Chobanov/DR; 128 (1), The Granger Collection/TopFoto; 128 (4), World History Archive/TopFoto; 128 (6), Piyathep/DR; 128 (7), robertharding/CO; 128 (8), The Granger Collection/TopFoto; 128 (11), Stefano Bianchetti/CO; 128 (12), The Granger Collection/TopFoto; 129 (14), Leemage/GI; 129 (15), Robert Miller/DR; 129 (20), Gavran333/DR; 129 (18), Asian Art & Archaeology, Inc./CO; 129 (21), Leemage/GI; 129 (23), David S. Holloway/GI; 130 (UP), Louie Psihoyos/CO; 130 (LO), Jaime Chirinos/Science Photo Library; 130-131 (CTR), Source/NGS Archives; 131 (LO), Jose Antonio PE—AS/Science Photo Library; 131 (UP), Roger Harris/Science Photo Library; 132-133 (Background), Milind Ketkar/DR; 133 (LO), Timplaru Constantin Razvan/DR; 134-135 (Background), Aspen Photo/SS; 134 (LO), Lisa Mckown/DR; 134 (UP), Borislav Bajkic/DR; 135 (UP LE), Chen Ws/SS; 135 (LO), Robert Fullerton/DR; 135 (UP RT), Reuters/CO; 136 (Background), Don Heiny/CO; 138-139 (Background), Lonely/SS; 138 (LO), Peter Endig/dpa/CO; 138 (UP), Lee Celano/Reuters/CO; 139 (LO RT), 2005 TopFoto; 139 (CTR), Scanrail/DR; 139 (LO LE), Lindsey Parnaby/epa/CO; 139 (UP LE), Henning Kaiser/dpa/CO; 140 (1), TopFoto; 140 (3), Digitalstormcinema/DR; 140 (5), Oleksii Lukin/DR; 140 (6), National Pictures/TopFoto; 140 (8), Silver Screen Collection/GI; 140 (10), TopFoto; 141 (12), Fototeca Storica Nazionale/GI; 141 (13), Rafael Ben-ari/DR; 141 (16), Topham Picturepoint/TopFoto; 141 (17), Edith Layland/DR; 141 (20), Lindsey Parnaby/epa/CO; 141 (21), The Granger Collection/TopFoto; 141 (22), The Granger Collection/TopFoto; 142 (UP), Bambi L. Dingman/DR; 142 (CTR), Paper Rodeo/CO; 142 (LO), Richard T. Nowitz/CO; 142-143 (CTR), Paul Kline/GI; 143 (CTR), Pete Niesen/SS; 143 (UP), Joe Belanger/SS; 143 (LO), Fredrik Von Erichsen/epa/CO; 144-145 (Background), maodesign/GI; 146-147 (Background), Kathy Kay/SS; 146 (CTR), kzww/SS; 146 (LO), Kjersti Joergensen/SS; 146 (UP LE), Mor3no/DR; 146 (UP RT), Michael Ansell/DR; 147 (LO), Vivilweb/DR; 147 (UP), Mike2focus/DR; 148 (UP), simone mescolini/SS; 150 (CTR), Nikolai Sorokin/DR; 150 (LO), Danny Smythe/DR; 150 (UP), Janian Mcmillan/DR; 150-151 (Background), Dean Lewins/epa/CO; 151 (LO), Brian Pohorylo/Icon SMI/CO; 151 (UP), Christopher Morris/CO; 152-153 (Background), JaySi/SS; 152 (CTR), Naluphoto/DR; 152 (LO), Ikonoklastfotografie/DR; 152 (UP), Bruno Rosa/DR; 153 (LO), Andreanita/DR; 153 (UP), Porbital/DR; 154 (1), Stbernardstudio/DR; 154 (3), Peternile/DR; 154 (4), LauraD/SS; 154 (6), Reuters/CO; 154 (8), Volodymyr Byrdyak/DR; 154 (9), Tom Wang/DR; 154 (10), Izanbar/DR; 155 (11), Alessandro Pinna/DR; 155 (13), Mirkorosenau/DR; 155 (19), Corey A. Ford/DR; 155 (20), Jamesbox/DR; 155 (21), Litton Entertainment/Splash News/CO; 155 (22), Lawson Wood/CO; 155 (24), Brian J. Skerry/CO; 155 (25), Luca Santilli/DR; 156 (UP), Moviestore/Rex Features; 156-157 (CTR), Peter Lovás/DR; 156 (LO), The Granger Collection, New York/TopFoto; 157 (UP), Richard Thomas/DR; 157 (LO), Karen Kasmauski/Science Faction/CO; 157 (CTR), Penguin Random House; 158-159 (Background), Brett Critchley/DR; 160 (LO), The Granger Collection/TopFoto; 160 (UP), 2000 Topham Picturepoint/TopFoto; 160 (LO), World History Archive/TopFoto; 160-161 (Background), kriangkrai wangjai/SS; 161 (UP), The Granger Collection/TopFoto; 161 (CTR), The Granger Collection/TopFoto; 162 (LO RT), Dmitry Ezepov/DR; 162 (UP), Ken Backer/DR; 162-163 (Background), Africa Studio/SS; 162 (LO LE), cdrin/SS; 163 (LO), Lebedinski/DR; 163 (LO), Lebedinski/DR; 163 (UP), Mark Large/ANL/Rex Features; 164 (1), Aaron Kohr/DR; 164 (3), Alexander Kharchenko/DR; 164 (4), Olga Popova/DR; 164 (6), NASA/Bryan Allen/CO; 164 (8), Ghadel/DR; 164 (9), Roger Ressmeyer/CO; 164 (10), Dave Yoder/National Geographic Creative/CO; 164 (11), STScI/NASA/CO; 165 (12), Steve Nagy/Design Pics/CO; 165 (17), Corey Ford/Stocktrek Images/CO; 165 (20), Fatmanphotography/DR; 165 (22), Nora Good/Masterfile/CO; 165 (25), Dr. Seth Shostak/Science Photo Library; 166 (CTR), Pamela Mcadams/DR; 166 (LO), Photodeti/DR; 166 (UP), Michiko Ishida/DR; 166-167 (Background), Matthew Benoit/SS; 167 (LO), Ksena2009/DR; 167 (UP), Isselee/DR; 168 (UP), CO; 168 (LO), The Granger Collection/TopFoto; 168-169 (CTR), The Granger Collection/TopFoto; 169 (LO), Louie Psihoyos/CO; 169 (UP), Louie Psihoyos/CO; 170-171 (Background), Nomadsoul1/DR; 172 (LO), Thomaspajot/DR; 172 (UP), Leemage/CO; 172-173 (Background), Roger-Viollet/TopFoto; 172 (CTR), Miriam & Ira D. Wallach Division of Art, Prints & Photographs/New York Public Library/Science Photo Library; 173 (CTR), Smileus/DR; 173 (LO), Anna Kucherova/DR; 173 (UP), World History Archive/TopFoto; 174 (LO), Andrey Pavlov/DR; 174 (UP), Andrey Pavlov/DR; 176 (LO), Sergey Skleznev/DR; 176 (UP LE), Gary Blakeley/DR; 176 (UP RT), Cory Richards/National Geographic Creative/CO; 176-177 (Background), Williamju/DR; 177 (LO), Alanmc/DR; 177 (UP), WireImage/GI; 178 (2), Adfoto/DR; 178 (4), Wrangel/DR; 178 (5), Attila Jandi/DR; 178 (6), Rafael Ben-ari/DR; 178 (9), Demerzel21/DR; 178 (10), Susana Machicao/DR; 178 (11), Batuque/DR; 179 (13), Photojogtom/DR; 179 (15), Ricardo Martinez/RooM the Agency/CO; 179 (17), Daniel Raustadt/DR; 179 (18), Mgkuijpers/DR; 179 (21), Kevin Dunleavy/DR; 179 (22), Natalija Berg/DR; 179 (24), Eduardo Gonzalez Diaz/DR; 179 (25), Christophe Dupont Elise/Icon SMI/CO; 180 (CTR), Percent/DR; 180 (UP), Blackslide/DR; 180 (LO), Nik Wheeler/CO; 180-181 (CTR), Buena Vista Images/GI; 181 (CTR), Neil Bradfield/DR; 181 (LO), Sarah2/DR; 181 (UP), Catz/SS; 182-183 (Background), Christian Bertrand/DR; 184 (UP LE), Dundja/DR; 184-185 (Background), Paul McKinnon/SS; 184 (UP RT), Gamma-Rapho/GI; 184 (LO), Wojtek Buss/Robert Harding; 185 (CTR), Plottyphoto/DR; 185 (LO), Albertoloyo/DR; 185 (UP), Afagundes/DR; 186-187 (Background), Briancweed/DR; 188 (UP), Monika Wisniewska/DR; 188-189 (Background), Science Picture Co./CO; 189 (CTR RT), Dule964/DR; 189 (UP LE), Nevinates/DR; 189 (CTR LE), MorganOliver/DR; 189 (LO), Minden Pictures/GI; 190 (1), Dino Vournas/Reuters/CO; 190 (2), Jamie Cross/DR; 190 (3), Jonathan Blair/Royal BC Museum/CO; 190 (4), Jonathan Blair/Royal BC Museum/CO; 191 (7), Sergey Kelin/DR; 190 (9), Paul Topp/DR; 190 (10), Frank Sommariva/imageBROKER/CO; 191 (11), Georgios Kollidas/DR; 191 (14), actionplus sports images/TopFoto; 191 (16), Linncurrie/DR; 191 (18), Kguzel/DR; 191 (19), Kevin Schafer/CO; 191 (20), adoc-photos/CO; 191 (22), Chenp/DR; 191 (24), Peter Van Dam/DR; 191 (25), Sean Pavone/DR; 192 (CTR), Leonidikan/DR; 192 (UP), Isselee/DR; 192 (LO), Mark Raycroft/Minden Pictures/CO; 192-193 (CTR), Esben Hansen/DR; 193 (LO), Mdorottya/DR; 193 (UP), Larisa Lofitskaya/DR; 193 (CTR), Srohmeyer/Animal Planet/Splash/Splash News/CO; 194-195 (Background), Stephen B. Goodwin/SS; 196 (LO), Brackishnewzealand/DR; 196 (UP), The Gallery Collection/CO; 196-197 (Background), Mihai-Bogdan Lazar/SS; 197 (LO), Robwilson39/DR; 197 (UP RT), CO; 197 (UP LE), John Sanford & David Parker/Science Photo Library; 198 (CTR), Idambeer/DR; 198 (LO), Nivi/DR; 198 (UP), Videowokart/DR; 198-199 (Background), Ivan Mateev/SS; 198 (UP), Videowokart/DR; 199 (LO), Daniel Schoenen/Daniel Schönen/Look-foto/CO; 199 (UP), Juri Samsonov/DR; 200 (2), Mikephotos/DR; 200 (3), Bettmann/CO; 200 (4), Dr. Seth Shostak/Science Photo Library; 200 (5), Bettmann/CO; 200 (6), Alexandr Malyshev/DR; 200 (11), Paramount Pictures/Sunset Boulevard/CO; 200 (CTR LE), Pixelrobot/DR; 201 (12), Andrey Armyagov/DR; 201 (13), Eugen Dobric/DR; 201 (17), NASA/Science Faction/CO; 201 (18), Brent Olson/DR; 201 (19), Vjanez/DR; 201 (21), CO; 201 (23), Olgany/DR; 201 (24), Andrzej Wojcicki/Science Photo Library/CO; 202 (LO), Brooklyn Museum/CO; 202-203 (Background), Olesja Yaremchuk/SS; 202 (UP), Graphica-Artis/CO; 203 (UP), Sandro Vannini/CO; 203 (LO), Source/NGS Archives; 204-205 (Background), Jose Gil/SS; 204 (LO), Lee Snider Photo Images/SS; 204 (UP LE), Ekaterina Pokrovsky/SS; 204 (UP RT), AFP/GI; 205 (UP), Gong Bing/Xinhua Press/CO; 205 (LO LE), Hilllander/DR; 205 (LO RT), Scott Van Blarcom/DR; 206 (2), 3000ad/DR; 206 (4), 2005 Charles Walker/TopFoto; 206 (8), Envision/CO; 206 (9), Leah Bignell/Design Pics/CO; 206 (10), Aero Graphics, Inc./CO; 206 (12), Timbrk/DR; 207 (13), CO; 207 (16-Background), Alex Makarenko/SS; 207 (16), I4lcocl2/DR; 207 (18), Sunset Boulevard/CO; 207 (20), Jack Pitney/Demotix/CO; 207 (21), Rachid Dahnoun/Aurora Open/CO; 207 (22), Brian Cahn/ZUMA Press/CO; 207 (23), Kenny Tong/DR; 208-209 (Background), Sergey Novikov/SS; 211 (LO), Andreyfire/DR; 212-213 (Background), A.RICARDO/SS; 212 (CTR), Offstocker/DR; 213 (CTR), Neil270/DR; 213 (LO LE), EmeraldUmbrellaStudio/DR; 213 (LO RT), Carpaumar/DR; 213 (UP), Samantha Tan/DR; 214 (LO), Photoeuphoria/DR; 215 (LO), Amero/SS; 215 (CTR), Percent/DR; 215 (UP LE), Isselee/DR; 215 (UP RT), Rozenn Leard/DR

AWESOME CREDiTS

This book was created for National Geographic Partners by Bender Richardson White.

The publisher gratefully acknowledges the writers of this book: Julie Beer, Sarah Wassner Flynn, Suzanne Francis, Michelle Harris, and Alison Pearce Stevens; photo editors Jeff Heimsath and Sharon Dortenzio; project editors Nancy Honovich and Karina Hamilainen; and project managers Lionel Bender, Becky Baines, and Ariane Szu-Tu.

James Hiscott, Jr., Art Director
Ben White, Designer

Since 1888, the National Geographic Society has funded more than 12,000 research, exploration, and preservation projects around the world. The Society receives funds from National Geographic Partners LLC, funded in part by your purchase. A portion of the proceeds from this book supports this vital work.

For more information, visit www.natgeo.com/info, call 1-800-647-5463, or write to the following address:
National Geographic Partners
1145 17th Street N.W.
Washington, D.C. 20036-4688 U.S.A.

Visit us online at nationalgeographic.com/books

For librarians and teachers: ngchildrensbooks.org

More for kids from National Geographic:
kids.nationalgeographic.com

For information about special discounts for bulk purchases, please contact National Geographic Books Special Sales:
ngspecsales@ngs.org

For rights or permissions inquiries, please contact National Geographic Books Subsidary Rights:
ngbookrights@ngs.org

Hardcover ISBN: 978-1-4263-2452-9
Library edition ISBN: 978-1-4263-2453-6

Printed in China
16/RRDS/1

CENTRAL PARK

Over one hundred and fifty years ago, when New Yorkers decided they needed a park, they held a competition for its design. The winning entry (by Frederick Law Olmsted and Calvert Vaux) created the first park in America to look like a natural setting rather than a formal garden. The park is two and one-half miles long and one-half mile wide. Horse-drawn carts brought in ten million loads of dirt to create flat open fields for concerts, hilly woods for hiking, and lakes for boating, swimming, and ice skating.

HUDSON RIVER

CENTRAL PARK

hrysler Building

MANHATTAN

HARLEM RIVER

NEW YORK CITY

New York City is the largest city in the United States and a world center for trade, industry, and culture. The city spreads over five areas called boroughs: Manhattan, Queens, Brooklyn, the Bronx, and Staten Island. Bailey and Margot live in the oldest and most important borough, Manhattan.

The BRONX

MANHATTAN ISLAND

Manhattan Island lies between the Hudson River and the East River, right in the center of New York City. The first people to live on Manhattan were the Algonquin Indians. They sold the island 400 years ago to Dutch settlers, who began the city and called it New Amsterdam. In 1664 (48 years later) the British got Manhattan Island from the Dutch and changed the city's name to New York. The island became part of the English colonies. The last change came after the American Revolution, when the colonists won independence and the island became part of the new nation, the United States of America.

QUEENS

Bailey's Birthday

Written by **Elizabeth Happy**

Illustrated by **Andra Chase**

MarshMedia, Kansas City, Missouri

For Adrienne, my muse.

*Special thanks to Beth Blackshire
from Andra Chase.*

Published by **MARSH**media
              A Division of Marsh Film Enterprises, Inc.
              P. O. Box 8082
              Shawnee Mission, KS 66208

Library of Congress Cataloging-in-Publication Data
Happy, Elizabeth.
    Bailey's birthday/written by Elizabeth Happy; illustrated
by Andra Chase.
          p.   cm.
    Summary: Bailey the dalmatian hopes to receive wonderful presents on his birthday until he learns that spending time with people who love him is the greatest gift of all. Includes information on the history and sights of New York City.
    ISBN 1-55942-059-6
    [1. Dalmatian dog—Fiction. 2. Dogs—Fiction. 3. Birthdays—Fiction. 4. Gifts—Fiction. 5. New York (N.Y.)—Fiction.] I. Chase, Andra, ill. II. Title.
PZ7.H1997Bai 1994   93-32519
[E]—dc20

Book layout by *Cirrus Design*

Printed in Hong Kong

Bailey waited. Sitting absolutely still, he fixed his eyes on the front door.

Suddenly Margot burst through it, home from school. She flung her backpack on the couch and dashed straight to her room. Bailey shot after her.

"Bailey!" demanded Margot, as he leaped on her bed. "Do you know what's coming?"

"WHAT? Oh wonderful WHAT?" thought Bailey, squirming with joy.

"Birthdays!" she announced. "Only seventeen days till my birthday."

"That's great!" panted Bailey.

"That's terrible. I can't wait!" Margot hugged Bailey. "It's your birthday, too. I got you last year for my birthday, so we'll celebrate together. I'll be seven, and you'll be one."

Margot snapped on Bailey's leash. "And it's Nicki's birthday next week. We're almost twins. It's the Great Birthday Month," she declared grandly.

Nicki and her dog, Claudia, were waiting outside the apartment building. With the two dogs pulling them forward, Margot and Nicki headed to Central Park.

The park was a wonderful blend of wilderness and city bustle. Swans glided across the Lake, disturbing the reflections of soaring skyscrapers. Horses clapped down the streets, pulling their carriages. Daffodils shook their yellow heads at bankers and lawyers. Musicians played Beethoven in the Sheep Meadow.

Margot and Claudia directed their attention to the sky. They loved anything that flew — kites, model airplanes, soaring falcons.

When they arrived at the Pond, the girls sat on the bank. The Pond was a favorite oasis for migrating geese.

Bailey sat beside Claudia. "I'm getting a birthday," he said.

"So is Nicki," Claudia replied. "And she always gets FABULOUS presents."

"Presents?" gasped Bailey. "You get presents?"

"You bet," said Claudia. "I'm sure you'll get lots."

"Wow!" Bailey jumped up.

He spun round and round until his leash encircled his legs and he tumbled on his side.

"Bailey!" Margot tried to untangle the leash. She shook her head. "What a silly dog."

At dusk, they started back to their neighborhood of narrow brownstones and tall apartment buildings. It was evening rush hour. Traffic was dense and horns honked in a frenzied clamor. Gayle, Margot's mother, would be returning home from work and greeting Harry, Margot's dad, with a kiss. Bailey wanted a kiss, too. He bounded down the street. When Margot unlocked their front door, Bailey raced for the kitchen.

"Eight calls today," Harry was telling Gayle, "and no one is hiring."

"Hi, Special Dog," he added when Bailey nuzzled his hand.

"Guess what Nicki's getting for her birthday," Margot cried. "A telescope! It's supposed to be a secret, but Nicki saw the box in the closet." Margot laughed. "Bailey, we just have to be good for seventeen days before we get all our presents, too."

Bailey was ecstatic. He thumped his tail against the wall. Why hadn't he heard about birthdays before?

Margot went to do homework while Harry finished making dinner. He stood by the stove and rubbed Bailey's stomach with his foot. "Not good right now for presents," he murmured.

"WHAT?" Bailey sat up quickly. What wasn't good for presents? He crawled under the table to think. Margot was going to be good for seventeen days. Nicki was already good enough to get a telescope. "I have to be good to get presents," he decided. "Harry's telling me I have to be a better dog!"

That night, Bailey's manners were impeccable!

He remembered: NOT to stand in his water dish while eating dinner.

He remembered: NOT to bark and spiral into the air when Aunt Syl dropped in and was taking off her coat.

Later, while everybody slept, Bailey crept out of his basket in the kitchen and sidled over to the couch.

Then he remembered: NOT to sink into the soft pillows.

He shuffled back miserably to his basket. "I'll never get to sleep," he thought, curling up, "and I'll never manage this for seventeen days!" Bailey was wrong.

He did fall asleep. Early the next morning, a loud CLANG! from the street below woke him.

Bailey sprang to the window. "They're delivering my presents!" he said. But all he saw were garbage collectors emptying garbage cans into their big truck.

16

"Haven't been good enough yet," he decided.

That afternoon, Margot and Nicki again headed to Central Park. Bailey and Claudia mushed ahead on their leashes.

At Heckscher Ball Field, two people were flying model airplanes. Miniature biplanes buzzed and bobbed overhead like fluttering moths.

The girls sat on a bench to watch. Claudia plopped beside Bailey.

"Can't wait," sighed Claudia.

"For what?" asked Bailey.

"For Nicki's birthday party. There'll be balloons and a white rabbit. Someone pulls him out of a hat." She tossed her head haughtily. "I'm sure he's for me."

"Wow! You must be acting awfully good."

"Of course."

"Margot and I are trying to be good," Bailey said and added with a sigh, "It's so hard."

"Not for me," said Claudia serenely.

19

A small red biplane dived in for a landing near the dogs. Claudia bolted forward, yapping.

"Claudia, here Claudia," Nicki shouted, coaxing Claudia back to the bench.

The plane scared Bailey, too, but he forced himself to stay calm. After all, he was certain that barking hysterically wouldn't earn him any birthday presents.

Ten days later, Margot took Bailey to Nicki's birthday party.

Claudia was right. Balloons were everywhere. Most dazzling of all was a black-caped magician who pulled two white rabbits from a tall hat.

After the magic show, a neighborhood bakery delivered a giant cake. Decorating its top was a peregrine falcon, drawn with gray and brown icing.

22

Colorfully-wrapped gifts covered the dining room table. Nicki tore through the presents — a poster of astronaut Sally Ride, a battery-powered planetarium, a kit of paper airplanes. Nicki squealed when she opened the heavy box with the telescope.

"What a glorious thing is a birthday," thought Bailey. Except when Claudia had to stay in the kitchen for eating ribbons, Bailey enjoyed the party. That night Bailey dreamed of his own glorious birthday — just seven days away.

Every day, Margot crossed a square off her calendar. Not many remained. Bailey hadn't barked once in the apartment nor scratched on a single door.

"Is Bailey sick?" asked Margot. "He's so calm lately."

That was good. People always used to flap their arms at him, shouting, "DOWN, Bailey. Be calm!"

"Here come the presents," he thought, rolling on his back.

23

Finally, one morning, Margot ran through the apartment calling, "Wake up! It's my BIRTHDAY!"

Harry flung on an apron and spent the morning in the kitchen. From time to time, he threw his voice into a Tyrolean yodel. Bailey joined in.

Aunt Syl arrived for lunch.

"Here's your present," she said to Margot. It was a solar system that stuck on the ceiling and glowed in the dark.

"Don't forget mine!" thought Bailey.

Harry and Gayle gave Margot a brilliant orange Delta kite.

"Singularity!" said Margot.

25

Harry turned to Bailey. "For you, a matching collar." He tied a bright orange bandanna around the dog's neck.

Then Harry brought out a triple-chocolate cake.

"Let's cut the cake!" Margot shouted. She put a slice of cake in front of Bailey. "We'll celebrate together." Bailey threw back his head and let the delicious cake fall down his throat. "Here's your present from me," Margot said, kissing Bailey between his ears.

Bailey waited for more . . . for packages . . . for colorful wrapping . . . for heavy boxes tied with ribbons.

Nothing came.

"A bandanna? A kiss? Where are all my presents?" He sank to the floor with his head between his paws. "I'm bad," he howled.

"What's the matter, Bailey?" asked Margot.

"Too much cake?" asked Harry, rubbing Bailey's stomach.

Gayle scratched his neck. "We're lucky to have you."

Later, the family rode the Staten Island Ferry. Sea gulls circled overhead, shrieking. Freighters full of cargo slipped off the horizon on their long ocean journey. The ferry passed the Statue of Liberty, silhouetted against the red stripes of a setting sun. Slowly the city began to blink. Skyscraper lights flickered on: the Chrysler Building, the Empire State Building, the Twin Towers.

Margot ate a hot dog. "Here," she said, giving Bailey half. "I've already got the Best Dog. Are you having a happy birthday?"

Bailey answered "yes" by licking everyone's face.

That night, curled up at the foot of Margot's bed, Bailey lay awake, thinking. Life is unpredictable, even if you are good. He *had* been good, and yet he'd gotten only a kiss and a bandanna. He'd expected much more. Still, this was probably the happiest day of his life. Bailey had had a wonderful day — a day spent with the people who loved him.

Suddenly, Margot sat up in bed. "Bailey!" she said. "There are only twelve months till our NEXT birthday."

"ANOTHER BIRTHDAY?" Bailey could hardly believe it.
"That's great," she sighed, her voice getting sleepy.
"That's terrible," panted Bailey. "I can't wait!"

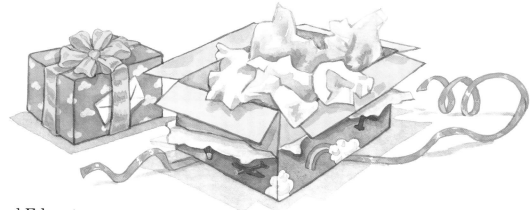

Dear Parents and Educators:

How shall young people measure their worth or "goodness"? By the material rewards and praise they receive? By the successful outcomes of their endeavors?

Depending upon outside reinforcement for appropriate behavior can be emotionally dangerous for children because, as Bailey finds out, life is unpredictable. Circumstances such as family traditions, values, or financial situations may limit the number of gifts we receive. There may not always be a caring companion close at hand to offer praise or congratulations. Even the best played games can be lost, and studying hard for a test doesn't assure an A.

The story of Bailey and his birthday celebration helps children understand that "goodness" is measured from the inside out. And ***Bailey's Birthday*** encourages young people to look beyond wrapped packages to appreciate gifts from the hearts of people who care for them. Love, acceptance, and a sense of belonging are the most precious gifts of all.

Here are some questions you might ask to help children think about the message of ***Bailey's Birthday***:

- Why does Margot's father say that it is not a good time for gifts?
- Why does Bailey try to be a good dog?
- What birthday gifts did Nicki receive? What gifts did Margot receive?
- How were Nicki's and Margot's gifts alike? How were they different?
- Why was Bailey's birthday one of the happiest days of his life?
- Has there ever been a time when you did not get a gift you wanted or expected? How did you feel?

Here are some things you can do to help children see gift giving in its proper perspective:

- Discuss with children how family customs and financial situations affect the gifts children give and receive.
- Explore ways of showing affection on special occasions apart from gift giving.
- Model a healthy attitude toward giving, being careful to separate decisions about gifts from evaluations of behavior.

Available from MarshMedia

Storybooks — Hardcover with dust jacket and full-color illustrations throughout. $16.95 each.

Videos — The original story and illustrations combined with dramatic narration, music, and sound effects. $59.95 each.

Activity Books — Softcover collections of games, puzzles, maps, and project ideas designed for each title. $16.95 each.

Bailey's Birthday, written by Elizabeth Happy, illustrated by Andra Chase. 32 pages. (MarshMedia) ISBN 1-55942-059-6.

Bailey's Birthday video. 18:00 run time. (MarshMedia) ISBN 1-55942-060-X.

Clarissa, written by Carol Talley, illustrated by Itoko Maeno. 32 pages. (MarshMedia) ISBN 1-55942-014-6.

Clarissa video. 13:00 run time. (MarshMedia) ISBN 1-55942-023-5.

Gumbo Goes Downtown, written by Carol Talley, illustrated by Itoko Maeno. 32 pages. (MarshMedia) ISBN 1-55942-042-1.

Gumbo Goes Downtown video. 18:00 run time. (MarshMedia) ISBN 1-55942-043-X.

Hana's Year, written by Carol Talley, illustrated by Itoko Maeno. 32 pages. (MarshMedia) ISBN 1-55942-034-0.

Hana's Year video. 17:10 run time. (MarshMedia) ISBN 1-55942-035-9.

Jomo and Mata, written by Alyssa Chase, illustrated by Andra Chase. 32 pages. (MarshMedia) ISBN 1-55942-051-0.

Jomo and Mata video. 18:56 run time. (MarshMedia) ISBN 1-55942-052-9.

Kiki and the Cuckoo, written by Elizabeth Happy, illustrated by Andra Chase. 32 pages. (MarshMedia) ISBN 1-55942-038-3.

Kiki and the Cuckoo video. 14:30 run time. (MarshMedia) ISBN 1-55942-039-1.

Kylie's Concert, written by Patty Sheehan, illustrated by Itoko Maeno. 32 pages. (MarshMedia) ISBN 1-55942-046-4.

Kylie's Concert video. 17:20 run time. (MarshMedia) ISBN 1-55942-047-2.

Kylie's Song, written by Patty Sheehan, illustrated by Itoko Maeno. 32 pages. (Advocacy Press) ISBN 0-911655-19-0.

Kylie's Song video. 12:00 run time. (MarshMedia) ISBN 1-55942-021-9.

Minou, written by Mindy Bingham, illustrated by Itoko Maeno. 64 pages. (Advocacy Press) ISBN 0-911655-36-0.

Minou video. 18:30 run time. (MarshMedia) ISBN 1-55942-015-4.

My Way Sally, written by Mindy Bingham and Penelope Paine, illustrated by Itoko Maeno. 48 pages. (Advocacy Press) ISBN 0-911655-27-1.

My Way Sally video. 19:30 run time. (MarshMedia) ISBN 1-55942-017-0.

Papa Piccolo, written by Carol Talley, illustrated by Itoko Maeno. 32 pages. (MarshMedia) ISBN 1-55942-028-6.

Papa Piccolo video. 18:00 run time. (MarshMedia) ISBN 1-55942-029-4.

Pequeña the Burro, written by Jami Parkison, illustrated by Itoko Maeno. 32 pages. (MarshMedia) ISBN 1-55942-055-3.

Pequeña the Burro video. 18:00 run time (MarshMedia) ISBN 1-55942-056-1.

Time for Horatio, written by Penelope Paine, illustrated by Itoko Maeno. 48 pages. (Advocacy Press) ISBN 0-911655-33-6.

Time for Horatio video. 19:00 run time. (MarshMedia) ISBN 1-55942-026-X.

Tonia the Tree, written by Sandy Stryker, illustrated by Itoko Maeno. 32 pages. (Advocacy Press) ISBN 0-911655-16-6.

Tonia the Tree video. 12:10 run time. (MarshMedia) ISBN 1-55942-019-7.

You can find storybooks at better bookstores. Or you may order storybooks, videos, and activity books direct by sending a check for the amount shown plus $2.50 per item for shipping to MarshMedia, P. O. Box 8082, Shawnee Mission, Kansas 66208, or by calling 1-800-821-3303.

MarshMedia has been publishing high-quality, award-winning learning materials for children since 1969. To receive a free catalog, call 1-800-821-3303.

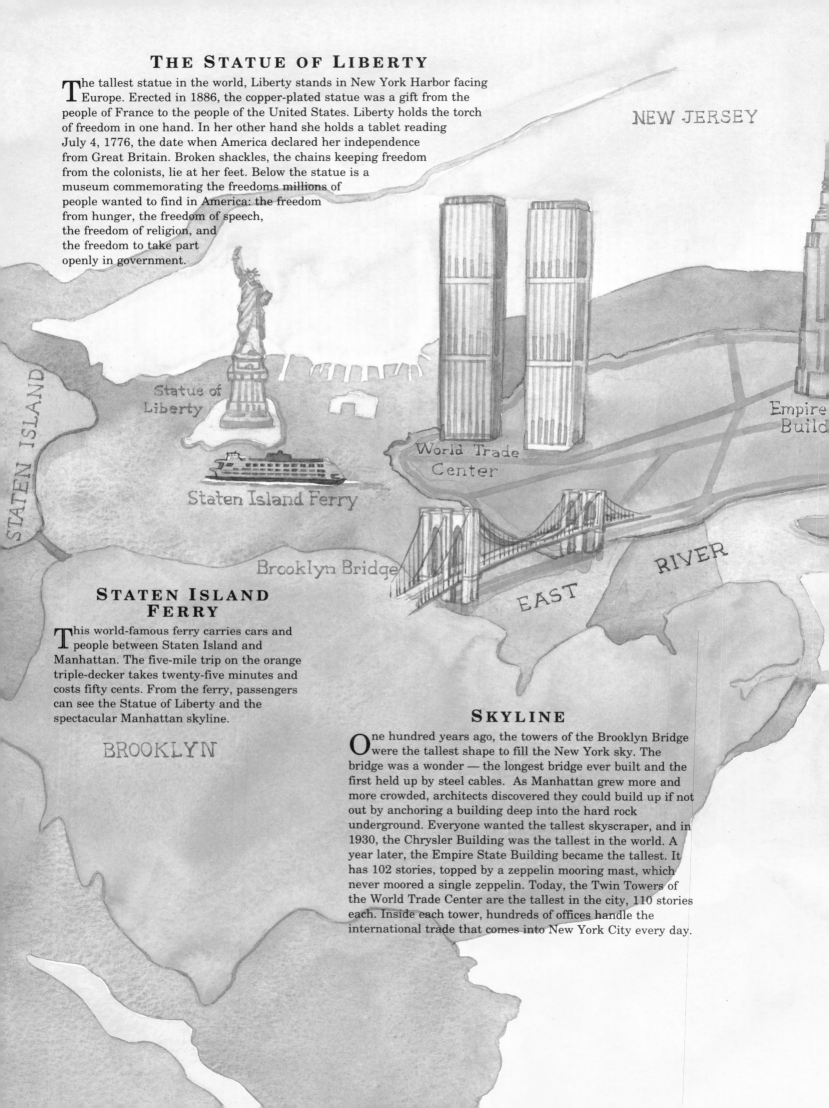

THE STATUE OF LIBERTY

The tallest statue in the world, Liberty stands in New York Harbor facing Europe. Erected in 1886, the copper-plated statue was a gift from the people of France to the people of the United States. Liberty holds the torch of freedom in one hand. In her other hand she holds a tablet reading July 4, 1776, the date when America declared her independence from Great Britain. Broken shackles, the chains keeping freedom from the colonists, lie at her feet. Below the statue is a museum commemorating the freedoms millions of people wanted to find in America: the freedom from hunger, the freedom of speech, the freedom of religion, and the freedom to take part openly in government.

NEW JERSEY

STATEN ISLAND

Statue of Liberty

World Trade Center

Empire Build

Staten Island Ferry

Brooklyn Bridge

EAST

RIVER

STATEN ISLAND FERRY

This world-famous ferry carries cars and people between Staten Island and Manhattan. The five-mile trip on the orange triple-decker takes twenty-five minutes and costs fifty cents. From the ferry, passengers can see the Statue of Liberty and the spectacular Manhattan skyline.

BROOKLYN

SKYLINE

One hundred years ago, the towers of the Brooklyn Bridge were the tallest shape to fill the New York sky. The bridge was a wonder — the longest bridge ever built and the first held up by steel cables. As Manhattan grew more and more crowded, architects discovered they could build up if not out by anchoring a building deep into the hard rock underground. Everyone wanted the tallest skyscraper, and in 1930, the Chrysler Building was the tallest in the world. A year later, the Empire State Building became the tallest. It has 102 stories, topped by a zeppelin mooring mast, which never moored a single zeppelin. Today, the Twin Towers of the World Trade Center are the tallest in the city, 110 stories each. Inside each tower, hundreds of offices handle the international trade that comes into New York City every day.